The Advanced Backpacker

The Advanced Backpacker

A Handbook of Year-Round, Long-Distance Hiking

Chris Townsend

RAGGED MOUNTAIN PRESS / McGRAW-HILL

Camden, Maine • New York • San Francisco • Washington, D.C. • Auckland
Bogotá • Caracas • Lisbon • London • Madrid • Mexico City • Milan
Montreal • New Delhi • San Juan • Singapore • Sydney • Tokyo • Toronto

Ragged Mountain Press

A Division of The McGraw·Hill Companies

Permissions to reprint previously published material appear on pages vii–viii, which constitute an extension of the copyright page.

10 9 8 7 6 5 4 3 2 1

Library of Congress Cataloging-in-Publication Data
Townsend, Chris, 1949–
    The advanced backpacker / Chris Townsend.
        p.   cm.
    Includes index.
    ISBN 0-07-135756-4
    1. Backpacking—Handbooks, manuals, etc.
      I. Title.

GV199.6.T68 2000
796.51—dc21   00-031071

Questions regarding the content of this book should be addressed to
Ragged Mountain Press
P.O. Box 220
Camden, ME 04843
www.raggedmountainpress.com

Questions regarding the ordering of this book should be addressed to
The McGraw-Hill Companies
Customer Service Department
P.O. Box 547
Blacklick, OH 43004
Retail customers: 1-800-262-4729
Bookstores: 1-800-722-4726

This book is printed on 70-lb. Citation by Quebecor Printing, Fairfield, PA

Design by Joyce C. Weston
All photography by Chris Townsend
Production by Kristin Goble, PerfecType
Production coordination by Dan Kirchoff
Edited by Tom McCarthy and Jane M. Curran

To Denise Thorn

Contents

Acknowledgments

Over the years a host of people, both friends and strangers, have provided information and assistance on my long walks. Thanking them all individually is impossible. Indeed, I do not even know the names of all of them.

Here I'd like to thank those who have given me specific assistance with long-distance hiking and with my writing and photography. I am, of course, solely responsible for the views and information in this book and also for any mistakes.

First must be my partner, Denise Thorn, who read through the drafts of this book and made many useful suggestions as well as corrections. The book is better for her involvement. I'd also like to thank Denise and my stepdaughter Hazel for their love, support, and companionship.

Many people in outdoor companies have provided me with information for my writing and equipment for my long walks. I would particularly like to thank Chris Brasher of the Brasher Boot Company for his support and for the many discussions we have had about lightweight equipment, as well as for his superbly comfortable boots; Steve Laycock of Pertex, also for support plus excellent fabrics; equipment designer Aarn Tate for the opportunity to try prototype packs and for our discussions on design; Craghoppers, makers of innovative packs based on Aarn's designs; and Julian Miles of Kathmandu Trekking for his lightweight tarps.

My thanks to Phil Oren for his work on boot fitting, which has changed my views completely and solved my fitting problems. On this same topic I have also learned much from Gordon Fraser of Mountain Sports UK, Jeff Gray of Superfeet, and boot expert Bob Rose.

Ray and Jenny Jardine have contributed greatly to my knowledge of ultralight hiking.

I'd like to thank writer and long-distance hiker Karen Berger for information on the Arizona Trail and the opportunity to exchange views (and sometimes moans!) with someone working in the same field.

Cameron McNeish, editor of *TGO* magazine, has published much of my work. I've also hiked with him and *TGO* deputy editor John Manning and had long discussions with both on all aspects of backpacking.

Long exchanges of views, mostly by e-mail but sometimes in the wilds, with writer and walker Dave Hewitt about everything from peakbagging to outdoor writing have also been very helpful.

Finally, I would like to thank Tom McCarthy, Jane M. Curran, Dan Kirchoff, and D. A. Oliver at Ragged Mountain Press for their support and their hard work in editing and producing this book.

Epigraphs on chapter-opening pages are reprinted as follows:

Page ix from *Camping and Woodcraft* by Horace Kephart, University of Tennessee Press, 1988.

Page 1 from *A Sand County Almanac: And Sketches Here and There*, by Aldo Leopold, copyright 1949, 1977 by Oxford University Press, Inc. Used by permission of Oxford University Press, Inc.

Page 9 © 1987 by Cindy Ross. Reprinted by permission from *Journey on the Crest* by Cindy Ross. Published by the Mountaineers, Seattle.

Page 20 from *Backpacking in Alps and Pyrenees* copyright © Showell Styles 1976, reproduced by permission of Curtis Brown Ltd., London.

Page 40 from Laura Waterman and Guy Waterman, *Backwoods Ethics: Environmental Issues for Hikers and Campers*, reprinted with permission of Countryman Press.

Page 66 from M. John Fayhee, *Along the Arizona Trail*, reprinted with permission of the author.

Page 102 from Karen Berger and Daniel R. Smith, *Where the Waters Divide: A Walk along America's Continental Divide*, reprinted with permission of Countryman Press.

Page 135 from John Muir, *Travels in Alaska*.

Page 189 from Colin Fletcher, *The Thousand-Mile Summer*, Vintage Books, a division of Random House, Inc.

Page 222 from Robert Service, "The Men That Don't Fit In," *The Spell of the Yukon*.

Page 244 from *Beyond the Wall* by Edward Abbey, © 1984 by Edward Abbey. Reprinted by permission of Henry Holt and Company, LLC, and of Don Congdon Associates.

Sunset in the Scottish Highlands.

Introduction

This instinct for a free life in the open is as natural and wholesome as the gratification of hunger and thirst and love. It is Nature's recall to the simple mode of existence she intended us for.

— Horace Kephart,

Camping and Woodcraft

Hiking is my passion, especially walking long-distance in wilderness areas, and has been all my adult life. In the many years since my first long walk, a 17-day journey along the 270-mile Pennine Way, a footpath along the moorland spine of England, I've endeavored to spend as much time as possible in wild country. During that time I've walked the 2,600-mile Pacific Crest Trail, the 3,000-mile Continental Divide Trail, the 800-mile Arizona Trail, 1,600 miles end to end along the Canadian Rockies, 1,000 miles south to north through Yukon Territory, 1,300 miles south to north through the mountains of Norway and Sweden, 1,250 miles from Land's End to John O'Groats in Great Britain, and 1,600 miles over the 517 summits over 3,000 feet in the Scottish Highlands. There have been as well many other walks not quite so long in many different places and countries ranging from the Grand Canyon to the Alps, Iceland to Nepal.

These walks have given me great pleasure and satisfaction and wonderful feelings of joy and excitement. I've learned a little about the natural world and, I think, something about myself. I've also at times been soaked, sunburned, frozen, thirsty, hungry, footsore, and exhausted. Tents have blown down, trails have been lost, and rivers and snowbanks have been fallen into.

All this experience means I have learned enough about long-distance hiking in wild places, and made enough mistakes, for my knowledge to perhaps be of use to others. There is much more for me to learn, of course. Indeed, I learn something new every time I go for a walk. But if the idea of spending weeks, perhaps months, walking and living in the wilderness attracts you, then my thoughts may well be of value.

Although novice backpackers may find much of interest here, this book isn't really designed for them. They would do better to look at my *Backpacker's Handbook* (Ragged Mountain Press), which covers all aspects of backpacking. Inevitably there may be some overlap between the two books, but in this book I've assumed a basic knowledge of camping and hiking techniques and equipment and a little backpacking experience. This book is for those who want to go beyond the weekend away or the week spent camping not far from a road and who want to venture further into the wilderness, walking longer distances and staying out for more nights. I've also looked at how to plan and undertake hikes in far-off distant places. Because the book is based on my own experience of long-distance hiking, some of the stories have appeared elsewhere in books about my hikes. If you hear an echo here and there, I apologize.

The question may be asked whether there is a need for a book like this. My reply is that although there are people who successfully complete long hikes without much preparation, they are rare. The dropout rate on popular long walks such as the Appalachian and Pacific Crest Trails is very high. Many hikers give up in the first hundred miles. Clearly there is a need for advice. There are many books on backpacking but few on long-distance backpacking. I fervently hope that this addition to the literature will help some to achieve their goals.

This book may encourage people who would otherwise not have thought to try long-distance hiking and to experience what it is like to live in the wilds for long periods. If so, I am pleased. That is part of my intention. Concern is sometimes expressed that there are too many people in the wilderness, that we are "loving it to death." I disagree. Although some places are very popular and can get crowded, most wilderness areas are not. And even where there are many people, the landscape is usually no more than a little ragged, a little tarnished looking. There is no comparison between an overwide trail or a flattened, well-used camping site and a clear-cut forest or a strip-mined mountainside. The real threats to the wilderness come from logging, mining, overgrazing, dams, downhill ski resorts, mass tourism developments, and other large-scale projects. Who opposes these schemes? Often it is people who have learned to love wild places by walking and camping in them, by treating them softly and leaving little trace of their passing. Long-distance hikers frequently feel they must give something back to the wilderness that has given them so much joy, and they become involved in environmental work and campaigning. In the words of one of the greatest long-distance wilderness walkers, John Muir, they want to "do something for wilderness and make the mountains glad." If no one understands the value of remote, wild places, who will speak out when they are threatened? If long-distance walking leads to an understanding of the need for wilderness, then that is enough to justify encouraging it.

Although the real threats to the wilderness come from industry—not hikers—those of us who walk the wild places should do so as lightly as possible, leaving little trace of our passing. There are techniques for doing so, and I've described them in this book. Long-distance hikers in particular should take care of the land through which they pass. We are privileged to experience the most beautiful and spectacular places on the planet. In return, we should help to maintain and preserve those places for the sake of those who come after us and the creatures and plants whose homes they are.

Inspiration and Reality

Only the mountain has lived long enough to listen objectively to the howl of the wolf.

— Aldo Leopold,

A Sand County Almanac

The first bright rays of the sun are just touching the jagged rim of the mountains silhouetted high above as you open your eyes. A whitening of frost covers the sleeping bag, and your breath is visible in the sharp air of dawn. Sitting up, you shiver slightly and quickly pull on a fleece jacket and a warm hat. Gazing around, you watch the mountains turn from gray to gold and red as the sun touches them. The solid black of the night is replaced by a complexity of cliffs, ridges, and gullies. The warm light slides down the slopes to touch the tops of the trees. Slowly the somber forest fills with light and life, brightness and color. There is no better way to start a day, you think, but you need a hot drink to warm up your sluggish muscles and thoughts.

The stove stands ready next to the groundsheet. (For the purposes of this story you are not in an area where bears are a problem.) You make a few strokes with the pump and open the valve a bit. A thin thread of fuel spurts out and dribbles down the side of the burner. You close the valve and then light the tiny pool of white gas with a flick of a butane lighter. By the time you've filled a small

Boot prints in the sand, Sandwood Bay, Scotland.

pot with water, the flame is beginning to die so you open the valve again. The sudden roar startles a couple of gray jays that fly squawking from a nearby tree. The familiar ritual of lighting the stove is always pleasing and welcoming, the modern equivalent of lighting the campfire. Breakfast is a hot drink and some cold cereal. By the time you've finished eating, the sun has reached your camp and you can feel its warmth suffusing your body. The sleeping bag is draped over a warm and sunny boulder to dry; then you start to pack up.

The trail leads across open ground a short way and then into a forest. At the trees' edge you turn and look back. The patch of bare ground where you camped is no more than a gray smear on the edge of the meadow, just as it was when you first saw it, but now it holds a place in your memory. I lived there, you think, before turning and striding into the cool dark forest, relishing the shafts of sunlight that slant down through the canopy above, sharply illuminating leaves, patches of bark, and spider's webs. Eventually you climb out of the trees and traverse upward across a rocky slope to a high pass where there's a splendid view of mountains and forest without end. Fit from weeks in the wilds, you find the walking so effortless you barely think about it as you follow the faint trail as it climbs, flicking your eyes ahead to check where to put your feet and enjoying the rhythm of movement, the natural and familiar feeling of wilderness walking. Not really thinking but rather absorbing all that lies around you, you register a change in the rocks from soft crumbling sandstone to harder angular quartzite, notice the layout of the basin below the pass, and pick out the lake near which you plan on camping. You sit on a rock as you lunch on cheese, crackers, granola bars, and water. A bird of prey far above catches your eye. The mini-binoculars you keep in your shirt pocket reveal it to be an eagle, and you watch entranced as it glides above the mountains without a flicker of its wings. Descending from the pass, you come to the first wind-flattened, stunted pines creeping across the rocky ground, outliers of the vast

forest below. Soon the trees rise up all around, tall and magnificent. As you walk through this natural cathedral, you become aware that you haven't thought of anything in particular for many hours, yet you feel very content.

A glimpse of water through the trees marks the edge of the lake. Back in the woods well away from the shore you spot a large clearing. On the edge of it lies a flat, dusty patch of ground beside a large boulder. Those unused to wilderness camping would pass it by with barely a glance, not that they would venture so far into the wilds anyway, but to you it looks like a potential home. A scattering of trees rises behind the rock while in front the scrub-dotted ground falls away gently a few hundred yards to a small creek that soon disappears into the trees on its way to the now-hidden lake. On the far side of the valley the forest rises to the base of steep mountains, their serrated rocky tops spattered with the last remnants of the winter's snow. When you reach this place you immediately do two important things: You lie down on the ground to check that it's flat and that there are no sharp stones or twigs that might puncture your ground cloth or poke you in the back during the night. Then you note the sun, well down now toward the top of the slope behind the big boulder. Slipping your compass out of your shirt pocket, you find the bearing for the sunrise. You already worked out when you were planning your route that the sun should be far across the valley in a shallow low gap between the mountains, but it's best to check. Early morning sun is always welcome.

Setting up your camp is a simple procedure that is quickly done, as it has been on so many nights before. First you glance skyward. Still no clouds. A roof shouldn't be needed. If it does rain, you know you can have your tarp pitched, using trekking poles as supports, in a few seconds. Leaning your pack against the boulder, you pull a groundsheet out and lay it down, smoothing out the creases. A foam sleeping pad goes on top, followed by a sleeping bag. More gear comes out of the pack: the stove, a fuel bottle, pans and cutlery in a little stuff sack, a larger bag full of dehydrated food. You place these items to one side of the sleeping bag. You remove a scrunched-up nylon water bag from inside the pans, shake it out, and wander down to the creek to quickly fill the bag from a small cascade of fresh, cold mountain water. You pause to glance up the line of sparkling water as it chatters over small stones, wild water falling down from the heights, one of the delights of the wilderness.

Back in camp, you sit down on your foam pad and lean back against your pack. All you can see is mountain, meadow, and forest, a perfect world. You lay out your kitchen next to the groundsheet and light the stove. A pot of water goes on, and you are soon sipping a hot drink while your dinner gently simmers. Staring into the slowly darkening sky, you suddenly realize you're feeling chilly dressed in just shirt and shorts. The sun is near the horizon now, and long shadows are creeping over the landscape. You pull your fleece jacket out of your pack and slip it on, zipping it up tight at the neck. Taking your shoes off, you slide your bare legs into the sleeping bag. Soon you start to feel comfortably warm again.

Entranced by the setting sun and the gorgeous red and purple bands that are spreading across the sky, you almost forget about dinner, but soon hunger reasserts itself, and you sample the bubbling brown stew. It's cooked. You settle back against your pack and eat your stew absentmindedly, your attention held by the darkening silhouette of the mountains and the deepening blue of the sky.

Warm and well fed, you almost fall asleep sitting up. You wake just enough to find your headlamp and place it in a shoe so you can find it in the dark. Then you stuff your fleece jacket into a stuff sack to make a pillow and pull the sleeping bag up around your shoulders. Within minutes you're sound asleep.

Another day in the wilderness has come to an end, another day of truly living, of being in touch with yourself and the world of which you are a part. And the great joy is in knowing that

In the Tombstone Mountains in Yukon Territory.

tomorrow will be the same, and the next day, and the day after that and on through the weeks and months.

There comes a point on a long hike when both beginning and end seem far away in both time and distance, when walking in the wilderness becomes what you do, becomes your way of life. That's the difference between a long-distance hike and a shorter walk. The latter is a break from everyday life; the former becomes everyday life. On hikes of two or three weeks I only begin to feel I live in the wilderness. But once I'm out for over a month, there is a subtle shift from being outside to being inside the wild. So, for me, a long-distance hike is one lasting at least a month, and preferably several months or more. And it's about time just as much as, if not more than, distance. How far I walk varies with the terrain, the amount of ascent, the steepness of the climbs, and the weight carried. That said, in a month I expect to walk, on average, around 300 to 500 miles, so I'd give that as the lower distance for a long-distance hike. The upper end? As far as you like. Three thousand miles—approximately!—is the farthest I've hiked in one journey, and that took five and a half months.

Hiking for months on end is the ideal, the dream. Of course, it's not possible to do that often or even at all for many who would still like to consider themselves long-distance hikers. Two weeks away is a more reasonable time, and while the deep experience of hiking as a way of life can only be glimpsed in such a period, the basics of long-distance hiking can be enjoyed. If you set out on a journey of a week or more intending to move on almost every day and with a given route to complete, then you have begun long-distance hiking.

Porters in the Keha Lungpa Valley, Western Himalaya, Nepal.

REASONS WHY

But why undertake such long journeys on foot? There are numerous reasons, for long-distance hiking has many pleasures. The sense of achievement on finishing successfully is an obvious one, and the desire for that is often what keeps me going when the weather is bad or my feet ache. Virtually all long-distance hikes have a goal, a destination to aim for that, when reached, marks the completion of the walk. Once there is a beginning and an end, the journey becomes a quest, a seeking of a distant object, one far enough away as to seem out of reach without great effort. The end becomes symbolic of the fulfillment of the journey, a summing up of the process that takes you there. The explicit purpose of the walk is the connecting of the start with the finish, though it is between those boundaries that the real meaning is to be found. It would, of course, be possible simply to set off walking with no definite destination in mind, but I would guess that few do this. Certainly my one attempt

to do so, on a two-week hike, ended in a very desultory fashion and taught me that I need the superficial target of a finish point even though I know that the main enjoyment of the walk lies in the journey, not in reaching the destination.

The challenge of a quest to be undertaken is often the stimulus that starts the long process of preparing for a long-distance hike. Once that spark is lit, it can take you to far-off places and lead to wonderful adventures, as any true quest should. To be a real challenge, the journey should be long and difficult enough to make completing it uncertain. That applies, I think, to any really long-distance hike, no matter how many you have completed in the past. There are so many variables involved that you can never be sure that the end will be reached. The importance of challenge may wane, however, after one or two long-distance hikes. The pleasure of walking for long periods in the wilderness may then be such that you simply want to repeat it, the destination merely a necessary finish point. Those for whom the challenging aspect of a long-distance hike is central may re-create it, even on the same trail, by trying to do it faster, in winter, with minimal equipment, or even by hiking it twice without a break.

Even without doing this, the challenges of a long-distance hike are many. Beyond the basic challenge of the distance to be walked, there are the weather and the terrain. On any long walk there will always be some stormy weather; on some hikes there will be a great deal of it. There'll be tough terrain to deal with, too— steep and rocky perhaps, or densely forested. Sometimes the hardest terrain and the worst weather will coincide, requiring both good backpacking skills and strength of will. Slogging through heavy rain or fighting through dense brush do not at the time seem good reasons for undertaking a long-distance hike. Afterward, however, there is a real feeling of achievement, a glow of satisfaction at having overcome such difficulties.

Important though the challenge of terrain, weather, and distance may be, for me it's the journey itself that is really fulfilling. The deepest joy is in the immersion in the natural world, in living simply in the wilderness for a long period of time, in connecting with nature so that I feel part of it. As the days and weeks pass, I find I become more attuned to the life around me, noticing more and, gradually, understanding more. The noise of the forest or the mountains starts to mean something as I slowly learn to distinguish between the wind sighing in the grasses and an animal rustling the bushes and to hear the individual songs of birds above the rush of a creek. My senses sharpen; I pick up distant noises I wouldn't have heard the first few days out and catch brief movements out of the corner of my eye as I watch the land more closely. The shape and form of the landscape becomes clearer as details are noted and relationships perceived. I see more, and what I see, I see more deeply and appreciate more profoundly. I become more alert, more part of the country I walk through. After a few weeks I cease to be aware of this, for it has become natural, part of who I am.

On the larger scale there is the appreciation of the wholeness of a place, the way its parts fit together and also how different ecosystems merge into each other. Curiosity about landscape, about what lies over the next hill, around the next bend in the river, is an essential part of all wilderness hiking. On a long-distance hike you are able to see what a whole mountain range is like. Walking the length of the Canadian Rockies showed me the integrity of the range in a way that books or words couldn't do. As well as understanding this intellectually, I felt it deep inside me and knew it physically, for I had seen it day after day, mile after mile. On the Pacific Crest Trail I experienced the landscape of southern California as it rose from desert to mountain and back again before finally soaring to the Sierra Nevada; in turn, these mountains then faded away into lower wooded hills in the northern part of the state and then rose again to the Cascade Mountains in Oregon and Washington. This gave me a coherent idea of how the

A rocky trail beside the Tuolumne River in the High Sierra.

different landscapes fitted together, how they blended into each other and were really part of a continuum.

There is delight, too, in the physical fitness that comes only after weeks and weeks of walking. The body works at its best when used every day, and the feeling this gives is tremendous. The miles pass more quickly; the hills are easier to climb. I become more aware of what I can do, too, knowing just how far I can go in a day, how long it will take to climb to a pass. At times walking becomes effortless, and I can walk for hours at a time without any awareness of physical effort or tiredness. The body simply flows over the landscape.

The challenge of long-distance hiking goes beyond fitness; a connection also develops between the body and the land. I find I walk more efficiently, more naturally, when I've been hiking for many days. I'm more adept at reading the land ahead and adjusting my stride to accommodate it. Brief glances show me well in advance where to place my feet, and I do this without consciously thinking about it so I can observe my surroundings while I walk. Many hikers watch every step, especially on rough ground, rarely glancing up to look round them. They haven't internalized how to walk without constant watching, probably because they haven't undertaken a long-distance hike and so have never had the time for walking in the wilds to become natural. I now retain this ability so that even on day hikes I mostly walk without consciously looking where I'm planting my feet, at least on safe terrain. Because of this I see more, much more, than those who need to check every step. This is not something I set out to learn—it's just one of the benefits of long-distance hiking, developed gradually over the months and years.

Mental fitness also comes with a shedding of the stresses and pressures of modern life. Self-confidence and self-knowledge grow with the journey, leading to a wonderful sense of well-being and the feeling that anything is possible. All this works in combination, of course. Being physically fit means the walking becomes easier and requires less concentration, so there is more energy for observing the surroundings and therefore more enjoyment and involvement.

The modern urban world is fast, complex, competitive, and always concerned with what happens next. There is always more to do than there is time. The landscape and even the light are mostly artificial. This can be exciting, but all too often it is frustrating, stressful, and exhausting. In contrast, hiking for weeks or months at a time in an unspoiled natural environment is a simple, repetitive activity that leads to calmness and psychological well-being, a feeling of wholeness, of being a complete person. Each day follows the same pattern, linking in with natural rhythms—walk in the light, sleep in the dark, eat when hungry, take shelter from storms. Only the details are different. I get a great pleasure from this simplicity, from the basic pattern of walk and camp, walk and camp. It is good to escape the rush of the modern world and for a period of time to live a quieter, more basic life. Problems and worries subside as the days go by; they are put into perspective by the elemental activity of putting one foot in front of the other hour after hour, day after day. And on returning from the wilds, restored and revitalized by the experience, I find civilization can be much easier to deal with; indeed, aspects of it can seem very desirable.

Some of the attraction of this simple life lies in its immediacy, in the fact that you live only in the present or the very near future. What matters comes down to how far you will walk that day, where you will camp, where the next water is, where you will stop for a rest or a snack. With life reduced, literally, to walking pace, anything more than a few hours ahead is too far in the future to worry about.

Part of the pleasure of simplicity lies in the satisfaction of being self-reliant, of carrying everything I need on my back. It may be only a relatively short time between each resupply point, but for that period I am self-sufficient,

dependent on no one but myself. This is significant, too. On a long-distance hike you are in control of your life. No external schedules or demands impose on your time; no one controls what you do and when you do it. It is up to you how you plan and carry out your hike.

The act and art of camping are important, too. There is a simple delight in creating a temporary home every day in a different place, in knowing you can make a comfortable, habitable space in a few minutes, a space where you can cook, eat, keep warm, and sleep protected from bad weather. There is also joy in the freedom of not having to reach a certain destination, in carrying your house on your back, able to set it down when and where you choose. Again this is different on a long hike than on a short one. Once I've been out for a few weeks I cease to wonder where I'll find a site and how quickly camp can be set up. Camping techniques become almost automatic, as the same actions are repeated time after time.

When all this comes together, when the walking seems effortless and the niggling worries that can bedevil short hikes and that are always present at the start of long hikes have faded from the mind, a state can sometimes be reached that can be described only as a form of ego loss, as a merging with the wild. Awareness of nature is heightened even while awareness of the self ceases. When this occurs, I can walk for hours acutely sensitive to all that is going on around me. Everything seems sharper, clearer, more real. I feel more alive, more in contact with the world, because my thoughts, the voices in my head, have ceased and are no longer acting as a barrier between myself and what lies outside. This is a very intense experience that some might call spiritual. I can't invoke this feeling, and it only occurs on long-distance hikes.

It also mostly occurs when I am alone in the wilderness, but I know that not all people like complete solitude; many value companionship on their hikes. The company of others often becomes a significant aspect of a long-distance hike. This doesn't mean just the company of hiking partners, though that can be important. It also means the friendship of those met along the way, both other hikers and, in particular, local people who offer assistance in many forms—rides to resupply points, food, lodging, and general encouragement. This "trail magic," as it's often called, can be inspirational and heartening, leading to a positive view of humanity, in contrast to the negative one handed down by the news media. Trekkers in Nepal frequently say that the most memorable part of their trip wasn't the scenery, spectacular though that is, but the local people, especially the Sherpas. They enthuse about how generous, friendly, and kind the Sherpas are. My own experiences in Nepal concur with this. However, I've also found the same qualities in local people along the Pacific Crest Trail, in the Canadian Rockies and the Yukon, in the Pyrenees and the Scottish Highlands—indeed, everywhere I've hiked long distances. A stranger on foot, carrying all he (or she) needs on his back, isn't seen as a threat but rather as a person with interesting tales to tell, a person who is to be admired for what he is doing and therefore worthy of assistance and friendship. I first found this out not in the Himalayan mountains or the Yukon wilderness but in the gentle country lanes and fields of rural England. I was on my first long-distance walk, a 1,250-mile journey from the points farthest apart on the British mainland, Land's End and John O'Groats. Finding places to camp in settled lowland farming areas where campgrounds and indeed walkers were rare loomed as a major problem when I set out. However, I soon discovered that I only had to pop into a bar and start chatting to the locals, and offers of places to camp would soon be made, along with suggestions as to the best route to take, which footpaths were passable, and whether farmer so-and-so's dogs or bull was to be trusted.

A long-distance walk doesn't really end when the hiking stops either. It is too intense and significant an experience for that, too much a major part of your life. Only afterward does a walk take on a completeness, a self-contained unity. It grows in the mind and gives joy and satisfaction long after the last step is taken. Different aspects of the walk—a sunset, a fleeting encounter with a wild animal, a campsite in the rain—can float into your mind years later. Thoughts and experiences deepen and become part of you, perhaps changing and certainly deepening your outlook on life, your personal philosophy, how you view yourself. In this sense a long-distance walk is not something to be undertaken lightly—it can have profound effects on the rest of your life.

2

Long Trails

They ask me: "Why hike the Pacific
Crest Trail, Mexico to Canada, for two
thousand, six hundred miles?"

All I can say is: "How can I not?"

— Cindy Ross, *Journey on the Crest*

The choice of destinations for the long-distance hiker is vast. In this chapter I outline some of the long trails in the United States and Canada (the rest of the world is the subject of chapter 3). Although I've hiked some of these trails, there are many I haven't been on. Doing the research for this chapter has made me want to hike many of the remaining ones, however.

Not all long trails are ideal for long-distance hikers, who generally want to spend most of their time in wild country. Some are close to or in towns and are more suited to short day hikes or cycling, while others follow paved roads for long sections. Here I've selected trails that should give a satisfying wilderness adventure. They vary enormously, of course. Some are well-blazed and well-maintained trails, with supply points that are fairly close together. Others are hardly marked at all and may not even be present on the ground in places, making for a more adventurous time for the experienced hiker but a potential nightmare for the novice. Different hikers like different landscapes, and there are forest trails, mountain trails, desert trails, lakeshore trails, wetland trails, and trails that include a little of all of these.

Tunnel Falls on the Eagle Creek Trail, an optional diversion from the Pacific Crest Trail in northern Oregon.

Thoughts on a 1,000-Mile Trek

In far northwest Canada lies a great and virtually unknown wilderness: 186,300 square miles of forest, lake, mountain, and tundra split by the great rivers Peel, Porcupine, Pelly, Stewart, and, mightiest of all, the Yukon, for which the territory is named. This is the land of the Klondike gold rush of 1898, the land that inspired Jack London's Call of the Wild and the poems of Robert Service—a wild, unspoiled land where grizzly bears and timber wolves still roam free. Yukon Territory is a land where untouched nature still dominates, barely brushed by the twentieth century. There are few such places left.

I knew well the argument that solo hiking in a remote wilderness was foolhardy, dangerous, even irresponsible, but I knew even more the great rewards that awaited, rewards that could hardly be glimpsed by those who walk in groups. Alone, I would be able to open myself up to the wilderness, to ready all my senses for what was offered, to learn what the mountains and forests, the rivers and lakes, had to teach me. I was not going to observe the land from the outside, to view it as a series of picture postcards, but rather to become part of it, to feel the harmony with the natural world that comes only after days alone. This was the real purpose of the walk, and the linking of two points on the map was merely an excuse to satisfy the rational part of me and to keep me moving each day.

— adapted from
Walking the Yukon

If any of these trails catches your imagination, more information can be obtained from guidebooks, hiker's accounts, trail organizations, and land managers (see the Resources chapter for details).

UNITED STATES

Triple Crown

There are three great long-distance trails in the United States that most long-distance hikers think of first. The original, best known, and most popular is the Appalachian Trail in the eastern states; the other two are the Pacific Crest Trail in the Far West and the Continental Divide Trail in the Rocky Mountains. The three together form the "Triple Crown," an award given by the American Long Distance Hiking Association–West (ALDHA-West) to hikers who have completed all three.

Appalachian National Scenic Trail

The Appalachian Trail (AT) was the first National Scenic Trail and is run by the National Park Service. It runs some 2,160 miles along the crest of the Appalachian Mountains from Springer Mountain in Georgia to Mount Katahdin in Maine. The idea for the AT was conceived by Benton MacKaye in 1921, but it was 1937 before the trail was completed. Eleven years later, in 1948, Earl Shaffer made the first continuous end-to-end hike. Fifty years later he through-hiked the trail again, an astonishing feat. Since Shaffer's first hike thousands of people have hiked end-to-end, and millions more have hiked sections of the AT. Today over two hundred people a year hike end-to-end, and many more set out to do so. Due to its popularity, the AT is sometimes called "the people trail." Through-hikers sometimes say that other hikers are the best feature of the trail.

The AT is a forest trail, dubbed the "long green tunnel" by some, though some sections are above timberline, such as that in the White Mountains in New Hampshire. Because it's a hiking-only trail, it takes a more direct line up and down hills than trails that are also designed for horses or mountain bikes, so the fact that much of it is in the trees doesn't mean that it's an easy hike. The AT is complete from end-to-end, and most of the land to either side is protected. The trail is well maintained and marked with the famous white blaze. Maintenance is carried out by volunteers working through the Appalachian Trail Conference. Shelters are located along the trail at close enough intervals that hikers can stay in one every night. These shelters can get crowded, however, so carrying a tent is advisable.

Only once on the AT, in the aptly named 100-Mile Wilderness, is the distance between supply points or road crossings as much as 100 miles. This means hikers can resupply fairly often so even those with low daily mileage shouldn't need to carry more than a week's supply of food at a time. Most through-hikers spend five to six months on the AT, starting in late March or April in the south and following the spring northward.

Pacific Crest National Scenic Trail

The Pacific Crest Trail (PCT) is a spectacular trail running 2,638 miles from Mexico to Canada through the deserts and transverse ranges of southern California, the Sierra Nevada range in central and northern California, and the Cascade

Mountains in Oregon and Washington. The idea for the trail was first proposed by Clinton C. Clarke in 1932. It was quickly accepted, and over the summers of 1935 to 1938 Warren L. Rogers led teams of young people along the whole of the proposed route. The PCT became the second trail designated a National Scenic Trail.

There is tremendous variety of scenery along the PCT from the hot deserts of southern California through the dense coniferous forests of the lower mountain slopes to the rocky terrain of many above-timberline passes, the highest of which is the 13,180-foot Forester Pass. In the High Sierra the trail runs through an alpine landscape, while in Oregon and southern Washington it runs past a long line of isolated strato-volcanoes—the Three Sisters, Mount Hood, Mount Adams, Mount Rainier—before finishing in the glaciated and very steep and rugged North Cascades. En route the PCT passes through 25 national forests and 7 national parks including Kings Canyon–Sequoia, Yosemite, and Rainier. Eighty percent of the PCT is on publicly owned land.

Forest camp with a tarp pitched as an open-ended ridge.

Crossing a patch of snow on the Pacific Crest Trail in northern California, with Mount Shasta on the horizon.

Much of the PCT is in country that is quite remote for the lower 48 states so there are long distances between resupply points, meaning a choice has to be made between heavy loads or high daily mileage. The trail is designed for horses as well as hikers so the grade is never very steep. On a through-hike, though, there's a good chance of encountering snow at some times and very hot temperatures at others. In the desert, water is a major concern, with two days' worth having to be carried at times, whereas in the mountains rainstorms and even blizzards can be a problem. To hike the PCT a full panoply of backpacking skills is needed.

Most hikers start in the south in April, hoping that by the time they reach the High Sierra, after approximately 500 miles, the bulk of the winter's snow will have melted. The early start is needed so that the North Cascades will be reached in September, before the next winter begins. Of course, high-mileage hikers can start later and avoid the snow, though they then have the pressure of maintaining that mileage throughout. Hiking north to south is much harder, as there will probably be much snow in the North Cascades until late June or early July, which means a late start on the hike, and the first snows may arrive in the High Sierra in October. High daily mileage will be needed to avoid this.

Continental Divide National Scenic Trail
The Continental Divide Trail (CDT) is the vision of Jim Wolf, who has worked for decades to see the trail established. It's the longest of the three big trails, at 3,200 miles. This is even more of an approximation than other trail mileage, as the CDT is not yet complete, although it was designated a National Scenic Trail back in 1978. It follows the U.S. watershed through Montana, Wyoming, Colorado, and New Mexico from Canada to Mexico. Most of the route is in the Rocky Mountains, but at the southern end the

trail descends to the heat of the desert. Like the PCT, the CDT passes through a wide variety of terrain, from low desert through forests to alpine tundra, making it a marvelously diverse hike. Along the way you'll see magnificent forests, alpine mountain ranges, glaciers, beautiful lakes, and desert mesas. There are also a surprising number of historical relics along the route, such as the abandoned dwellings of Native Americans, traces of the journeys of Lewis and Clark, the wagon ruts of the Oregon Trail, old mines, and trappers' cabins. Among the many scenic areas the CDT passes through are Glacier National Park, the Bob Marshal Wilderness, the Wind River Range, Yellowstone National Park, Rocky Mountain National Park, the Indian Peaks Wilderness, the Mount Massive Wilderness, the Weminuche Wilderness, and the Gila Wilderness.

Around two-thirds of the trail is now complete, though much of this isn't marked as the CDT. In places, particularly in southern Wyoming and New Mexico, the through-hiker has to link old roads, abandoned trails, and cross-country sections. This makes for an adventurous journey where good route finding and cross-country skills are necessary. Few people set out to through-hike the CDT. And in many areas few hikers set out on shorter trips due to the remoteness of much of the terrain. At times you can hike for days and meet no one along the trail, though in areas like Yellowstone and the Wind River there will be many others about. The

Climbing old snow in the Bob Marshal Wilderness in Montana on the Continental Divide Trail.

CDT is not a trail for those who like the camaraderie of trail life, but it's superb for those for whom solitude is important.

An Awesome Bear

I had not ventured far into the broad valley when I spotted a black object a quarter of a mile away to the west that looked suspiciously like a large animal. Through my binoculars I saw a dark grizzly bear foraging, I guessed, for berries. Because I was alone in the wilderness this bear was awe-inspiring and frightening. I felt privileged to see it since only a few hundred grizzlies inhabit the whole of the Ogilvies. Compared with the better-known coastal bears of Alaska and British Columbia, the northern Yukon grizzlies are small, the males reaching no more than five hundred pounds, females two-thirds of that, because of the sparse food available. Knowing these details didn't detract from the bear's impressiveness. Meeting the unchallenged lord of the mountains, the ultimate symbol of wilderness, can never be less than exhilarating.

— adapted from
Walking the Yukon

There haven't been enough through-hikers for a consensus to emerge as to whether it is easiest to hike south to north or north to south on the CDT. Either way, unless a very high daily mileage is maintained, snow will be found somewhere along the trail. Most of the few hikers who have done the CDT have taken five to six months. Hiking north means starting in April, which avoids the hottest weather in the desert but which means there is still likely to be snow in the San Juan Mountains in southern Colorado. The first snow of the next winter may fall on you in the northern Rockies, as you are unlikely to be there before September. Going south, as I did, the earliest practical start time is June, when the last snow will probably still be present in the mountains of Montana. However, a June start means going through the Colorado Rockies in September and October, when the first snows of the next winter are likely to begin. Given this chance of encountering snow, plus the scarcity of resupply points, which makes heavy packs inevitable at times, the remoteness of much of the trail, the lack of a good trail in many places, and the general ruggedness of the terrain, the CDT is undoubtedly the most difficult of the big three trails.

Other Long Trails

The Long Trail

James P. Taylor, founder of the Green Mountain Club in Vermont, first thought of the idea of a series of connecting trails, a long trail, through Vermont from Massachusetts to Canada in 1910. No other similar trails existed, so this was a visionary concept. The Long Trail became the first ever long-distance hiking trail. Although some sections were open before then, it wasn't until 1930 that the whole trail was completed. The Long Trail is 265 miles long and follows the ridge crest of the mountains, with many steep ascents and descents. The southern part of the trail coincides with the Appalachian Trail, and similar to the AT, there are shelters spaced a day's hike apart. These can be crowded, so carrying a tent or tarp is advisable. Black flies plague the Green Mountains early in the summer, so late July, August, and early fall, when the foliage is at its most spectacular, are reckoned to be the best times to hike the trail.

John Muir Trail

In 1892 Sierra Club member Theodore S. Solomons came up with the idea for a trail that followed the spine of the Sierra Nevada, keeping as close to the crest as possible. Club members explored possible routes over the next two decades for what was then known as the High Sierra Trail. However, after John Muir, then the president of the Sierra Club, died in 1915, it was decided to change the name to the John Muir Trail (JMT) in his honor. Trail construction was begun soon afterward, but the trail wasn't completed until 1938.

The resulting trail is probably one of the most spectacular and beautiful in the world. For 211

Monument 78

The trail winds through the wet forest, the dripping vegetation soaking the legs. A small clearing appears with a stone obelisk in the center of it. Monument 78, the northern end of the Pacific Crest Trail. "USA" it says on one side, "Canada" on the other. It has taken 5½ months to reach here, all the way from Mexico. You've experienced 2,600 miles of desert, mountain, and forest, 2,600 miles of glorious, awesome nature, 2,600 miles of adventure and excitement, delight, and pleasure. At times it has been hard and tiring. At times you have been wet, cold, exhausted, hungry, and thirsty. But those times fade away in comparison to the intensity of spending so long on a journey through the wilds, a journey in which you have reconnected with nature and yourself. Monument 78 marks the end but not the destination. The walk was not about reaching here—it was about what happened during the process of reaching here. And that will be with you forever.

miles it runs through the High Sierra, past soaring granite peaks and domes and through magnificent pristine conifer forests.

Starting in Yosemite Valley, the JMT climbs east into the High Sierra then turns south over a series of above-timberline passes ranging from 11,000 to 13,000 feet before finishing on 14,494-foot-high Mount Whitney, the highest peak in the contiguous United States. The descent from the summit adds a minimum of 11 miles to the hike. For much of the route the JMT takes the same line as the Pacific Crest Trail.

The JMT is a very popular route, so would-be hikers need to apply early for permits. In summer the weather in the Sierra Nevada is generally warm and dry, giving it perhaps the best climate for such a high range in the world. The JMT is well maintained and not too steep, but for 140 miles no roads are crossed. There are a couple of resupply points that can be easily reached by side trails, but even if these are used, heavy loads will need to be carried. Hikers also have to deal with black bears, which are used to raiding campsites for food. In the winter and spring the route is usually deep under snow, making it the province of the experienced ski tourer.

Pacific Northwest Trail

The Pacific Northwest Trail (PNT) is still very much in the making, although long sections are open to hikers. The idea behind the trail is to link the Continental Divide with the Pacific Ocean. In doing so, it also links the CDT with the PCT, opening up the intriguing and challenging possibility of combining the two big trails into one very long hike (approaching 7,000 miles for the entire trail system). The proposed route of the PNT is 1,100 miles long and runs through Montana, Idaho, and Washington, mostly in very remote mountain and forest country. Ron Strickland, the founder of the trail, has written a guidebook to the PNT (available on computer diskette), and it has been through-hiked by a few determined hikers. Summer is the time to go, and good cross-country hiking and navigation skills are required. A look at the PNT on the map suggests this is a superb wilderness route.

Solitude

With no sign of a path, I plunged into the willow swamps and stagnant backwaters behind my camp, not a pleasant start to the day. Once I escaped them I found the flat shady forest rich in vegetation and mostly free of the deadfall that impedes progress. The walking was almost hypnotic in the still silence of the trees. The only sounds were the infrequent chatter of a squirrel and the faint hum of insects in the occasional sunny clearing. I thought about loneliness, something others seem to feel should be a problem on a long solo walk. I have never found this to be so. In my journal I wrote, "How can you be lonely here? This is the heart of life. A place to be content and at peace while the work of nature, so superior to our efforts, goes on all around."

— from *Walking the Yukon*

Colorado Trail

The Colorado Trail runs for 471 miles through the Rocky Mountains from Denver to Durango. First conceived in 1973, the trail was completed in 1987. For some of the way the Colorado Trail and the Continental Divide Trail share the same route, though in places the CDT takes a higher line, closer to the divide itself. The Colorado Trail goes through some of the most impressive scenery in the Colorado Rockies, with long sections above timberline. As you'd expect for Colorado, this is a high trail, much of it above 10,000 feet and with a high point of 13,334 feet at Coney Summit in the San Juan Mountains. This means that large portions of the trail are snow-covered for much of the year. Through-hikers can start in late June at the Denver end; this is 70 miles from timberline, so it'll take you a while to reach the high country. Durango, however, is fewer than 20 miles from timberline. Early July is a better time for starting there if you want to avoid the snow.

Arizona Trail

The idea for a trail running through Arizona from Utah to Mexico first came to schoolteacher Dale Shewalter in the early 1970s. However, it

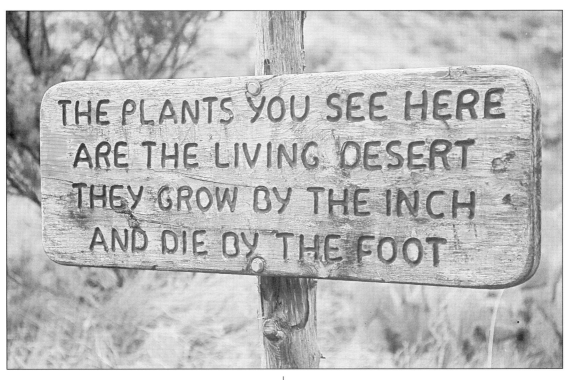

Tread carefully in the desert, advises a sign in the Grand Canyon.

was 1985 before he put his proposal forward, after spending 24 days hiking part of the planned route. Work on the Arizona Trail (AZT) began soon afterward and is still ongoing, as the trail is not yet complete. When finished, it will be at least 780 miles long, 85 percent of it on public lands, mostly national forests.

As the trail crosses a series of small but steep mountain ranges, it's a roller-coaster of a route, climbing up and over each range as well as descending in and out of several canyons, including the Grand Canyon. The low point is 2,000 feet, the high point 9,000 feet. The terrain varies from hot subtropical desert through grasslands and chaparral to subalpine forests. Overall, though, this is a desert trail with the associated heat and shortage of water. The summer is extremely hot at low elevations, while in the winter there can be snow on the highest sections, making autumn and spring the best times

for through-hiking the trail. Because the trail isn't finished yet (500 miles have been completed so far), hikers have to plan their own routes in some places. My hike along this exciting and spectacular trail was about 800 miles long.

North Country National Scenic Trail
When finished, the North Country Trail will be one of the longest trails in the United States. How long is not certain—the National Park Service estimate is 4,200 miles. The trail runs from the Adirondack Mountains in New York to the Missouri River in North Dakota and travels through the states of Pennsylvania, Ohio, Michigan, Wisconsin, and Minnesota. Over half the trail has been completed. Much of the North Country Trail is in forests, but there are also mountain summits, wetlands, lakeshores, farmland, and grasslands along the way. The length of the trail, which means that winter is likely to be encountered at both ends, and the lack of development make this a very challenging and difficult trail. Very few people have

Dawn and Dusk

The sun sets and the sun rises. We all take this for granted, though we mostly never see either event. Out in the wilds, though, the power and significance of the sun's appearance and disappearance are felt more strongly. And when a brilliant wash of color over the sky accompanies the sun's coming or going, it can be awe-inspiring, a powerful reminder of the glory of the natural world.

Sunset is a time of reflection and quiet. The day's hiking is over, and it is time for rest. Sunsets may blaze at first with color, but slowly the reds and yellows deepen and darken, their brightness fading as they merge with the deepening blue of the sky, a strangely calming and relaxing process.

Sunrise, in contrast, is invigorating and stimulating. The first faint gray light brightens and strengthens as the power of the sun increases. The black silhouettes of mountains, lakes, and trees develop details and color, a monochrome world becoming brilliant with intensifying shades of red, green, and blue. As the sun rises into the sky and the glory of its first appearance fades into the stark light of day, the sleepiness of the night is thrown off, and it is time to begin.

---

section-hiked the route from end to end, and still fewer have through-hiked it. The first to do so in a single season was Carolyn Hoffman in 1978, accompanied by Lou Ann Fellows for all but a couple of hundred miles. Hoffman took 222 days to hike the trail.

Sierra High Route
The Sierra High Route is just what the name suggests, a high-level hike along the High Sierra. The route's originator and author of a guidebook, Steve Roper, describes it as "a rugged alternative to the John Muir Trail." The route is 195 miles long, beginning in Kings Canyon in the southern Sierra and finishing at Twin Lakes near the northeast boundary of Yosemite National Park. Almost half of the route is on trails; the rest is cross-country. Virtually all of it is on or above timberline, between 9,000 and 11,500 feet. The route runs through the gloriously scenic high country of Kings Canyon–Sequoia and Yosemite National Parks, often via little-used passes, and it looks to be a superb hike for the experienced backpacker.

Florida National Scenic Trail
Not all hikers like ascents; indeed, some dislike them intensely. The Florida Trail is made for such people. Not yet complete, it will eventually run for 1,300 miles from Big Cypress National Preserve in southern Florida to the Gulf Islands National Seashore in western Florida. So far, 950

miles of the trail have been completed. This is a low-level trail and a wet one, in that it crosses a wide variety of wetlands and swamps, though there are drier pine forests in places. This is the only trail where you have to join the local trail association if you want to hike the entire length, as some private lands that lie on the route are only open to association members.

Iditarod National Historic Trail
Famous for its annual dogsled race, the Iditarod Trail in Alaska is also open to ski backpackers and, in a few places, summer hikers. The total length is 2,264 miles, but this is for a network of trails rather than one continuous trail. The basic route from Seward in southern Alaska to Nome in western Alaska is 938 miles long. The Iditarod follows trails established by prospectors in the late nineteenth and early twentieth centuries. It's not a mountain route; rather, it follows river valleys, crossing many wetlands along the way. Much of the terrain is not passable on foot in summer, so this is very much a winter trail as then the rivers and marshes are frozen. It's also a trail for the experienced winter traveler able to cope with bitter winter temperatures as low as −40°F.

Great Western Trail
This exciting-sounding trail is still in the planning stage and does not yet exist on the ground. When it does, the Great Western Trail will run

from Mexico to Canada through Arizona, Utah, Wyoming, Montana, and Idaho. The proposed trail corridor is 3,783 miles long. This should be a superb route through some of the finest scenery in the West, though it seems likely that parts of the trail will be open to off-road vehicles. There is, of course, nothing to stop anyone from hiking his or her own route through these states already.

American Discovery Trail

Stretching 6,356 miles from the Atlantic to the Pacific, the American Discovery Trail (ADT), opened in summer 2000, is the longest trail in the United States as well as the first to run from coast to coast. The brainchild of *Backpacker* magazine and the American Hiking Society, the ADT is an amazing creation. En route from Point Reyes National Seashore in California to Cape Henlopen State Park in Delaware the ADT crosses 15 states and the District of Columbia, 14 national

The U.S.–Canadian border at Waterton Lakes National Park, the start of the Continental Divide Trail, the Great Divide Trail, and the Pacific Northwest Trail.

parks, and 16 national forests. The ADT isn't wholly a wilderness trail. Part of its purpose is to link communities, so it passes through small towns and cities as well as wild areas, linking up over 200 local, regional, and national trails. Through-hiking the whole trail would be a major achievement, while hiking long sections would be challenging. The 2,000 miles from the Rocky Mountains to the Pacific Ocean through Colorado, Utah, Nevada, and California looks to be a fine hike for those who like wilderness.

CANADA

Great Divide Trail

The Great Divide Trail (GDT) through the Canadian Rockies close to the watershed of Canada was first proposed in 1967. Some construction work was done in the 1970s, but since then little has happened officially. However, during the 1990s Dustin and Julia Lynx explored a 900-mile GDT route along already existing trails from Alberta's Waterton Lakes National Park (where the Continental Divide Trail also begins) north to Kakwa Lake Provincial Park and wrote a guidebook describing this route. I hiked a some-

Encounter with Otters

The small, shaded, lily-dotted pool, deep in the forest, barely merited a glance as I hiked past, intent on reaching the more obviously attractive mountains of the Three Sisters, enticing glimpses of which I kept catching through the trees. Then a slight movement made me look closer. An otter was swimming across the pool, three cubs following her. Carefully and quietly I sat down, not daring to remove my pack, and watched. No more than a few dozen feet away the otters swam and dived. Occasionally they looked my way but seemed curious and wary rather than afraid. They dived together, arching their backs in the air. Occasionally I could see their sleek bodies under the water, the fur white with air bubbles, as they swam close to me. They communicated with loud hissing or hard breathing sounds and high-pitched squeaks. There seemed no purpose to their swimming other than pleasure, though I guess it was good training for the cubs. Once they lay draped over a small rock in the middle of the pool, totally relaxed in the sunshine, and after half an hour, as I quietly departed, they climbed out onto a log. Watching them was an absorbing experience. Everything else vanished, my hike, the time, where I was. All that existed was the wood, the water, and the otters. The Three Sisters, so urgently desired so shortly before, were totally forgotten.

what different route from Waterton to Kakwa in 1988 on my length of the Canadian Rockies walk. The GDT is not marked as such on the ground, and as the Lynxes point out, there is a choice of trails in places. The Canadian Rockies comprise one of the most spectacular mountain ranges in the world, and most of this region is still unspoiled wilderness, making the GDT a marvelous and highly recommended trail.

Bruce Trail

The 500-mile Bruce Trail, completed in 1967, was the first long-distance trail in Canada. Wholly situated in the province of Ontario, it follows the Niagara Escarpment from Queenston, near Niagara Falls, to Tobermory, at the end of the Bruce Peninsula in Georgian Bay. This is mostly a forest and lake route. There are shelters and campsites along the whole route. A ferry at Tobermory can be taken to connect the Bruce Trail with the Voyageur Trail at its eastern terminus.

Voyageur Trail

The Voyageur Trail is planned to run 700 miles in Ontario from South Baymouth on Manitoulin Island in Lake Huron north along the north shore of Lake Superior to Thunder Bay. At present, 375 miles of the trail exist. The rugged coastline of Lake Superior has high cliffs and pebble beaches backed by deciduous and coniferous forests. The trail runs through Lake Superior Provincial Park and Pukaskwa National Park, a wilderness of forests, hills, pebble beaches, and rocky coves.

Canol Heritage Trail

The Canol Heritage Trail is unusual in that although it passes through very remote wilderness country, it follows the remains of the Canol Road and pipeline. These were built between 1942 and 1944 to transport oil across the Mackenzie Mountains from the oilfields of the Northwest Territories to the Yukon Territory and the Alaska Highway as part of plans to protect Alaska from attack in World War II. The project was abandoned shortly after completion. Now overgrown and eroded, the road has become a hiking trail that climbs over the Mackenzie Mountains from Norman Wells on the Mackenzie River in the Northwest Territories to Ross River in the Yukon, a distance of 222 miles. The high point on the trail is 5,500 feet.

The Canol Trail is a serious route. There are several river crossings where the road bridges have been washed away, and these can be impassable after heavy rain. All supplies have to be carried. This is a true wilderness hike for the experienced backpacker.

Svalbard reindeer on the arctic island of Spitsbergen.

3

Further Afield

There is just one moment when carrying a
thirty-pound pack is purest pleasure unalloyed:
the moment when you first shoulder the pack after
twenty-four hours of hoicking it on and off ships
and in and out of trains.

— Showell Styles, *Backpacking in Alps
and Pyrenees*

There are myriad opportunities for long-distance hiking in the United States and Canada. No one could hike more than a small fraction of what is possible. Even so, adventurous backpackers may start wondering what it's like to hike in other countries, may wonder what the Alps are like or the Himalaya. Experiencing different cultures, meeting people whose lifestyles are very different, and visiting towns and cities unlike those of home can be a fascinating adventure. The landscapes may also be strange: great granite walls rising out of icy fjords in Greenland; brown moorlands above old industrial towns on the Pennine Way in England; the highest mountains in the world soaring above Sherpa villages and green forests in Nepal. Hiking may involve traveling with pack animals or porters and sleeping in mountain lodges or even hotels every night rather than the self-sufficient backpacking of North America, though that can be practiced in most places as well.

PLANNING

Good planning is even more necessary for hiking abroad than it is at home. The suggestions given in chapter 4, Preparation and Planning, all hold true, but there are also some specific recommendations that can ease foreign travel. The first is to begin planning earlier than you would for a trip at home. There is more to do, and it can take longer to get information from other countries—never mind the waiting for visas, tickets, and other documents. A good book to consult is Ellen Dudley's *The Savvy Adventure Traveler*.

INFORMATION

Not so long ago information about many hiking destinations abroad was sparse and hard to find. Now with the World Wide Web and myriad guidebooks there are few areas without fairly detailed information. Finding it still requires a bit more effort and time than researching a hike at home, though. See also Finding Information, pages 56–58, and the Resources chapter for tips and sources.

The World Wide Web has many useful sites, with <www.gorp.com> a good starting place. As well as information on various regions and accounts of hikes and other adventures you can find links to other sites and sources of information. Guidebooks can be bought from such sites as <www.adventuroustraveler.com> and <www.amazon.com>, too.

Inspirational books packed with photographs of hiking destinations and brief details of hikes are useful when trying to decide where you want to go. The latest one of these is *Classic Treks*, edited by Bill Birkett. Older books worth seeking out are *Classic Walks of the World*, edited by Walt Unsworth, and *Trekking: Great Walks of the World*, edited by John Cleare.

Once you know where you want to go, guidebooks are an excellent starting point for gathering information and planning your hike. They fall into two categories. General guides will tell you all about a country or region and the requirements for traveling there, whereas trail and trekking guides give details of hiking routes and areas. Books from such publishers as Lonely Planet and Bradt cover both general and specific information, while the Sierra Club and the Mountaineers publish hiking guides to many areas. It's advisable to check the publication dates of trail guides and to remember that the writer will have last researched the trail a year or two before that date. Guides for less popular areas may not be updated very often. Older trail guides can still be useful, especially if they are all there are, but you need to allow for changes occurring since they were written. On a hike in the French Alps I discovered the 10-year-old trail guide I used didn't show a major new road over a mountain pass. This caused me to change my route, as I would have had to walk along the road for many miles if I'd followed the guidebook. The book also didn't show several trail relocations and was inaccurate regarding accommodations and facilities in the villages I passed through. However, the maps I used were up-to-date and showed the changes to trails and roads, and having more facilities along the way than I had anticipated was a bonus. It's not always like that. During a hike along the Pennine Way in England I headed down a sodden boggy hillside

Inoculations

Inoculations are likely to be needed for many developing countries. They may have to be administered many weeks before you go, and you may need several inoculations that can't be given at the same time, so it is essential to find out early what is required—at least six months before you go. Information on necessary inoculations can be obtained from the Centers for Disease Control's International Travelers' Hotline (404-332-4559) or Web site (<www.cdc.gov/travel/>). And when you're traveling, don't forget to take your inoculation certificates with you.

Overcoming Language Barriers

Speech is the primary form of communication between human beings. So when we can't understand someone or be understood by them, it can be disturbing, especially when you or the other person is in need of information or help. Sign language is the only recourse if you have no words in common, and even a few signs will be very helpful. Creativity is needed to use sign language well along with any props you have. A map may be useful as people will often recognize place-names even if they're not familiar with maps. If you point in the distance and at a place on the map, a nod probably means that yes, it is in that direction. Food and other supplies can be bought and accommodations booked by pointing and miming if necessary. You just have to be patient and accept that you may not always get exactly what you want.

Learning a few words of the language before you visit a country will make communication much easier, however. Local people may well be more helpful if you've obviously made an attempt at learning at least a few words of their language, too. A phrase book can come in handy. There are many that are light enough to take on a hike.

in driving rain toward a road, looking forward to hot food and drink at a café at the road crossing that was recommended in the trail guide. As I approached the road, I was disappointed to see the charred remains of a wooden building. The café had burned down a few years earlier. There was no other building in sight.

I would also suggest reading hiking stories, especially long-distance hiking stories, about the countries you are thinking of visiting, if any are available (the Resources chapter includes a whole section on such books). There's nothing like a personal account to capture the atmosphere of a place, the details of what it's like to be there.

MAPS

Maps vary enormously from country to country. Most Western European countries are well mapped. In Britain the Ordnance Survey (OS) publishes detailed 1:50,000 and 1:25,000 topographic maps of the whole country, while Harveys Maps publish special 1:40,000 and 1:25,000 topo maps of popular hiking areas. In France the 1:25,000 IGN Serie Bleue maps have hiking trails (Grandes Randonnées) marked clearly on them, plus mountain lodges and other facilities. In many developing countries the maps are not as good. In Nepal many maps are based on very old surveys and are lacking in detail. On a trek across the remote region of Dolpo, I used simple 1:250,000 maps with few spot heights. When these are the only maps available, a trail guide is very useful. Using minimal maps whose accuracy is dubious does add a sense of discovery and exploration to a hike, though. It can be exciting not to be sure whether there is a way down from a high pass or whether there's a trail down a valley. Such doubts have to be built into your planning, of course, so you have time to change your route or retreat if necessary.

Web bookstores like the Adventurous Traveler can supply maps for foreign countries. Trail guides to specific areas usually give sources for maps.

HEALTH

Before undertaking a long hike abroad a sensible precaution is to have a medical checkup so any potential problems can be detected and treated at home. Tell your doctor where you're going and what you'll be doing—hiking in remote areas is very different from traveling to popular tourist places—and get advice on what medicines you should carry. Up-to-date information is very important, for medical hazards can change quickly. The Web site of the World Health Organization, <*www.who.ch/welcome.html*>, contains information for travelers (see Resources).

At least six months in advance of the trip you'll need to find out if any vaccinations are needed. For Western Europe, Australia, and New Zealand, these aren't likely to be necessary. For countries in Asia, Africa, and South America, vaccinations are usually essential. Some are requirements of entry; others are merely advisable. The Centers for Disease Control and Prevention (CDC) publish an annual country-by-country list of immunizations and other precautions required or recommended. Local health departments usually have copies of this. The CDC also has an International Travelers' Hotline (404-332-4559) and a Web site *<www.cdc.gov/travel.html>*. Immunization records should be carried with you. Some countries may require certificates to show you have been immunized. If you need several vaccinations, these may have to be staggered over a period of months, so you need to find out early what inoculations you need.

In many countries malaria is a major cause for concern. Antimalaria medication has to be started a few weeks in advance of a trip and continued after you come home. Malaria pills aren't total preventives, though. Where malaria is a threat, you'll need repellent and mosquito-proof clothing plus a tent with insect netting on the doors or a mosquito net to sleep under.

Water is the biggest threat to health in many developing countries, for it may contain viruses that can kill or disable you. Chemical disinfection is the only sure way to kill viruses. A filter alone is not enough. See pages 98–101 for details of water treatment. Remember, too, that tap water is often untreated as is the water used to wash fruit and vegetables, which should always be peeled before being eaten. The only time I have had a severe stomach disorder was in Katmandu, when I wasn't even hiking. I suspect it was caused by brushing my teeth with tap water in my hotel room.

First-aid supplies may be hard to come by in some countries, so it's a good idea to bring a more comprehensive kit than you would carry at home. In developing countries disposable syringes are worth carrying in case injections are

Essential Information

In case of loss, theft, or damage, lists of the details of essential documents should be carried separately so you have the information if it is needed. Also leave a list at home as a backup.

- passport number with date and place of issue
- credit card numbers
- bank telephone numbers
- camera equipment with serial numbers
- insurance policy numbers plus telephone numbers for claims emergency
- medical telephone number
- doctor's name and telephone number
- consulate and embassy addresses and telephone numbers
- plane ticket booking reference number
- plane ticket serial number and date of issue
- dates and times of flights
- telephone and booking numbers of the flight-booking agent
- telephone code for home
- telephone codes for countries to be visited
- contact address, if possible

needed. I also like to take broadband antibiotics and prescription painkillers accompanied by copies of the prescriptions in case I'm asked to explain what they are to an official.

PAPERWORK

The essential item needed for travel abroad is, of course, a passport. For some countries you'll need an entry visa or a hiking permit as well. Check with the relevant embassy for this. The U.S. State Department can also supply information on visas and other requirements. You'll need a photograph for your passport and possibly for visas and permits. If you carry several passport photographs, you won't be caught out if you find you need one for a permit.

You'll also need health and travel insurance. Make sure this covers hiking and backpacking and mountain rescue in the country you're visiting. General travel insurance doesn't usually cover hiking, and many health policies don't cover foreign travel. It's wise to keep documents on your person when traveling and when in any shared accommodation or eating places used while hiking. I carry mine in a small, flat nylon pouch hung around my neck or kept in an inside pocket. In case your documents are lost or stolen or you have an accident or become ill, it's best to carry a list of important information separate from the other paperwork. Leave a copy of this at home, too, in case people there need the information. This list could include the items listed in the Essential Information sidebar, page 23.

Along with this list you should leave at home as detailed an itinerary as possible, including dates when you expect to phone home, or send a card, letter, e-mail, or fax. At the same time remember that postal services and phone networks vary widely across the world. It might take a few days or a few months for a letter to arrive, depending on where you mail it. At least with a phone you know whether you've gotten through or not. Many places, including some remote locations, now have Internet or cyber cafés from which you can send e-mail messages.

MONEY

Foreign currency can be carried in different forms for security. Cash, credit cards, bankcards, and traveler's checks are the options available. Cash is needed for small purchases and in remote places where nothing else will be accepted. Buying currency before you set out is a good idea so you're not desperately seeking a bank or foreign exchange when you arrive tired and jet-lagged in a strange country. On a long trip you won't want to carry all the cash you might need over several months, so knowing the whereabouts of banks and exchange bureaus is sensible. If you do carry a large amount of cash, I suggest splitting it into separate amounts and carrying these in different places. Always having some small denomination notes is a good idea so you don't end up trying to buy a cup of coffee with the equivalent of a $50 bill.

A credit card is safer than cash and can be used for many purchases, sometimes in surprising places. You can pay for food and accommodations in unstaffed huts deep in the backcountry in Norway simply by filling in a credit card slip and dropping it in a box. Indeed, this method is preferred, as a box full of slips isn't attractive to thieves. Credit cards can also be

Hiring a Guide

Hikers who don't want to join an organized trek may need a guide or perhaps a porter to assist them in their journey in areas such as the Himalaya. In some areas a guide may be a requirement. Finding guides and porters can take time, so it's best to allow a day or so for this. Guides can be found through trekking companies, tourist bureaus, magazine advertisements, and park officials, or other authorities for the area. Asking other hikers, either directly or via Internet newsgroups, is a good way to assess whether a guide is likely to be good. A trekking company with a good reputation should be able to recommend competent people, too.

If you do hire someone, sort out all the details of what is involved in advance. What are they expected to do? How much will they be paid? Find out, too, if tipping is usual and, if so, how much. Do they bring their own food, or do you provide it? Can food be bought en route? Who supplies tents and other equipment? Sort out how sanitation, water, and rubbish will be dealt with and what fuel will be used to ensure a minimum impact hike.

Guides, of course, should always be able to speak some English as you have to be able to communicate with them. Porters may not be able to speak any English, so those arrangements have to be made through a trekking agency.

Walls of Mist

The eerie silence and closed-in feeling of walking through dense mist high in the mountains is strange and otherworldly. Gray tendrils of air slide over the ground and around trees or rocks. Sometimes the mist is wet, and droplets of moisture coat everything, materializing out of the air. The air has a sense of solidity to it. It almost feels as though you can reach out and touch it, though you know there is nothing there.

Mists usually fade away, but they can stop abruptly. I first experienced this on the Pennine Way in England. Following the path in thick mist across open moorland beside a lake, I suddenly walked out of the cool, damp mist into clear, dry, warm air. Startled, I turned and looked back. A white wall rose into the sky just a few feet away. I walked in and out of the mist a few times, intrigued by this seemingly inexplicable phenomenon.

I have most often experienced this on the crest of the Pyrenees. In these mountains moist, cool air rises up out of the forested French valleys to the north and meets hot, dry air coming up from the arid, dusty Spanish plains. Sometimes the balance between the two is such that they simply stop where they touch, neither able to push the other forward. Often this actually occurs on the border, the French mists hanging motionless as they come up against the wall of Spanish heat. Following the High Level Route, which winds along or close to the border, crossing it many times, you can dip in and out the mist, a curious sensation.

---

used to buy cash in banks or withdraw it from automatic teller machines (ATMs). (On a long trip make sure you've arranged for your home contact or your bank to pay your credit card bill every month.)

Bankcards can also be used to withdraw money from ATMs or a bank as long as your bank is part of the same international network. Often this is the way to get the best exchange rate. With both credit cards and bankcards there's a fee for withdrawing cash, so it's best to take out a fair amount at one go rather than make many small withdrawals.

Traveler's checks can also be exchanged for cash in banks as well as used for direct payments. In remote areas they may not be accepted, however. Checks in U.S. dollars are best in developing countries. In Europe checks in the currency of the country you're visiting are more readily accepted. If you carry traveler's checks, take the receipts as well, stored separately, and leave a copy of them at home in case of loss. You should also keep track of how many you have used. Traveler's checks are expensive and a bit of a hassle. I must admit I haven't used them for many years, since most places that accept them also take credit cards.

In some countries you have to change a certain amount of cash and spend it before you leave. (Currencies where this is the case aren't usually worth anything outside the country anyway.) Regulations change rapidly, so up-to-date information should be obtained just before your trip. Countries with these regulations are usually places with severe economic problems. Dollars are of great value in these places.

TRANSPORT

Fast, efficient aircraft can whisk you across the oceans from one modern airport to another. Once you leave that sealed, sanitized world, it can be quite an adventure just reaching the start of your hike, however. Getting to your starting point might involve long vehicle journeys down rut-filled dirt roads or flights through mountain gorges in tiny aircraft or over twisting glaciers in a helicopter. Some of these journeys can be wonderful and exciting; others can be truly terrifying. On a trip to Nepal I was driven from Katmandu to the town of Nepalgunj along narrow, winding, bumpy dirt roads in a lurching taxi with sagging suspension. We left Katmandu at dusk to descend hairpin bends in the growing dark,

Being dropped from a fishing boat at the head of a fjord in southwest Greenland.

seeing the many lorries crawling up the mountainside only at the last minute, as most had no lights. Although I was very tired from a long flight, fear kept me awake for the whole hot, sweaty 11-hour journey, whereas my companion, owner of the trekking company organizing the trip, slept soundly for hours. I guess he was used to it.

One of the most spectacular journeys I've undertaken was in southwest Greenland. From the little settlement of Nanortalik, itself reachable only by air or sea, we were taken fifty miles up Tasermuilt Fjord on a small fishing boat. Bits of iceberg bobbed around us as we sailed up the fjord past huge granite walls and spires, some of them soaring 5,000 feet into the sky, a wild, fantastic sight. At the head of the fjord a 4,000-foot icefall tumbled down from the vast inland ice sheet in a tangled mass of contorted blocks of green-blue ice. We were put ashore by small

dinghy and left with the knowledge that we were there alone until the boat came back in two weeks' time, a strange feeling.

On the helicopter flight to Nanortalik we had hugged the coast as it was misty, so we'd seen little. On the way back just the peaks around the fjord were cloud covered. The helicopter flight was in bright sunshine, and the pilot took a spectacular inland route flying low above long winding glaciers. A huge waterfall crashed down the cliffs at the head of one of these ice rivers. Just as I was wondering how the pilot was going to avoid it, I suddenly found myself looking straight down at the surging water as the helicopter was flipped on its side in order to make the abrupt turn.

Some journeys, especially ones by train, can be a delight, a relaxing way to ease into the wilds. Flights take you from cities to remote places very abruptly, leaving a feeling of surprise at the sudden transition. Trains are more gradual, especially if you take a sleeper. One of my favorite journeys is the night train from Stockholm in southern Sweden to arctic Lapland. The last views you have before falling asleep are of suburbs and brown farmland. But when you wake, you look out at huge pine forests, long shining lakes and rivers, and distant snow-covered mountains, a vast northern landscape.

Although all the details of your journey can be worked out at home and the tickets booked in advance, don't expect journeys to run smoothly everywhere. Due to a whole host of reasons, delays are common in some countries. In others the weather may play a part. Many airports don't have radar and may not be accessible in storms. That's the case with Nassasuaq in Greenland. When I flew there, I knew that if the clouds closed in we would probably have to divert to Reykjavik in Iceland and wait there until the weather changed. In fact, we landed just as the weather began to deteriorate. A group waiting to fly out then spent most of a day waiting for it to clear. Although it can be frustrating to have to wait longer than expected to reach the start of your hike, it's best to regard any holdups as part of the adventure. There's nothing you can do about them anyway. I carry a few paperbacks to pass away the time during delays. Secondhand books that you don't mind leaving behind are best.

Public transport is generally reliable in Europe, and you can often start hiking from the bus or train station. A few weeks before writing this I hiked the GR58 long-distance trail in the Queyras region of the French Alps. I traveled south from Paris on a sleeper train that arrived at the start of the hike at 7:30 in the morning. I literally stepped off the train and started hiking. In developing countries public transport is often more erratic, with timetables rarely, if ever, adhered to. If there is no public transport, it's worth inquiring at your hostel or hotel and at any tourist information offices as there will almost certainly be locals who run vans or buses that will take you where you want to go.

Renting a car would seem to be a way to avoid public transport delays. It can be in some countries as long as you feel comfortable driving on strange roads after a long flight. You also need to think about what you'll do with the car while you're hiking. I've never rented a car abroad.

GEAR

Hiking gear is much the same wherever you go—or at least the same gear will work everywhere. If you travel much, you'll notice some differences. For instance, in Sweden and Finland a hiker in leather or fabric hiking boots stands out, for the locals usually hike in high-topped green rubber boots.

Gear needs to be appropriate to the expected conditions, of course. In the Dolpo region of Nepal I hiked in sandals, shorts, T-shirt, and sun hat most days as it was hot and sunny. Once the sun went down, it became very cold very quickly, however, so during the evenings and early mornings I wore a thermal shirt, fleece jacket, down jacket, fleece hat, and long pants with long underwear underneath. Night temperatures were between 2°F and 30°F, so I was glad to have my warm sleeping bag, too. On the 17,000-foot passes we crossed, I often wore a wind shirt to cut the cool breeze, but I never once needed the light rain jacket I'd brought.

In complete contrast to this was a spring trip to the remote island of Spitsbergen high in the arctic at 78°N latitude. Here the daytime temperature

Political Instability

Political stability is the norm in Western countries, but this is not the case in many parts of the world. Many regions are volatile, and a country that is calm and seemingly stable one day can burst into civil war or revolution the next. The kidnapping of visitors for ransom or as a bargaining tool, although rare, does occur at times. Violence against people from other countries is possible, too. You can minimize the risk of such events by staying away from potentially dangerous regions. To find out which regions to avoid, get up-to-date information from the State Department's Travel Warnings and Consular Information Sheets Web site, <www.travel.state.gov/travel_warnings.html>, or phone their Emergency Center, 202-647-5225.

Approaching Charkabhot

Dusty red rock mountains rise above; below, far below, a dark twist of river, the Barbung Khola, runs. The narrow stony trail descends slowly, approaching the rushing waters. Ahead a cloud of dust rises into the clear sky. Beyond it a fortress stands on a rocky bluff above the river, a fortress decorated with a mass of ragged white flags, a fortress made up of stone buildings with narrow slots for windows and flat roofs on which dry cracked firewood is stacked in large piles. This is the village of Charkabhot, high in the remote Dolpo region of the Nepalese Himalaya.

As we approach, figures can be seen moving in the swirling cloud, raising and lowering their arms, apparently beating the ground with long poles with loose flapping paddles on the end of them. These are villagers threshing the corn crop. Others are sieving the husks. A pall of corn debris hangs in the air.

rarely went above the freezing level and was mostly below. The coldest night was –5°F. Most days I wore thick bibs over long underwear, a thin thermal shirt, a stretch fleece top, a lightweight fleece jacket, a waterproof-breathable jacket, a fleece-lined cap, liner gloves, and thick pile-lined windproof gloves. In camp I added a down jacket and insulated booties. On one day we crossed a pass straight into a blizzard that was so cold I pulled my hood up over my hat and donned a neck gaiter and still barely felt warm. In that storm, ice formed on any exposed skin, nostrils and eyelids froze, and the edges of hats and hoods turned white with frozen condensation from our breath. Yet 3,500 feet was the highest I reached on Spitsbergen, some 14,000 feet lower than in Nepal.

Though gear you already own will almost certainly do for the hiking, an extra bag is useful for getting your gear to the start of the walk. Packs may be wonderful on your back, but they aren't ideal for air travel due to all the straps hanging from them, which can get caught in conveyor belts and may be used to haul the pack about by baggage handlers. A duffel bag big enough for your pack and other items like boots and trekking poles (and anything you may buy to take home) will protect your gear and is much more likely to survive airline baggage handlers intact. Once you're at your destination, the duffel can be deposited in the airport's stored luggage area if you're flying out from the same airport or else at a hotel where you'll be staying. If you are flying out from a different place, you'll need to mail your bag to yourself. I put street clothes and shoes in the duffel, too. They're nice to travel in and even nicer to don at the end of the hike. If you're on a trip where porters carry the loads, your duffel may well be needed by them and so will go on the walk with you.

If you don't use a duffel bag, your pack can be protected to some extent by tightening all straps and tying down the ends so they don't flap. Hip-belts can either be fastened around the back of the pack or removed and placed inside. Cord or even sticky tape could be wound around the pack, or you could put it in a couple of garbage sacks and tape these shut. I've never done the last as I have seen packs arriving on the carousel with the garbage sacks shredded into strips of black plastic. I've also traveled with someone whose brand-new pack arrived with broken buckles and torn fabric at the start of a trip. A duffel bag is best.

The only item of gear that could be a problem abroad is your stove, both in terms of flying with it and finding fuel for it. Stoves are covered in detail beginning on page 160. Here I'll just point out that airlines outside the United States and Canada seem to be happy to carry empty stoves and fuel bottles. I've never been told I couldn't do this, though a few times I have been asked if I was carrying fuel. If you're heading for developing countries, don't expect to find clean fuel—dirty kerosene is most common. A field-maintainable multifuel stove plus a filter funnel is just about essential. For other countries, find out what the locals use. In France, Camping Gaz cartridges are the standard and can be found everywhere, so a stove that fits these is a good idea. In Scandinavia, alcohol stoves are very popular, and Peak 1/Primus/Optimus style resealable cartridges can be found in many places. White gas is very rare and expensive outside North America. You might find Coleman Fuel in outdoor stores, but that's about it. Also find out what fuels are called in the countries you're visiting. It can be confusing. For example, kerosene is called *paraffin* in Britain but *petrol* in France. Petrol, however, refers to automotive gasoline in Britain.

CULTURE

Different cultures can be overwhelming, confusing, even scary at first. I can remember arriving in Katmandu for the first time and finding the noisy bustle in the narrow, crowded streets quite startling. I didn't know how to deal with the

A duffel bag big enough to hold your pack is a good way to protect your gear when traveling.

street vendors who beseeched me to buy their wares, and the volume of noise was disorienting. After a few days I had accepted it, though I never became used to it.

As visitors in someone else's land, hikers from abroad should respect local customs. First, that means finding out what they are, which can be done from good guidebooks to the area. If in doubt, politeness and watching locals to see how they act often helps. Even if they don't react when you commit a faux pas, local people will usually have more respect for you if you know or show you want to learn their customs. In Dolpo I quickly learned that the Sherpas always walked past *mani* (prayer) walls (lines of engraved stones), on the right and that they prefer everyone to do the same, for this is a mark of respect. If you appear to have inadvertently committed an offense, an apology may help. Even if the words aren't understood, the gestures and tone of voice probably will be.

Hikers visiting some developing countries will have to come to terms with the obvious and

A Short Hike in Greenland

Beside some cascades a rough path climbs steeply upward to the rocky Mellemlandet ridge. A narrow terrace passes above the dark waters of a lake, then the path leads onto the crest of the ridge and offers a sudden and magnificent view down to the cracked blue-tinged ice of the Kiagtût Sermiat glacier far below. The winding gray-white curve of the ice riddled with crevasses stretches away into the far distance where snowy peaks mark the edge of the Inland Ice, the vast ice cap that covers most of Greenland. On Mellemlandet (which means, literally, "place between the land") you can pause and view the ice for a while, staring in awe at the vast untouched wilderness that stretches away into the horizon to the east.

huge discrepancies of wealth between them and the people of the country. Nepal, for example, is one of the poorest countries in the world. It is impossible for Westerners to conceive how the majority of the people live. The gap between visiting hikers and the porters who carry their belongings is vast. However disturbed you may feel at the difference in wealth, the answer is not to respond to begging by children and others. Creating a culture of dependency will not help. It is far better to donate money to charities working in these countries to help the people help themselves and to lobby Western governments to cancel debts of developing nations and to enable favorable trading conditions. Disabled beggars and others who clearly depend on handouts are a different matter. I'd rather give a little to them and risk being conned by someone perfectly fit and healthy who makes a career out of begging than to ignore their need.

Language is another issue. Everyone does *not* speak English. This is particularly so in the more remote places that hikers visit. Even a few words of the local language can be helpful and are usually appreciated by local people. Phrase books give instruction in basic statements or questions, and guidebooks often have brief language primers. I'm as bad with foreign languages as anyone is, but I do try to learn some basic phrases or at least words of greeting. My minimal, appallingly pronounced French has proved sufficient on solo hikes in the Alps and Pyrenees for booking rooms, buying food, and talking after a fashion to local people. Sometimes, though, sign language has to be used. In the Queyras Alps I was descending from a high pass late in the day close to the French–Italian border when I met two gaudily dressed men carrying large packs and pushing heavily laden bicycles up the steep, rocky path. As soon as they saw me they both began talking loudly and excitedly in Italian, a language I don't know at all but that I could just recognize. (The logos on their clothing were a clue, as was the proximity of Italy.) I muttered in French, "Pardon—je ne comprends pas." They looked blank, probably due to their having no idea what language I was trying to speak, and spoke more loudly, waving their hands toward the pass. "English," I said. They looked at me, apparently astonished. One tapped his watch and pointed at the pass. "Far?" he asked, dragging an English word from his subconscious. I held up a finger and pointed at the pass and where I was and then indicated that it would be two hours to the pass. They seemed to understand, thanked me profusely, and went on.

The language of hiking itself has cultural differences that international hikers may find useful to know. In Britain and some other European countries, Australia, and New Zealand the term *backpacker* is often used, particularly in the media and by nonhikers, to describe someone, usually young, who travels with a rucksack by hitchhiking or public transport. Someone once posted a query to an Internet newsgroup devoted to hiking asking for advice about backpacking in Australia. A reply came back from an Australian that if the person meant traveling round the country by bus and thumb and spending a lot of time getting drunk, which is what backpackers did, this was the wrong newsgroup, but if they were interested in hiking, they should look for *bushwalking* information. In Britain, though, *bushwalking* means nothing. Because most of the wildest country is high up, *hillwalking* is the common term there. *Trekking* is used for multiday hikes, usually with porters or pack animals, in places like the Himalaya.

FOOD

For a trip of a few weeks or less you could take all your hiking food with you from home, though you'd have to check in advance what foodstuffs are allowed to be brought into the country you are visiting. However, for longer trips, and most people going abroad will be doing longer trips, this isn't really feasible. You could ship all your food and then mail it to yourself, but this would be expensive and time-consuming. It would be better to plan on buying food when you arrive, either enough to get you to the next supply point or, if supplies along the way are unlikely, all you need. In the latter case you can then mail the food to yourself.

In Europe, Australia, and New Zealand you'll find many of the same foods as at home. Even in countries where you can't read the language, you'll recognize many brand names and labels. In big cities in developing countries you'll find some of the same items, too. However, in smaller places much of the food will probably be unfamiliar. This I find one of the attractions of different countries. Experimenting with new foods can be exciting and entertaining, if sometimes a little startling when something turns out to be completely different from what is expected. Choosing food for a long hike can be an interesting exercise when you can't read the names, ingredients, or cooking times on food packets and even more so when foods are sold loose and come with no packaging anyway. When you don't know how long something will take to cook, remember to carry extra fuel for your stove.

SAFETY

Concerns about safety are only natural when traveling far from home. Generally most of the

Enchantment in the Encantados

The climb from the lake led us into a dense mist, unusual in the normally hot and sunny Spanish Pyrenees. The trail was clear though, winding up the mountainside to the grassy saddle of the Port de Caldes. As we paused at this pass, the mist began to move, swirling and eddying around us. Pale rock towers and pinnacles started to solidify in front of us and then faded away again into the moving gray air. Below, patches of green grass and the dark edge of a lake began to materialize. Slowly, with the mist returning and retreating in erratic waves, the jagged mountain walls across the deep gulf before us became firm and hard, changing from phantasms and fantastical shapes into real but no less dramatic or impressive mountains. We were entering the Encantados, the Enchanted Mountains.

---

wild areas hikers visit are safe from threats of theft, assault or kidnapping. Cities at home are probably more dangerous. Political and social conditions can change quickly, though. Up-to-date information about the risks in various countries you're thinking of visiting will tell you whether a war has just broken out or if a revolution is brewing, so perhaps you'd better go elsewhere. This information is available from the U.S. State Department's Citizen's Emergency Center (202-647-5225). You can also check out the State Department's Travel Warnings and Consular Information Sheets Web site, *<www.travel.state.gov/travel_warnings.html>*.

The best advice is to take the same precautions in a foreign country that you would when traveling at home. Keep valuables on your person somewhere hard to reach, and don't leave your pack unattended in places where it could be stolen. The laid-back attitude that may be fine in small settlements—leaving your pack outside the door when you go into a post office or a café, leaving gear on a picnic table in camp while you're away—is risky in larger towns and cities. When you travel to and from a hike, zippers on duffel bags and pack compartments can be padlocked together to discourage pilfering. You can even buy a slash-proof, chain-mail-like, steel mesh pack cover (Pacsafe by Outpac Designs), which could be useful in areas where theft is common. Remember your gear is valuable. In a developing country it can be worth a fortune, and you may stand out as a very rich foreigner. Be particularly careful with cameras, as these are obvious targets for thieves. Don't think that you are safe and can relax your guard once you get home, either. Some friends of mine traveled halfway across the world without losing anything, only to have some valuable gear stolen in the bus station in their hometown when they left it unattended.

Overall, however, don't let fears of theft or attack dominate your travels abroad. Most hikers encounter no problems at all.

GROUP HIKES

If all this planning and data collecting seem too much like hard work, you could go on an organized trip with an adventure travel company or a hiking club, a university, or other noncommercial body. The Sierra Club, for example, has a program of overseas adventures. On such a trip, all the travel arrangements, route planning, and food supplies will be arranged for you, and there will be a guide to do the navigation and route finding. In many areas such as the Himalaya or the Andes, porters or pack animals will carry your belongings. Porters may pitch your tent, too, and a cook crew will provide meals. All you basically have to do is hike. In other areas you may have to carry your own gear and help out with setting up camp and preparing meals. An organized trip is to some extent less of a challenge than one that you plan yourself, though they do vary. On standard, well-traveled routes there may be little sense of adventure, though the trek can still be very enjoyable. On trips into remote, little-visited areas, especially trips where you can contribute to route finding or campsite selection, an organized trek can still be a challenging experience.

On an organized trek you will be hiking with people you haven't met before, which some people like but others don't. You'll also be tied to an itinerary you had no say in planning. If you're happy with this, that's fine—but if you prefer to lead and have control over your hike, you may find a guided trip frustrating.

If you do decide on an organized trip, research the options carefully. Find out whether trekking companies that offer trips to the places you want to visit have a good reputation and what the arrangements are in event of an accident or serious illness. To see which trips suit you, you'll need to know how many people will be involved, including any porters. On an organized trek in Nepal I hiked with 9 others and a support crew numbering more than 30, which

Crossing the Arctic Circle

Small birch trees dotted the flat tundra. In the distance, rounded brown hills, their tops spattered with snow, rose above the sparse forest. The narrow trail, a dark beaten strip, ran through low vegetation—bilberry, heather, moor grasses—that in late August was already turning red as the short summer slowly faded away. On a ragged wooden sign nailed to a post the word *Polecirklen* was scrawled. Here in the wilds of northern Sweden on the Kungsleden long-distance path there was none of the razzmatazz found where highways cross the Arctic Circle—no visitor centers, information boards, or cafés—just this simple crude sign. It was enough. More than enough in fact, for being here was not about crossing artificial boundaries but about living close to nature, about feeling part of the wilderness. The arctic creeps up gradually, the changes in the environment coming slowly. There's no line that says here the arctic starts, and all is different now. Nature doesn't work like that. This is something the walker lives, moving slowly through the landscape and noticing, feeling, the slow transition from one ecosystem to another.

made for a very large group. What distance will be covered each day? Because of the size of the group on that Nepal trek and the weight of the porters' loads, we averaged only 7 to 10 miles a day, which allowed masses of time for observing wildlife, exploring off the trail, and taking photographs. Also ask how many days will be spent hiking and how many in motorized transport. On some treks more time can be spent traveling in buses and trucks than hiking. You'll also want to know what sort of accommodations will be used—tents or lodges—and whether you'll be putting up tents yourself. Will porters or pack animals be used, or will you carry your own gear? Is there a cook crew, or does everyone help with meal preparation? You should also be told how difficult the hiking is and the weather you're likely to encounter. There should be a gear list so you know what to bring. Finally, inquire about the environmental policies of the trekking company and how they treat porters, if used. Are stoves used for cooking? Cooking over wood fires for and by trekkers has contributed to deforestation in some countries such as Nepal. Is all garbage either burned or packed out? What equipment is supplied to porters in the way of clothing, footwear, and shelter?

MAKING YOUR OWN WAY

If you decide organized treks are not for you and you'd rather do the planning yourself, you'll have the freedom to do the hike as you like. In some countries you can still make use of some of the same services as organized trips. In Katmandu, for example, there are many trekking companies that can outfit a trek for you with porters, cook crew, food, camping equipment, and guide. You can employ just one or two porters to help carry your supplies, or you can book the whole package. A translator may be useful to help you communicate with locals, buy food, and arrange accommodations. Do check just what the outfitter has provided and remember that on this sort of trip you make the decisions. Some friends of mine used a company in

Katmandu to outfit a trek. After a few days they noticed that one porter had a big load that was never unpacked. "What's that?" they asked. "A dining tent," they were told. "Leave it here, and we'll pick it up on the way back," said my friends. "We've never needed a dining tent before, and we don't need one now."

TRAILS AND TREKS AROUND THE WORLD

Describing the possibilities for hiking worldwide could fill several books. Here I've outlined a few ideas, with an emphasis on long-distance and remote country hikes.

Access to wild country varies from country to country. If you're planning any cross-country hiking, you need to find out if it is allowed where you want to go. Wild camping is restricted in some areas, too.

The Himalaya and Karakorum

These two great central Asian mountain ranges contain the highest mountains in the world, making them a big attraction for trekkers and climbers. The Himalaya ("abode of snow") is sandwiched between India and Tibet and is 1,500 miles long and about 90 miles wide. Nine of the ten highest peaks in the world are found in the Himalaya, including, of course, Mount Everest at 29,028 feet. The Himalaya spreads across northern India, Pakistan, Tibet, Nepal, and Bhutan. The Karakorum lies north of the western end of the Himalaya and is about 250 miles long. It includes K2, the second highest mountain in the world at 28,244 feet.

Hikers can trek as far as the feet of these giant mountains. Only climbers can go further. The most popular treks are the 50-mile hike to the Everest base camp, which usually takes around two weeks, and the 150-mile Annapurna Circuit, around the 10th highest mountain in the world, which generally takes three to four weeks. Both these hikes can be lengthened or shortened, depending on where you start and whether you take any side trips. They are very popular, and

Trekkers' camp at 13,500 feet, Dho village, Dolpo, Nepal.

you will meet many other hikers of all nationalities. The Annapurna Circuit, in fact, is the most popular trek in Nepal. Because of this popularity, you can stay in "tea houses" or other accommodations every night, though there are plenty of campsites.

If you'd rather go somewhere less crowded, there are many other possible treks that will reveal the stupendous high mountains. On my trek in Dolpo, which began at Jupal and finished in Jomsom, I saw both Dhaulagiri, the seventh highest mountain in the world, and Annapurna, and I can say that these magnificent peaks are truly awe-inspiring.

Trekking in the Himalaya isn't just about the high mountains, though; it's also about the beautiful valleys, the forests, the deep gorges, the villages, the religious sites, and the people. Below the snowline the Himalaya is not a wilderness in the sense of an unpopulated area.

There are many villages, and the trails you hike along are the roads between these. The Karakorum is different, a wilder, more remote area with no people living in the heart of the range. I have never been there, but it is high on my list of places to visit. Although Nepal is a Hindu kingdom, the religion of the hill people is Buddhism. You'll pass *mani* walls, *chortens* (monuments), and *gompas* (monasteries), and you'll find colorful prayer flags on the passes. You'll meet yak trains carrying goods between villages and maybe see barley harvested and threshed by hand. The traditional self-sufficient agriculture practiced here is very different to that of home.

It is, of course, possible to link trails in the Himalaya to make longer journeys. You could even hike the whole length of the range, a journey that has been done a number of times and that must be one of the ultimate long-distance hikes.

Europe

Although crowded and small compared with North America, Europe still has some excellent hikes through beautiful landscapes. In many mountain areas—the Alps, the Pyrenees, the Norwegian and Swedish mountains—chains of lodges offer accommodations, so you can travel light. In fact, in some very popular areas like much of the Swiss Alps and some parts of the French Alps, camping in the wilds is forbidden in order to reduce the impact, and huts must be used. Mostly, though, you can still camp in the wilds, and this is what I prefer to do, relishing the freedom and the contact with nature that it gives, even though it means a heavier pack.

The Alps

The Alps are the highest range in western Europe (18,475-foot Elbruz in the Caucasus in eastern Europe is the highest peak in Europe) and very famous, being the birthplace of mountaineering and the word *alpine*. The Alps stretch for over 600 miles in a great arc from Austria in the east to France in the west.

The Alps are laced with trails, so it's easy to link them together to make long routes. The most famous and popular trail is the 120-mile Tour de Mont Blanc that encircles the highest peak in the Alps (15,766 feet) and passes through France, Italy, and Switzerland (*tour* is French for a circular route). Also popular but much longer is La Grande Traversée des Alpes:

GR5 that runs north to south through the French Alps from Lake Geneva to the Mediterranean Sea, a distance of some 400 miles. GR stands for Grandes Randonnées ("big walks"), and there are around 25,000 miles of them in France, all maintained by the Fédération Française de la Randonnée Pédestre (FFRP), or French Hiking Federation. The GR5 itself is the southern part of the 1,294-mile European E2 route that runs from the North Sea coast of the Netherlands to the Mediterranean Sea near the town of Nice.

Other long hikes in the Alps include the Walker's Haute Route from Chamonix in France to Zermatt in Switzerland, both famous mountain towns, a hike that goes past Mont Blanc and the famous Matterhorn and parallels the ski mountaineer's Haute Route. This route is 120 miles long with over 35,000 feet of ascent. Most people spend a couple of weeks on the hike. A longer east-to-west route is the Alpine Pass Route through Switzerland. This covers 200 miles and crosses 16 high passes with 60,000 feet of ascent. En route you will pass by dramatic alpine mountains such as the Eiger, the Jungfrau, and the Wetterhorn.

In the central parts of the Alps the mountain summits are out of reach of the hiker, since the terrain is very steep and rocky and includes crossing many glaciers and permanent snowfields. In some less well known regions, though,

Margins

Deep in a forest or the middle of a moor the land is unchanging on the grand scale; the differences, and the interest, are in the details. Each tree is unique and worth looking at. Each undulating wave of the moor varies from all the others, the pattern of vegetation matching the gentle rise and fall of the land hidden below it. It's the same in the heart of a vast snowfield or out on a glacier or on a mountain ridge. The big changes come on the margins of the land, in the places where one landscape gives way, sometimes abruptly, sometimes gradually, to another. These are exciting places, where water and forest, lake and cliff, desert and river, meet. Things happen here more quickly. Water erodes a bank, and the shape of the meadow beside it changes, wind crops the edge of the forest, boulders fall from the cliff into the valley below. The different landscapes flow into each other, trees growing high up in a sheltered cirque but not on the exposed ridges edging it. A watercourse surrounded by greenery ripples through a dry, stony desert, the plants slowly dwindling in height and becoming more scattered as their distance from the water increases.

A narrow mountain ridge in the Queyras Alps, France.

vated land in most areas. You should, of course, follow any restrictions that may apply, such as those in the Pyrenees National Park in France, where camping is only allowed at least an hour's walk from any road.

The Pyrenees

Forming the border between France and Spain, the Pyrenees run for 250 miles from the Atlantic Ocean to the Mediterranean Sea. Two trails run the length of the range. The 435-mile GR10 is the lower of the two and stays on the French side of the border. The Pyrenean High Route is about 375 miles long and follows the border as closely as possible, staying mostly in France but dipping into Spain occasionally. On both routes you can stay in accommodations every night, but I feel this would be to waste the opportunity to camp high in these beautiful mountains. I think the Pyrenees are better suited to backpacking than the Alps, as you can get deeper into the mountains, and indeed climb many of them, without mountaineering skills or equipment. Overall they are wilder and less developed than the Alps.

Norway and Sweden

Although much lower than the Alps and Pyrenees (the highest peak is 8,098-foot Galdhopiggen in the Jotunheim ("home of the giants") in Norway), the mountains of northern Scandinavia are wilder and more remote, stretching as they do well above the Arctic Circle. In places you can be three or four days' walk from the nearest road, something impossible in other European mountain ranges. Norway is approximately 1,000 miles long and has a coastline estimated at 30,000 miles. In width it varies between 275 and just 4 miles. To the east lies Sweden, with its own mountains running south to north. Norway covers some 150,000 square miles, of which 70 percent is classified as mountainous and only 4 percent is cultivated. Sweden is a much larger country, but only 25 percent of it is mountainous. In both countries you have a legal right to walk anywhere you want on uncultivated land and camp anywhere as long as it's not near a building. In Norway this comes under the Great

the summits are accessible. One such is the Queyras in southwestern France on the border with Italy. The Tour du Queyras (GR58) circles through this region for around 125 miles, depending on the exact route taken, and gives opportunities to climb a dozen or more peaks in the range of 8,000 to 10,500 feet. It's a lovely route and much quieter than some of the more popular trails through the higher mountains.

All these hikes pass through spectacular mountain landscapes, but they are not wilderness walks. The valleys are cultivated, and the hiker will reach villages frequently. Every night can be spent under a roof. However, those who prefer nights in the wilds can still find secluded campsites high in the mountains above culti-

Open Air Charter; in Sweden it's called *Allman-sratten*. This gives great freedom in planning long-distance hikes, a freedom I used to advantage on my 1,300-mile hike south to north through these countries. There are mountain lodges in many areas, but I mostly camped.

The Scandinavian mountains are northern ranges with the vastness and sense of space of the Arctic. They are sparsely populated and the nearest in feel to the wildernesses of North America, especially in Lapland in the far north. Trails in both countries usually have excellent waymarks, with cairns and red-painted marks on rocks, trees, and buildings. There are more signposts in Sweden, where blue-finger posts indicate directions. Most trails lead between mountain lodges and are not given names or numbers. In Swedish Lapland, however, there is the 270-mile Kungsleden ("king's way"), a marvelous trail that runs through beautiful birch forest, over arctic tundra,

The northern end of the Kungsleden in Abisko National Park, Sweden.

past vast lakes (some of which have to be crossed in a rowboat or by ferry), and along deep mountain valleys. At the northern end the Kungsleden runs past Kebnekaise, at 6,943 feet the highest mountain in Sweden and in Scandinavia north of the Arctic Circle.

Britain
Although small, Britain has a surprising amount of country suitable for hiking. The north and west regions are quite hilly and rugged, with famous walking areas like the Lake District in England, Snowdonia in Wales, and the Scottish Highlands. Only in the Highlands, though, can you get far from a road and feel you are in remote country.

Britain has many long-distance trails and thousands of miles of footpaths that can be linked to make long routes. In the Scottish Highlands you can walk just about anywhere on uncultivated ground, which it mostly is, and can easily make your own long-distance routes, as I did when I walked 1,700 miles over all the

A hiker looks over the gulf of High Cup on the Pennine Way in England.

summits more than 3,000 feet high in Scotland. An excellent way to experience the area is to walk west to east across the Highlands from the Irish Sea to the North Sea. There is no "official" route, but there are many you can plan yourself. I've walked seven different ones, ranging in length from 175 to 350 miles.

The most famous long-distance path in Britain is the 270-mile Pennine Way, which runs up the line of moorland hills that stretch up the center of northern England. Like many walks in Britain, it has historical as well as scenic interest, running for a few miles along Hadrian's Wall, built by the Romans on the northern boundary of the Roman Empire to keep out the hostile Pictish tribes to the north, and still remarkably intact in places.

The longest trail in Britain is the South West Coast Path that runs 525 miles round the rugged, rocky coastline of Cornwall, Devon, and Dorset. In Scotland the longest path is the 220-mile Southern Upland Way, which runs through the rolling hills in the southern part of the country just north of the border with England. Much shorter at 92 miles but much more popular is the West Highland Way, which runs from the outskirts of the city of Glasgow to the town of Fort William below Ben Nevis, which at 4,406 feet is the highest summit in Britain.

If you want to see the wide variety of scenery found in Britain, you could plan a walk from the farthest-apart points on the main island, Land's End in southwest England and John O'Groats in northeast Scotland. My first long-distance walk was to hike for 1,250 miles between these two points.

The Arctic

Some of the wildest, remotest, and unspoiled country left in the world lies in the far north, in Greenland, Svalbard (Spitsbergen), Iceland, northern Canada, and Alaska. I've included the last two regions because, although they are part

In the Beginning

A young man, burdened with a huge pack and tense with nervous anticipation (though trying to look cool and experienced), takes his first steps through the Edale Meadows at the start of England's Pennine Way. Ahead lies Kinder Scout, a dark, brooding moorland plateau and a steep ascent up the rocky ravine of Grindsbrook Clough. As the path climbs, the pack feels heavier and heavier, and the young man wonders how he ever thought he could walk the 270 miles to Scotland and the end of the trail.

Seventeen days later I stood at the finish, pleased but also disappointed. I didn't want the hiking to stop; I wanted to go on, to see what was over the next hill, the next pass, and to keep the closeness to nature, the feeling of being part of the wilds that had grown during the journey. I had found what I wanted to do, what mat-tered more than anything else. I didn't stop hiking, of course. Since that first journey I have covered thousands and thousands of miles on trails in many different countries, but that first 270 miles, that Pennine Way hike, was in a way the most important hike because it was the first, because it was then that I discovered the importance of backpacking, of spending days and weeks in the wilds.

of North America, hiking there is a totally different experience from hiking in the contiguous United States or in southern Canada.

These lands are vast. You can be weeks away from the nearest road. The population is tiny, too—half a million in Alaska's 586,000 square miles, 30,000 in the 186,300 square miles of Canada's Yukon Territory—and you can walk for weeks without seeing any other people. The group of islands called Svalbard, of which Spitsbergen is the largest, covers 24,209 square miles and has a population of around 6,000. Greenland is the largest island in the world, 840,000 square miles in size and stretching 1,660 miles from south to north. Most of Greenland is covered by a vast ice sheet, but around the coasts and along the fjords there are mountains and valleys accessible to adventurous hikers. My one trip to Greenland, to which I've already referred, is the only time I've felt isolated in the wilds, for I knew that we were effectively stranded until the boat came back to pick us up. Surrounded as we were by the sea, huge cliffs, and the inland ice, walking or skiing out would have been very difficult. During the 10 days we spent in that area we did not see another person nor did we hear or see a plane pass overhead.

A trip to the far north requires careful planning, especially with regard to resupply and transportation. Stores and roads are few and far between. When I hiked south to north through the Yukon, opportunities for resupply were a major determining factor in the route I planned. On that solo hike I went for nine and a half days without seeing or speaking to another human being, the longest I have ever done so.

The above descriptions only touch on the possibilities for hiking worldwide. Africa, South America, Australia, New Zealand, and many other areas offer huge opportunities just waiting to be taken. For the hiker, it's still a big world. And traveling on foot is the best way to really experience it.

4

Preparation and Planning

It's not just sitting on a remote summit that matters. It's how hard it was to get there. It's the fact that you got there on your own power, testing your knowledge and experience of the woods trails, your judgment, your physical condition, and most of all your drive and desire to overcome the difficulties.

— Laura and Guy Waterman,
Backwoods Ethics

It's possible to set out on a long-distance hike with no preparation or planning. Some people who do so even complete their hikes. The vast majority of people, however, will enjoy their hikes much more and be far more likely to reach their intended destinations if they prepare beforehand.

Given that most people who set out on long-distance hikes don't get very far, it seems fair to assume that their preparation has not been ideal. As an example, during my first few weeks on the Pacific Crest Trail I was surprised that many of the other would-be through-hikers I met hadn't expected snow in the mountains in April and didn't have the skills or the equipment to deal with it. I never saw most of those hikers again along the trail, and I doubt many of them got very far. With better planning they'd have known that snow was likely and would've been able to prepare for it. Knowing

Descending a faint, rough mountain trail in the Rio Ara Valley in the Spanish Pyrenees.

what to expect in the way of weather and terrain and having the skills to deal with it are important for a successful hike.

BUILDING UP TO A LONG-DISTANCE HIKE

Success and enjoyment on a long-distance hike are more likely if you already have a fair amount of backpacking experience, including some trips of more than a few days. This is the only way to get a taste of long-distance hiking and find out if you like it. If you're longing to go home after a week out, then a six-month trip is probably not for you, at least not yet. As well as developing self-knowledge, shorter hikes are also ways to develop skills and find out about equipment. A blizzard in the San Bernardino Mountains on the Pacific Crest Trail is not the ideal place to learn how to use a map and compass, nor is a week of rain on the Appalachian Trail the best time to learn how to camp comfortably when it's wet.

All this may seem obvious, but it's surprising how many would-be long-distance hikers think they can complete a long trail without much in the way of backpacking skills or experience. A few may do so, but they will certainly enjoy their hike less and suffer more than those with some experience. Most will find their lack of ability too great a handicap. Think of any other outdoor pursuit—perhaps rock climbing or skiing. A novice doesn't expect to climb the hardest routes straight away or ski the steepest runs. A long-distance hike is the backpacker's equivalent. Backpacking isn't as technically difficult as rock climbing or downhill skiing, of course, but doing it well still requires practice.

A gradual build-up of experience is the best way to prepare; it's an apprenticeship, in fact. Teaching yourself isn't difficult, but you can learn more quickly by going out with a hiking club or even taking a course. I learned a great deal at meetings of the U.K. Backpacker's Club when I was a novice.

I began with day hikes and weekend camps at campgrounds, followed by weekend backpack-

ing trips and then a 17-day, 270-mile hike up England's Pennine Way. This moorland walk was so satisfying that I wanted to try something longer. Two years later I walked from Land's End to John O'Groats, the farthest apart points on the British mainland, a distance of 1,250 miles that took 71 days. At the end of that walk I can remember standing on the cliffs of the north coast of Scotland and staring out over the ocean, wishing I had farther to walk. I knew then that long-distance hiking was for me. I doubt, though, that if I'd set out 10 years earlier I'd have finished the walk or wanted to do another one.

GETTING IN SHAPE

Fitness is essential for long-distance hiking. The fitter you are, the more you'll enjoy the walk and the more likely you'll be to complete it. If you're not fit, you can ease into a walk, very gradually increasing the daily mileage over the first few weeks and taking plenty of days off so your aching muscles can recover. You probably won't enjoy that period, though, and you'll miss much as your lack of fitness will dominate your days. Also, injuries are more likely to occur if you're unfit, since stiff muscles and ligaments tear more easily, and you're more likely to stumble and trip over things when you're exhausted. You'll also find that stormy weather and difficult terrain are harder to deal with if you're unfit. It's far better to be fit when you start. You can't get fit quickly—it takes many months to get in shape. If you're not already fit, I'd suggest you start your training as long in advance of a hike as you can, four or five months at the least.

Be realistic about your level of fitness. It's too easy to think you're fit and don't need to do any training. You may indeed be fit enough for short hikes, but long-distance hiking is much more strenuous, for it involves walking all day, every day, usually with plenty of ascent and descent. I've known hikers and wilderness travelers certain of their fitness reduced to total exhaustion after a week or so out. In one case I was assured by a skier accompanying me on a fairly arduous

Weekends spent backpacking, such as at this large backcountry campground in the Canadian Rockies, are preparation for longer hikes.

hut-to-hut tour in the Norwegian mountains that he was perfectly fit. A week later we had an 18-mile ski over two passes right into a big storm. This skier was so tired he was reduced to a crawl, and we nearly had to spend an uncomfortable and cold night out on the trail. By having others ferry his pack for him and by taking far longer than we needed, we managed to reach the hut by nightfall. Afterward the skier admitted that he'd had no exercise for the last year but believed he was fit anyway.

I've met others who've believed the same convenient myth. Unfortunately, it's simply not true. If you stop exercising, your fitness level will drop. Having been fit a year or more ago doesn't mean you are fit now. And regaining fitness takes time. The older you are, the longer it takes.

You also need the right sort of fitness. Backpacking requires good aerobic capacity,

strong leg and back muscles, good balance, and stamina. Regular long walks are the ideal way to achieve this. Cycling, running, cross-country skiing, and swimming are all useful, too, especially if done slowly and continuously. Short bursts of speed aren't so helpful, for these do little for developing stamina, aerobic capacity, or the muscles needed for walking hour after hour.

Carrying a load is one of the biggest causes of misery for many long-distance hikers. Although this is often because too much is being carried, even a moderate load can be tiring if you're not used to it. Carrying a pack while you train is therefore good preparation. However, in urban areas you might feel that carrying a large pack attracts attention and looks odd. To get around this, you can carry small dense objects in a small pack. I first came across this idea in John Hillaby's *Journey through Britain*, the story of a walk from Land's End to John O'Groats and a book that helped inspire me to try long-distance hiking. Hillaby trained for this 1,100-mile walk by walking each weekday into the center of

London, where he worked, for the three months before the walk, carrying weights sewn into a flat rucksack so it didn't look strange.

Ideally, of course, you should regularly go on day hikes with a pack and take short backpacking trips whenever possible, a good way to become familiar with techniques and gear as well as to get fit. This isn't possible for everybody of course. If not, any aerobic exercise is better than none, and it will be all the better if you can manage to carry a bit of a load as well.

Wilderness travel means hiking over all sorts of rough terrain at all sorts of angles. A good sense of balance is a great help, especially when you're threading your way through a mass of fallen trees or stepping from boulder to boulder across a creek. Good balance can change walking over such terrain from a lurching, tiring stumble to a careful, energy-saving dance. It can also reduce the chances of an injury from a fall or from twisting an ankle or a knee. Your balance can be improved by walking on rough ground whenever possible. Running is even better, for you have to react faster to changes in the terrain. An exercise for improving balance is simply to stand on one leg, holding the other foot behind you with one hand, and stay as still as possible.

Hiking over rough terrain also stretches your ankles and leg muscles so they become more flexible, less likely to stiffen and tear, and able to adjust to different positions, which again lessens the chance of injuries and reduces the likelihood of aching muscles. Stretching exercises can also help, especially calf stretching, the only one I do regularly. There are various ways to do this. I place my hands against a solid object (a wall at home, a tree or boulder in the wilds) and lean forward, pushing against it. I then place one leg in front of the other with the front knee bent and straighten the back leg, keeping the heel on the ground. You should feel a slight pull on the calf when you do this. Hold for half a minute or so and then repeat with the other leg. Any stretching should be slow and gentle.

Whatever form of training you do, do it regularly, even if only for short periods. Nothing for

Good fitness is needed for climbing a snow slope on Mount Baden-Powell in the San Gabriel Mountains in California on the Pacific Crest Trail.

six weeks and then a 40-mile backpacking trip over two days will tire you out and do little for your overall fitness. You want a body that is used to exercising every day. You might find that it helps to plan your training and keep a log of what you do. Don't set high targets at the beginning, though. Failing to achieve them can lead to disappointment and feelings of failure, and attempting to do too much too quickly can lead to injury. Build up slowly to the distances you expect to hike each day, increasing the load you carry at the same time. Walking can be done every day. And do take rest days from arduous exercise such as running. These are essential if your training is to have the desired effect and not result in injury or exhaustion.

The other important point is to do something you enjoy so that you'll keep doing it. I don't actually like the word *training*; it implies a boring routine. Preparing for a long-distance hike should be fun, not drudgery. I hike regularly, from a few hours at a time to a few days, but I do these hikes for their own sake, not as "training" for a longer hike. It just so happens that these shorter hikes help keep me prepared for the long ones. I also go Nordic skiing in the winter, take occasional cycle rides, and collect and cut fallen timber (with an ax and bow saw, not a chainsaw) for the stove in our house. All these help keep me fit, but none are done as training activities.

I live in the country, though, which gives much greater opportunities for outdoor exercise than life in a city. If you don't like hiking, running, or cycling around city streets or parks, then you could exercise in a gymnasium or fitness center. In my view this isn't as useful as regular walks with a pack, but it's better than nothing. I did once spend several nights a week for five months working out in a fitness center before a long-distance hike, while still taking my usual walks. I can't say that it improved my fitness noticeably, but the hiker who has worked out regularly will be better prepared than one who has done little if any exercise. The fact remains, though, that the best way to prepare for a long-distance hike is to hike with a pack over rough terrain. Other exercise is better than nothing, but hiking is the best preparation for hiking.

MIND GAMES

Long-distance hiking is at least as much a mental challenge as a physical one. The most important ingredient for successfully completing a long-distance hike is your will to do so. Experience, skill, equipment, money, and time may all play a part, but none of them will be any use if you don't really want to succeed, if you're not really determined to finish.

It's important to think about why you want to do a long walk. The better your understanding of your motivation and what the hike will involve, the more prepared you will be. Just knowing the hike sounds good and you want to do it isn't enough. What do you think it will be like, what do you want it to be like, what are your expectations? What do you hope to get out of it? What do you expect to put into it? What are you prepared to put in? A long-distance hike is a big commitment. Do it half-heartedly, and you probably won't complete the journey. Make it the main purpose of your life, the goal of your desires, the thing you want to do to the exclusion of everything else; put your whole self into it, in fact, and you probably will reach the finish. Even more importantly, you'll get far more out of it; you'll learn more about nature and more about yourself.

In particular, you need to be prepared for problems and difficulties, for the times things don't go right, when the weather is dull and wet, when your feet hurt, when there are no views, when you wonder what the hell you're doing there. Such times will come, believe me. If you expect the whole hike to be a pleasant wander through beautiful scenery under a shining sun, then you will be very disappointed. And disappointment can nag away at you, destroying resolve and undermining confidence and motivation. Aching shoulders and sore feet can do the same, and so can wet and stormy weather. If you've thought about these things beforehand, you can decide how you will deal with them. Accept that there will be days when things don't work out as hoped. There are bound to be. Do you go through months of life at other times with no difficulties, no days that you'd rather forget? Trail life isn't that different. However, on the trail such times are often shorter than off the trail, as the problems are usually simpler, more easily understood, and more easily solved.

Because I know in advance there will be days that won't go so well, I'm prepared to deal with them. If I've already set out for the day, I keep hiking, knowing that the bad times won't last. I know, too, that I will keep going, that I won't give up. At times this knowledge can be reduced to a tiny thought in the back of my mind, but it's always there. I may stop early, deciding that a long rest in camp will do me good, or if a town stop isn't far away, I may go on to it and then have a longer rest than planned. I may decide to stay in lodgings rather than camp. It's surprising what a day of luxury can do.

Depressing days can be caused by a host of different things including prolonged rain, minor ailments, a poor diet, lack of proper sleep, sore feet, sore hips, and aching shoulders. It's always worth trying to work out why you're feeling gloomy. The reason may be obvious, such as blistered feet, or obscure, such as your diet or a minor illness. On my walk through the Yukon I had a couple of days when I felt lifeless, with no appetite and generally uninterested in the walk. I couldn't work out why until the physical symptoms of a cold manifested themselves. Although the cold became worse over the next few days, I

Following a marked route in the Jotunheim National Park in Norway.

felt psychologically better because I knew the cause. And when I got to a town, I had an extra day off while I recovered.

On another occasion, during my walk south to north through the mountains of Norway and Sweden, I was feeling particularly grim as I approached a small village in the steady rain that had been falling for days. I was fed up with constantly hiking in rain jacket and trousers, fed up with boots that squelched with every step, fed up with all my gear feeling damp, and fed up with seeing little but mist rolling over the hills and a rain-sodden landscape. My curt journal entry sums it up: "Rain all the way. Tops in low cloud. Dull & gloomy. A head down slog." It really was one of those "why am I doing this?" days. The weather didn't help, but the main reason was that it had been 10 days since I'd had a day off, 10 days during which I'd walked 175 miles mostly cross-country over very rough terrain and in mostly wet weather. I was, simply, in need of a rest. The village had a small hotel. I hadn't intended to stop

there, but I checked in anyway, with a feeling of relief that told me it was the right thing to do. By the middle of the next afternoon I was completely refreshed and keen to continue the walk.

LAYOVER DAYS

Preparing for minor illness or tiredness means accepting that at times the best thing to do is to take some time off. I learned this the hard way. When I began long-distance hiking I intended walking all day every day. This uninformed plan didn't last long, for I found that unless I took time off every so often I felt as though I was slowly winding down, gradually becoming less and less efficient at hiking. I soon discovered that a rest every now and then had a wonderful rejuvenating effect. Knowing this, I now plan to rest a while every week or 10 days. I usually do this at supply points, which makes sense because there are always chores to do that take time anyway. To me, resting from hiking means just that, not hiking, rather than doing nothing. A rest doesn't necessarily mean taking a whole day off from the trail. Often it means hiking for a few hours to the resupply point and then taking the rest of the day off. Or if I arrive late in the day, I may postpone leaving until the next afternoon and again walk a shorter distance than on a full hiking day. If I feel the need, though, I will take a whole day off. That I find is usually enough. If I stay longer, I get restless.

Although I would advise building layover days into your plans, how often you should take them is a personal matter. Everyone is different. Some people like a whole day off every week; others never rest for more than a half day. Of course, it takes time to find out what suits you, so until you're sure how much rest is best for you, I'd suggest planning for a layover day every week.

You can have layover days in the backcountry, of course. Sometimes I do this because the weather is bad, but sometimes there is something about a spot that catches my emotions and makes me feel I want to stay there a while. To do this requires having enough food to make it to the next resupply point. At resupply points you can pick up extra food you've put in your supply box, buy food from a store, or, more usually, dine in a restaurant.

SOLO OR NOT

Most people hike with one or more companions, yet many long-distance hikers, especially those who do several long-distance walks, travel solo by preference, as I do. There are many reasons for this. To start with, it can be hard to find a partner with whom you get on sufficiently well so that spending many months on the trail together seems a good idea. Unless you have a regular hiking partner who wants to do a long hike with you, it's much simpler to go alone. However, going solo just because you can't find a partner is not a good idea. Solo hiking is not for everyone. You need to be happy, very happy, with your own company, even when it's been raining for days or you haven't seen a trail sign for hours. You have to take sole responsibility for your own safety and well-being. There's no one else to go for help in case of injury or sickness. There's also no one else to make camp when you're tired or cook dinner or sort out the route finding. There's no one to share the good times either, no one to share the excitement or pleasure. The most important thing of all, though, is that you need to be immune to loneliness. I know an experienced backpacker who once set out to walk solo coast to coast across the Scottish Highlands, a two-week hike that was well within his capabilities. He gave up after walking less than half way for the simple reason that he couldn't cope with being alone. Without company he couldn't enjoy the walk. How would you feel if you hadn't spoken to anyone or maybe even seen anyone for several days? It can happen, especially on less popular trails. I would certainly advise anyone thinking of undertaking a long-distance walk alone to do some shorter solo walks first to see how they get on. I also wouldn't advise novices to go solo, either. Experience and skill are even more necessary if you're heading into the wilds for long periods alone.

Solo hiking has great rewards, however. Alone you can become absorbed into the country through which you hike, noticing and feeling far more, as there is no one else to distract you. I can enjoy hiking with companions, but I never feel the closeness to nature that I get when going solo. Solo hikers are quieter and less conspicuous, too, making it likely that they'll see more wildlife than groups. Decision making is simple when you're alone, as there's no one to consult. It's up to you how far and how fast you walk, how often and for how long you rest, when and where you camp, what time you start, what time you stop. Hike nonstop for hours? Fine. Sit and watch a rippling creek for hours? Also fine. The freedom to do this can be very liberating.

CHOOSING A COMPANION

If you hike with one or more companions, you need to think carefully about what this involves.

How well do you know the others? How much hiking have you shared? How many camps? You'll probably be together 24 hours a day the whole time. You'll be together when you're cold, wet, exhausted, hungry. Habits that are normally only minor irritations can swell into major hassles when you're never apart. Long-distance hiking can put a huge strain on relationships. I know a few friendships that have ended on the trail. At the same time, people who are very close and really good friends can support each other through difficult periods and gain great joy from sharing the high points and the overall satisfaction of long-distance hiking.

You need to talk over the hike with any prospective companion. Your aims need to be the same, and by that I don't mean just that you both want to do a certain hike. You have to want to do it the same way. Fast and light or heavy and slow? Many layover days or no layover days? You have to agree to walk the same distance every day and to camp in the same places. Though people often do, you don't have to walk together, share

Occasional Companions

Rather than hike the whole trail with companions, you may have friends who can hike with you for only some of the route, as I had for the first 500 miles of the CDT. I've also had people join me several times for much shorter sections of my hikes. Usually we arrange to meet at a resupply point, and usually we succeed. Once I arranged to meet a friend at a stream junction in the middle of a lonely glen in the Scottish Highlands. He was arriving by bus and walking in from the nearest road by way of a pass while I was hiking in over the hills. I had to shorten my planned route to arrive the right afternoon, but I still remember the feelings

of delight and amazement as I neared the rendezvous to see my friend approaching me from the other direction.

Meetings haven't always worked out so well, though. On my first long-distance hike, from Land's End to John O'Groats, I had arranged to meet a friend on a campground in the small town of Chepstow at the start of the Offa's Dyke long-distance path that runs along the border between England and Wales. I duly arrived and pitched my tent at the campground. There was no sign of my friend. Maybe he'd arrive late, I thought. Morning came, and still he wasn't there. I phoned home to discover he'd been in touch the previous

evening—from Chepstow. An inquiry revealed that there were two campgrounds in the town, something that hadn't occurred to me. I hastened over to the other campground to discover that Graham had started out two hours previously. I hurried after him, though not so fast that I couldn't enjoy the beautiful woodland, the spring flowers, and the cliffs overlooking the river Wye. Late in the afternoon I found an arrow made from twigs in the mud at a trail junction. It pointed down a side trail to the ruins of Tintern Abbey. Guessing Graham had made it, I followed the pointer and met him just starting back up the trail.

Solo hikers are likely to notice and feel close to wildlife, such as these reindeer in Lapland.

rest stops, or even cook and eat together. Hiking speed can be a big problem. If you do get fed up with trying to catch up with your partners or with waiting for them, try hiking at your own speed and meeting up at lunch or camp spots. Make sure, though, that you each have a map or guidebook and that you agree exactly on where you'll meet up. It's also wise to have some contingency plans in case of failure to meet up. How long and where do you wait before hiking out for help? If you fail to meet at one rendezvous, where is the next one? The last thing you want is to be separated from your companions and not know what to do.

Even with these arrangements it's advisable to wait at any junctions where the route isn't clear. I learned this the hard way. For the first 500 miles of the Continental Divide Trail I had a companion (a hiker whom I'd met on the PCT and with whom I traveled through the High Sierra—trail friendships can last). I tended to hike slightly faster than he did and often pulled ahead. At one point I strode past a trail junction, glancing at the map to check I was going the right way, and into a meadow where we'd agreed to stop for lunch. After waiting there a while I grew uneasy and headed back up the trail, only to meet a furious Scott storming down it. Without a map he'd taken the wrong turn at the junction and had gone a fair way uphill before he realized he shouldn't be climbing and turned back. Quite rightly he felt I should have waited at the junction. I didn't make that mistake again.

What if you don't want to go alone, but you don't already have a partner or friend to hike with? There are two options. You can set out alone, hoping that you'll find a companion along the way, which is fairly likely on popular trails like the Appalachian or Pacific Crest. On the PCT I met with several people in the first few weeks who were keen to hike with others, and I ended up teaming up for safety with three others, previously hiking as a pair and alone, to go through the snowbound High Sierra. Different hiking styles caused us to split up again after we were through the snow—though there was no acrimony in this. I went back to solo hiking though I could have had company for the whole trail. Mainly this was because I felt like being alone again after weeks with companions. However, it was also because I wanted to hike further and for longer each day than two of my companions, but I didn't want to set off so early in the morning as the other one.

If the chance of finding a companion along the way sounds too hit or miss or if you're hiking a trail where this is unlikely, then you should seek a companion in advance. This can often be done through the organization that looks after the route or perhaps through Internet Web sites and newsgroups. For example, the *Appalachian Trailway News*, the journal of the Appalachian Trail Conference, has a Hiking Partners section where people advertise for companions. It would also be worthwhile to join a long-distance hikers' group such as the Appalachian Long Distance Hikers Association or the American Long Distance Hiking Association–West or an organization that supports the trail you want to hike, such as the Pacific Crest Trail Association or the Continental Divide Trail Society (see the Resources chapter for the addresses of these and other organizations). Their newsletters may contain information about people looking for hiking partners, and if you attend their meetings or annual gatherings you have the opportunity to meet many other long-distance hikers.

If you look for companions via advertisements, it is of course important that you check out would-be hiking partners very carefully. Ideally, you should meet them and take a short hike together. If this isn't possible, talking on the phone should at least establish some form of rapport. When searching for a hiking partner make it clear what your aims and experience are and what your plan is for the hike. Prospective companions need to have an idea of what you are like and why and how you want to do the hike.

One advantage of hiking with a companion is that you can share the load, taking one shelter, one stove, one pan set, one repair kit, and so on. However, this means you really are dependent on each other. If you decide to hike separately, new gear has to be obtained; if one person drops out, the other is left with a heavier than necessary load to carry. Having all your own gear makes you independent and able to hike alone at short notice. I'd suggest doing this unless you know your companion very well indeed.

LEAVING WORD

Long-distance hiking isn't a dangerous activity, and most hikers have no serious problems. However, accidents can happen. If you fail to reach a supply point and want someone to come and look for you, it helps if they know where you might be. Details of your route should be left with whoever is acting as base for you. They should also know when to expect to hear from you and how long to wait and what to do if you don't check in. This is especially important for solo hikers, as there's no one to go and get help if you are injured or sick. The more remote the area, the more important this is, as there'll be less chance of being found by other hikers.

Ideally your route plan should include bad weather and escape options, too. If your set route seems unsafe, you shouldn't push yourself to continue just because it's the route you're expected to follow. If you abandon your set route, you should let your contact know as soon as possible.

HIKING STYLE

There are various ways to undertake a long-distance hike. How you do so is very much a personal choice. There is no right or wrong way to hike a trail. Others may feel that their way of hiking is somehow superior to yours. That's their problem; don't let it bother you. To quote a well-worn Appalachian Trail adage, "hike your own hike." There are no rules except the ones that you set yourself.

It's important to be honest about your hiking style though, both with yourself and with others. If you don't, you may find your hike collapsing in confusion. Changing your aims is, of course, fine as long as you admit that's what you're doing and that you're happy doing so. Think hard before you do something irrevocable like accepting a lift or skipping a section. Are you sure you won't regret it? It might be better to suffer a little more at the time than to feel later that you've compromised your ideals. It's hard to kid yourself that you're sticking to your aims if you're not.

There's also nothing that will alienate other hikers more than the feeling that you're not telling the truth about how you're hiking. When four of us teamed up to go through the still snowbound High Sierra on the Pacific Crest Trail, we were approached by another hiker asking if he could come with us. After a short discussion we refused because we didn't feel we could rely on him, and the last thing we wanted was someone who couldn't cope. It was very hard to turn down a request from a fellow hiker, but we all felt unhappy about having him along. The reason was that his story of how he'd hiked this far didn't make sense. We'd seen him on and off for several weeks, usually in a town stop when we arrived and still there when we left. He explained that ranger friends had told him about shortcuts, so he could hike between places more quickly than we could, but he could never give any details of these routes. Because we didn't believe him, we weren't prepared to have him as a companion.

Through-Hiking

The most obvious and the simplest way to hike a route is to start at one end and walk to the other, known as *through-hiking*. That's what I've always done, as the feel of continuity this gives to a walk is very important to me. Indeed, the only rule I make for myself on a long hike is to walk every step of the way. I have at times stopped hiking and taken a ride in order to resupply, but I've always rejoined the walk at the same point,

which I'm always careful to mark so I can be sure of finding it.

If you're hiking a well-established trail such as the AT or the PCT, the question arises as to how closely you should stick to the "official" route. Some people like to follow it exactly, always returning to the same point when they leave the trail to resupply, even if there are loops that can be hiked, so the walk remains continuous. Personally, although I want my hikes to be continuous, I'm not bothered about sticking to the precise line of the trail. If I can hike out to a resupply point along a side trail and then hike back in along another one to join the main trail further along, that's fine with me. It's only when I take a ride to a resupply point that I return to the spot where I left the main trail. If there's something worth seeing near the trail, I like to make a diversion to it, too. Trails don't always visit the most scenic places. An example can be found on the PCT in northern Oregon. Because this trail is designed for horses as well as hikers, it avoids the wonderful but narrow Eagle Creek Trail, which winds around cliffs and behind the spectacular Tunnel Falls. I hiked the Eagle Creek Trail rather than the official route, and it remains one of the high points of my PCT hike in Oregon. Perhaps I'm not bothered by deviating from official trails because most of the long-distance hikes I've done have been on routes I've planned myself; there is no set route, no trail markers, no guidebook.

Alternative Routes and Flip-Flopping

Most long-distance trails are not designed with through-hikers in mind. In particular, the length of the longest trails usually means that a through-hike will involve traveling in wintry weather at some point unless you do high daily mileage. However, most hikers probably start out intending to through-hike. Conditions along the way can change this, though, especially ones for which you're not prepared. Some of the hikers I mentioned earlier who were surprised by the snow in the High Sierra on the PCT skipped the snow and went north to do lower snow-free parts of the trail first before returning and hiking the Sierra when the snow was gone. A few hiked up the highway in Owens Valley to the east of the mountains, which did maintain the continuity of the walk, while one went and sat on a beach for a month while the snow melted. Only one hiker managed a continuous wilderness hike while avoiding the Sierra. He crossed Owens Valley, hiked along the White Mountains, and then returned to the Sierra north of the snow. It was an imaginative solution, inspired, he told me when I caught up with him later in Washington State, by Colin Fletcher's wonderful book *The Thousand-Mile Summer,* which tells the story of the author's hike north along the length of California.

Flip-flopping, as doing a hike in noncontinuous sections is often called, certainly means you can avoid difficulties like snow, but I imagine it could also give a disjointed feel to a hike. My inclination, if conditions make a section too dangerous or impassable (which means impassable to you with your skill level and equipment rather than absolutely impassable), is to find an easier route so as to keep the walk continuous. That's what I've often done on the walks I've planned myself. Many times in areas like the Yukon or the northern Canadian Rockies I've not known until I arrived in a place where possible routes lay anyway, so I keep my hiking routes flexible.

Running Out of Time

Another problem with through-hiking can arise if you find yourself running out of time, either because you have to be home by a certain date or because winter is approaching and will close the trail. There are three possibilities here. One is to hike as far as you can and then stop, planning to return and hike the rest in the future. Or if the approach of winter is the problem, you could hike along a lower, still passable route, perhaps again intending to come back and hike the higher route some other time. Both these have the advantages of maintaining the conti-

nuity of the route. The third option, skipping a section that doesn't look all that interesting, disrupts the continuity, but some people are happy with it. Two of my PCT Sierra companions did this in northern California when they realized they hadn't enough time left to complete the trail before one of them had to be home. They hitchhiked around a couple hundred miles of the trail and then continued hiking. In this case the tactic was successful, but I would think it could lead to a breakdown of the whole idea of a long-distance hike. If you hitchhike once, why not do it again the next time a section seems dull or perhaps because the weather is wet? This way a long hike could become a series of short hikes, which, of course, would be fine if you decided you were happy with that. However, if it's not what you set out to do, it could lead to a slow collapse of morale and motivation and leave you feeling dissatisfied and possibly even a failure.

Slackpacking

Confusingly, *slackpacking* is a term that now has two different meanings. Originally it was coined by a group of AT hikers to mean taking a long time over a hike, with low-mileage days and plenty of time to look around and enjoy where you are. One of the hikers involved, o.d. coyote, says that slackpacking is "to attempt to backpack in a manner that is never trying, difficult or tense but in a slowly free-flowing way that drifts with whatever currents of interest, attraction or stimulation are blowing at that moment" (see his excellent feature, "Slackpacking Revisited"). o.d. coyote doesn't see slackpacking as better than other forms of hiking (something I inadvertently implied in *The Backpacker's Handbook* and for which I apologize) but rather as one option among many, all of them valid, that happens to suit some hikers.

However, *slackpacking* is now also used to mean hiking with a support team who ferry your gear to the next road crossing so you can travel light, often with no more than a daypack. This obviously works best on trails in less remote areas. Slackpacking in this sense has become so popular on some trails that commercial services operate to transport your goods. Maybe it should be called supported or pack-free hiking.

True slackpacking and pack-free hiking are both bona fide ways to undertake a long-distance hike. There is nothing ethically superior (or inferior, for that matter) about hiking a trail quickly or carrying a full pack the whole way, though some would have you believe so.

Fast Packing, Speed Hiking, and Power Hiking

Some hikers like to cover many miles a day and finish a trail in a relatively short time. Part of the pleasure of the hike lies in the distance covered each day and the speed with which the hike is completed. To do this these hikers carry light packs and walk for long hours, spending a minimum time in camp. If you enjoy moving fast through the wilderness, this may be the style for you. I've dabbled with this approach, trying it for a few days at a time, and although I can see the pleasure that can be gained from moving fast, I find it too restrictive and disciplined an approach. An occasional relatively high mileage day (which means 20 plus miles for me) is fine, but I wouldn't want to try and do it every day. I like to vary each day according to how I feel, within the limits of needing to reach the next resupply point in a certain time, so I don't plan high-mileage days. Long-distance hiking also involves more than the walking for me. I like to spend time in camp or at rest stops soaking in my surroundings.

There are two basic approaches to high-mileage hiking. One is to cover the distance by walking for long hours and spending little time in camp or at rest stops, rather than by moving very fast. The other is to walk as fast as possible and thus do more miles per hour. This second approach reaches its logical conclusion in trail running. Runners carry very little and rely on support teams and vehicles as support. This, I think, is going beyond the definition of long-distance hiking.

Section Hiking

Many people don't have the time or perhaps the desire to hike continuously for many months but would still like to complete a long-distance trail. Section hiking is the way to do this. For really long trails this could make for a more enjoyable hike. Take the PCT, for example. To through-hike it you either have to maintain a high daily mileage or else risk dealing with wintry conditions at the start and the finish. Split the hike into two, and each section fits nicely into a summer season. Of course, if you divide a route into sections, they can be as short or long as you like. In central Washington State I met a hiker doing the PCT in weeklong bites, one each summer. It had taken him four years to reach this point and at his present rate of progress would take him another twenty-eight to finish. That's not long-distance hiking, of course, but it is hiking a long-distance trail. This hiker was continuing his walk each year at the point he'd stopped the year before, but of course you don't have to do this. An advantage of section hiking is that you can visit each part of the trail at the time of year it's at its best, avoiding the snow, cold, rain, heat, bugs, and any other discomforting factors with which through-hikers have to deal.

Flexibility and Enjoyment

Too rigid an approach to hiking can, in my opinion, reduce or even destroy feelings of enjoyment and connection with nature. Many, many years ago on a hike along the Pennine Way, England's most famous long-distance path, I met up with a father and son near the end of the trail. As we spoke, I found that they were doing the trail in a totally different way than I was, hiking on a strict schedule of 10 hours and 20 miles a day with no deviations. There are many places close to the trail worth seeing, places recommended in the trail guides. They had seen none of these, making it clear that to deviate from the strict route was in their view not really walking the Pennine Way. I was visiting these places and walking as far and for as long each day as I felt like, so in their eyes I was not a serious walker. I was carrying far more than I would now on such a walk, but they had much bigger packs than I, in part because the father was carrying a gallon of water (in a very wet area) and they had lots of heavy food such as glass jars of jam. Now if they were enjoying their hike, this would be okay, but they weren't—they were miserable. The father looked exhausted, too, and had a swollen tendon. Sticking to their rigid schedule, the very schedule that had probably destroyed any joy they might have found in the walk, was all they had left. It had become important to them to believe that theirs was the only way to hike the trail, the *true way,* and that hiking it in a different way didn't count. If they didn't believe this, there was no justification for their suffering. I left them hoping they managed to finish, as that would be the only pleasure they gained from the hike.

Hike, then, in the way that suits you, but remember that you own the hike, it doesn't own

Checking the map while hiking cross-country in the Ogilvie Mountains in Yukon Territory.

you. If it isn't working out the way you'd like, change the way you hike.

COSTS

In day-to-day terms, long-distance hiking is not an expensive pursuit. Most days you spend nothing. An often-quoted estimate is that to hike a long-distance trail costs $1.00 to $1.50 per mile. So a few thousand dollars could see you through any of the country's long trails. You can spend a lot more, of course. Some people, with care, will be able to get by with less.

In advance of your hike you'll need money for food supplies, gear, maps, guidebooks, and any permits and land use fees that may be required. Supply boxes have to be mailed, so you'll need money for postage, too. I'll look at food supplies separately in chapter 5, but the cheapest way to eat is to buy in bulk and then repackage the food yourself. Of course, you would still buy food if you weren't hiking, so this is only spending money in advance that you would spend

Supplies for six days bought from a small store in Sweden.

anyway. Food for a long-distance hike doesn't need to cost any more than the food you'd eat at home, though it is possible to spend a great deal if you live mainly or exclusively off the most expensive freeze-dried meals.

You'll need money for transportation at either end of the trail, for train, taxi, bus, or plane fares or for gas, if you drive. You could hitchhike, but this isn't wise in terms of safety. It's also hard to plan your itinerary when you don't know when you'll reach the start of the hike.

On the trail itself, money is needed only at resupply points. How much depends on how you live when in town. Stay at a campground or in a hiker's hostel and eat food from a supermarket, and you won't need much. Stay in a motel and eat in diners, and you'll need a bit more. Stay in a hotel and eat in more expensive restaurants, and you'll need more still. Money will also be needed for postage to mail supplies ahead or back home, to send letters and cards to friends, and to wash your clothes at a laundry. You should also have a bit of money available in case you need extra trail food or to replace or repair items of gear.

None of these things cost much individually (unless you have to replace an expensive bit of equipment), but the amount does add up over a period of months. Budgeting can be done by dividing the funds you have by the number of town stops you'll be making, including the first and last days of the hike. I'd then add 10 percent and keep it as a reserve just in case something unforeseen happens.

Think about what you'll want to do when you reach a town, too. It's easy to plan on camping every night of a trip before you set out. That was my intention when I began long-distance hiking. How good will your resolve be when you arrive in a town after days of rain with all your gear damp? It's hard then to resist a night in a hostel or motel and nice to be able to afford it. The same applies even more to food. Few if any hikers can resist eating in restaurants when in town. After a week of trail food most hikers find restaurants just impossible to pass by.

The longest I've been out between town stops is 23 days. That was on the PCT between Kennedy Meadows and Mammoth Lakes in the snow-covered High Sierra. It didn't take quite that long to hike between the two towns, for we took a day off to climb Mount Whitney and I waited with most of the gear for two days while my companions went out to collect a cache they'd planted before the hike. But for 23 days I lived on dried food, and by the end of that period not quite enough dried food either. By the time we reached Mammoth Lakes, we'd been thinking and talking of nothing but food for days. The moment we arrived in town we headed straight for a restaurant and had a huge meal. Setting up camp and showering came next, but we were back in the same restaurant just a few hours later. Another huge meal went down easily. We stayed in Mammoth for nearly two days, during which time we just ate and ate. This was an extreme example, our huge appetites being due to the length and strenuous nature of the hike through the High Sierra (I say *hike*, but we were using snowshoes or skis most of the time and crampons much of the rest).

Even when not undertaking such long, hard journeys, long-distance hikers do work up big appetites, and town stops are the places to fill up, so it's wise to allocate funds for this. All-you-can-eat places are very popular with long-distance hikers and well worth seeking out. I can remember one pizza place in Butte, Montana, a resupply town near the Continental Divide Trail, where I met up with a 14-strong group also hiking that trail. We stayed for hours, and by the time we departed they had only salad left.

Spending on the trail is one thing, but how do you afford the whole trip in the first place, in terms of both time and money? I've talked to many people who've told me how envious they are of my trips and that they'd love to do a long hike but . . . So often there's a "but," so often they "know" they can't do it. If you really want to

do a long hike, if it's a consuming passion that is far more important than anything else is, then you can do it. Some circumstances may mean that you have to wait a while, of course, but most can be worked around eventually if you're really determined.

Choosing to do a long-distance hike will probably mean giving up something else—unless you're wealthy, of course. It comes down to priorities. How important is that new car, new sound system, new house? What do you want to do with your life? Some committed long-distance hikers work to hike, leaving their jobs once they have enough money for the next trip. Others find jobs from which they can take long periods of unpaid leave or regular sabbaticals or look for jobs that give long vacations. The interval between college and work is a popular one to use for long-distance hiking, as is a break between jobs. In addition, there are more and more retired folk heading for the trails.

I'm often asked how I can afford to do so many long hikes. By making them my life, I reply. My first long-distance hike was undertaken during unpaid time off from working as a sales assistant in an outdoor gear store. Afterward I knew that I wanted to do more, many more, such hikes and that I had to find a way to make this possible. A small inheritance enabled me to undertake a second long hike. When I made this hike I'd already started to communicate my joy in hiking and experiencing the wild country by writing about it. Over the years since that hike my work has become a mixture of writing, photography, illustrated talks, instructing, leading hikes and ski tours, gear testing, and consulting. Making long-distance hiking a priority meant the money I earned I spent on hiking, and for many years I owned neither a house nor a car. I didn't have any financial commitments either. Hiking has become the mainstay of what I do, rather than a holiday activity. Being self-employed means I am able to take time off whenever I can afford it, while the fact that I've spent years reviewing gear both for magazine reviews and as a consultant to various companies means sponsorship is sometimes available. Living like this isn't a way to get rich in the monetary sense, but in terms of experience I feel immensely wealthy.

FINDING INFORMATION

To plan a long-distance hike, you need to know what maps and guidebooks are available, how to get to the start and back from the finish, where resupply points are and what facilities they have, what the climate and terrain are like, whether there are any access problems or permit requirements, and if any specific factors apply such as potential problems with animals, a lack of water, or the likelihood of extremes of weather.

How easy it is to obtain this information depends on the hike you're doing. The Appalachian Trail is the most popular long-distance hike by far, and there are abundant excellent resources available, many of them published by and still more available from the Appalachian Trail Conference. There are planning guides listing the distances between all supply points so you can quickly work out an itinerary based on the daily mileage you are planning. There are detailed guidebooks and maps and books of advice on what to carry and how to undertake the hike. Much of this can be found on various Web sites as well. This information is updated frequently, some of it every year. A fair amount of information is also available for the Pacific Crest Trail, much less for the not-yet-complete Continental Divide Trail, and less still for most other trails. It can take time to collect all the information you need and then to plan your hike, especially for the less popular, less documented trails. I'd allow many months to do so, preferably a half a year or more. A good sourcebook to start with is Ed Sobey's *The Whole Backpacker's Catalog*, which is packed with information including addresses and Web sites for trail organizations, hiking clubs, gear companies, national and state parks, and wilderness areas.

The World Wide Web is now a major tool for research, with a huge amount of information on trails and wild areas available. After Ed Sobey's book it's the first place I look when I start to research a hike. Many useful sites are listed in the Resources chapter at the back of this book, but new ones appear so frequently that it's always worth doing a search so you don't miss any. Good sites often have links to other useful sites, of course, but this doesn't always happen. The Web is useful for finding out addresses, what guidebooks and maps are available and where to get them, permit requirements, land use fees and regulations (whether campfires are permitted, where you can camp), and much more. For some areas you can apply for permits by e-mail from a Web site.

Although much information can be downloaded from the Web, you'll still need maps and probably trail guides. As well as giving route details, the latter usually contain much of the other information you need and give contacts for obtaining the rest. However, these guides can never be fully up to date, nor can they provide all the information you need. Also, trail guides usually describe the route only in one direction. That's fine if that's the way you want to go. Following trail guides backward is awkward, however, which is why most people hike the trail the way the guide describes.

Maps can often be quite out of date, too, even if printed out from a CD-ROM or downloaded from the Web, which is possible for many areas. Trails, even national scenic trails, often don't appear on maps, especially topographic maps, as it can be decades since these were last revised. The answer for those trails where topo maps are needed is to draw the route on the map with a marker pen. I did this for the Continental Divide Trail, which doesn't appear on many maps and in places doesn't exist on the ground either, and for the long routes I've planned myself. I didn't do it for the Pacific Crest Trail as the guidebooks contain maps with the route marked.

CDs that give you an overview of the area sometimes contain useful information as well, though they're best used for inspiration rather than detailed planning.

Unless you find a Web site that is really comprehensive and gives you all the information you require, you'll probably need to contact land management agencies by letter, e-mail, or phone for up-to-date advice and information. In return, you'll almost certainly get a mass of material, much of it irrelevant to your needs, which you'll have to dig through to find the data you need. In my experience local offices and ranger stations of the National Park Service, Forest Service, and the Bureau of Land Management are the best places to contact. Central offices usually have only very general information, though they can point you to the local office. On a really long trail like the Continental Divide, this can mean you'll need to contact dozens of offices. It's also worth contacting tourist offices, both local and state, for information on state parks, campgrounds, transportation, and facilities at supply points.

The people with whom you deal in government and state agencies will probably know little or nothing about long-distance hiking, so don't expect answers to specific hiking questions. The information they can provide is aimed at car tourists, day hikers, and perhaps short-stay backpackers. It's up to you to interpret it for long-distance hiking. For the big-name trails like the AT and the PCT, this isn't a problem, since the trail organizations can provide all the information you need. In areas where hikers are less common or unheard of, organization staff may try to put you off, because to them what you are proposing sounds highly dangerous. When I approached Yukon Tourism for information, they were initially horrified at my plans and told me that my proposed hike through Yukon Territory was very hazardous and that I had little chance of completing it or even surviving. At the very least, they said, I should employ a guide. However, once I'd explained my background and the amount of hiking I'd done, they were extremely helpful, especially with regard to resupply, a big problem in the Yukon, where there are few roads or settlements.

On another occasion when I wrote to a tourism office about a proposed long-distance hike in the Southwest, which I am still hoping to undertake, I was told that my plan was "physically impossible." The tourism representative went on to tell me that "an Englishman whose name I cannot recall attempted to hike through the inner Grand Canyon. He survived, barely, to write a book called *Walking through Time.*" The reference is to Colin Fletcher's *The Man Who Walked through Time,* the story of his through-hike of Grand Canyon National Park. To say he barely survived is completely inaccurate. The book is a celebration of the Grand Canyon and of wilderness hiking, not a survival epic. I wasn't, anyway, planning to replicate his walk. Again, though, a more detailed account of my experience and my plans evoked a change of attitude. A second letter from the same person, rather than trying to put me off, provided details of post offices and public transportation and even information about a possible river ford.

From these and other contacts I learned that it is best to provide full details of your hiking experience and your plans when approaching organizations so that they take you seriously. It is understandable that they will try to discourage what sounds like a crazy scheme. It's up to you to convince them you have the experience and ability to carry out your hike safely. You also need to be careful in interpreting what they tell you. Although a general dismissal of your plans as impossible or dangerous can be taken with a grain of salt, more specific information on hazards should be looked at seriously. The tourist officer mentioned above told me that a river I wanted to cross "becomes quite shallow about 5–10 miles from the point where it enters the lake and can usually be forded. Even so, unexpected rain can change conditions, and the area is known to have quite a bit of quicksand. I believe you should be prepared to walk the full eighteen miles to a bridge." From this I would plan to have enough supplies and time to do the extra mileage plus whatever mileage was necessary on the far side of the bridge to rejoin my route in case I couldn't ford the river.

Finally, when people have been helpful and taken the time to assist you with your planning, it seems polite and friendly to write and thank them. This may well help other hikers when they make inquiries, too.

ITINERARY

The itinerary of a long-distance hike is based on three factors: the length of the hike, the amount of time you have available, and the whereabouts of resupply points (the details of resupply are covered on pages 87–90). Once you know how many days you want to devote to the hike, you can work out how many miles you'll need to average per day. Remember when doing this that layover days need to be excluded. If you've done previous hikes, short or long, you should have an idea how far you can comfortably hike in a day, so you'll know if the figure you come

Sorting out supply boxes at a campground in the rain in Yukon Territory.

up with looks feasible. If you know you can walk 20 miles a day over the sort of terrain the trail traverses and you enjoy doing so, then planning that distance per day is fine. However, if you normally hike only 12 miles a day and you've never hiked 20 miles, or if the few 20-mile days you've done have been tiring, then a 20-mile-a-day schedule is almost bound to result in failure and disappointment. If your proposed daily mileage seems too high, then you need either to allow more time for the hike or to plan a shorter route to bring down the mileage to a figure that better suits you. Whatever figure you come up with, it's wise to leave some days free so that if part of the walk takes longer than expected, you don't have to give up hope of finishing it or push yourself constantly trying to get back on schedule.

Long-distance hikes break down into shorter ones between resupply points. Getting the planning right here is the key. If it's 100 miles between supply points and your average daily mileage is 20 miles, you'll need food for 5 days;

if it's 10 miles, you'll need food for 10 days. The latter means a heavier pack when you set off, but you'll need to walk only half as far each day. If you're not sure how far you can walk in a day, err on the cautious side and plan for a low daily mileage. It's better to reach a supply point with a few days' food left than to run out before you get there. You don't want to carry more food than necessary, though, so if you do find you're walking further each day than originally planned, adjust your plans accordingly and carry less food.

It is possible to plan a detailed itinerary giving the daily mileage, each night's campsite, and the number of days between resupply points so that you know exactly where you should be each day, how far you'll walk, and even for how long. For me, however, such a detailed plan takes away from the freedom of a walk and makes it feel a tad too regimented. I like to have the flexibility to vary the hike according to how I feel or what the weather is doing or what the terrain is like. If I find a beautiful spot to camp, a place that calls to me to stop and experience it more fully, I like to be able to do so even if I haven't completed a set mileage. My itinerary for a long-distance hike lists supply points, the distances between them, and how much food I need at each supply point based on an average daily mileage, but I don't put in proposed overnight camps. A computer spreadsheet can be used to compile such an itinerary, though you can do your planning with a simple word-processing program or even pen and paper.

To plan how much food you need at each supply point means you have to estimate an average daily mileage. That doesn't mean you have to do exactly that mileage each day, though I have met hikers who do this. On any given day I may do far more or far less than the mileage I need to average over the whole period between supply points. To take that 100-mile example again, planning to hike it in 5 days means carrying 5 days' food and averaging 20 miles a day or running out of food before I reach the next supply point. However, I may walk 10 miles one day

and 30 on another. And I often take an extra day's supplies, too, so I have the option of staying out longer. That takes the pressure off so if the weather or terrain makes averaging a certain mileage difficult, I can simply do a little less. I find this approach more versatile than a more rigid itinerary. If the terrain is gentle, the trail good, and the weather fine, I'll probably hike further than if the terrain is rough or the trail hard to follow. However, in stormy or very wet weather I often hike further than on fine days because I stop less often and for shorter periods of time. I hike fastest on paved roads, partly due to the flat smooth surface but also because I don't like road walking and want to get it over with as quickly as possible. Overall this means adapting to the prevailing conditions rather than sticking to a fixed schedule regardless of what the day brings. After all, for me the point of the hike is to gain the most from each day, to fully enjoy where I am, not to reach the end as fast as possible or meet a preplanned schedule.

My daily mileage also varies because the weight of my load changes. When I leave a resupply point with a week's food and fuel, my pack is around 15 pounds heavier than when I arrive at the next supply point. That's enough to affect how far I find it comfortable to walk. I also get fitter during a walk, so my daily mileage goes up after a few months.

PLANNING YOUR OWN ROUTES

Once you have some experience of long-distance hiking, you may want to plan your own routes rather than follow long trails. This opens up the areas where you can hike, as many places don't have long-distance trails or even, in some cases, any trails at all. It's also immensely satisfying to plan and then follow your own route (see chapters 2 and 3 for a discussion of possible destinations).

Putting together your own long-distance route is, of course, harder than following a set trail. Once you've decided where you want to go, you

Climbing steep scrub-covered slopes in southwest Greenland.

have to gather as much information as you can and then work out a route that looks feasible on the maps. This isn't too difficult if you're linking trails, and there's a good chance you'll be able to follow the route as planned. Chances are, though, that even if your route mostly follows trails, there'll be sections where you have to go cross-country, for not all the trails will link up. In other areas there may be no trails at all. At least on the map, that is—you may find trails on the ground, which can be confusing since you won't know where they go unless you have local information.

When I hiked the length of the Canadian Rockies, there were virtually no trails marked on the maps for the northern half of the hike, so I simply planned a route that followed valleys and crossed passes and that didn't look too steep, hoping that I'd be able to follow it when I got there. In many places I did so, but in others I used trails made by hunting parties, often being given the information by local outfitters I met. Because trail hiking is easier than going cross-country, I followed these trails where they existed, rather than my original route. In other places I discovered that my route didn't take the best cross-country line. Often it was easier to climb above timberline and hike along open mountainsides than to thrash through dense vegetation in the valley bottoms.

Finding a trail where none was expected can be heartening if the terrain is difficult. That's if the trail goes the right way. It's very tempting to follow a trail because it's there, even if it doesn't go exactly where you'd like it to go. I've done this a few times and had to retrace my steps when I finally admitted to myself that it really wasn't going in the right direction. This happened on my hike through Canada's Yukon Territory when I was following a river valley where the going was very difficult due to muskeg swamps, dense forests full of deadfall, and steep brush-choked slopes. After two days of slowly struggling through this, I was delighted to come upon a clear trail that led, eventually and after disappearing into a swamp at one point, to a wider track. This went in the right direction for a short while but then turned the wrong way. Reluctant to abandon it, I kept on until I had to admit the track was not going to turn back again, and I had to retrace my steps, having walked an unnecessary four miles. It's better to abandon a trail that goes the wrong way sooner rather than later, though it can be difficult to do so when the alternative is difficult bushwhacking.

In other places trails marked on the map may no longer exist on the ground or may be very hard to follow even if they do exist. Again, it makes more sense to pick out the easiest cross-country route rather than to spend time and effort searching for signs of a trail.

When planning cross-country routes like this, it's best to accept that your intended route is only a tentative idea and to be prepared to change it whenever it seems best to do so. Even better is to look forward to doing this. Teasing out a route through wild country feels like real exploration and seems much more adventurous than following a trail. You have to be adaptable and accept there will be difficulties and that at times you'll need to backtrack and that at others your progress may be extremely slow. On that Yukon walk I hiked cross-country much of the time, and my final route was very different from the one I'd planned back home. How confident those bold yellow lines crossing the maps had looked! In reality, I sometimes wasn't even on the same map sheets my planned route crossed, never mind anywhere near the route itself.

Although large-scale maps (1:24,000, 1:25,000, 1:50,000 and 1:62,500, depending on where you go) are the best to use while hiking, for the initial route planning they're not so desirable because so many are needed and you don't get an overview of the whole area. For your planning, small-scale maps, such as 1:250,000, are better. In the United States the DeLorme Atlas and Gazetteer Series that have all the 1:250,000 maps for a state in one book are excellent. I use marker pens to draw my proposed route on the map—apart from the route being useful with planning distances and resupply points, it acts as a reminder of where I intended hiking when I actually get there. On a number of occasions, though, as I stood at the foot of a steep ascent or below a rocky ridge, I have stared at a yellow line streaking across my map and have wondered how I ever thought this could be a feasible hiking route!

If you're planning routes that link trails, any available trail guides are useful. I planned most of the southern half of my Canadian Rockies walk using *The Canadian Rockies Trail Guide*, by Brian Patton and Bart Robinson.

The whereabouts of possible resupply points has to be taken into account when planning your own route. Indeed, the location of supply points may determine where your route goes. It certainly did on my Yukon walk, where I had to plan on coming out of the wilderness to a settlement or road to resupply. Only on one occasion was I able to stay in the backcountry for a period longer than I could carry food for, and that was because I arranged with a tour-boat operator to take supplies for me down the Yukon River to a prearranged meeting point. The advantage of this arrangement was that I was able to go deeper into the wilderness because I was able to stay out for 20 days between roads. The disadvantage was that I arrived at the rendezvous three days before my supplies and had to wait.

Planning your own route can take a great deal of time and effort, so much so that you may feel lost in the logistics and wonder why you got into this. It's worth the effort, though, and this frustration fades away once you start hiking and the real adventure begins.

TIME AND SPEED

How far you walk in a day is dependent to some extent on how fast you walk but even more on how long you walk—not just how many hours you're out between camps but also how many of those hours you actually spend hiking. Long rest stops and time spent taking photographs, watching wildlife, or fiddling with gear can all quickly eat away at hiking time.

Hiking, especially with a heavy load or on rugged terrain, is not a fast activity. Three miles an hour is a good average on a well-maintained, fairly level trail. Some people can manage four miles an hour, but how long they can keep it up is another matter. I once measured my pace against mileposts when walking on a flat paved road in the Great Divide Basin on the Continental Divide and found it to be 3.75 miles per hour without rest stops. I couldn't do that on a trail unless it was very smooth and flat. Most hiking is not on the flat or the smooth but on much rougher and often steeper terrain. Also, on that occasion I was hiking hard and fast because I wanted to get off that road and back into wilderness country. Normally on trails and easy cross-country terrain I estimate my speed at 2 to 2.5 miles per hour. This speed declines when the going gets rough, sometimes to as little as half a mile an hour.

An old but useful formula (developed in 1892 by the Scottish mountaineer W. Naismith) allows an hour for every 3 miles of distance and a half-hour for every 1,000 feet of ascent, not including stops. Thus a 9-mile hike with 3,000 feet of ascent will take 4.5 hours, not 3 hours, an average of 2 miles per hour. Calculations like this are only approximate, however. Extremely rugged ground, strong headwinds, difficult river crossings, problems with route finding, and other difficulties can all slow you down. Even so, I find Naismith's formula to be accurate enough for me to use for my planning.

If you keep records of your mileage, you can look back and see the distance covered on previous hikes and base your planning on this. My figures are remarkably consistent. On the Pacific Crest Trail, the end-to-end of the Canadian Rockies walk, and the end-to-end of the Scandinavian walk I averaged 16 miles a day, while on the Continental Divide Trail it was 16.5 miles a day. This figure drops down to 12.5 miles per day for the end-to-end of the Yukon walk, mainly, I think, because I was mostly hiking cross-country over difficult terrain. On the walk over all the Scottish 3,000-foot summits I averaged 15.5 miles a day. That walk was hard because much of it was cross-country and involved 575,000 feet of ascent. However, to compensate for that I carried a much lighter load (averaging 30 lbs.) than on the other hikes, partly because I could resupply frequently. These figures exclude rest days.

Working from these figures, I now plan on averaging 16 miles a day on trails and 12 on hard cross-country terrain. As I said above, I don't intend to do the exact mileage every day, however. Looking at my daily logs for those walks, I see that on the shortest day I covered just 3 miles while on several occasions I walked 30 miles.

Putting accurate figures on how far you walk is very difficult to do. Because maps are flat, the distance shown between two points is accurate only if the ground is also flat. Map miles are nearly always less than the miles you actually hike because the ascents and descents are longer than shown on the map. As the table below shows, the steeper the ascents and descents are, the longer they are.

Additional Distance Hiked for Slopes of Different Angles over 1 Mile on the Map

Slope Angle	Height Gained in Feet	Additional Distance Traveled	
		Percentage	Feet
10°	930	1.5	80'
20°	1,920	6.5	340'
30°	3,050	15.5	815'
40°	4,435	31.0	1,615'
50°	6,295	56.0	2,936'
60°	9,146	100.0	5,280'

Ground with a slope of over 40 degrees is very steep and only rarely climbed by hikers. Trails on steep slopes usually climb in switchbacks, which can be another cause of underestimated mileage, as the switchbacks will cover much more ground than the straight-line map distance. Distance can be estimated in a number of ways. You can run a length of string along the route on the map and then measure this. I've always found this an irritating and frustrating method, however, and have never had much success with it, for I find it hard to keep the string in place. On maps with grid squares you can count the number of squares the route crosses and call this the distance hiked, hoping that the squares crossed only in one corner and those where the route crosses diagonally or winds all over the place will cancel each other out. Probably the most accurate method is to use a map measurer, which has a little wheel that you run along the route. The distance can then be read off against the correct scale (most map measurers have several scales so they can be used with different maps).

Trail guides usually give distances, but these

Put on windproof clothing at rest stops if it's cool and breezy.

are not necessarily any more accurate than your own measurements. It depends on how they were obtained. Often it is by counting grid squares, operating a map measure, or even using a piece of string. Occasionally the writer will have wheeled a measuring wheel along the route, which should give a pretty accurate result but which must be very tedious to do.

Rest Stops

Every hiker stops to rest during the day—how often is a personal matter. Some hikers advise stopping for 5 minutes every hour, others for 10. This obviously works for them, but I'm not so organized. I stop when and where I want to, rather than according to the clock. Often I pick an obvious point, such as a pass or a hilltop or a lake, somewhere where spending a few minutes will probably reveal something about the land or its inhabitants. Sometimes, though, I encounter a view, an animal, or a tree that so overwhelms me I just have to stop. When I finally move on, I feel amazingly refreshed and invigorated by the experience.

In wet and windy weather I look for shelter when I want a rest. Big trees and large overhanging boulders attract me then, so when I see a good one, I stop. Sometimes I will walk for some time after I've decided I'd like a rest, maybe an hour or more, until I find shelter, rather than halt in the storm. It's surprising how often the boulder just up ahead can look like a great place to stop until I reach it. If I can't find anywhere and I'm carrying a tarp, I may pitch this. Otherwise I have a very brief halt, just long enough to eat something and drink a little water.

However, when it's sunny I may stop for quite some time if I find a spot I really like or where there are animals or birds to watch. It is often said that rest stops should be kept short; otherwise your muscles will stiffen up, and you'll find it hard to go on. All I can say is that I've never found this to be so. If I was so tired I thought I might have trouble continuing my hike, I'd be more inclined to stop and make camp than to stop for a rest.

During a day I may rest a dozen times or just a couple, depending on the weather, the weight I'm carrying, and how I'm feeling. There are days when my spirits and my body come together, and I can walk effortlessly for hours at a time, almost oblivious of my body. I'm not going to break that rhythm by sticking to a rigid schedule of rest stops. On other days when I'm plodding along and my spirits fail to soar or even rise a little, I may stop often. I'll probably make camp early as well.

However often you stop to rest, it's important to make the most of the time and rest your legs. Mostly just sitting down and having something to eat and drink is enough. However, if your legs are feeling tired or feeling swollen or heavy, which isn't conducive to getting you going again, you can relieve this by sitting down with your legs extended straight in front of you. Even better, prop your feet up on a rock or log and lie down for a short while. The old idea of putting your feet up to relax after physical exercise is a very good one. A boulder or tree will do as a backrest, or you can use your pack, propping it up with trekking poles if you have them. This really can make a big difference. Sometimes when I've arrived at a town and gone into a café for a meal, my legs start aching after I've been sitting down for a while because I haven't elevated my feet.

In addition to full rest stops where I take my pack off and sit down, I have many shorter stops to check the map, take photographs, or look at something interesting. One reason I don't plan a high daily mileage is so that I can do this and not feel I have to keep moving all the time.

EASING INTO THE HIKE

Whatever distance you plan on averaging over the whole hike, it's wise not to aim to do this the first few days or even weeks out. Starting a long-distance hike means a sudden change to a new way of life, and it can be difficult to cope with this. It is possibly one of the main reasons why so many hikers give up early in their journey. It is better to ease yourself gently into the hike. That means mentally as well as physically. The rewards of the hike will come slowly; you won't feel in touch with nature or yourself immediately. In fact, you may feel the opposite, unsure of why you're there, uncertain of the wildness around you, and no longer sure this is what you want to do. Keep hold of your dream and keep going, and this will pass.

I find I need what I think of as an easing-in or breaking-in period (other long-distance hikers have their own descriptions—Colin Fletcher talks of a "shakedown cruise," Ray Jardine of "trail shock"). On a hike of a few weeks this lasts a few days; on a multimonth hike it can last a few weeks. During this period I find myself worrying about things I may have forgotten or about whether I'll find somewhere to camp or water to drink or myriad other things. Mostly I think this is displacement— what I'm really worrying about is the enormity of what I've set out to do. Can I really hike 1,000, 2,000, 3,000, or however many miles? Surely not!

Pushing too hard early on can exacerbate these worries, leading to a feeling that failure is inevitable, that your dreams will become nightmares. The answer is to slow down and gradually get used to being a full-time hiker. If necessary, take a day off. I find that as the first few weeks pass, the concerns fade and I start to live in the present rather than the unknown of the future. I start to realize that I will find campsites and water and the route. I stop thinking about the length of the hike and how far away the finish is. It doesn't matter, I realize—only today's hike matters.

WHEN TO GO

The best time for hiking long-distance trails is often only a few months long. This is true for the big three, the Appalachian, Pacific Crest, and Continental Divide Trails. To through-hike these means either maintaining a high daily mileage or, as most people do, dealing with the vestiges of winter early on in the hike and the beginning of the next winter toward the end. How difficult this is depends on just how long you're planning on taking for the hike, how late the snow lasts, and how soon it returns. As already mentioned, I had to hike through deep snow in the High Sierra on the Pacific Crest Trail. At the northern end in Washington State there were only the first flurries of the next winter's snow, but there was a great deal of rain. On the Continental Divide I had deep snow at the start in the northern Rockies and then again in the Colorado Rockies. In both places I had to take a lower route at times. In retrospect, I suspect that if I'd gone south to north instead of north to south I'd have had fewer problems. I could've started much earlier (I began in June), as the first 500 miles are in the deserts of New Mexico, and I would've reached Colorado after most or all of the snow had gone. Then I would've been hiking the northern end of the trail before the next winter's snow began.

Finding out what weather to expect is advisable, but it's also advisable not to be surprised if the weather is not exactly as expected. On the end-to-end of the Canadian Rockies walk I was told several times how unfortunate it was that I was there during a summer that was wetter than normal (though from my British perspective the summer was warm and sunny!). On the Pacific Crest Trail there was much more snow than normal in the High Sierra, whereas on the Continental Divide Trail the first snows in the fall arrived very early. "Normal" weather actually seems quite rare!

A remote mountain shelter, known as a *bothy*, in the Scottish Highlands.

Food, Water, and Resupply

I always carry with me soy sauce, bacon bits, parmesan cheese, curry, olive oil, garlic powder, boullion, and oregano. With those items, I figure I can make a tasty meal out of dirt and grass if necessary.

— M. John Fayhee, *Along the Arizona Trail*

The thought of a hot, tasty, filling meal can keep you going at the end of a long day. If you find yourself flagging with a few miles still to go to a campsite, a quick snack can revive your tired legs. Food is very important for the success of a long-distance hike, far more important than which brand of pack you carry or which fleece jacket you wear.

The problem for long-distance hikers is to select food that is tasty, nutritious, and full of energy while being lightweight and low in bulk. If you're out for only a few days, the weight of your food isn't that important, unless you're planning on moving fast and covering many miles; nor is the balance or quality. Any deficiency in your diet won't matter much over a short period of time. On a long-distance hike, though, your food is your fuel, the stuff that keeps you going and keeps your body in good repair. Eating properly and well is very important for a successful hike. You can complete a hike on an inadequate diet, but it will be harder and you probably won't enjoy it so much. It's more likely that you'll give up. The weight and bulk of that food matters, too, for on most long-distance hikes there will be times when supplies for several days, maybe even a week or longer, will have to be carried.

Good food means food you enjoy eating as well as food that is good for you and light in weight. A nutritious diet that you don't enjoy, or even worse that you dislike, will be bad for morale. You'll probably end up not eating much of it anyway. That's what happened to me on my Canadian Rockies walk on which I had 12 varieties of lightweight dried main meals. These were carefully balanced, free from artificial chemicals, and made from wholesome ingredients. They also all had the same mushy texture and uninteresting taste. Long before the end of the walk I found I couldn't face eating them anymore, even when laced with garlic and curry powder to make them more edible. Instead I ate instant noodles mixed with packet soups that were not as good for me but that tasted far better. The mistake I made was not to try the meals on short trips beforehand. Advice is often given to try trail meals at home, but I find this unrealistic. What tastes fine in camp after a day's hiking often isn't very appealing at home.

Here I've outlined my thoughts on food for long-distance hiking and listed what I eat and why. Of course, food is very much a matter of personal preference, but it is important to have a diet that aids your hike rather than hinders it. Over years of long-distance hiking I've developed a diet that keeps me going and keeps me healthy. Remember, poor nutrition or unpalatable food can spoil the enjoyment of a hike and maybe even cause you to give up. Good food should be part of the pleasure of a hike. I hope my ideas will provide some suggestions for finding a diet that works for you. Be prepared to experiment and to reject foods that you don't

like or that don't seem to give you the energy to keep hiking. I'd never again risk buying large quantities of untried food for a long-distance hike.

CALORIES

As well as being tasty, nutritious, and light in weight, food for long-distance hiking needs to be packed with energy, which is measured in calories. Strictly speaking, the calorie used for food is a great calorie or *kilocalorie*—that is, a thousand calories—which is the amount of heat needed to raise the temperature of 1 kilogram of water by 1°C. A small calorie is the amount of heat needed to raise the temperature of 1 gram by 1°C. Kilocalories are also known as *Calories* with a capital C. Calories are transformed by the digestive system into energy that enables you to keep going. Too few calories, and you'll slowly run out of steam—not in a matter of hours or perhaps even days, but certainly in a matter of weeks. Adults need around 2,000 to 2,500 calories a day for normal activities that aren't very strenuous. Long-distance hiking is very strenuous, however, so far more calories are required.

How many calories you require depends on how much energy you are expending and on your metabolism, the chemical process by which food is utilized by your body for cell building and for energy. Everyone's metabolism runs at a different rate, though generally the more exercise you get and the more fit you are, the higher your metabolism, which means you'll burn up food quickly.

Working out the calories I consume on trips, I found that I need around 4,000 calories per day for the first few weeks. After that my appetite goes up, and I need at least 5,000 calories, an amount that then stays constant until the end of the hike. That's in temperate weather. In very cold and stormy conditions even more calories are needed, some of them just to keep warm.

Because metabolism varies so much from person to person, it's impossible to say how many calories a day any individual will need for a long-distance hike. This can be seen from the experience of Will Steger's dogsled expedition to the North Pole (see *North to the Pole* by Will Steger). The number of daily calories eaten by members of the expedition ranged from 4,500 to 8,000. Rations were apportioned in equal amounts, but as Steger puts it, "meals were informally reapportioned according to need on a daily basis."

Smaller people often need fewer calories than larger people, but this isn't always the case, and it certainly isn't a good basis for planning supplies. I once led a two-week hut-to-hut ski tour in Norway on which one of the participants was a small, wiry trail runner and orienteer. His appetite was enormous! He had to eat often, too. Despite his having snacked constantly all day, as soon as we reached a hut he would fetch a packet of cookies from the store and eat the lot. On the same trip was a fairly heavily built man with a sedentary job. Everybody was given a candy supply at the start of the trip to eat as snacks. Two days before the end of the tour this man emptied all his candy bars on the hut table. He announced that he was fed up with carrying the candy and that anyone who wanted could take them. He hadn't eaten even one bar while several other people had finished their supply. The bars rapidly disappeared off that table.

Only experience will show you how many calories you need for long-distance hiking. Until you find this out, it's best to take slightly more food than you think you'll need rather than less. Then if you find yourself arriving at supply points with food left over, you can reduce the amount you carry.

Although it is interesting and can be useful to know how many calories your foods contain, it isn't essential. I don't calculate in detail the calorie content of foods when planning food supplies. I know roughly the energy value of the foods I choose and that I should carry around 2 to 2.5 pounds of food per day. Basically, if you can hike every day without running out of energy, you should be eating enough. You shouldn't feel desperately hungry either, though most long-distance hikers do feel hunger, especially when nearing a supply point. Part of the reason for this is, I think, due to the low-bulk nature of much backpacking food, part due to not having quite enough calories.

A constant supply of energy is needed when hiking, so a steady supply of calories should be consumed. This means it's best to eat at regular intervals during the day, rather than have one long lunch stop. I eat small snacks at least every few hours as well as stopping for a couple of longer breaks.

FOOD COMPOSITION AND QUALITY

Calorie content alone isn't enough to provide nutrition. If it were, you could survive purely on very high-calorie foods, which means fats, for these have more than twice as many calories as carbohydrates and protein (9 calories per gram as opposed to 4). You can't, however, subsist on a diet of pure fat. Fat is digested slowly and releases its energy slowly, which is not what you want for hiking. It's also hard to digest during exercise. Just imagine hiking on a diet of margarine, butter, cheese, oils, eggs, nuts, and chocolate.

Fat is needed in the body, though, but not in large quantities. Its slow release of energy helps keep you warm during cold nights, so most of the fat in your diet is best eaten in the evening, which also overcomes the digestion problem. Fat is stored in the body as reserve energy and is released if your calorie intake is less than required for your energy expenditure. Most of these reserves are usually burned up during the first few weeks of hiking, which is why your appetite may go up. Polyunsaturated fats, found in many vegetable oils, margarine, and low-fat spreads, and monounsaturated fats like olive oil are reckoned to be better for you than saturated fats like butter, cheese, whole milk, lard, chocolate, and animal-fat margarine.

Protein builds and renews muscles and body tissue. During digestion, protein is broken down into amino acids of which eight are essential for health. Proteins that contain all of these are known as complete proteins and are found in meat, eggs, and dairy products. Grains and legumes contain incomplete proteins, as they don't have all the essential amino acids. However, complete proteins can be created by combining different incomplete proteins. Thus peanut butter on wheat bread or a grain- and bean-based stew provide all the amino acids. Protein is either used immediately for muscle renewal or stored as fat, so it's best eaten regularly in small amounts.

The food that powers the long-distance hiker along the trail is carbohydrate. This is what keeps you going and gives you energy. Carbohydrate comes in two basic forms: sugars and starches. Sugars are called simple carbohydrates and include ordinary table sugar or sucrose, dextrose, glucose, fructose, and honey. Simple carbohydrates are quickly digested and provide rapid bursts of energy. However, this energy doesn't last and quickly leads to a sudden feeling of being drained of energy, known as a sugar crash or sugar low. If you need a quick energy boost, perhaps toward the end of a long day, sugar-rich foods will provide it, but you should eat some other food with the sugar or soon afterward to avoid the slump that follows.

What the long-distance hiker really needs are complex carbohydrates or starches, which are found in grains, vegetables, and legumes (beans and peas). These release their energy over a much longer period of time than sugars and don't lead to a sudden slump. Complex carbohydrates are stored in the liver and muscles as glycogen, which is then broken down into glucose when energy is required. Restoring the glycogen used up while hiking is very important. Complex carbohydrates also contain fiber, minerals, and vitamins, all of which the hiker needs. Fiber is needed to prevent constipation, something long-distance hikers are prone to due to the lack of fresh fruit and vegetables in the diet.

Overall, some 70 percent of food for long-distance hiking should consist of carbohydrates,

mainly starches, with the other 30 percent split roughly equally between protein and fat.

Vitamins and minerals are needed only in tiny quantities, but they are essential. On trips of less than a month hikers probably don't need to bother about them as long as they are eating a balanced diet of high-quality food. On longer trips, though, a lack of fresh food could mean a vitamin or mineral deficiency. Multivitamin and mineral tablets can be taken to avoid this. I'd also suggest eating plenty of fresh food when in towns and carrying some for at least the first day out from a supply point. I've taken vitamin and mineral tablets on most but not all of my long-distance hikes. Although I can't say what difference they made, and I didn't notice the lack of them on the longest hike I've done, the Continental Divide Trail, I'll still take them on future hikes. They are very light and low in bulk; taking them does no harm and could do some good, including improving your long-term health.

The quality of food as well as its composition should be considered. Modern industrial food manufacturing produces far too much food that is denatured and adulterated with chemicals in the form of preservatives, flavorings, and color. Foods that haven't had nutritious components removed and that are free of additives are best, especially if they are also organic, which means produced without the use of chemical fertilizers, pesticides, fungicides, or, in the case of animals, chemical feed and hormones.

Grains suffer particularly from being denatured, a process obliquely referred to as refined. Refined white flour is nowhere near as nutritious as whole-grain flour due to the removal of the bran and wheat germ. Many commercial brands of other grains such as oats, rice, corn, rye, buckwheat, and barley are also treated the same way. I look for those described as whole-grain as this means nothing has been removed. Labels should be checked to see that a food that looks whole-grain really is. Brown bread is often made from white flour dyed with caramel rather than whole-grain flour. Refined grain products usually have lots of additives, too, many of them preservatives and flavorings, though some are intended to restore a little of what has been lost. It always strikes me as ironic when I read the long list of ingredients on bread made from white flour and see that bran has been added.

In general, I seek out unprocessed (or low-processed), additive-free natural foods. This is what I mostly eat at home and have done for decades. I certainly don't want to eat less nutritious food on a long-distance hike when I am physically working much harder. If the food is organic, that's even better.

FRESH FRUIT AND VEGETABLES

The healthiest diet is generally accepted to be one containing plenty of fresh fruit and vegetables. Unfortunately these are heavy and bulky, and most don't survive well in a pack. Dried fruits still contain much of the goodness they had when fresh so I always carry some of these. Dried vegetables are better than none at all. Dinner entrees usually contain dehydrated or freeze-dried vegetables. If I make up my own, I often add dried onions or peas.

I don't like going without fresh products for long, however. One that is lightweight and compact and that really adds flavor to a meal is garlic, so I usually carry this. A small onion sometimes finds its way into my pack as well. I often leave supply points with some fresh fruit—apples and oranges are the easiest to carry without risking damage—that I eat the first day or so. Of course, salad vegetables and fruit can be bought from stores at supply points for immediate consumption, and if you dine in restaurants, you can eat plenty of salads and cooked vegetables there as well.

DEHYDRATED AND FREEZE-DRIED FOOD

Fresh food of all types, not just fruit and vegetables, is the healthiest food to eat. However, the weight and bulk plus the problems of keeping it fresh and in good condition mean it's not ideal for long-distance hiking. The main reason for all these disadvantages is the water content: remove that and you have food that is lightweight, compact, durable, and long lasting. (Canned food survives in the pack okay, but it's also heavy and bulky, as you have to carry the weight of the can as well as the water inside it.)

Dried food is the most practical for long-distance hiking. Caloric value isn't changed by removing moisture, nor is much of the nutritional content. However, some dried foods have chemicals added and are made from denatured foods. Again, check the labels. I have eaten dried foods most evenings on all my long-distance hikes without any adverse effects, but I have been careful to choose those with no or few additives and made from nonrefined foods so that they are as nutritious as possible. When choosing dried meals I plan on 6 to 8 ounces dry weight for an evening meal, regardless of how many servings the packet claims to have. If a meal is less than this weight, I know I'll have to supplement it or else eat two packets at once.

There are different methods of drying food. The simplest and oldest is sun drying. Fruit dried in this way is delicious. I particularly like sun-dried bananas. Most dried food is dehydrated by exposure to hot air blown into a spinning drum or else through a series of trays. Commercially available dehydrated food varies enormously in quality. Some reconstitutes well and is quite tasty, but much produces a bland mush that barely resembles the original fresh food because the cell structure has been damaged.

Home dehydrating is a way to produce good quality dried food. This is not something I've ever done, though I keep meaning to get around to it, but I have eaten excellent food dried this way by friends. You can dry cooked foods, so cooking times are short, though a period of presoaking may be needed. There are several makes of home dehydrators available, all consisting of racks of trays and a fan that runs off an electric motor. You could even build your own dehydrator. You can find out how from Alan Kesselheim's *Trail Food*, which also tells you how to dry food, including complete meals.

Spray-dried foods such as instant coffee, dried milk, and cheese powder are produced by the food being sprayed into a hot air–filled cylinder at high speed. Freeze-drying, a complex and expensive process developed originally to produce food for astronauts, involves first flash-freezing the food so the water in it turns to tiny crystals too small to damage the cell structure and then putting the frozen food into a vacuum at a low temperature, where the ice vaporizes without turning into water first. Because the structure of the food isn't damaged during freeze-drying, it reconstitutes well and is often tastier than dehydrated food.

RAW FOODS

Cooked foods are not essential and don't have any more calories than cold or raw food. Indeed, cooking can destroy some vitamins and reduce the nutritional value of some foods. Hot food, however, is psychologically appealing, especially at the end of a tiring day and when the weather is cold. So although I could probably save weight by leaving my stove and cooking equipment at home, I don't. There may be no more calories in it than in a cold meal, but I really enjoy those first mouthfuls of hot soup or stew in the evening, and they seem to have an almost immediate warming and restorative effect.

WEIGHT

On a long trip you can't skimp on food or you'll run out of energy. I carry 2 to 2.5 pounds of food for each day, and most long-distance hikers seem to do the same. That means food for a week will weigh 14 to 18 pounds or so, and for two weeks, 28 to 36 pounds, the most I would now ever consider carrying. This is where your daily mileage and the whereabouts of supply points become important. To go back to the 100-mile example used on pages 58–59, if you hike this distance in 5 days, you need to carry around 12 pounds of food, but if you hike it in 10 days, you'll need 24 pounds of food, a big difference.

The most I have ever carried was an unbelievable (and many years later even I find it hard to believe) 44 pounds of food on the 23-day crossing of the High Sierra on the Pacific Crest Trail. Combined with a pack including snowshoes, ice, ax, crampons, and cold-weather clothing plus all the fuel needed for the stove, I set off with a load that weighed at least 100 pounds, a crazy amount that I couldn't get on my back without sitting down. My only excuse for such a weight is that I didn't know what carrying it would be like. I soon found out. It was so heavy I had to get the weight off my legs at least once an hour or they went numb. The enormous energy requirements of carrying such a load meant that the food, which worked out to 1.9 pounds a day, wasn't enough, anyway, so I arrived at the end of that section very hungry indeed. I've not done that since and wouldn't do so again. Two weeks of food is the absolute most I'm now prepared to carry, and that's only if I really can't resupply more often.

COOKING TIMES AND METHODS

Many otherwise good foods have long cooking times that make them unsuited to long-distance hiking. At the end of a long day when your energy reserves are in need of replenishment, sitting and watching a meal simmer for half an hour or more is not appealing. Long cooking times means more stove fuel is needed, too, so more weight has to be carried.

Foods that cook quickly are a particularly good idea on hikes that will take you to moderately high altitudes for any length of time, such as the Pacific Crest and Continental Divide Trails. Because of the drop in air pressure, the boiling point of water drops with the rise in altitude at a rate of 9°F for every 5,000 feet. And for every drop of 9°F, cooking time almost doubles. So at 10,000 feet food takes nearly four times as long to cook as it does at sea level. Meals that are already fully or at least mostly cooked and that need only heating up and simmering a short while are best for cooking at high altitude.

I prefer such meals anyway. I have no desire to spend much time cooking on a long-distance hike—there's too much else to do. I look for meals that require just the addition of boiling water or that need to be simmered for 10 to 15 minutes at most.

With some foods, such as dried vegetables and soy products such as textured vegetable protein, soaking in cold water can reduce cooking times. You can't do this with most pasta or rice unless you want them to turn into a soggy mush, but you can add rice and quick-cook pasta to boiling water, turn the heat off, and leave the pot until it's cooked, with a lid on to keep the heat in. This saves fuel, if not time.

As well as checking for cooking time, I also read food packets for cooking instructions. Because I want to keep my cooking simple and quick and to carry the minimum of cookware, I look for meals that need cooking in only one pot of boiling water for a short time. Once two pots are needed it's too complicated, especially because I have only one burner. Adding different ingredients at different times is fine, though.

On long-distance hikes I don't fry or bake either, since I don't want to carry the extra items needed to do so—nor do I want to have to clean up a greasy pan used for frying food. If you do want to bake, there are two very light backpacker's ovens available that I've used with success on short trips: the Ultralight Outback Oven, which weighs 7 ounces, and the Ultralight BakePacker at 4 ounces. The first requires a stove with a controllable flame but is more versatile than the simpler BakePacker, which is simply a metal grid that you place in your pan and on which you can steam-bake foods in a plastic bag.

If you don't want to forego baked and fried foods but don't want to spend too much time preparing them, a good book to consult is Dorcas S. Miller's *Backcountry Cooking*. This has a good selection of quick-cook recipes.

SOURCES

Supermarkets and groceries can provide all the food you need at reasonable cost, especially if you buy in bulk. However, much supermarket food is laden with chemicals and contains white flour and other denatured grains. More wholesome foods are available, and it seems that their availability is increasing. Read the labels to check what you're getting. Look for carbohydrate, protein, and fat ratios, too. Many processed foods are very high in fats and sugars and low in complex carbohydrates.

Natural and health food stores are a great source of low-processed and additive-free foods of all types and also dried fruits, nuts, and grain bars. Lightweight, low-bulk, freeze-dried and dehydrated hiker's meals can be found in outdoor supply stores. Often they can be bought directly from the producers by mail order as well. Some companies will even drop-ship purchases to post offices along the trail (see pages 88–90).

If you'll be using supply boxes (see pages 88–90), you can save money by buying food in bulk. A large sack of muesli or box of pasta costs less than lots of smaller packets. The penalty, of course, is that you'll have to repack it into smaller amounts.

MY FOOD CHOICES

I'm mostly vegetarian (which is to say that I'll eat fish or meat if there's nothing else available, but otherwise I don't) so my choice of food doesn't include meat or fish. My meals are based on obtaining protein from other sources.

Staples

Although I try to have a varied diet, I almost always carry the following items.

Instant Nonfat or Low-Fat Dried Milk
This is a versatile food that I use on breakfast cereals and as a whitener for some hot drinks. It can also be added to main meals for more calories or flavor and as a thickener. There are various types

Breakfast at a campsite at Charkabhot village, Dolpo, Nepal.

of dried milk and milk look-alikes. The latter are made mainly from vegetable fat and usually contain a lot of additives and very little, if any, actual milk. I prefer milk powder with nothing added. Milkman is my favorite brand, as it has a touch of fat that does make it taste better than ones with no fat. Dried milk is available in cartons of various sizes and in packets, usually ones that make a quart of milk. I buy the latter by choice, but if just cartons are available, I look for the 7-ounce size, which makes 3.5 pints, and transfer the powder to a plastic bag. A quart packet will last for three days, a 7-ounce carton for a week. I rarely make the milk up on its own, but instead I stir spoonfuls of the powder into my muesli or hot drink.

Sugar

I use sugar in some hot drinks and on muesli and granola if they're not sweetened. Two ounces a day is ample. I prefer raw cane sugar, but white will do. A hot, sweet drink is a good source of fast calories and warmth if you're cold and wet, though some complex carbohydrates should be eaten at the same time or soon afterward to avoid a sugar crash.

Muesli

I have muesli for breakfast at home and on the trail. Four ounces a day with the addition of dried milk (0.3 to 0.6 ounce) and a little sugar (around half an ounce) and perhaps some extra dried fruit if I have any keeps me going through the first few hours of hiking. I don't feel the need for hot food in the morning unless it's very cold, and I certainly don't want to be bothered making pancakes or other foods that take time to prepare. On frosty mornings muesli can be heated up to make a sort of porridge. It does stick to the pan, though, so you need to stir it constantly. Even if you do this, some will still probably adhere like glue to the sides of the pan. Soaking the pan in cold water helps make the cleaning a bit easier.

Muesli can be eaten at any time of day. If I've had a long day and don't want to be bothered cooking, I sometimes eat a bowl for dinner. I look for muesli made from whole grains and with plenty of dried fruit in it. Occasionally I eat granola instead, as long as it's made from whole grains and doesn't contain lots of additives, as much granola does.

Trail Mix or Gorp

Having a snack food that can be carried in a pocket and eaten while hiking is useful in stormy weather when you need to eat but don't want to stop. I find trail mix ideal for this and for munching on any time I want a snack. I also like the fact that the mixture can be varied, so it doesn't always taste the same. Every hiker has their favorite ingredients. Because I have a sweet tooth, I prefer trail mix that is rich in dried fruit, especially papaya, pineapple, dates, and raisins. Some nuts and seeds are fine for me, but not too many. I also sometimes add chocolate chips, butterscotch chips, carob chips, M&Ms, and even handfuls of granola. I allot 2 or 3 ounces per day, but it often doesn't last until the next resupply station. The trail mix high in sugars that I like is good for a quick energy boost but not for long-term energy, so I would never make it the main part of the food I eat between camps. Add more nuts and seeds or granola to give it a higher content of more complex carbohydrates and fats.

Dried Fruit

In addition to the dried fruit in my trail mix, I frequently carry other dried fruit such as sun-dried bananas, which come in 8-ounce blocks and taste delicious, and apple rings. I also like fruit leathers, those strips of pressed fruit that weigh little and have a really fresh taste. Grape is my favorite flavor.

Grain and Fruit Bars

I used to eat several candy bars a day, but for many years now I have replaced these with grain and mixed grain and fruit bars because these contain more complex carbohydrates and less sugar and fat. My favorite bars by far are made by the

Intermountain Trading Company of California and appear under the Bear Valley label. There are four varieties: Fruit 'n' Nut Pemmican Bar, Carob Pemmican Bar, Coconut Almond Meal Pack Bar, and Sesame Lemon Meal Pack Bar, with calorie contents varying between 415 and 470 calories. Given that they only weigh 3.75 ounces, these bars have a high energy content. The ingredients are compressed so the bars don't crumble when carried in the pack. They have a coarse, baked texture like a cake rather than being chewy like many energy bars, which makes them easy to eat and very tasty. They're healthy, as well; they're made from whole grains with no additives and contain all essential amino acids, so they're a good protein source. The fat content is low, too. The ingredients are similar, but the bars have distinctive tastes. The Fruit 'n' Nut Bar, as an example, contains malted corn and barley, nonfat milk, honey, wheat germ, raisins, walnuts, soy flour, soy oil, wheat bran, pecan nuts, and grape juice. I discovered these bars on the Pacific Crest Trail and enjoyed them so much that I then ate at least one a day on the Continental Divide Trail. I'd have eaten more if I'd had them, so on the Yukon walk I ate two or more a day. I never got tired of them. Bear Valley bars can be found in natural food stores, outdoor equipment stores, and some supermarkets and grocery stores.

When I can't get Bear Valley bars (I've never found them in Europe), I buy other grain and fruit bars, often under the name *flapjack* (which means a sweet oat-based cookie). I like soft-baked bars rather than hard ones. I've tried many of the so-called energy bars available, but they don't seem to give me more of a boost than the Bear Valley bars or other grain bars that don't make the same hard-to-believe claims. Many energy bars are also often full of additives and simple sugars. Some have a dense texture and don't crumble or come apart easily in the mouth, so eating them can be hard work. I sometimes think the calories they contain are needed to provide the energy for chewing them! Lots of water is needed with them, too, as they're often very dry. In the cold they set like concrete and are a good way to break your teeth unless you carry them close to the skin to keep them soft. Given that the taste is often bland and the price usually high, I can't see any reason for long-distance hikers to eat these bars. The only ones I'd make an exception for are Clif Bars and Balance Bars, which have a good taste and a soft texture.

Bread and Bread Substitutes

I really miss bread on long-distance hikes and sometimes carry a small whole-grain loaf if weight and space allow. This is eaten the first couple of days out so it doesn't get too squashed or go stale. Most of the time, though, I carry more durable, lower-bulk alternatives. Whole-grain tortillas and pita bread come in resealable plastic bags and will last for a week or so if kept cool, which means storing them deep in the pack in hot weather. It's still wise to keep an eye out for mold. Biting into moldy bread is extremely unpleasant, as I unfortunately know from doing so once in the dark. I plan on two tortillas or pita breads per day.

Crackers, biscuits, and crispbread are long-lasting bread substitutes but need to be carried carefully if you don't want to end up with a packet of crumbs. Again, I try to find whole-grain varieties. I admit I'm not very fond of crackers, but they're the best alternative to bread when you have to carry food for a week or more because they are lightweight and low in bulk, as well as durable. Six to ten crackers, depending on size, are my daily supply. Oat crackers (Scottish oatcakes) are my favorites. Six of these weigh 2.5 ounces and contain 275 calories.

Spreads

Most bread and crackers are dry and bland if eaten on their own. I always carry some form of spread to put on them, usually a squeeze tube of cheese or vegetable paté, sometimes a plastic bottle of jam or honey. Glass jars are far too heavy, not to mention the risk of breakage, whereas plastic tubs are generally not strong enough and are likely to crack. Whatever container a spread comes in, I always carry it in a plastic bag so that if it does break, the contents don't spread themselves over other items in the pack. Peanut butter is another good choice, and meat eaters may like to carry paté, salami, or other spiced sausage.

Cheese

A small amount of a cheese such as cheddar can add taste and calories to many savory meals and can also be eaten as a trail snack with crackers or bread. I usually plan for 2 ounces a day. Cheese keeps well as long as it's cool. In hot weather I eat it in the first few days after leaving a supply point. Hard dry cheeses like Parmesan last longer in the heat than moister ones like cheddar. Powdered cheese is useful for adding to pasta or soup, and I sometimes carry a small carton of Parmesan.

Packet Soups

Soups are a good way to restore liquid, and I usually eat a bowl before having my main meal. They can also be used to add flavor to a bland meal or can even be used as the main sauce. I did this most evenings on my walk through Norway and Sweden on which I resupplied from stores along the way. There wasn't much choice in the tiny settlements I passed through, but I could always get pasta and packet soups, so the two mixed together made up my main meals. Instant soups are the easiest to prepare, but the portions and calorie content are tiny—7 ounces when rehydrated and around 120 calories—so I usually eat two at once when I carry them. A packet weighs only about an ounce, so the weight is incidental. Health food stores sometimes carry additive-free instant soups, but most of those found in supermarkets and grocery stores are chemical-laden concoctions, which I try to avoid. They're also very high in salt. Noninstant packets of soup can also have a dubious list of ingredients, but some, such as those from AlpineAire, are fairly good.

Pasta

Pasta in all its forms—macaroni, spaghetti, vermicelli—is an excellent source of complex carbohydrates. Because it's also lightweight and easily cooked, it's excellent as the main component of the hiker's dinner. I eat far more pasta than any other carbohydrate. I carry pasta on trips on which I'm making up my own meals and also prefer pasta-based prepared meals when I carry those. I prefer whole-grain pasta for its taste and because it's much more nutritious than that made from white flour, but I'll eat the latter if it's all I can get. I plan on 4 ounces of dry pasta a day. Mixed with a little cheese or dried milk powder, some dried vegetables, a few herbs and spices, and maybe a dash of pesto or tomato purée, pasta makes a simple, tasty meal that I never tire of eating. Packet soups can be used as a sauce as well, mixed in with the pasta after the latter has cooked. Dried pasta sauces could be used instead; some of these are quite tasty, but they are often packed full of additives.

When buying pasta I look at the cooking time and the bulk. Most pasta cooks in well under 10 minutes, and you can get no-cook pasta from AlpineAire. Short-cut or small elbow macaroni, tiny stars and shells, and spaghetti take up the least space in your pack. I don't carry spaghetti, however, because it's hard to eat with a spoon, and I don't carry a fork.

The instructions for cooking pasta nearly always call for boiling it in lots of water and then draining surplus water off. This isn't necessary as long as you stir the pasta frequently to stop it from sticking. I cook pasta in just enough water that there is sufficient left to mix in any dried ingredients such as milk powder or instant soup and allow them to rehydrate. That way no water or fuel is wasted.

Dried Vegetables

Vegetables can add flavor and color to any meal. Some, though, need a long soaking or simmering time. If it's more than 10 minutes, it's too long for me. My favorite dried vegetables are onions, mushrooms, and sun-dried tomatoes.

Seasonings

A selection of herbs and spices can add zest to any meal and can even be used to rescue a particularly unpalatable one. I normally carry small amounts of garlic powder, curry or chili powder, black pepper, and mixed herbs. I don't carry salt, as most dried meals are salty enough for my taste. Rather than garlic powder, I often carry fresh garlic, which is tastier and can easily be sliced with a pocketknife and then crushed on a pan lid with knife blade. When weight isn't important, I sometimes carry squeeze tubes of tomato purée and pesto. Dried pesto is available, too.

Specialist Backpacking Meals

Meals specially designed for outdoor use are convenient, but they can be quite expensive. Most are freeze-dried and quick and easy to prepare, just requiring the addition of boiling water and perhaps a short simmering time. Note that convenience and quick cooking are major selling points for these foods, so the packets often indicate the minimum amount of water and the shortest cooking time required to make the meals just about edible. A little more water and a bit more cooking time can often make the meals far more palatable. I cook these meals until the contents seem fully rehydrated, rather than when the claimed cooking time is up, and I add extra water if necessary.

Many prepared meals are made from refined grains and are full of chemical additives. Some use additive-free and low-processed foods, and the numbers of these are increasing. One of the first producers in this field was AlpineAire, whose meals I've been eating for many years. I discovered them when hiking the Pacific Crest Trail and found them so tasty and filling that I then ate them almost exclusively on the Continental Divide Trail and the Yukon walk. To prepare these meals (*cook* is too fancy a word here), you just add the meal to boiling water and then wait for 7 to 10 minutes. AlpineAire entrées include meat and fish dishes as well as vegetarian ones. A meatless example is the Mountain Chili, which contains cooked freeze-dried pinto beans, soy protein, tomato powder, cornmeal, freeze-dried corn, spices, bell peppers, onions, and salt. The dry weight is 6 ounces for a packet said to contain two servings, though a hungry long-distance hiker should have no problem eating the entire amount. I certainly don't. It gives 30 ounces of food when hydrated and provides 680 calories.

Harvest Foodworks of Ontario, Canada, also offers dried meals free from additives. They are very tasty but do take a bit more preparation than the AlpineAire dishes, so I've eaten them only occasionally. Natural High from Richmoor and Uncle John's Foods are also additive free, but I have tried neither. Stove makers MSR have a range of gourmet foods that are organic as well as additive free. They also come in burnable brown paper packets rather than foil or plastic. The ones I've tried are quite tasty. Backpacker's Pantry and Mountain House also offer some tasty meals, many of which are additive free.

Occasional Foods

I occasionally carry some of the following other foods, either for variety or because they were all I could get at a resupply point.

Cooking over Trangia alcohol stoves at a backcountry site in the Spanish Pyrenees.

Oatmeal

This is my choice for breakfast if I can't get muesli or granola. Instant oatmeal is the easiest and quickest to prepare, but I don't find it very filling or tasty. I'd rather spend a little more time making proper porridge from whole-grain oats.

Candy Bars and Chocolate

I once snacked on these every day, but now I eat them only occasionally, preferring the complex carbohydrates of grain bars to the high-fat, high-sugar content of candy bars and chocolate. If they're all I can get, I eat them more often.

Margarine

I used to always carry margarine, using it as a spread on bread and crackers and also putting some in evening meals. However, now that I am trying to have a high-carbohydrate, low-fat diet, I have stopped doing so. It's awkward to carry, messy if it spills, and high in weight due to the high water content. Very occasionally I carry tiny tubs of margarine (the sort you get in restaurants), but mostly I do without. And I don't miss

it. If meals call for the addition of margarine or butter, I add a little cheese. The exception to this is on winter trips when more calories are needed. Then margarine is a useful food to carry with you.

Desserts

Soup and a main meal are enough for me in summer, enough in the sense of the amount of food preparation I want to do as well as in the amount of food. In winter, however, when the nights are long and cold and there's plenty of time for cooking, especially as the stove provides some warmth, I sometimes carry desserts such as instant custard and instant puddings for more calories. Because the days are short, I eat less during the day, and so the weight of the desserts is balanced by carrying fewer trail snacks.

Dehydrated Potato

Instant potatoes are great for fast meals because they simply require the addition of boiling water. There are many varieties, some containing nothing much but potato, some containing various chemical additives. Flavored potatoes are more likely to have additives than plain ones. I find plain instant potatoes bland, but they can be made more palatable by adding cheese, milk powder, spices, garlic, and dried vegetables. A friend used to add instant soups as flavoring, but after seeing the lurid green mush produced by mixing potato powder with green pea soup, I never adopted this myself! I sometimes carry one or two packets of instant potatoes so I have something very quick to prepare for really long days at the end of which I just want to eat and go to sleep. On those occasions the taste of what I eat isn't that important anyway.

Rice

The problem with rice as a hiking food is that most of the quick-cook varieties are made from polished rice with most of the nutrients removed. Brown rice with nothing removed is much tastier and much better for you but takes 40 minutes to cook. Brown rice that cooks in ten minutes is available, and I sometimes carry this as an alternative to pasta. I usually use it to make curries with dried vegetables and spices.

Couscous

This crushed wheat is another food that is useful for fast meals, for you just add it to boiling water and let it sit for a few minutes. It's just about tasteless, but anything can be added to it, from cheese to curry powder. Again, whole-grain versions are available.

Instant Refried Beans

Beans and other legumes take far too long to cook to be of use to the long-distance hiker. However, instant refried beans can be the basis of a good meal, especially if added to rice or couscous to make complete proteins. I've carried them only occasionally, but I might do so more in future when I can find varieties without additives.

Textured Vegetable Protein (TVP)

This meat substitute contains all eight amino acids, so it is a good protein source. It comes in the form of chunks and mince. The chunks take a bit too long to cook for hiking use, but the mince cooks very quickly and is a good addition to any meal. TVP is tasteless on its own but quickly absorbs flavors. If you cook it in a tasty sauce, it's fine. Flavored TVP, such as bacon bits, is available, but the flavors and colors are usually artificial, so I avoid it. Two ounces a day is adequate for TVP.

Complete Meals

Packaged meals that contain all the ingredients are easy to prepare, though cooking times can be long. However, most supermarket ready-made meals, including that old standby macaroni and cheese, are made from refined foods and con-tain additives, so I tend to avoid them except for occasional meals. They're often high in fat, too. I used to eat Ramen noodles quite often because they cook so quickly, but I've stopped doing so because many brands are made from white flour, are high in fat, and contain flavor packets that are full of salt and monosodium glutamate (MSG). I occasionally eat Westbrae Ramen noodles, which are made from whole-grain flour, though they still contain a lot of fat. They're found in some supermarkets and health-food stores. You can also get Chinese or Japanese noodles without flavor packets. If you want macaroni and cheese, Fantastic Foods makes an additive-free version that tastes OK. The 5-ounce packet isn't very filling, though, so two packets are needed plus extra cheese and milk to make a meal adequate for a hungry hiker. Fantastic Foods also makes other mixes from grains, beans, and vegetables that are additive free. These portions are also on the small side, so again I'd recommend two packets. I find them a bit bland and in need of spicing up, but I would buy them in preference to chemical concoctions. Dorcas Miller in her excellent book *Good Food for Camp and Trail* says that Fantastic Foods' Potatoes Au Gratin was the only supermarket mix of that type she could find that didn't contain additives.

MENU PLANNING

It is possible to plan a hiking menu in detail, listing exactly what you will eat each day for each meal. I don't do this, as I prefer to allow a little room for spontaneity. I can decide what I feel like eating at the time. It also means I can adjust my diet to the conditions. On a day of rain and wind I may munch lots of trail mix and a few grain bars, carried in a pocket, while hiking rather than stopping to spread something on crackers or bread. At the end of a long, tiring day I may just have soup and bread and not bother with a main meal. On cold days I occasionally get the stove out at lunchtime and have some warming soup. The food planning I do is to ensure that I have enough food for the time I'll be out and that it is balanced between break-

fast, lunch, and dinner foods. Overall my menu provides at least 4,000 calories a day, split roughly into 800 calories for breakfast, 1,600 for lunch, and 1,600 for dinner, and weighing approximately 35 to 40 ounces.

The table below is a sample planning menu for a week.

RUNNING OUT OF FOOD

If your food planning is accurate, your supplies are in the right place, and you protect your food from animals (see the section on food storage on page 83) you shouldn't run short of food. What happens though if you do? How long can you go without food and keep hiking? Longer than you might think from my experience. I've arrived at supply points quite hungry on numerous occasions, having almost run out of food with a day to go, but only once have I really had to hike for days on very little food. This happened during my end-to-end hike in the Canadian Rockies in an area where I couldn't walk out in a day or two. When my supply box failed to turn up, the only time this has ever happened, I bought food from a supermarket. I couldn't, however, find any replacement topo maps. I was in a small town far from anywhere and with no public transportation, so I phoned around trying to order some maps by mail. Eventually the Canadian Forest Service offered to send me some. What arrived was a bundle of almost incomprehensible blown-up aerial photographs and a blue and white 1:250,000-scale map. As it had taken a week to sort out getting these, I dumped the aerial photos, which I couldn't relate to the map, and continued my hike, hoping the map would be adequate. It was

Breakfast	Lunch	Dinner
muesli, 28 oz.	trail mix, 20 oz.	packet soups, 7 x 14 oz.
dried milk, 14 oz.	sun-dried bananas, 16 oz.	freeze-dried entrées, 3 x 21 oz.
sugar, 14 oz.	grain bars x 14, 52 oz.	pasta, 16 oz.
	oat crackers x 42, 18 oz.	cheese, 14 oz.
	vegetable paté, 16 oz.	seasonings, 4 oz.
		dried vegetables, 8 oz.
		TVP, 8 oz.

Drinks: herbal/fruit teabags, fruit crystals/decaffeinated coffee, 4 oz.   Total Weight: 271 ounces (16.5 lbs.)

roughly 250 mostly trail-less miles to the next supply point. Unsurprisingly I was unable to plan a proper route with such a basic large-scale map, and once I got disoriented I was never sure exactly where I was for almost six days, though I knew which direction I needed to walk. The supplies I'd bought to replace the missing ones didn't prove as filling, and I had to ration them drastically for the final five days of mostly hard bushwhacking in dense forest, eating a mere fraction of what I normally ate per day. I became extremely hungry but didn't run out of energy, probably because I was very fit, having been hiking for over two months over a distance of 800 miles, and because the weather was dry and fairly warm. Knowing that I can hike with very little food for five days or so is reassuring, though I would much rather never have to do so again.

Unless you're hiking in remote areas, if your supplies run low, you can usually hike out to a road or town in one or two days, resupply your food, and then return to the trail. In the case described above, continuing along the direction of my hike was actually the quickest way to reach a road. Of course, I should have checked in advance that my supplies had arrived. And instead of waiting for maps to arrive by mail, I should have either taken a taxi (expensive but probably no more so than staying in town a week) or hitchhiked to a place where I could buy maps.

DRINKS

Water is the best liquid for the hiker. It's discussed in detail starting on page 92. What I'm talking about here is flavoring for those times when you don't want to drink plain water—that is, coffee, tea, herbal tea, hot chocolate and cocoa, fruit crystals, and energy drinks.

I used to be a big coffee drinker—a caffeine addict, in fact. I drank less coffee when hiking than when at home simply because I didn't want to stop during the day long enough to make it. But I was still barely able to wake up in the morning without a large mug of coffee, and it took another one to get me going. Until I'd had my coffee I barely noticed the world around me. And when I stopped to make camp, coffee was the first thing I wanted. Yet caffeine is a diuretic—that is, it increases the output of urine—so it's worse than useless for fluid replacement. It's also a stimulant that increases heart rate and causes blood pressure to rise. I decided to give up coffee because I didn't feel the amount I was drinking was good for me and because I had failed at cutting back on my consumption due to the cravings engendered when I didn't have a cup at a time I was used to having one. It was actually easier to give up completely than to cut back. Not drinking coffee when hiking has made a noticeable difference. I don't wake up in the morning feeling the only thing I'm interested in is a mug of coffee. Some days I don't even have anything to drink for quite a while. I'm more aware of my surroundings immediately when I wake, and sometimes I prefer to observe nature coming to life rather than immediately cranking my stove into action. At the end of the day I can now relax and wander round my campsite, getting a feel for where I am rather than fixating on having a mug of coffee. Overall I feel that giving up caffeine allows me to be more in touch with the wilds as well as being healthier.

I still drink coffee, but only decaffeinated. As well as instant decaffeinated coffee, I now carry various herbal teas and fruit crystals, as long as they are pure fruit and not chemical concoctions. I also sometimes carry ingredients for hot chocolate, though I am aware this does contain caffeine. I don't drink it every day, however, so I'm not concerned about becoming addicted to it.

I drink only water while actually hiking, so I don't carry much in the way of drinks, since I need them only for mornings and evenings. Enough for three or four mugs a day is adequate. I don't usually bother with energy or sports drinks, even though they're supposed to help you rehydrate more quickly and efficiently. I've experimented with these, and they don't seem to give me any extra energy or quench my thirst any

Alcohol

A cool beer is welcome when arriving in a town after a week or more on the trail. And a glass of wine can be a nice accompaniment to a restaurant meal. However, I'm careful how much alcohol I drink and when I drink it. Alcohol is a much stronger diuretic than coffee, so it's unwise to drink it if you're at all dehydrated, as it'll only make the condition worse. Better to gulp down lots of water and leave the alcohol until later, when you'll probably enjoy it more. Eating with alcohol mitigates the effects, too. Beer on an empty stomach at the end of a day on the trail can have a powerful effect.

Too much alcohol dehydrates you and can mean leaving a supply point feeling as though you need a rest rather than as though you've had one. Hiking and hangovers don't go well together.

better than water. In fact, some are quite sickly and leave me feeling that I need a drink of something less sweet. At the start of a two-week hike in the Grand Canyon, a place where you need to drink large quantities to avoid dehydration because of the heat, I bought two one-quart bottles of a sports drink. I drank those in the first few hours as I descended into the furnace of the lower canyon. They tasted okay, if a little sweet. After they were gone, though, I drank plain water and found it even more refreshing. The main benefit I gained from buying the sports drinks was that the bottles were useful for carrying extra water. Sports drinks may work for much more energetic pursuits like running or cycle racing, but I don't think they're necessary for hiking. I'm also dubious about the amount of sugar and chemicals found in some of these drinks. Water is best. I used to carry powdered drinks to disguise the taste of iodine-treated water before I discovered that dissolving vitamin C (ascorbic acid) in the water neutralized the taste. Nowadays I don't carry iodine, either. For more on water and water treatment, see the Water and Treating Water sections beginning on page 92.

On hikes in bitter winter weather, when lakes and streams are frozen, and any open water is so close to freezing it sets your teeth on edge and leaves you gasping when you drink it, I carry a vacuum flask so I can have a hot drink during the day. I now use a tough stainless steel flask, having broken several glass ones (always when full, too). The problem with steel flasks is the weight; my 1-pint flask weighs 18.5 ounces. When it's really cold I feel it's worth the weight, though. I fill it with hot water at night so I have some water for breakfast and don't need to melt snow. I usually mix fruit crystals (lemon and blackcurrant ones are very refreshing) with the water because I don't find warm water very appetizing. I carry the flask only when I expect prolonged extreme cold, though. In spring I exchange it for a foam insulated water bottle cover. My Outdoor Research one holds a quart-size Nalgene bottle and weighs just 4 ounces. The total weight of bottle and cover is half that of my steel flask, but it holds twice as much. Water doesn't stay as hot as in a flask, but it does stay warm all day, which is fine with fruit crystals in it, though probably not so good if you prefer tea or coffee. On long hot spring days when plenty of water is needed but streams are still frozen, snow can be added to the bottle, a little at a time, to keep it topped.

PACKAGING

Many foods come wrapped in an unnecessary abundance of wasteful packaging that adds to the weight and the bulk. This is best stripped away and the contents packed in a simple plastic bag, the standard item for carrying hiking foodstuffs. Zipper-lock bags are preferable to twist-tie ones as they're easier to use. Different sizes are useful, as are spares. Any items that could cause a mess if spilled, such as sugar, dried milk, dehydrated potato flakes, and other loose powdery items I double-bag. Items that don't have to be repackaged, like packet soups and grain bars, can be kept together in bags so they don't get crushed and so you can quickly check what you have left. Rather than using one big bag, I keep them in several smaller ones. The only items I keep in

Supplies for ten people for eight days before repackaging.

their original cardboard containers are crackers, as these crumble too easily if not protected.

Cooking instructions can be cut or torn off packets and placed in the plastic bag with the ingredients. Labeling foods that could be mistaken for something else is wise, too. I well remember an incident on a backpacking trip I was leading when, at a rest stop, one of the participants offered to make a hot drink for everyone. He then handed out rather murky looking mugs of tea and coffee. The drinks tasted strange and had a gritty texture, and the bottom of each mug was full of thick sludge. A quick investigation showed that he'd inadvertently used potato flakes instead of dried milk.

Small items like herbs and spices can be stored in small plastic bottles. I use empty vitamin containers. Larger bottles aren't as good due to their bulk. Plastic bags take up almost no room when empty and are easy to pack when full.

To keep together all the plastic bags of food, I store them in nylon stuff sacks (which weigh around 4 ounces each). On trips where I'll need to carry a week's supply of food or more at a time, I use two nylon sacks rather than one. It's easier to pack two smaller sacks in my backpack and easier to find items in them. Lunch and snack foods, which are quite bulky, go in one stuff sack, breakfast and dinner material in the other. Food I'll be eating that day goes in an outside pocket of the pack, usually the one in the lid, stored together in a large plastic bag.

If you're using bear-resistant canisters (see pages 85–86), care is needed to squeeze all the air out of plastic bags and really get them as small and flat as possible if you want to fit in the six days of food that the smallest size canister is claimed to hold. If you'll be using these containers, you also want to carry the lowest bulk foods you can find.

Plastic bags are not very environmentally friendly, especially if used just once and then discarded. I reuse bags until they split, rinsing them out when necessary. Ones with holes can still be used to keep grain bars together. Paper bags are an alternative, but they tear easily in the pack and aren't any more environmentally friendly than the plastic bags unless they're made of recycled paper.

FOOD STORAGE IN CAMP

If I'm not hiking in an area where bears may be a problem, I usually store my food in my tent, under my tarp, or close to me if sleeping under the stars. This gives me easy access to it and means I should hear if an animal tries to raid it. I don't like leaving my food in my pack, since sharp teeth and claws can soon tear through the fabric, and many animals know that packs often contain food.

In areas where there are regularly used backcountry campsites, many animals and birds have learned that there is often food in these places and so have become regular visitors. This is only natural on their part. Animals will always seek out the easiest source of food. However, becoming dependent on hikers' supplies isn't good for them, as well as being a nuisance for you. The food itself isn't what they normally eat and is likely to be bad for them. The packaging certainly is harmful, and many animals eat this, sometimes clogging their stomachs with indigestible plastic and foil so they then starve. It is in their interests as well as yours to keep your food away from them. The easiest way to do this is not to camp on or near popular sites (see discussion of campsite selection on pages 217–19). In some areas using these sites is required by the authorities, however. This is the case in the national parks in the Canadian Rockies and in some U.S. parks like the Grand Canyon. Popular sites in the latter have posts on which to hang your food, and park regulations say that all food and plastic bags must be packed away when not in use. Starving mule deer with stomachs full of plastic have had to be shot in the Grand Canyon, so the regulations do have a purpose.

I found mice the biggest problem in the Grand Canyon. During a two-week hike there I slept under the stars the first few nights but soon started using the tent when mice running over me during the night kept waking me up. Even at little-used sites I suspended my food bags from branches if there were any or kept them in the tent to keep the mice from them. I never lost any food.

Protecting Food Supplies from Bears

Bears are magnificent creatures, synonymous with true wilderness. Seeing one is a wonderful experience. However, the very power and size that makes them so impressive also makes them potentially frightening. Many long-distance trails pass through black bear country, including the Appalachian, Pacific Crest, and Continental Divide Trails. Grizzly bears are also found in places along the last trail as well as in many areas of western Canada and Alaska. Many hikers are terrified of bears even though they are unlikely even to see one. The risks involved in camping in bear country are not great as long as certain precautions are followed. I've spent countless nights in bear country, and only once did a bear visit my campsite. (For bear encounters while hiking, see page 215.)

Bear country doesn't necessarily mean bear problems. Only in some very popular areas, usually national parks, do bears get used to raiding campsites, Yosemite National Park being a notorious case. In other areas the bears are still wild and will usually stay well out of your way. Where bears have become used to eating hikers' food (and other items like sunscreen, toothpaste, soap, and garbage), it is necessary to protect your food from them for their sakes as well as for yours. Bears that raid campsites regularly, especially roadside ones, may end up being drugged from a dart gun and then relocated in a remote area. If they return and repeat the behavior, which to them is only natural, they are often shot, as is any bear that harms a human being.

The traditional way to keep food from bears is to hang it from a high branch. However, this method, known as *bearbagging*, isn't very effective in many areas now, partly because it can be difficult to do properly, and when done improperly the bears can easily get your food, and partly because the bears have figured out how to circumvent it.

There are three basic ways to bearbag food supplies. Which method is best depends on whether bears are likely to raid campsites, where you are camping, and which bears are found there. The first method is fine in areas where problems with bears are unlikely. It involves suspending your food at least 12 feet above the ground, 10 feet away from the trunk of the tree, and 6 feet below the branch. To do this you tie a rock to one end of a line (it's easier to put the rock in a small bag first) about 50 feet long (I use standard parachute cord) and a stuff sack con-

Counterbalancing food bags in the High Sierra on the Pacific Crest Trail.

taining your food to the other end. Then you chuck the rock over a long branch about 20 feet up, haul up the stuff sack, and tie off the line round the trunk of the tree. In grizzly bear country hanging your food very high is more important than having it far from the trunk of the tree, since grizzlies don't climb well but can reach high. Black bears are good climbers, however, so bags too near the trunk of a tree will be easy for them to get.

A more secure method for protecting your food and also one that works in areas where there aren't any branches long enough for the above method is to suspend the food bag between two trees about 25 feet apart. This is done by attaching the food bag to the center of your line, throwing a rock attached to the line over a branch, and tying it off around the trunk of the tree. Next you throw the other end of the line over a branch on the other tree, haul the food up into the air, and tie off the line. This prevents a black bear from climbing out on the branch from which your food is hanging and trying to get it.

In much of the High Sierra, including along the Pacific Crest Trail, where bears raid popular campsites nightly, neither of the above methods is enough. The bears know that if they break the cord, the bag of food they can see will fall to the ground. For these bears the food must be *counterbalanced*, which means both ends of the line must be at least 12 feet above the ground, 10 feet from the trunk of the tree, and 6 feet below the branch. This means having two stuff sacks of roughly equal weight. The first one is hauled right up to the branch and then any loose line is pushed into the second one before it is hurled up into the air, ideally with the result that both bags end up at the same height. If you leave a loop of line just poking out of the top of one of the bags, this can be hooked with a trekking pole or a stick to get the bag back down.

Bearbagging by any method can be difficult and can take hours to get right. At the end of a long day it can be a tiresome chore. You have to find the right tree to start with, which is not always easy in dense forest. Often the line gets snarled up and can't be retrieved, so it remains hanging from the branch, an unsightly piece of litter. Too many campsites are marked by long lines of tangled cord with rocks on one end hanging from branches. If you haven't any extra cord, this leaves you with the problem of how to protect your food. Also, throwing cord over a branch and then hauling up a heavy food bag can damage or even break the branch. I've been startled a number of times when a big branch that looked perfectly solid and healthy crashed to the ground at my feet as soon as it bore the weight of my food bag. In some places like the High Sierra even counterbalancing is no longer that effective anyway, as bears have worked out many ingenious strategies to get the food they can see and smell, including breaking the branch from which it's hanging.

If you have a very heavy food bag, it may be extremely difficult to haul it up due to the friction of the cord over the branch. A thicker line would help, but this means more weight and bulk to carry. On the Canadian Rockies walk, where I sometimes had to bearbag 25 to 30 pounds of food, I tied the end of a line to a thick stick, held this across my stomach and walked away from the branch, pulling up the bag behind me. Pulling at an angle rather than from below the branch reduces the friction. It also means that if the branch breaks, it doesn't land on your head. The closest I've come to serious injury in bear country has been from bear-bagging rather than bears. On the Continental Divide Trail I shared a campsite in Glacier National Park with some other hikers, including two fishermen who had a week's supply of canned food. There was a steel cable to hang food from. The problem was getting their food, stored in a pack, up there. With four others hauling on the line, I pushed the pack up from below, only to see it swing wildly and then come crashing down, narrowly missing me as I jumped out of the way. The line had snapped. A second attempt, with me standing well out of the way, broke the line again and we succeeded only

Bear pole at a backcountry campsite in Banff National Park in the Canadian Rockies.

by going to a stronger line. Ironically enough, after all our effort, another angler left a large fish he'd caught on a low rock overnight. It was still there in the morning.

Because bearbagging often fails, many park managers now advise using bear-resistant containers instead. These weigh around 3 pounds for the smallest size, which will hold six days food for one person if you have low-bulk food and pack it in very carefully. Being round and solid, they are awkward to pack, but they are said to be effective. The weight and bulk mean I would be reluctant to use them on a really long hike unless it was legally required, as it now is in some places such as Denali National Park in Alaska and Kluane National Park in Yukon Territory.

My one use of bear containers was on a two-week hike with a friend in Yosemite, where we certainly found them much preferable to hanging food. We saw no bears on that trip and never, as far as I know, had one visit any of our camps. However, I don't think the main reason for this was the containers but rather the fact that we avoided popular campsites. Only once during the whole trip did we camp anywhere near anybody else. We did, though, meet people who had lost food to bears or spent nights awake trying to keep the bears away. One hiker we met invited us to come and camp near him beside a lake. He told us that there were other people there and also that bears came into the camp every night. Needless to say, we camped elsewhere. Bears will go where food is normally to be found, which means campsites that are used most nights. Camp where other people usually don't, and you'll probably not have any problems with bears. (See page 217 for more on campsite selection.) This is especially true if you don't cook very aromatic or greasy food, or if you stop to cook and eat but then walk on and camp later. If you do cook in camp, as I usually do, it should be done at least 100 feet downwind of where you'll sleep. Food should be hung that far away as well.

I would particularly avoid any campsite with garbage in it, as any leftover foods plus the smell are likely to attract bears. I've only once had a bear visit a camp, and this one was, I suspect, used to doing so in search of food. This occurred in Jasper National Park on my Canadian Rockies end-to-end walk. I'd arrived at a campsite after a long rainy day to find it strewn with trash, some of it food scraps. I burned what I could, but this was difficult, since it was soaking wet from the rain. I cooked in the campsite but set my tent up back in the woods much further away than I usually did. The next morning I was having breakfast under a tree, since it was raining again,

when a black bear poked its face out of some bushes about 20 feet away. I jumped up and shouted, and it backed off into the bushes, though not far. I made more noise, including blowing my safety whistle, and it eventually disappeared into the forest. The fact that it didn't race off immediately, as had other black bears I'd encountered, made me think this was a bear used to raiding campsites, so I packed up and left in case it came back.

It's also worth checking campsites for signs of bears, such as droppings, paw prints, and trees or stumps raked by claws. In Glacier National Park on the Continental Divide Trail I remember arriving at a campsite to find a signboard almost totally shredded by a bear's claws. As it was late in the day, my companion and I camped there anyway, only to learn later that a grizzly had been seen there just the day before. Since then, if there's bear sign, I move on.

Where black bears are to be found but where there's no record of them raiding campsites, I don't hang my food. On the Pacific Crest Trail I hung my food in the High Sierra but otherwise kept my food near me at night just outside my shelter, since no other areas seemed to have problems with bears. If I heard a movement during the night, I switched on my flashlight and made a noise. At various times I was disturbed by mice, deer, and porcupines, but never by a bear. I did see a few bears on the PCT, but they always ran off fast, and none came into my camps.

On sections of the Continental Divide Trail (Glacier and Yellowstone National Parks in particular) and throughout the Canadian Rockies and Yukon walks, I was in grizzly bear country. Though encounters with grizzlies are far fewer than with black bears, and even when they occur nothing usually happens, the potential for being hurt is greater, for grizzly bears are more aggressive and less predictable than black bears.

In grizzly country I don't sleep with my food nearby, and I always bearbag it if this is possible. In some national parks, such as those in the Canadian Rockies, backcountry campsites, which hikers are required to use, have either poles with pulleys for your food or bars between trees from which to suspend your food. In other areas I've bearbagged my food where the trees were big enough. In the northern Yukon, though, the trees were often either too small or nonexistent. There I split my food between two stuff sacks, carried each one at least a hundred yards in opposite directions from each other and my camp, and left them on the ground under some low bushes. Only once did any animal raid my food, and then it was something very small that took very little. If there are big boulders or cliffs around, food bags can be stored high in cracks or on ledges or even lowered from the top, as bears are not good rock climbers.

I also don't cook in or near my tent in grizzly country, and I make sure before the trip that my tent doesn't smell of food. Because the smell is probably what initially attracts bears, foods without much odor, such as dried and especially freeze-dried foods, are a good idea. Keeping foods sealed in plastic minimizes the smell. If you don't finish a meal, the scraps should be bagged up and stored with the food.

RESUPPLY

On any hike longer than a week or so, you have to work out how to resupply with food and other items. Your route plan should give the locations and number of days apart of possible resupply points. Once you know this, you can plan what needs to go into each supply package and how you will collect them.

On well-established trails like the AT and the PCT, lists of supply points with details of facilities can be found in planning and trail guides and obtained from trail organizations. For less popular or unfinished trails and for your own routes, more research is usually needed to find where supply points are. Local tourist offices are useful here, as they should be able to tell you where post offices are located, along with supermarkets and grocery stores.

Once you know how far apart supply points are and what daily mileage you are planning to do, you can work out how many days' worth of food are needed at each supply point. To use the 100-mile example again, if that's the distance between two supply points and you hike 10 miles a day, you'll need 10 days' worth of food, but if you travel 20 miles a day, you'll need only 5 days' worth of food. Layover days away from resupply points need to be included, of course, so if you're going to spend a day not hiking in the backcountry, add that to the total. If you come up with a figure higher than two weeks' worth of food for any section, I'd look for an additional supply point or consider placing a cache so you can reduce the amount you have to carry. I prefer to resupply at least once a week if I can and certainly once every 10 days. I have in the past carried horrendous amounts of supplies, such as the 23 days' worth of food described on page 71. As I said, I wouldn't do this again, and I don't recommend it.

Using every possible resupply point is the way to keep the weight carried as low as possible. Choices still have to be made, however. Many resupply points are not actually on the trail but some miles away. How far out of your way are you prepared to go to resupply? If it'll take a day to get to a supply point and back, is it worth it? If it's the only supply point in a three- or four-week section of trail, then using it is just about essential. However, if another supply point much nearer the trail is only a few days further away, then it might be worth skipping the supply point that will take you farther off the trail.

Resupplying As You Go

The simplest way to resupply is to buy your food along the way. This cuts out the time and effort of planning your supplies in advance. If there are plenty of stores on or near your route, this is quite feasible, but it doesn't work well everywhere. I hiked for a while on the Pacific Crest Trail with a hiker who had previously supplied along the way with success on the Appalachian Trail. However, on the PCT he found that many of the stores on or near the trail carried very little food suitable for hiking, so he was often forced to carry foods that were heavy and took a long time to cook. Because of this he arranged for his family back in New Jersey to send out occasional food parcels.

I resupplied from stores on my hike along the length of Norway and Sweden. I knew that most grocery stores sold quick-cook pasta, packet soups, and oatmeal and that most of the lodges in the mountains, of which there are many, sold foods suitable for hiking. Even so, I had a somewhat limited diet compared with trips when I've planned my food in advance, as there wasn't much choice. Also, at times I had to buy larger quantities than I needed when smaller amounts weren't available. I did the same on the Arizona Trail but found a greater choice of suitable foods though I still had to buy more than I needed.

I do usually plan on buying some supplies en route, which cuts down on the weight and therefore mailing costs of my supply boxes and shortens the time needed to sort and pack food in advance. Spending money in local stores also supports the communities you pass through and helps give hikers a good name. Because dehydrated meals are the hardest to obtain in stores along the way, I plan on buying snack foods and perhaps breakfast cereals as I hike, but not evening meals. On the PCT and CDT I bought most of my lunch and breakfast foods along the way. In remoter areas, like the northern Canadian Rockies and the Yukon, I could do this in only a very few places.

When I am restocking en route, I compile a shopping list for each resupply point as I go along and as I run out of things so that I can shop as quickly and efficiently as possible. At times, a store may not have something I want, in which case I have to go without or select something different. Trying different foods is an advantage of shopping as you go, as is not having to eat foods again that you dislike.

Supply Boxes

The best way to ensure you have the supplies you want is to pack them beforehand and have them sent to supply points. Using your itinerary, you can make lists of all the food supplies needed at each supply point, purchase the food in advance, and pack it in strong cardboard boxes. I mark each box on the outside with the name of the supply point to avoid confusion. In addition to food, I pack maps, guidebook sections, first-aid items, toiletries, socks, spare footwear, paperback books, film and film-processing mailers, and any other needed items in the supply boxes. Goods should be packed tightly to avoid damage in transit. Avoid sending perishable foods because they'll probably spoil. Food will need to be sorted into the right amounts for each section of the hike and then repackaged. This task takes a surprising amount of time, so plan to do it well in advance of the start of the hike. Arranging and packing supply boxes also takes up room. You'll need to do this somewhere where no one is going to object to piles of food and equipment scattered everywhere. A hundred or more days' worth of food takes up a large area.

Sending Supply Boxes

Boxes can be mailed to post offices on or near the trail. They should be addressed to yourself *c/o General Delivery* in North America and *Poste Restante* in Europe. Mark them *Hold for Hiker* and list the expected collection date plus a return address. If the boxes have supplies for more than one person, all the names should be listed on each box so that any of you can collect it. Remember you'll probably need to show some form of identification, such as a driver's license, before a post office clerk will let you have a box.

You can't mail all the boxes you'll need for a long hike before you set out because post offices will hold items for only about a month (the holding time varies from post office to post office, so check in advance). Someone at home will have to mail most of the boxes for you. If you're far from home or don't have anyone who can do this, you could use a professional service. There are mail forwarders who will handle boxes for you, and some food suppliers will also do this. I've never used a mail forwarder, but when I hiked the PCT Trail Foods of North Hollywood drop-shipped my food for me. Before the hike I visited the company to put other items like maps and guidebooks into the supply boxes. This worked very well—all my supplies turned up when and where I wanted them. On the CDT I ordered much of my food from AlpineAire and again arranged for them to drop-ship it to me. In this case I wasn't able to add other items to the boxes, so these had to be sent separately. If you use a company to mail supply boxes for you, you need to explain carefully exactly what you are doing and when each box is needed.

An alternative way of sending supply boxes if you haven't anyone to do this for you is to mail them as you go along. At the time of writing I am planning a hike along the Arizona Trail. On arriving in Arizona I plan to buy enough food for the first three or four weeks. Except for those supplies needed at the start of the hike, this food will be packed and sent to post offices on or near the route that I will be able to visit during the first month of the walk and that are roughly a week or so apart. At the end of that month I will visit the nearest town where I can buy supplies and repeat the process. Doing this means I won't have to rely on whatever I can buy in small stores along the way nor rely on a company to mail my supplies. (In actual fact I ended up resupplying with food along the way and sending a running supply box ahead with maps, films, and other items in it.)

The advantage of having someone at home mail your boxes is that you can leave the boxes open so you can have items added or removed if necessary. For this to work well, you and your mailing person need to have lists of the contents of each box. It's also a good idea to have a separate box containing items you might need at some stage, such as spare footwear and replacement items of equipment, so that when you need something, it can easily be found. It is irritating for the person doing all these chores for you if you have to phone up to explain that the pack you want sent to you is probably stored in the closet in the spare room or possibly in the attic.

When you use post offices, it's best to find out the hours of service in advance and then plan your itinerary to fit with these hours. Arriving early Saturday afternoon to discover that the post office closed at noon and doesn't reopen until Monday morning stops your hike for nearly two days. It's fine if you've planned for this, but not if you want to keep walking. In many small communities there is a post office counter inside a store, rather than a separate post office. These tend to keep longer hours than regular post offices and will often let you collect your parcel when the post office is officially shut but the store is still open.

You'll have to make other arrangements if you plan to hike in a place where there are no post office facilities. On some trails there may be local businesses, such as outfitters, lodges, or cafés, that will hold supply boxes for a fee. Some of these may be in small settlements that don't have post offices or situated on roads many miles from the nearest town. Others are located in the backcountry at the end of long dirt roads. I used several of these on the Continental Divide Trail where there are long sections between towns and roads. It's a good way to stay in the wilds and not have to make long diversions away from the trail to reach a town. Another advantage is that you can usually collect your box whenever you arrive, but a disadvantage is that you can't mail anything from these supply points. Often there are other facilities available at these businesses, such as accommodations or meals. By using these services you'll help keep the owners of these businesses happy and help ensure that the service will remain for future hikers. Note that places far from a post office may only accept UPS parcels. Information about these places can usually be found in guides to the trail or obtained from the trail organization.

Ranger stations may hold supplies for you, too, and may even carry them into the backcountry so you can pick them up at a remote cabin. These services won't be advertised, but it's always worth inquiring. On the Canadian Rockies walk I was able to hike a 17-day section without starting out with a very heavy load because I had a supply box waiting at a backcountry warden station.

In really remote areas it may take a fair amount of research to find people who'll hold supplies for you. It's worth the effort. I discovered this in the northern Canadian Rockies, where some of the outfitters who run hunting camps in the backcountry would have taken in supplies for me if I'd asked. I wish I'd done so, as it would have saved me carrying a lot of weight. On the Yukon walk I had supplies taken down the Yukon River for me to a riverside campsite by a commercial riverboat, enabling me to stay in the wilds for 20 days. On the far northern section of that walk where there were no post offices and only one tiny settlement, I arranged for supply boxes to be dropped at highway maintenance depots by a tour bus. The contacts for these services were found for me by Yukon Tourism.

In general, the way to find places to hold supplies is to phone around, starting with the tourist information office, if there is one. If you're planning on staying in a hotel or guesthouse or wilderness lodge, the owners will probably hold a supply box for you. Ask when you book. Other places may do so for a fee, which you should always offer to pay.

Returning Boxes

Often at supply points you'll have items to send home, such as gear that is no longer needed, books you've read, and maps and guidebook extracts for the section of trail you've just walked. These can be packed into the supply box you've just emptied. I put a small amount of parcel tape and some address labels in supply boxes to make mailing them home easier. I thought of this after I'd bought full rolls of tape on several occasions, most of which I then left in the store as I didn't want to carry the weight.

If you decide not to complete a hike, you'll need to contact any remaining supply points and arrange for the return of your boxes. Phone them to find out what the charge will be and then send them the money and a mailing label.

Family and Friends

If your hike is in an area where you have family or friends and they are happy to help out, you could have them bring out supply boxes to road crossings and trailheads. On my hike over the Scottish mountains my partner, Denise Thorn, drove thousands of miles on everything from main roads to narrow twisting single-track roads to bring supplies to remote road ends. She also delivered boxes to campsites, cafés, and hotels in places where there were no post offices. This made a huge difference, as the only alternatives would have been to hike out regularly to post offices and towns, which would have added many days to the walk, or cache food in advance, which would have involved many days as well. People who bring out supplies could then hike with you for a day or more. In places they could hike in with your supplies and meet you in the backcountry. Care needs to be taken to ensure you know exactly where you're meeting if you do this (see Occasional Companions on page 47).

Self-Delivery

It would be possible to deliver food boxes to supply points yourself, though I've never done this. Obviously you would need to know which places (individuals, businesses, ranger stations, and the like) would hold boxes for you. Although I can't imagine delivering all the supplies for a long hike like this, you might want to take boxes out to one or two places that would be otherwise hard to reach.

The Running Supply Box

On my first long-distance hikes I sent home items I didn't need. Months later I often needed those items again and either had to buy replacements or have the original items sent back again at a cost in both time and money. On the Continental Divide Trail, for example, I sent home my gaiters and thick thermal shirt once I left behind the snow and cold of northern Montana. However, in Colorado I had more wintry weather to deal with, and I needed those items so I bought new ones. Now I use a running supply box that goes from post office to post office ahead of me. It may contain all sorts of things, from spare footwear and socks to boot wax, paperback books, first-aid items, a towel, and shampoo. Into this box go any items I don't think I'll need before the next supply point. Of course, a running supply box is only of use on hikes where there are plenty of post offices so that you're able to send it on ahead. Otherwise, you have to carry everything.

Caches

Caching food in the wilderness is an appealing idea. It means you can spend more time there and can minimize contact with civilization. However, it does have disadvantages. You have to hike in with the supplies, which takes time, and then stash them somewhere you can find them again and where they will be safe from animals. I'd be sure to take a GPS reading or compass bearings and a note of prominent landmarks and other features to help you find the supplies months later when the details have long faded from your mind. Protecting your supplies from wildlife can be a problem, as any packaging will have to be packed out. Metal drums and the like can't be used, yet the packaging needs to be animal proof. This means that in bear country, bearbagging will be necessary (see pages 83–84). In other places, supplies could be buried (I know people who've done this) or stored deep in brush. However carefully food was protected, I would still worry that it might not be there or that it would be badly damaged, which is one reason I would only cache supplies if there really were no other choice. Hiking with the worry that vital supplies might not be available doesn't sound fun.

Leaving a note with your supplies would be wise so that anyone who found them would know they hadn't been abandoned. I've only once cached food, and that was on a ski tour in the Canadian Rockies on which we left supplies halfway up a glacier, where there was no danger of animals finding them. We picked the food up a week later so we could still easily remember

where we'd left it. Not that finding our food was difficult—it was the only dark object for a long way in any direction.

Another problem you might have with caching food is the idea of visiting a place where you will be hiking later on. If my hike is in an area I've never visited before, I prefer that the area be totally new when I get there on foot. I don't want to see it for the first time when I arrive with a cache of supplies.

Having someone else cache food for me is not something I've done or would want to do. I just wouldn't feel comfortable relying on someone else to tell me where my supplies were. It would be too easy for me to misinterpret their directions or for them to overlook some crucial piece of information. The worries I'd feel about finding food I'd cached myself and about keeping animals from eating it would be multiplied many times if someone else had cached it for me. I guess I might feel a little more confident if both of us had been to the place together beforehand.

An alternative to having food cached in advance is to have supplies delivered by plane or helicopter. Though in many places this would be totally inappropriate and an intrusion, in really remote areas, like much of Alaska, bush planes are regularly used. Here again, you would have to know exactly where the drop would be made. You would need to be there well in advance of the drop and to have a signal system worked out so the pilot could spot you.

Hitchhiking

Some resupply points can be many miles from the trail. It's fine if there are side trails leading to them, but often you will have to walk along the highway or hitchhike. I would rather not hitchhike unless it's absolutely essential. I prefer to carry more food than to travel to a distant resupply point or to walk there and back if there is a trail or quiet back road. Hitchhiking, I find, breaks the flow of the journey.

If you do hitchhike, great care is needed. Rather than stand by the road with your thumb out, look for any drivers at the trailhead, especially those who look like hikers, and ask them for a ride, explaining what you are doing. Other hikers are often happy to give long-distance hikers a ride and hear about their adventures. Picking up hitchhikers is often perceived as hazardous, so don't be surprised if some people reject your request. Looking reasonably neat and tidy helps but doesn't guarantee success. On my walk in the Scottish mountains I hiked a long ridge with two companions, descending to a roadside inn. We'd traveled light, leaving the camping gear in my companions' car at the far end of the glen below the ridge. To retrieve the car, the owner, an accountant who looked highly respectable and inoffensive, approached a man who was just getting into his car and asked for a lift. The request was met with an alarmed "I can't take the risk." The next person asked was a hiker, who gladly provided a ride.

If there are any facilities at the trailhead, such as a ranger station, café, small store, or gas station, ask there about rides. On popular trails you may find that there are locals who often give rides to hikers. I found such people in several places on the Pacific Crest Trail. Also check whether there are local bus services, and consider phoning for a taxi if the distance isn't too great and you have the money. Walking on a busy highway is potentially very dangerous, perhaps the most dangerous part of a hike. If you do so, be very careful, face oncoming traffic, and be prepared to get off the road very quickly. Hikers have been killed by cars.

When sticking out your thumb is the only option, do so in a safe location where vehicles can easily stop. It's safest to hitchhike in pairs. With more than two people it's harder to get a lift, while solo hitchhikers are obviously more vulnerable. Don't feel obliged to take any ride that is offered, even if you've been waiting a long while. If you don't feel comfortable in any way with the person offering the ride, decline politely and walk away. Talking to the driver about where you're going gives you time to decide whether you want to take the ride or not. I've never felt threatened by anyone offering a lift, but I've had clearly drunk people offer me lifts on a number

of occasions. Once, many years ago when I was a student and hitchhiked everywhere, a friend and I accepted a lift late in the evening from a driver who turned out to be roaring drunk. He picked us up because he wanted a navigator to get him to the next bar. He had, he told us, just been thrown out of one bar, so he'd stolen the car in which we were riding to drive to the next bar. He may or may not have been lying, but he was certainly well out of control. His driving was frightening as he sped around blind corners on the wrong side of the road, the car swaying and skidding. Luckily the next village was only 10 miles or so away. Once we found a bar he stopped outside, and we got out and ran, relieved to still be alive. Since then I've been careful not to accept rides from anyone who seems to be drunk or who acts oddly in any way.

If you're returning from a supply point to the trail, it's worth asking in the places where you've stayed or shopped or eaten if anyone knows someone who'll give you a ride for a small payment or a tank of gas. In some remote areas arranging rides like this is normal practice. At the end of the Yukon walk I'd been given a ride to the arctic town of Inuvik in the Northwest Territories and needed to get to Dawson City in the Yukon Territory. I inquired about how to do this in the hotel in which I stayed, and they arranged a lift for me with one of the other guests, a standard procedure I gathered, in return for my paying for the gas.

WATER

Your body is about 70 percent water. Lose more than a very little of that amount, and your body doesn't work as efficiently. Even without exercise you lose 1 to 2 quarts of water every day (about 2.5 percent of the total water in your body) in your breath, urine, and perspiration and through your digestive system. Perspiring heavily increases this amount greatly. Lose 5 to 10 quarts, and you'll be seriously ill; lose 12 to 15 quarts, and you'll die. To stay fit and healthy, long-distance hikers need to drink enough water so that their

Plenty of water is essential for the long-distance hiker.

intake matches their output. And that can be a lot of water on a hot day.

When hiking it is very easy to become dehydrated, which is unpleasant at first and can quickly become serious. The initial symptoms of dehydration are thirst and a dry mouth. Urine becomes darker in color and decreases in quantity (it should be light-colored and copious). If you don't do anything to counter dehydration, you'll probably start suffering from headaches and constipation next. If, as many hikers do, you drink some water but not enough, these symptoms will persist and may get worse. You'll feel dull, too, and your brain won't work very well, which is hardly conducive to enjoying the hike

or being in touch with nature. Without any water for just a few days in very hot weather, you'll die from heatstroke, as your body can no longer keep cool by sweating. In cooler weather you can survive longer, especially if you don't exercise, but kidney failure will eventually occur.

Once the symptoms described above start to appear, you are already dehydrated and need to start drinking large amounts of water or other liquids immediately (preferably not coffee, tea, hot chocolate, or alcohol, as these are diuretics). Water alone is fine but doesn't contain electrolytes, such as sodium chloride (table salt), potassium, and bicarbonate. These electrolytes are lost along with water and must be replaced, for they are essential for the body to function properly. Various sports drinks contain electrolytes, but so do fruit crystals, soups, and other drinks that are much less expensive and that I've found perfectly adequate. One reason I have a bowl of soup most evenings is because it is a good way to replace salt. Various foods contain electrolytes, too. It is wise anyway to eat while rehydrating because too much plain water can cause water intoxication, which is actually due to a lack of salt and which can make you seriously ill or even kill you. Too much salt isn't good for you, either, so I would never take extra salt as a precaution, and I don't carry salt on its own. There's plenty of it in my food.

It is far better to avoid dehydration in the first place by drinking regularly. Don't wait until you feel thirsty. By then, it's too late.

The amount of water needed when hiking depends on a number of factors: how big you are, how hot and dry the weather is, and how much energy you're expending. When it's cool and cloudy, a quart or two of water may be all you need to drink when hiking, but on a hot, sunny day you may need a quart an hour. That's apart from what you drink in camp, where you also need water for cooking and washing. I need at least 2 quarts of water for camp use, but 4 quarts or more are better. I estimate my total water needs as varying between 5 and 12 quarts per day. Water is heavy, weighing over 2 pounds a quart, so this means 10 to 24 pounds per day if carried, which is why I try to avoid carrying any more water than necessary. In hot, desert regions it may be necessary to carry water for a day or two, but that's really the maximum that's feasible.

To Drink or Not to Drink

How safe though is it to drink water from springs or streams or other surface water? There's no easy answer, as it depends on where the water sources are and what has been happening around them. In cultivated areas where there are farms, commercial forestry, mines, and any sort of industry, surface water will almost certainly be polluted with runoff and discharges from these operations that may contain pesticides, herbicides, heavy metals, sewage, and more. In such areas, and they do occur on long-distance trails though they're not common, I wouldn't drink any water that hadn't come out of a tap or that I hadn't brought from somewhere else or bought from a store.

Water in the wilderness is different. Here, clean water can still be found. The difficulty is in identifying it. Even the cleanest-looking water may contain microscopic living organisms—bacteria and protozoa—that can cause severe stomach upsets and in some cases more serious illnesses. The most infamous of these parasites are *Cryptosporidium* and, particularly, *giardia*, but there are others.

Cryptosporidium is a protozoan that exists in a resistant cyst form in water. When ingested it may cause severe diarrhea and sickness called *cryptosporidiosis*. There is no effective treatment, but healthy people should recover fairly quickly.

Giardia lamblia, another protozoan, attaches itself to the walls of the intestines and can cause a digestive illness called *giardiasis*. The symptoms include diarrhea and foul-smelling feces, plus a general feeling of weakness and being unwell. It can be treated with various antibiotics but in a healthy adult will clear up in 7 to 10 days even if not treated. Most people don't exhibit symptoms even after ingesting giardia anyway. In the stan-

dard work *Medicine for Mountaineering* (edited by James A. Wilkerson), Fred T. Darvill, M.D., says that "in one incident carefully studied by the Centers for Disease Control, disruption in a city's water disinfection system allowed the entire population to consume water heavily contaminated with giardia. Only eleven percent of the exposed population developed symptomatic disease, although forty-six percent had organisms in their stools."

Those who catch giardiasis report that it is extremely unpleasant. It's not going to kill or disable you, though, and you can continue hiking while suffering from giardiasis, but you may not want to. According to *Medicine for Mountaineering*, it appears that most people develop an immunity to giardiasis after the first occurrence, so you're unlikely to catch it again. There are many causes of diarrhea other than giardiasis. The latter is often blamed when it's not actually the cause.

Giardia lamblia is excreted in the feces of humans and other mammals in the form of cysts that can then get washed into surface water. These cysts can also live in the air, and there is some evidence that a significant way for giardiasis to be spread is via hands, utensils, or food rather than drinking water. If you or other hikers don't wash your hands thoroughly after defecating, there may be cysts on your hands that can then be transferred to mugs, plates, cutlery, or food. Sharing food or utensils can then transfer the cysts to other people. It only takes one person not washing his or her hands for giardia to spread.

Roland Mueser interviewed many through-hikers on the Appalachian Trail for his interesting book, *Long-Distance Hiking*. Of the 134 hikers who responded to questions about water treatment, roughly a third of those who didn't treat their water said they suffered gastrointestinal illness, as did a third of those who used iodine, a third of those who used filters, and a third of those who boiled their water. Of those who did get sick, only 8 had giardiasis. For these hikers, treating the water didn't seem to be an effective way of avoiding stomach upsets. Mueser suggests that the illnesses were perhaps caused by the sharing of food and utensils or by not washing cutlery, mugs, and bowls thoroughly. Hygiene, he thinks, is probably more important than water treatment. As I usually walk solo and have mostly done hikes in little-frequented areas, sharing food and utensils is unusual for me. I also eat and drink from my pans rather than using a plate or mug. These are washed after every meal, but unlike plates and mugs, they are also thoroughly cleaned by having water boiled in them for cooking and hot drinks. I'm careful to keep my hands clean, too. Maybe that's why I've stayed well despite not treating most of the water I use.

This is backed up by a study published in the journal *Wilderness and Environmental Medicine* and reported in *Backpacker* magazine that concludes that giardia is mostly transmitted "by direct oral-fecal or food-borne transmission not by contaminated drinking water." The authors of the report found hardly any evidence that giardia in water was a cause of illness in hikers and said that it was "an extraordinarily rare event," the likelihood of which was comparable to a shark attack. They also note that "most backpackers religiously treat water from alpine streams and lakes as though it were straight from the sewers of Calcutta, yet they routinely tolerate crusty cookware and body grime as part of the outdoor experience." The view that giardia isn't actually that common in wilderness water is backed up by Darvill, again noting in *Medicine for Mountaineering* that "frantic alarms about the perils of giardiasis have aroused exaggerated concern about this infestation. Governmental agencies, particularly the U.S. Park Service and the National Forest Service, have filtered hundreds of gallons of water from wilderness streams, found one or two organisms (far less than enough to be infective), and erected garish signs proclaiming the water 'hazardous.'"

The standard way to avoid *Giardia lamblia* and *Cryptosporidium* is to filter water or treat it with chemical purifiers. If the main cause of gastrointestinal illness isn't contaminated water, this is the wrong approach. Spending time washing your hands and your cooking and eating equipment properly is probably more important than spending time filtering water.

None of the organisms found in water in western Europe or North America is likely to threaten your life or disable you. That isn't the case in Africa and Asia, where bacteria that can cause dysentery and cholera, and viruses that can cause hepatitis, polio, and other serious diseases are found in the water. In such places, water treatment is essential. That treatment must purify the water—that is, must kill everything in it. Note that some filters don't remove viruses. When I went on an organized trek in Nepal, all vegetables and fruit were washed in iodine-treated water, and iodine was used to purify all drinking water. Personal hygiene is still important, though, and a bowl of warm washing water and some soap were placed outside the dining tent before each meal so diners could wash their hands before handling food or utensils.

If you do suffer from giardiasis, and you need to visit a doctor to have this diagnosis confirmed, it can be cured by the antibiotics metronidazole (Flagyl) and quinacrine (Atabrine). With any diarrhea, whatever the cause, it is important to drink plenty of fluids to make up for those lost. Antidiarrhea treatments are available, but most experts advise against these as they may impede recovery.

Water Sources

Being able to identify likely sources of clean water is important. No water sources can be guaranteed to be safe, of course, but some are far more likely to be safe than others.

Even if you do treat all your water, I would still advise taking water from sources that are as clean as possible. That way if your filter or water container isn't as clean as it could be, or if you don't get the amount of chemicals correct, you still stand a good chance of not getting sick. I suspect that treating water, especially with filters, lulls many hikers into the proverbial false sense of security so they are prepared to drink any water as long as they've treated it. I'm not convinced that the small, relatively fragile filters used by hikers are capable of removing heavy concentrations of contaminants day after day after day or that hikers are able to keep these filters clean enough to ensure they work effectively.

Whether you treat all your water or not is a personal decision. I only treat water when there is an obvious source of contamination, which means rarely. On my European hikes I've never treated water. Nor did I do so in the Canadian Rockies or the Yukon. However, on the Continental Divide Trail and the Pacific Crest Trail I did use chemical treatments (iodine on the CDT, chlorine on the PCT) when drinking from stock ponds in the desert and from streams in areas heavily grazed by cattle. For me there is nothing more delightful or refreshing on a hot day than to plunge my face into a clear, cold mountain stream and take in great gulps of the pure, fresh water. Drinking directly from backcountry water gives me great pleasure and makes a physical contact with the natural world that I am very loath to abandon. My joy in the wilderness would be diminished if I started regarding all water as potentially harmful. I am, though, very careful in selecting water sources.

As I've already said, I wouldn't trust any water in areas that have been developed in any way. In the wilderness it's different, though. When you are considering how clean a backcountry water source is, the first thing to consider is what lies above it. Check the map for this—the sources of potential pollution may be many miles away. If there are campsites, mountain lodges, or livestock, especially cattle, above the water, then it would be best not to drink the water. If you have to drink it, you should treat it, for the chance of contamination from feces will probably be high. This applies even if the water is a clear, gurgling stream or a spring. How do you tell if there are cattle upstream? If there are cattle or signs of cattle downstream (the signs are usually obvious both to the eyes and the nose in the form of

dung), then unless there's a physical barrier such as a waterfall or a stock fence, the cattle will have wandered upstream.

Fast-running creeks above any contamination source are a good source of water. I drink from them regularly. Checking a little way upstream to see if there's a dead deer or other animal in the water is wise, though I don't always do this. Mountain lakes and pools may be safe to drink from as long as there is water flowing out of them and the water looks clear. I prefer, though, to take water from the outlet creek. Pools with no outlet and bottoms that look like they haven't been disturbed by moving water for a very long time are probably stagnant and should be avoided.

Debris in the water—twigs, bits of vegetation, insects—does not matter. It's harmless and can be easily filtered out with a clean bandanna or coffee filter. Brown-stained water is usually fine, too, as long it's flowing and there's no contamination source upstream. The discoloration comes from plants and is leached out during heavy rains.

High-country springs are my favorite water source. The sight of water bubbling up through the earth or spilling out through a hole in a bank is refreshing in itself. And the water always tastes wonderful. In low country, especially southwestern deserts, springs may be full of poisonous minerals. If there are no insects or vegetation in the water, or if the pool has crusty edges formed of deposited minerals, I'd be suspicious. Water from such springs tastes bitter. Unless the alternative is death from dehydration, don't drink it.

Knowing where to find water is very important. The reliability of sources matters, too, if you're in an area where water is scarce. On some hikes there are plenty of places to locate water. Often, though, sources may be widely spread. Some may be seasonal and others hard to find. Both the Continental Divide and Pacific Crest Trails go through areas where there isn't much water, and that's not just in the desert regions, either. However, for these trails the trail guides identify the whereabouts of water sources and their reliability, which makes planning easier.

Filling containers at a creek in the Grand Canyon, where hikers may have to carry a gallon or more of water a day.

Where water sources are a day's hike apart, it's best not to camp at one source and then carry all the water needed for a whole day to get you to the next water location. Instead, you can plan to arrive at the first source in the middle of the day, drink deeply and perhaps cook and eat a meal, and then, with water bottles full, walk on and have a dry camp. The next day you have to walk only half the distance to the next water source. Where sources are more than a day apart, there's no choice but to carry all your water for a long time. Even so, it's still best to plan to arrive at water locations during the day and then to drink plenty before moving on. On hikes where water is scarce throughout or for long sections, your whole itinerary should revolve around water sources.

On hikes in areas where there is little or no information about the location of water, you have to check your maps for water sources and make a careful study of the terrain. Learning where water is likely to be found in different places is very useful. In deserts, cottonwood trees and other greenery mark water, though it may not be on the surface. Small hollows in the rock hold water after rains or snowmelt, too. In any area look at the terrain and think where water would flow or settle. That's where to start searching. Although maps can help, you can't rely on them. Water marked on the map may not be there on the ground. And when there's no water marked on the map, it doesn't mean there isn't any. On the Yukon walk I hiked along the crest of some rolling hills. The map showed no water anywhere near my route. There were many good campsites, though, and I was reluctant to deviate a long way from my route to locate water. Toward the end of the day I started surveying the landscape carefully for signs of water. Soon I noticed two very slight dips in the terrain, minor undulations that I wouldn't have noticed normally. The map indicated that the depressions marked the heads of shallow valleys that led down to a distant creek. If there were any water in the area, it would collect below those dips. Leaving my pack, I headed down into the first draw with my water containers. A long search showed no sign of water, so I climbed back up and tried the other dip. This time I met with success. About 150 feet down the hillside there was a tiny pool under a seep in some moss. I filled my containers with water, returned to my pack, and made camp.

Taking water from tiny seeps like this requires care. Wide-mouthed bottles are the easiest to fill. Narrow-mouthed ones and soft water bags can be impossible, since you can't fit the edge of the mouth under the drips. These containers can be filled from a mug or wide-mouthed bottle. In order not to disturb dirt or break down the edges of the seep, the lip of the container should be pushed gently under the water. If the seep is really tiny, in a very narrow space, or without enough space below it for a water bottle or mug to fit, something will be needed to form a channel for the water to flow along into the container. A small curved piece of paper, plastic, or foil can be used for this. Usually, though, you can get the edge of a mug or bottle under the dripping water or into the pool below it. Remember that seeps are used by wildlife and may be needed by other hikers after you, so take great care not to damage them or trample the ground around them.

You can't smell water. Or if you can, it's not water you want to drink. You can hear water, though, even small trickles, and this is sometimes the best way to find water. Again in the Yukon I was descending steep slopes in dense forest with a creek not far away and was looking for somewhere to camp. As I thrashed down the hillside I lost the creek, which hardly mattered, as there was nowhere to make my camp. Suddenly and unexpectedly I came out into a large flat area with space for myriad tents. I had a campsite but no water. There was no chance of seeing water in this wooded terrain, and there were no obvious places where the creek might be, so I stopped and listened for it, turning my

head from side to side, trying to pick up any faint hint of running water. The whine of mosquitoes around my head made this difficult, but eventually I did detect a trickling sound. I went toward it and found the small creek, well concealed in a dense thicket of alder trees.

Just a few weeks before writing this book I was hiking the Grande Randonnées 58 circular trail in the Queyras Alps in France. At the very end of the summer season these mountains, which lie not far to the north of the Mediterranean Sea, are quite dry, and I'd already learned there was not much water above the valleys. At the end of one long day I found a good campsite. However, I had little water with me. The campsite was high above the last water I'd seen, and I didn't want to make a long descent and reascent to bring up supplies. There had to be water somewhere. I stood and listened, concentrating my mind and trying to cut out the noise of the breeze in the grasses and the call of birds. Then I heard it. A very faint trickle. But where was it? I turned my head back and forth trying to locate the direction of the slight noise but to no avail. Eventually I realized where it was. At my feet! Hidden in the grass I was standing on was a dark slash of earth with a thin sliver of water running down it. It was enough.

Another source of water is snow. Patches often remain long into the summer in mountain areas, and it can be worthwhile to divert over to them and stuff your containers full. If added to a little water and then shaken, snow will melt to some extent in a bottle. It certainly can be melted in a pan over a stove or fire. If you do collect snow, avoid any that is colored pink, as this is due to an algae that can upset your stomach.

TREATING WATER

It's always best to drink only water that is likely to be clean. If water seems dubious, keep going to the next clean source, if you can. However, if you know you'll be drinking water that could be contaminated, or if you decide you want to treat all your water anyway, just to be on the safe side, there are a number of options to render it safer.

Filters

When I've needed to treat water, I've always used chemical disinfectants because they are lightweight, easy to use, and inexpensive. I have, however, tested several filters. Doing so has not persuaded me to carry a filter on a long hike. Filters are heavy, bulky, complex, expensive, and slow to use. They can clog easily and are not easy to keep clean, which worries me. I found it difficult enough under test conditions to keep parts separate and away from untreated water. I can easily imagine arriving at a campsite in a storm after a long day and being too tired and in too much of a hurry to be scrupulous about filtering water.

Even so, most hikers who treat their water use filters. This doesn't make filters popular, however. Indeed, long-distance hikers probably complain about their filters more than about any other piece of gear. Experienced long-distance hiker Karen Berger describes filters as "easy winners in the category of most vilified equipment" in her *Advanced Backpacking*.

With filters, the size of the pores determines just what they will block, but any good filter should remove the bacteria and protozoa likely to be found in North American and Western European waters. Because filters can't remove viruses, chemical purification is also needed in areas where viruses are found. Some filters have a built-in chemical purifier for this reason.

There are two main styles of filters: pump filters and bottle-top filters. The first can be used to filter large quantities of water. However, they are heavy, bulky, and expensive, and they can be slow and awkward to use. They must be kept clean, too, which can be difficult when you're camping. Small filters that come fitted into the top of a water bottle are lighter, less expensive, and easier to use, but they purify only a bottleful of water at a time. This works fine for solo use while hiking but is not so useful in camp. They

Using a water filter.

are also slow to use. Note, too, that any filter is heavier once it's been used, since it is impossible to dry them out fully when hiking.

Filters must be used, cleaned, and stored exactly as stated in the instructions if they are to work properly. Pumping can be hard work, especially if much water is required. Eventually any filter will clog. This will happen sooner if very dirty water is used, so it's worth filtering out visible debris and sediment with a coffee filter or bandanna before putting water through a filter. Good filters should be maintainable on long hikes and should have cartridges that can be replaced. Even so, I would recommend carrying either a replacement cartridge, which is a heavy item, or chemical treatment drops or tablets as a backup in case your filter quits and leaves you without clean water.

An alternative to a pump filter is a gravity-feed filter. With these you suspend a water bag in the air so that the water can trickle down a tube, through a filter cartridge, and into a container. There's at least one commercial model on the market, which I've tried and which takes ten minutes to produce a quart of water, which is a lot slower than the quart per minute I got when pumping the same unit. You can, of course, do something else while the water is dripping through the gravity-feed filter, which is the great advantage. You can also make your own gravity-feed system. Ray Jardine describes how in *Beyond Backpacking*. If I were to use a filter, this is the type I would go for so I didn't have to spend time pumping.

Boiling

Boiling is a very effective way to purify water because all harmful organisms, including viruses, are killed before the water even reaches the boiling point. For that reason there's no need to boil water for several minutes, as is often suggested. Just bringing water to a rolling boil is enough. Boiling water is fine in camp when you're cooking anyway but hardly practical for all your water needs because of the time and fuel required. Unfortunately, boiled water tastes flat. One way to liven it up is to shake it up and then pour it back and forth between two containers to aerate it.

Chemical Purification

Chemical treatments come in the form of tablets or liquid. They are very lightweight, low in bulk, simple and quick to use (though you have to wait for them to take effect), and, if the right one is chosen, reliable. They're also inexpensive. There are some disadvantages, however: the taste, the presence of chemicals in your water, and the need to wait for them to work. Chemical treatments don't remove debris or sediment, so water may also need filtering, which can be done with a clean bandanna or handkerchief or just

by giving the sediment time to sink to the bottom. Even better is to use a paper coffee filter plus a filter holder. A plastic holder works but is awkward to pack and can break. I use a tough synthetic filter holder that folds flat. It's made by Ortlieb and weighs just 1.5 ounces. It can be wedged into the top of a wide-mouthed bottle or propped over a pan and held in place with a couple of tent pegs.

The standard chemical purifiers are iodine and chlorine. Of these, iodine is reckoned to be the more effective for wilderness use. Chlorine takes much longer to work and may be ineffective in water that is alkaline or has organic debris in it. The general assumption is that it's not reliable for use when hiking. Iodine is effective, but it needs at least 10 minutes to work before the water is safe to drink. Studies have shown that the longer the waiting period, the more effective it is, so it would be better to wait even longer than the recommended time. Purified water often tastes strongly of chemicals, which most people find foul. This taste can be minimized by adding neutralizing tablets (soluble vitamin C). These should only be added once the treatment has been in the water for at least the recommended time. They take about 5 minutes to work and remove most but not all of the taste of the purifier.

It's not certain that iodine will kill *Cryptosporidium* cysts, so it isn't the best treatment when these may be present (and there is no way of assessing this in the backcountry—you just have to guess). Iodine is sensitive to water temperature, so more is needed if the water is very cold. A longer waiting time is needed, too. Iodine also stains if spilled and has to be carried in a glass bottle, for it will leak from anything else. For most people it's perfectly safe in low doses, but anyone with a thyroid problem should consult a doctor before using it. I've used two types of iodine. Potable Aqua from Wisconsin Pharmacal, which I used on the Continental Divide Trail, is iodine in tablet form. A 3.5-ounce bottle contains 50 tablets. Once the bottle is opened, the tablets should be used within a few weeks, as they won't last. Several bottles would be needed for a long hike. Even if the bottle is unopened, the tablets have a short shelf life and need replacing every year. Polar Pure doesn't have this problem. It consists of iodine crystals in a small glass bottle to which water is added to make an iodine solution. A filter cone inside the bottle prevents the crystals from coming out when you add some of the solution to water. You then have to wait 20 minutes before the water should be safe to drink. A thermometer on the side of the bottle gives the temperature of the solution and tells you how many capfuls of solution to add to the water. The colder the solution, the more is needed. To kill giardia, the water to be treated must be at least 68°F, which is warm. Most wilderness water would need warming in the sun or heating on the stove to reach that temperature. One bottle of Polar Pure weighs 3 ounces before any water is added and will purify 2,000 quarts of water. I don't like carrying a glass bottle full of iodine solution however, especially because the liquid stains if it spills or leaks.

For years when I treated water I used iodine, but I've found a better alternative: Aquamira, which is lightweight, inexpensive, and easy to use and has no apparent disadvantages apart from having to wait for a while before treated water is safe to drink. I'd rather do something else while the treatment works than spend my time fiddling with a filter, however. Aquamira comes in two tiny plastic bottles, one containing the water treatment, which is 2 percent stabilized chlorine dioxide (a misleading name apparently, for the makers say chlorine as we know it does not exist in Aquamira), and the other an activator, which is 5 percent food-grade phosphoric acid. The combined weight is 2.5 ounces, and the bottles will purify 120 quarts. A mixing cap is fitted to one of the bottles. To purify a quart of water, you put seven drops of each liquid into the mixing cap and let them react for 5 minutes, during which time the mixture turns yellow. You then add the mixture to the water and wait 15 minutes (30 if *Cryptosporidium* may be present in the water). Mixing the two liquids is needed to activate the chlorine dioxide, which then releases the oxygen that kills all microorganisms, which are anaerobic and can't exist in high concentrations of oxygen. It's a slightly more complex process than that required for other chemical treatments, but it's the only one that is claimed to kill everything and that doesn't leave a residue of iodine or chlorine in the treated water. How it works I don't claim to understand, since I'm not a chemist, but no chlorine is released into the water. This means there's no aftertaste, so neutralizing tablets aren't required. There is a strong smell of chlorine immediately after purification, but if you leave the water container uncapped for a short while this disappears.

It is not possible, of course, to assess just how effective any water treatment is at removing contaminants from water without proper research by trained scientists. The claims of the product makers have to be taken on trust in a way that isn't so with other items of gear. If you don't get sick, it doesn't prove the treatment works, and if you do get sick, it doesn't prove it doesn't. In the first case none of the water treated may have been contaminated anyway. In the second the amount of chemicals used may have been inadequate, or part of the filter may have been in contact with contaminated water and transferred it to water that had been filtered. Treatment is a safeguard only. It doesn't guarantee water is safe to drink, which is why I emphasize choosing water sources very carefully.

A long glacier stretching through arctic tundra in Greenland.

6

Feet and Footwear

With 3,000 miles to walk—six million steps, as we figured the distance—a blister was a far more terrifying prospect than a rattlesnake.

— Karen Berger and Daniel R. Smith,
Where the Waters Divide

On a 2,000-mile hike you will take around 5,000,000 steps. Every day, week after week, month after month, you lift up and put down your feet, hour after hour, mile after mile. What you wear on those feet makes a huge difference to whether those millions of steps will be joyful or painful. Your footwear is the most important item of gear for comfort on the trail. Far more time and attention are needed to make sure you have the right footwear than is needed for other items of equipment. Yet many people don't realize just how important footwear is, as can be seen from the fact that aching, blistered feet are probably the greatest cause of misery on a long-distance hike and also a main reason why people give up without completing the hike. Getting your footwear right and sorting out any hint of a problem as soon as it occurs are crucial for an enjoyable hike.

Doing this is not always that easy, however. Several factors are involved, including the weight of your pack (see pages 136–38). But the key is making sure that you have the right footwear and that it fits properly. And properly means properly, not approximately or near enough. A poor fit almost certainly means that problems will occur. Allow plenty of time when fitting footwear, and don't purchase any footwear until you're absolutely certain it's right for you.

You may think your boots already fit. But if you suffer from blisters, hot spots, sore feet, bruised toes, or even sore knees or hips, then your boots probably could and should fit better. Unfortunately, until the late 1990s boot fitting was a fairly crude business, and few people ended up with a really good fit. Now, though, it is possible to have footwear fitted carefully by trained fitters who can achieve a near-perfect fit. Settle for no less. The first question to ask when buying footwear is whether the store has trained fitters. If not, go elsewhere.

PHIL OREN FITSYSTEM

The revolution in boot fitting for hikers comes in the main from one man, Phil Oren of Arizona, who has been involved professionally with outdoor footwear all his life. In 1985 Phil was planning to hike a long section of the Pacific Crest Trail. Because he already had severe foot problems, he had two pairs of boots specially made. Even so, these still needed to be modified to make them comfortable enough for long-distance hiking. However, despite his many years of involvement with the hiking footwear trade, Phil couldn't find a single outdoor recreation store in southern California, Arizona, or southern Nevada that could do this. Finally he went to a ski shop in Mammoth Lakes in the Sierra Nevada. Although the people there had never modified hiking boots and were concerned that their techniques would damage Phil's boots, he persuaded them to try because, as he said, "I cannot wear them as they are now."

One and a quarter hours later Phil had "the most comfortable footwear I had worn for 15 years." He then did a 150-mile hike with no foot problems at all, and the next year he and his wife hiked the PCT south from Bishop to the Mexican border, a distance of 751 miles. En route they met 29 hikers heading north who were hiking the whole trail. They all had what Phil described as "massive foot problems." This started Phil thinking that the way footwear was fitted had to be changed, and he began developing what he calls his *Fitsystem*. Since then he has spent his time refining this system, compiling a database of foot shapes and sizes, fitting shoes to feet, and teaching boot and footwear workshops to both retailers and the public. Phil says that his mission is "to revolutionize the way footwear fits people's feet, not just so that their feet are comfortable but also for the benefit of their whole well-being—their feet, knees and their backs." He is keen that designers understand fit better and build footwear that is more suited to people's feet. He has worked with companies to this end, and some are beginning to produce better-fitting footwear. Phil also feels that outdoor recreation stores have to be more professional in their fitting service and must understand that mass-produced footwear generally won't fit individual feet without modification.

I've had many boots and shoes fitted in the brief, traditional way, and I've had many problems with footwear that didn't fit properly. Until I met Phil Oren I didn't understand why this was the case. Indeed, I thought my footwear fitted as well as was possible. To minimize the problems, I went for footwear that was too big so that it didn't pinch my toes or rub anywhere. It didn't give much support either, so I relied on strong ankles and also, more recently, trekking poles to provide the stability my footwear should have given me. The Phil Oren way of fitting boots was a revelation to me and has totally changed my view of how boots should fit and should be fitted. After several years of using footwear fitted in this way, I'm convinced it is the only way to fit footwear for long-distance hiking.

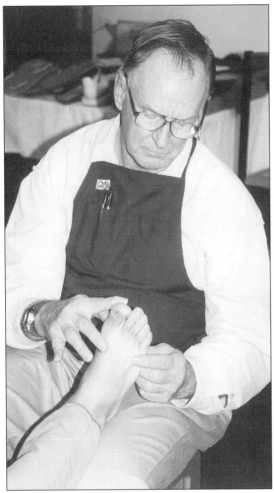

Boot fitting starts with foot examination, here performed by Phil Oren.

Staff at many stores don't know how to fit boots properly. Even worse, some store personnel have a faint grasp of boot-fitting techniques but not enough training or knowledge to do it correctly. Because of this, I detail below just how proper fitting works so you can see what you should be offered.

Feet First

First and foremost, the boot should be made to fit the foot, not the other way around. Fitting starts with the feet, not the footwear. By examin-

ing and measuring your feet, a trained boot fitter can tell what needs to be done to achieve as perfect a fit as possible. The customer enters the information on a Foot Measurement Chart while the fitter carries out the examination. When this is done for the first time, it can be an unnerving experience, as I found when Phil Oren examined my feet. By the time I'd written down "slightly hammered toes, Morton's toe, chubby toe and toe drift" and circled various places on the foot diagrams on the chart to show where I had calluses, the start of bunions, and other potential problems, I was wondering how I'd ever managed to walk anywhere. Next I stood up to put weight on my feet, and the news got even worse as Phil did what he called the *toe test*. He tried to lift a big toe off the ground with a finger placed under its tip. It wouldn't budge. Then he twisted my knee slightly outward and did the same again. This time the toe moved easily. "Over-pronation," he intoned. It sounded serious.

Biomechanics

To understand over-pronation, it's necessary to understand how the foot works. As you walk, the shape of the foot changes. Just before you put weight on it to take the next step it's in what is called the neutral position, with a high arch and instep. As your foot strikes the ground, it rolls slightly to the outside. This is called *supination*. Over-supination can occur but isn't a problem for most people. As more weight comes onto the foot, it rolls to the inside, and the instep and the arch drop slightly. This is *pronation* and helps the foot adapt to uneven surfaces. Next your foot should go back into neutral and perhaps even become slightly supinated so that you can stride off your big toe. However, what happens with many people is that the foot over-pronates instead. This means that rather than going back into neutral, the foot collapses to the inside, flattening and spreading out, which makes it unstable. You cannot spring off your toes but have to propel yourself from the inside of the foot.

When walking barefoot or in very soft footwear over rough ground, as our ancestors did and as many people in many countries still do, over-pronation doesn't occur. However, we usually walk on flat surfaces that give no support to the foot. This is a major cause of over-pronation. Over-pronation makes boot fitting difficult because the foot elongates when it flattens so it is a different size when weighted than when it's in the neutral position. The same boot can't fit both sizes properly. Elongation can be shown by drawing around the foot when it's unweighted and in the neutral position and then drawing with a different colored pen when the foot is weighted. The difference can be surprising. Over-pronation affects around 80 percent of people, so it must be considered when fitting boots. An over-pronated foot puts the knee out of alignment and stresses the whole skeleton. It can be the cause of knee, hip, and lower back

Feet come in all shapes and sizes.

problems, too, so it isn't a problem to be ignored, especially by long-distance hikers.

Measuring the Feet

To go back to the foot examination, the toe test is a good indicator of over-pronation. If the toe can't be lifted, it's because the foot has flattened out. The test doesn't give the fitter enough information, however. Next the feet must be measured. This is done with a Brannock Device, which measures the overall length from the heel to the toe and the width of the foot plus the heel-to-ball length—that is, to the point where the foot flexes. The latter is important, as boots should flex at the same point as your feet. Measurements should be made when sitting with the foot in the neutral position and when standing with the foot weighted. The socks you'll wear when hiking should be worn. Due to over-pronation, my feet measured size 9.25 (left foot)

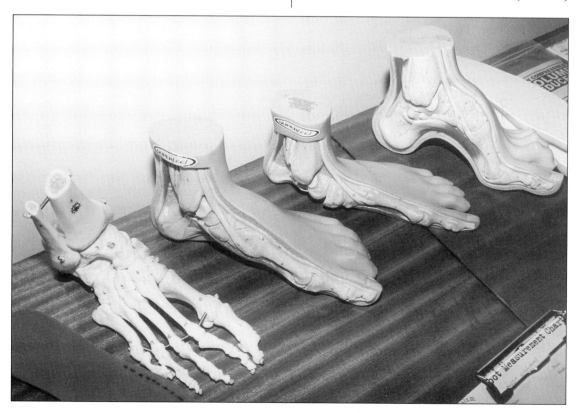

and 9.5 (right foot) in the heel-to-toe length and size 9.5 (both feet) from heel to ball when in neutral. When weighted they measured size 10+ (left foot) and 10.5+ (right foot) in the heel-to-toe length and 11.5 (both feet) from heel to ball. The width was EE+, slightly on the wide side.

In the past I'd always fitted boots to the larger weighted size. If I didn't do this, I found that as soon as I put weight on either foot, my toes were crushed into the toe of the boot as my foot elongated and flexed in front of where the boots flexed. This was because my heel-to-ball measurement is longer than my heel-to-toe length, common in men, and my feet over-pronate. However, footwear that fitted my elongated feet was actually too big and therefore gave little ankle support, especially when going downhill. Because my shoes were too large, my feet moved around, rubbing against the boots, which sometimes led to sore spots and blisters and always to holes in the heel linings.

Volume

Nor had I ever bothered with or even thought about the volume of boots. However, as both feet and boots are three-dimensional, their volume should be taken into account. There's no standard way of measuring foot or boot volume, though Phil Oren is working on this, but a good boot fitter should be able to come up with a fairly accurate estimate and should also know the relative volumes of the boots in stock. Phil Oren found my feet were medium double minus, which is on the low side. Most people's feet were low volume, he told me, but most boots were medium to high volume, with what he described as "ballonous" heels. He said my ankles were narrow and my Achilles tendons were extremely narrow, which presented another fitting problem.

Solving the Problems

Once the examination and measurement of the feet are complete, the fitter can make suggestions as to what is needed to get the right fit. In my case Phil told me I should be wearing size 9.5 or

10 footwear, depending on the exact fit, and that my feet needed stabilizing with special footbeds to overcome elongation. I needed thick socks and possibly volume adjusters and tongue depressors to fill out the volume unless I found some low-volume footwear. He also said my footwear would need modifying to take pressure off the raised and callused areas at the sides of my forefeet.

Footbeds

Virtually all hiking boots and shoes come with removable foam inserts, often called *footbeds*. The usual claims are that they cushion your feet well or keep your feet smelling sweet. What they don't do is support the foot. This can be easily checked by taking the footbed out of the boot and holding it down with a finger in the middle of the heel area. Next push against the inner side of the heel with another finger. If it flattens under the pressure of your finger, then it certainly won't support all your weight. I've tried this with footbeds from dozens of pairs of boots and shoes. Every one flattened with hardly any pressure. This means that they can't support and stabilize the foot and prevent elongation, which makes boot fitting impossible for anyone whose feet vary by a size or more between the neutral and pronated positions.

What is needed is a footbed with a firm rear section that doesn't deform under pressure and that supports the interior shelf of the heel bone. There are very few like this. The one I use and am happy to recommend is the Superfeet footbed. This comes in two forms, Trim to Fit and Custom Fit, both of which have a semi-rigid cradle around the heel that holds it in place and keeps the foot in neutral.

Trim to Fit footbeds come in a range of sizes and can be cut down to fit your boots. This doesn't give a precise fit, of course, but Phil Oren reckons they can stabilize your feet—that is, stop them from over-pronating and elongating—by 40 to 75 percent, depending on how good the overall fit of your boots is. If you have severe fitting problems (as, alas, I was told I have, with a two-size difference between my weighted and unweighted heel-to-ball lengths plus low-volume feet and narrow ankles), then Custom Fit Footbeds are a better choice. These should stabilize your feet by about 96 percent because they are made to fit you exactly. The process involves heating the footbeds, clamping them to your feet inside plastic bags, and then removing all the air from the bags. It's important that your feet are in neutral while this is done, so each foot should be held by the fitter in this position while the footbed is customized.

I've been using Superfeet footbeds for several years now and am amazed at the difference they make. First, I found that when I walked in them my feet pointed forward, whereas for years they'd pointed slightly outward. With no power in my toes due to the collapse of the arch, I'd been striding off the side of my big toe. With Superfeet, instead of a duck-footed, slightly knock-kneed walk, I have a longer, springier stride and now take fewer steps to walk the same distance. The second thing I've noticed is that I no longer wear holes in the heel linings of boots, something that always used to happen. This is because my feet don't slide forward when I put weight on them anymore, which causes the heels to rise, rubbing against the boot lining. I do enough walking that the skin on my heels is very hard, so it was the boot linings that suffered. Other people find heel blisters are the result. There's more too. Since I started using Superfeet and wearing boots that fitted properly, I haven't suffered from the sore knees that long stony descents often produced or the backache I sometimes had. This is because my feet, ankles, knees, and hips are all in alignment instead of being twisted, as they are when my feet overpronate. The effects of this can be seen by a simple test. Stand with your feet hip width apart and hold your arms out in front of you, one hand over the other. Then get a friend to slowly push down on your hands. Resisting the pressure will be very difficult, and you will probably wobble and feel unstable quite quickly. Next, stand on a pair of Superfeet and repeat the test. This time you should be able to resist the downward pressure quite easily. I've done this with a number of friends, and all have been surprised and impressed.

Finally, my feet, and especially my heels, now feel less hammered after hours spent pounding steep rocky terrain. This is because Superfeet prevent the fat pads under your heels from flattening when you walk, and these fat pads provide far better shock absorbency than any artificial material. This can be easily seen by having someone press firmly on the bottom of your unsupported heel. They'll find they can easily feel the heel bone. Then have them squeeze the fat pad under the heel from the sides and press again. This time the fat pad will prevent them pushing against the heel bone. The Superfeet footbeds hold your heels in this position so the fat pad can provide maximum cushioning. This can also be seen by removing footwear and socks, rising up on your toes, staying there for a few seconds, and then quickly letting your heels drop. The shock can be felt right up through your legs. Repeat the exercise, but this time with Superfeet under your feet. The difference is noticeable.

Volume Adjusters and Tongue Depressors

What do you do if your boots are too roomy? Stabilizing footbeds won't stop your feet sliding around in a boot if there's too much volume in it, so any extra space has to be filled. Volume adjusters are flat noncompressible neoprene rubber insoles that fit under the footbeds. Tongue depressors are softer foam pieces that go under the laces and force the tongue down on the foot. Both reduce the volume of boots, but finding a better fit in the first place is the preferable option. Extra and thicker socks can also be used to fill out boots.

Trying On Footwear

I'm convinced enough of the great value of Superfeet footbeds that I now use them in all my footwear and never go out of the house without them in my shoes. They're not the whole story, however. If they were, you could just buy a pair, slip them in your boots, and expect never to have foot problems again. Unfortunately, except for the lucky few, it's a bit more complicated than that. There is still the question of getting the best-fitting footwear. The key is to find a boot that fits your feet as closely as possible and then to modify it so it fits even better. Volume, width, and flex point all need taking into account.

The boot should fit the overall shape of your foot. Too often people buy boots that feel comfortable because they don't feel tight anywhere but that are too wide at the heel, have too much volume around the instep, and flex at a different point to their feet. They buy boots that, in fact, aren't the same shape as their foot at all and don't actually fit them. As long as the boot is a good fit overall, pressure points, heel spurs, bruised toes, and more can be dealt with by modifying the boots.

The size of boots should be based on the Brannock measurements. If you use stabilizing footbeds, you may find a smaller size than expected will fit. I now wear a whole size and a half smaller than I did before I started using Superfeet. Sizing isn't exact across makes or even across models in the same range, so don't be surprised if the size numbers vary in footwear that fits you. The numbers don't matter, the fit does.

Incline Board

The fit of all boots should be tested on an incline board, something any shop needs if they are to fit boots properly. This is simply a 20-degree ramp on which you stand, facing uphill initially. While you're in this position, the fitter checks that the heel fits properly and whether there is any loose fabric round the ankle, an indication that the volume of the boot is too high. It's important when doing this that the boots are laced up firmly, pushing the heels back into the heel cups.

I first used the incline board without adding stabilizing footbeds, volume adjusters, or tongue depressors to my boots. Pieces of tape were stuck over the exact flex points of the boots, and then the flex point of my foot (the head of the first metatarsal, for the technically minded) was marked as I faced uphill. It was almost the same

as that of the boot. Next I turned to face downhill on the board and jumped up and down. The results were startling. The flex points of my feet were now an inch ahead of those of the boots and my toes were crammed into the front of the boots. Holding the position was most uncomfortable, and it felt as though I was clinging to the board with my toes. If the boots had fitted properly, my feet should hardly have moved at all.

To try to solve this problem, the boots were fitted with footbeds, volume adjusters, and tongue depressors, and I tried the incline board again. There was no difference. These boots have just too much volume for you, said Phil Oren. I tried another pair. This time there was a marked change. After sliding forward an inch without the added items, my feet hardly moved once they were in place. I had a pair of boots that fitted. They felt a bit tight in the forefoot, though. That's where modification comes in, said Phil.

Modifying Footwear

Footwear is mass-produced, but feet aren't, so it's extremely unlikely that any boot or shoe will fit you perfectly straight off the shelf. Footwear that fits properly stops your foot moving inside it. However, to do this it must fit closely, which means there are likely to be points where you can feel pressure on your feet. The temptation then is to go for a bigger shoe, as loose-fitting shoes feel more comfortable. Unfortunately they don't support your feet very well.

The solution is to change the shape of the shoe where it presses on the foot. A skilled fitter has several different ways of modifying footwear. The most basic is with a device invented by expert boot maker and fitter Bob Rose called a rubbing bar. The shoe is placed over this bent metal rod, and the blunt end is used to push out the leather at the pressure point. Only tiny modifications are needed to effect a surprisingly different fit. I now have my own rubbing bar at home, and I modify just about all the footwear I test. And I've tested many, many pairs of boots and shoes in my work as an equipment reviewer for an outdoor magazine.

Lumps and protrusions inside footwear can be flattened out by hitting them with a convex hammer while the shoe is on the rubbing bar. Synthetic toe boxes, heel counters, and rands can be softened by putting them in boiling water (inside a plastic bag!) before using the rubbing bar. There are also more complicated hydraulic devices for modifying footwear. These are particularly useful with plastic boots but can be used with recalcitrant leather and fabric ones.

Such modification is important if a proper fit is to be obtained. Indeed, Phil Oren says that in one store that uses his Fitsystem, the Summit Hut in Tucson, Arizona, three out of every four pairs of boots sold are modified.

Future Fitting

I'd suggest having footwear properly fitted every time you buy, even if you're buying the same model. Although all the shoes from one batch may be the same, other batches may be made to slightly different tolerances or even on a different last or in a different factory. Materials and construction methods change, too, and different leathers may stretch more or less while types of toe closure or stitching can alter the shape slightly. If you use the same store, they can keep your details on file so you don't need to have your feet examined and measured every time, though doing so occasionally is worthwhile as your feet may change slightly over time. However, new footwear should always be tried on the incline board. If you use Superfeet or other special footbeds, take these along and fit them to footwear before you try it on. Wear the socks you'll use with the footwear, too. Stores often provide socks to wear when you try on footwear, but these may be thicker or thinner than the ones you'll be wearing. Allow plenty of time for fitting footwear and don't purchase a pair until you're certain the fit is excellent.

FOOTWEAR ON THE TRAIL

However well your footwear fits when new, you may still have problems on the trail. Although most modern hiking footwear doesn't need much of a break-in period, I'd suggest hiking for several days or more in any new footwear to see if any problems arise before heading out on a long trip. It's important to do this with a full pack, too. Footwear that feels fine with a light load may not do so with a heavier one. In the event that the footwear does rub or hurt your feet, take it back to the store and have the fit checked and any necessary modifications done. If that doesn't solve the problem, you have the wrong footwear.

Problem Footwear

Hikers with foot problems often say that it's not their boots but their feet that are the cause. "I

Rock hopping across a stream in the Scottish Highlands.

always get blisters," they say, or "My feet always ache." Not so. The cause is your footwear, and you can do something about it.

If at any time during a hike your feet start to hurt, you get blisters, or you start feeling twinges in your ankles, knees, or hips, don't soldier bravely on—you could wreck your walk. Unless you have slipped and twisted an ankle or knee or bruised your foot on a rock or injured yourself in some other way, your footwear is almost certainly to blame. As well as immediate relief, such as treating blisters (see page 112), I suggest changing your footwear. If you're carrying spare footwear, which I always do on a long hike and which I strongly recommend, hike in this instead. I've done so many times and found my aches fading away. Also consider replacing your footwear at the earliest possible opportunity. I've bought new footwear on several long hikes, though now I like to have replacement footwear waiting to be sent out when I need it or even ready in a supply box (see page 88). Even if it's the same model as the pair causing the problem, it may still be an improvement, though a different model would be preferable.

There are several reasons why footwear starts to cause problems. Most likely something internal that you can't see has broken down so that the footwear is rubbing somewhere or isn't properly supporting your feet anymore. Heel counters can slip sideways a little, tongues can twist, and midsoles collapse without you realizing it. The last is the most serious problem, for it means you're walking on an uneven platform, causing your foot and ankle to become slightly twisted. Occasionally I've suddenly developed foot pains or blisters in footwear that had been comfortable up to that point and that still looked in perfectly good condition. When this happens, the only solution is to replace the footwear. Remember, foot problems are virtually always caused by your footwear.

Hot Feet

A common problem is hot, sweaty feet, which can lead to blisters and sore spots as soft, damp skin is more easily damaged. Because hot feet swell, your footwear may feel tight and may pinch your feet and rub painfully, especially on a high-mileage day in hot weather. Taking your boots off can bring amazing relief as the heat is released and your feet start to cool down. Pouring cold water over them gives even greater relief. Until I realized that heavy boots and thick wool socks weren't the best hiking footwear for hot weather, how far I walked in a day was often limited by how hot and sore my feet became.

Lighter, very breathable footwear and thinner, moisture-transporting socks can solve the problem of hot feet. I discovered this in the deserts of southern California when I hiked the Pacific Crest Trail. Never having walked in desert terrain before, I set off in the sort of footwear in which I'd always hiked, 5-pound leather boots and heavy wool socks. By the end of the first day my feet felt as though they were on fire and going to explode. At first I removed the footbeds from the boots, which provided a little relief by allowing a bit of room for my swollen feet to expand. Even so, by the end of the second day I had four blisters on my feet that were very painful, a worrying situation with five months of walking ahead. Because of this, on the third day I walked in the running shoes I'd brought for camp and town wear and a thinner pair of socks. The relief was immediate. My feet felt much better, for the boots were far more comfortable on my back than on my feet. If I hadn't had the running shoes, I think I'd have had to leave the trail to buy more footwear. The weight and stiffness of the boots contributed to my discomfort, but I think the main problem was that the boots were too hot.

The answer then for hot, swollen feet is to change to lighter, cooler footwear. If this isn't possible, you can remove volume adjusters (but preferably not supportive footbeds), loosen laces, and change to a thinner pair of socks. You could wear no socks at all, something I've done at times in running shoes. Hikers who do high mileage in hot weather may find that this isn't enough relief and that even lightweight shoes feel too tight. New footwear is the answer, but

Air your feet whenever possible, as this hiker is doing at a rest stop in the High Sierra.

until you can acquire some, relief can be obtained by cutting sections out of your shoes. I've never done this, but I know high-mileage long-distance hikers and trail runners who have, and they report that it works. My alternative footwear in warm weather is sandals with adjustable straps that can be let out if necessary. Feet become far less hot and therefore less swollen in sandals, anyway.

Lacing

Lacing footwear properly is important for a good fit. If your laces are too loose, your feet will move about regardless of how well the footwear fits or whether you are using Superfeet or other supportive footbeds. Laces should be firm enough that your feet are pushed back into the heels of your footwear and held there. If you can't tighten the laces adequately, then the volume of the footwear is probably too high.

FOOT CARE

Despite the right footwear, the right socks, and a good fit, blisters and hot spots may still occur. It is vital that these are dealt with as soon as possible. It is all too easy to ignore a slight irritation, telling yourself you'll deal with it later, only to find when you do finally take your shoes off that you now have to deal with a plump blister. Far better to stop and put a dressing on that small red spot before it becomes a blister.

Friction is the immediate cause of rubbing or blisters, and you need to deal with it, too. Have your laces slackened off a little? Are there bits of grit or grass seeds in your boot? If you can't find any, check your sock, turning it inside out and feeling the area that covers the place on your foot where the rubbing occurs. Sometimes simply swapping socks from one foot to another can make a difference. If your socks are sweaty and matted, change to a clean pair. If you don't have a fresh pair available, try to rinse out a pair as soon as possible and make a mental note to wash your socks more often. If none of this works, change to your spare footwear. Finally, remember that it's better to stop early and rest your feet if you can't solve the problem rather than pushing on and making it worse. If the problem is severe, take a few days off at the next town and let the blisters heal. Don't forget to locate the source of the problem. If you don't, the blisters will return when you start walking again.

Treating Blisters

When you do get a blister, it needs treating. There are arguments for and against bursting blisters. However, if you're going to walk on a blister, it's better to burst it because then you have control of the process. Leaving the blister alone means it'll probably burst anyway, resulting in a sticky mess of clear fluid and blood in your shoes and a much greater danger of infection. It's also usually much more painful to walk on a fluid-filled blister than a drained one.

To burst a blister, sterilize a needle from your repair kit in a match or lighter flame and then pierce one edge of the blister. Roll the needle across the blister, squeezing out the liquid and wiping it up with a piece of tissue. Make sure you squeeze out every drop, or the blister will be very painful when you start walking again. If the blister is a large one or under hard skin, several needle holes may be needed.

Once drained, the blister should be swabbed with antiseptic or an antiseptic wipe and then covered with a dressing. Leave the skin in place over the drained blister; it will protect the area while new skin forms. There are many types of dressings that are suitable, from Band-Aids to duct tape to moleskin, but I've found the best to be Spenco's Second Skin. This is a gel that both helps the damaged area heal and minimizes the pain when you walk. Second Skin comes in sheets with protective coverings on each side. To use it, cut a piece a bit bigger than the area you want to cover, remove the protective layer from one side, place the gel onto your skin, remove the protection from the other side, and cover it with adhesive tape of some sort to hold it in

place. Second Skin is available both with and without strips of adhesive fabric. I prefer to buy it without these strips, for I find they don't stay in place very well. Micropore tape is better in my experience, so I carry a roll of this. Whatever you use, breathable fabric is best because it allows air to the wound, which helps speed up healing. As long as the Second Skin is in place and I am not suffering much pain from a blister, I leave it there. I only replace it if it slips or the pain doesn't ease off. If you're still in pain, don't simply stick more tape on top of the dressing. A thick wad of fabric can make the pain worse, not better, because there probably isn't room for it in your footwear. Instead, remove the dressing, check that all the fluid has been squeezed out of the blister, and then put on another dressing.

Second Skin is also a good dressing to put on hot spots to prevent them becoming blisters. Because the product is mostly liquid, it's important that the resealable package of Second Skin remains closed to prevent it from drying out. If this happens, you can revive Second Skin a little by sprinkling it with water.

The fastest way for blisters to heal is in the open air. If you have such bad blisters that they are interfering with the enjoyment of your hike, take two or three days off and keep your feet bare, without dressings on the blisters, as much of the time as possible.

Hardening and Washing

Looking after your feet properly reduces the chances of getting blisters and makes them less likely to hurt. Walking barefoot whenever possible is a good way to harden your feet, though take care to look where you're going. Wearing sandals is good for this, too. The various hardening methods for feet—rubbing alcohol and other liquids—are not something I've tried, but some people swear by them.

Make sure that your toenails are kept short and that you cut them square to prevent the edges from cutting into your toes. Wash your feet as often as you can during a hike, making sure you dry them thoroughly.

If you have calluses, using a foot file to remove them can help prevent blisters forming under them. Such blisters are very painful and hard to get rid of.

Resting

Feet need rest. They also need air. Whenever it's warm and dry enough, I remove my footwear and my socks at rest stops to let my feet cool and dry. I do the same in camp and walk about barefoot if the temperature and terrain allow. This is very refreshing and helps harden my feet. If my feet ache, I try and rest with them elevated on my pack or a log or rock since this allows the draining of the blood that has pooled in them and caused the aching, which in turn lets them cool and allows swellings to go down.

CHOOSING FOOTWEAR

Fit is the most important factor in choosing footwear, which is why I've discussed it in such detail before looking at types of footwear. Fit is not a matter of opinion. A shoe or boot either fits or it doesn't. What type of footwear you wear is a question of choice, however. In this section I give my choices and my reasons for them. Not all experienced long-distance hikers will agree. If you find a different approach than mine works, that's fine. It's not a question of right or wrong but rather a matter of finding what is most comfortable and efficient for you. What I'm not going to do is mention or recommend any particular brand or model of footwear. This is partly because models come and go rapidly, and even when a model stays around for a while it may be redesigned so much that only the name is really the same. The main reason, though, is that what fits me may well not fit you. The best shoe is the one that fits your feet. Never set your heart on Tough Guy Mountain Stompers or Neverslip Cliffgrippers because your best friend or favorite outdoor writer or world's top hiker recommends them. If they don't fit you, they're the wrong shoes.

The quality of your footwear does matter, though, and I would recommend buying from a specialist store with a good selection of models and knowledgeable staff. There's no need to pay a fortune for hiking footwear—indeed, the most expensive fully featured boots are usually unsuitable for long-distance hiking—but bargain-basement shoes probably won't last long or perform very well.

My view, and it's backed up by the experience of many other hikers, is that lightweight, flexible footwear is best for long-distance hiking. Many hikers change from heavy to light footwear during a long hike, and their comments indicate that this was a good move.

Weight

The heavier your footwear, the sooner your feet and legs will tire each day and the shorter the distance you will feel comfortable walking. I am a firm believer in this. Hikers not planning high daily mileage may say the weight of footwear isn't important, but I would rather do low-mileage days or stop early because I choose to, not because I am forced to do so by aching feet and tired legs. My view is reinforced regularly, as I often test boots that are heavier than I would wear by choice, and I always find that I cannot walk as far in them before my feet ache as I can in lighter footwear. The records I've kept on long hikes show the same. When you think about it, this makes perfect sense. At every step you lift the weight of your footwear. My stride is roughly two feet long. So I lift my feet around 2,500 times per mile. If I wear boots weighing 4 pounds a pair, I'm lifting around 10,000 pounds every mile. However, if instead I wear low-cut shoes weighing 1.5 pounds, then I lift only 3,750 pounds every mile. In the course of hiking 20 miles, that's 200,000 pounds lifted with 4-pound boots but only 75,000 pounds with 1.5-pound shoes, a big difference.

The often-quoted adage that a pound on your feet equals five on your back is true in its overall implications, even if the specific figures aren't necessarily accurate. I discovered that on the

Pacific Crest Trail when I ended up carrying my 5-pound boots and hiking in my 17-ounce running shoes. Although I could feel the addition to my load, the boots were less tiring to carry on my back than to wear on my feet.

How light you can go depends on where and when you're hiking. I've hiked in sandals in the Colorado Rockies, the Grand Canyon, the Himalaya, the French Alps, and the Scottish Highlands and in lightweight, low-cut shoes even more often, including thousands of miles of the Pacific Crest and Continental Divide Trails. In colder, wetter, more northern areas such as the Yukon, the northern Canadian Rockies, and Norway and Sweden, where I've done much off-trail hiking, I've worn medium weight (2.5 to 3.5 lb.) boots to provide more protection and warmth than shoes. Except in snow, I'm no longer convinced that this is so, however, and I would choose lighter footwear now.

Midweight leather boots suitable for winter hiking.

Ankle Support

A common argument in favor of heavy footwear and for wearing boots rather than low-cut shoes is that boots provide ankle protection. Although boots with very stiff high ankle cuffs do provide some ankle support, many hiking boots have fairly low soft cuffs that give little if any support. This isn't, in fact, a problem because what matters is that the foot is centered over the sole of the shoe and held there so that the ankle does not twist. This is done by having a firm heel counter (a shaped piece of material embedded in the heel of the boot or shoe) to cup the heel and keep it in place, which stops the ankle twisting from side to side. I once tried a pair of leather boots with high ankles but without heel counters and found my ankles turning over constantly. Because good-quality off-road running shoes and trail shoes have heel counters, boots aren't needed for ankle support. If your feet move in your shoes, heel counters alone won't do much, of course. This is where you can be

aided by supportive footbeds like Superfeet, which stabilize your feet.

If you're worried about weak ankles, the answer isn't to splint them into a stiff boot, which will ensure they don't get any stronger. Indeed, because they restrict how you walk, I suspect that stiff boots make ankle injuries more likely. Having footwear with good heel counters and using stabilizing footbeds are the ways to support your ankles. It's also worth strengthening your ankles before a long hike by exercising them. The best way to do this is to do a lot of training walks over rough ground.

Flexibility

I find flexible footwear the least tiring, most stable, and most comfortable footwear for long-distance hiking because it is the closest you can get to hiking barefoot without actually doing so.

Your feet are sensitive, complex, and very flexible, for they evolved originally for walking over the roughest of terrain, adapting to every change in the ground. It is very hard to twist an ankle in bare feet. When it's warm enough, I often walk short distances barefoot, a wonderfully sensuous experience. The texture of vegetation, stones, and sand feels marvelous, and I'm always amazed at how secure I feel. Care is needed when doing this to avoid kicking rocks or standing on sharp stones or sticks, of course, and I've never hiked very far barefoot. But after I hike in sandals for a few weeks, my feet are hard enough to walk about on surprisingly rough ground without feeling it.

Constrict your feet in shoes or boots, and you have far less knowledge about the terrain you're hiking over and you're less able to walk naturally. Stiff boots hold your feet in one position, so you have to waste energy fighting to make the boots flex with your feet. Because of this and because it is difficult to adapt to rough terrain, I think that boots with stiff soles are more likely to lead to injury than flexible footwear. The latter lets you adapt to the terrain, but stiff boots make you place your feet down the same way with each step, resulting in a steady hammering that

can jar your ankles, knees, and hips, especially on steep descents. With stiff footwear you have to stand on the edges when traversing steep slopes, which puts a great strain on the ankles. On ascents you tend to walk on your toes, which puts a strain on the foot, while on descents you come down on your heels, which causes jarring and shocks to your feet, ankles, and legs. In all these cases only part of your boot sole is in contact with the ground, which makes slips more likely as well as being unstable. With flexible shoes you can place the whole sole on the ground, using the flexibility of your feet and ankles to gain stability and support rather than trying to prevent their flexing by locking them in a stiff boot.

Flexible shoes are also more environmentally friendly. They are generally placed more gently on the ground because you walk on the whole of your foot. When you traverse, climb, or descend a slope just on your boot edges, toes, or heels, you tend to slam them into the ground to make a platform to stand on and to get better grip. This gouges and tears the ground, displacing stones and vegetation, compacting soil, and leaving indentations that can fill with water and start to erode. The damage done by one pair of boots is, of course, minimal, but multiply that by thousands of pairs every year in popular areas, and it can soon be significant. (Flexible shoes also have less damaging tread patterns, as discussed on page 119.)

There is a theory that stiff soles are needed because they protect your feet from stones and rocks. This isn't in fact so. What is needed is a sole that is hard and dense enough not to deform when placed on stones or rocks. Thin synthetic midsoles and thicker shock-absorbing midsoles both give this protection without needing to be stiff. It's also often said that stiff-soled boots are needed to support the weight of your pack. I've never understood this. I can't see why having stiff platforms under your feet that prevent them from adjusting to the terrain adds anything to support or stability. I've hiked thousands

Trail shoes are excellent for warm-weather hiking.

of miles in lightweight footwear carrying 50- to 60-pound loads without problems.

When hiking across steep snow, you need to be able to kick steps with the toes or edges of your boots or use crampons. A hiking boot with a semistiff sole can give support then. (See page 227 for more about hiking in snow.) If you may need such boots during a hike I'd suggest mailing them ahead and only wearing them when absolutely necessary.

LONGEVITY

It is very difficult to predict how long a pair of boots or shoes will last. When I wore heavy boots, a pair would last for 1,000 to 1,250 miles before the soles were worn out and they needed resoling. Running shoes, trail shoes, and light-weight boots have lasted anywhere from 400 to 1,000 miles. If you have them resoled once or

twice, it could be possible to wear one pair of heavy boots for an entire hike of more than 2,000 miles. It may seem easier and less expensive to do this, but I wouldn't recommend doing so for the reasons already cited regarding the benefits of changing footwear regularly and wearing lightweight footwear. Rather than thinking about how many miles you can squeeze out of a pair of shoes, you'd do better to have spare footwear ready to be sent out or already in supply boxes and to carry spare footwear with you to change into if there any problems.

SHOES, BOOTS, OR SANDALS?

There are four types of footwear I consider suitable for long-distance hiking: sandals, off-road running shoes, trail shoes, and lightweight boots. The last three all have similar features.

Features

There are many shoes and boots available that are suitable for long-distance hiking, but there also are a large number that aren't suitable, despite appearances.

With running shoes, the tread must be considered, for models designed for road running usually have soles that are too smooth to grip properly on rough ground. The sole also tends to be soft and spongy, great for protecting your feet when running along a flat, hard road but not very stable when hiking on steep, rugged terrain with a pack on your back. The relative weight of low-cut trail and off-road running shoes is important, too. Some trail shoes weigh as much as or more than many lightweight boots, which defeats one of the main points of wearing them. In my view, 2.25 pounds should be the maximum weight for a pair of size 10 men's shoes. Many good ones weigh far less. If you prefer hiking boots to shoes, there are many in the 2- to 2.5-pound range that are suitable.

Whether you choose leather footwear or a combination of fabric and leather is really a personal choice. I prefer fabric for warm weather, as I find it breathes better and dries more quickly when wet. Leather keeps out water longer, but once it's soaked it can take ages to dry. Single-piece leather boots do last longest, however, as there are no seams to split or fray. Seams can be protected on boots and shoes by coating them with a flexible epoxy. Unless you'll be hiking in very cold places, I'd avoid boots with much padding in the uppers because this makes footwear hot, slows drying time when wet, and adds unnecessary bulk and weight. Sewn-in tongues are useful, thought not essential, for keeping bits of debris out of your footwear.

I always check the flexibility of a shoe by bending it. If it's hard to bend with your hands, it'll be hard to bend with your feet, too, and more tiring to wear than a more flexible shoe. Unfortunately some trail shoes and many lightweight boots have stiff metal or synthetic shanks and very stiff midsoles that make them too rigid for long-distance hiking.

Lightweight mountaineering boots suitable for prolonged use with crampons.

Cushioning is important too. A polyurethane or EVA midsole will absorb some of the shock of walking, particularly on roads and hard surfaces, and will protect against stones and sticks. A hard sole with no cushioning will subject your feet to much more of a pounding.

However, soles that are too thin or soft won't protect your feet against bruising and pressure from rocks and sharp stones. A good sole will enable you to walk over stones without feeling them overly much. This matters on a long-distance hike. You can't check this by walking round on a smooth floor. Good stores should have a rock board for testing boots. There should be enough rocks for you to at least walk a few steps, and ideally a whole rocky trail would wind through the store. If you can feel the points of the rocks when you walk on the rock board, look for another pair of boots. Trying a different boot on each foot is a good way to compare how much protection they give.

To be avoided are midsoles that are very soft (they create a wobbly platform), very thick (they raise your feet too high above the ground), and wider than the uppers of the shoe (they also are unstable). The big problem with all these types of midsoles is that they increase leverage on the foot, which makes twisting an ankle more likely as well as making walking more tiring. Footwear that keeps your feet close to the ground and soles that are flush with the uppers are best.

Heel counters are essential to keep your ankle centered over the sole of the boot or shoe. All good hiking footwear has heel counters. Toe-caps, however, are optional. Many low-cut shoes have soft toes, which may be a concern to some people. If you walk carefully, you shouldn't hurt your toes anyway. I've never done so. But if you worry about this, there are trail shoes with toe bumpers just like those on lightweight boots.

Flexible footwear isn't very good for kicking steps in snow, of course, and crampons don't fit well either. For snow and ice, stiffer boots are needed. I was very glad to have my 5-pound boots in the High Sierra on the Pacific Crest Trail because the mountains were still snowbound, and I wore crampons and kicked steps frequently. Boots that heavy aren't needed, though. There are plenty of boots in the 2.5- to 3-pound range that are stiff enough. Full rigidity isn't required, just enough stiffness so that flexible hiking crampons won't fall off. Boot uppers also need to be fairly stiff so that crampon straps won't compress them.

Water Resistance

Many hikers are very concerned about keeping their feet dry, citing this as a reason they prefer boots to shoes. The truth is, though, that on a long hike it's simply not possible to keep your feet dry in prolonged wet weather. I've found the way to have dry feet for the maximum amount of time isn't to wear water-resistant or even water-proof footwear but to wear footwear that dries quickly. Even the most heavily waxed boots made from the most water-resistant leather will get saturated after a few days of walking in really wet conditions. And once wet they take days and days to dry. Fabric shoes may get wet quicker, but they dry much quicker, too, often in a matter of hours.

I particularly dislike waterproof-breathable linings or booties. They make footwear hotter and don't breathe very well when the outer material is soaked, resulting in sweaty feet. They are also very slow to dry when wet inside, since moisture can escape only at the ankle. They don't stay waterproof that long, either, usually leaking at the toes after a few weeks of wear. I suspect that miniscule particles of grit penetrate the lining and then puncture the waterproof-breathable membrane. I have worn lightweight boots with such linings on long-distance walks in wet places—the Scottish Highlands, Norway, and Sweden—and have had wet feet most of the time. I'd have been drier and more comfortable in footwear without such linings.

In really cold wet weather, when keeping feet warm and dry is important, there are better alternatives than waterproof linings (see Oversocks on page 127).

Hiking beside a mountain stream in the Cairngorm Mountains in Scotland.

Lacing

I've already mentioned that lacing footwear firmly is important (see Lacing on page 111). It's easier to do this with some lacing methods than others. Tunnel and pulley laces are great—one yank and the laces tighten from bottom to top. In fact, overtightening is more likely to occur with these laces than undertightening. On a number of occasions I've had to slacken off tunnel lacing because it was too tight across the instep. If you don't want any pressure on your instep due to protrusions or prominent veins, then you can feed the laces through the tunnels on the same side in this area rather than using cross lacing.

Although tunnel and pulley lacing are in my view the best system, they aren't found on that many boots or shoes. Of the other lacing methods, a combination of D rings and hooks is probably the most common. This is fine as long as at least half the lacing is by hooks. Tightening laces through a long set of D rings can be difficult and is liable to be done improperly. Some shoes have eyelets, and here, too, it can be difficult to tighten laces.

Outsole

Although having footwear with a tread that grips well is important, it's not something that requires too much thought for most hiking footwear comes with soles that work well on most terrain. There are many patterns, but all that really matters is that the tread has some depth to it. Very shallow treads won't last long and may not grip well anyway. I have a pair of trail shoes with a pattern of light dots that grip well on dry terrain but that slip on anything wet, especially muddy ground.

That said, thought should be given to the impact that hiking footwear has on the ground. Heavy boots usually have deep lugs, which tear up the ground more and remove more soil than lighter lugged soles. Heavily lugged soles don't necessarily offer more security. When clogged with soil, they are more likely to slip than soles with more widely spaced, shallower lugs. The type of sole found on most trail shoes and light-weight hiking boots is fairly kind to the ground, though I have found that some soles clog more easily than others.

Soles are made from different densities and compounds of rubber. Again knowing the details isn't important, but note that the life of a sole is dependent on the type of material used as well as the depth of the tread. Indeed, some shallow treads will outlast some deep ones. The type of compound also determines in part how well soles grip. Sticky rubber, which adheres well to rock (it was first used on rock-climbing shoes), is found on some footwear. The stickiness doesn't work on mud or wet grass, however, so a decent tread is still required.

Construction

There are various ways of constructing foot-wear, and I've not found one that is superior to any other for hiking. Most soles are cemented on these days so the intricacies of various stitching methods are mostly irrelevant. The first cemented soles sometimes delaminated, but this problem has been overcome and shouldn't happen with quality footwear.

Inexpensive shoes and boots, especially running and trail shoes, sometimes have fiberboard or cardboard insoles. These are often not very durable, especially if they get wet, and they can wrinkle and even disintegrate, leaving an uncomfortable, uneven surface. To check the insole, remove the footbed and look inside. (If the footbed is glued in place, you are not looking at a quality product.) If you see a flat section of what looks like cardboard or compressed fibers, that's what it probably is. A hard, shiny sur-

Lightweight fabric-suede boots are a good choice for three-season backpacking.

face means a synthetic insole. These are found in most hiking boots and come with different degrees of flexibility, with the most flexible being the best for long-distance hiking.

Durability and Longevity

A point often made in favor of heavy boots is that they last a long time. This is undoubtedly true, at least for most models, but it's not a good enough reason for hiking in such footwear. I'd rather have footwear that didn't last quite as long but that was far more comfortable for hiking. Quality light-weight footwear can last a surprisingly long time anyway. I wore a pair of lightweight boots on my end-to-end hike in Scandinavia that lasted for nearly 1,000 miles before I retired them when the tread was wearing out. And on the Pacific Crest Trail a pair of fabric-suede trail shoes saw me through the 1,000 miles of Oregon and Washington, though they were in tatters and the soles were almost worn flat at the finish. I'd had to have the stitching on the uppers repaired, too, but they did make it to the end. Overall, though,

Keep footwear in good condition, and it will last longer.

I wouldn't worry about how long your footwear will last. Comfort is what matters. I'd never rely on any one pair to last a long-distance hike anyway. Even if they didn't wear out, they might start to cause foot problems. Carrying a backup pair and having spare pairs ready to be sent out to you are the best precautions against footwear wearing out.

Care and Repair

Footwear will last longer if it's looked after. I don't carry boot wax or shoe polish with me, but I do put it in supply boxes so I can treat footwear during rest days. My preference is for the water-based products made by Nikwax, as these can be applied to wet footwear and will soak into the areas that need the wax most. The sponge applicator makes these easy to use, too. There are versions for leather, fabric/leather, and suede and Nubuck leather. I also like these products because they use water as a solvent, which is environmentally more friendly than chemical solvents.

Other than occasional waxing, I do little to my footwear when hiking. In the evenings I remove the footbeds so any moisture that has built up under them can disperse. I also open up the tongues so the shoes can air and the insides can dry at least a little. If footwear does get wet, it shouldn't be dried in too hot a place, which means keeping it out of a hot sun as well as away from campfires and indoor heaters. Footwear can be badly damaged by too much heat. I can remember arriving at a mountain hut in Norway in the pouring rain and having the warden whisk away my sodden boots, saying she'd dry them out. Only later did I discover she had put hot air blowers into each boot. They were certainly dry the next day, but after that treatment they sucked up moisture like sponges, no matter how much wax I rubbed into them. During a hike walking footwear dry is probably the best method.

SANDALS

People who are doubtful of the idea of hiking in shoes are often horrified at the idea of doing so in sandals. They shouldn't be. I've worn sandals on several hikes lasting a couple of weeks and found them excellent, though I haven't worn them on a longer venture yet. Others have, however. I know hikers who've through-hiked the Appalachian Trail and the 900-mile length of the Atlas Mountains in Morocco in sandals.

Just any sandal won't do, of course. For a start you need straps round the ankle to help hold the heel down and stop the foot sliding about. A good grip is needed, too, and a cushioning midsole. Sports sandals supply these features, and there are many good models available. Although it seems unlikely, footbeds like Superfeet can be fitted successfully to some san-

Sandals are cool to walk in when it's hot, as seen here in the Grand Canyon.

dals. Even so, heel support in a sandal is far less than in a shoe with a good heel cup. People who over-pronate excessively would probably be more comfortable wearing lightweight shoes rather than sandals.

The great advantages of sandals are their breathability and coolness. Swollen, sweaty, overheated feet are things of the past when you hike in sandals. You don't need to worry about keeping your feet or footwear dry, either, sloshing straight through creeks and knowing they'll dry very quickly. Another result is hard, tough feet.

Sandals are fine on trails and on rocky and bare ground. However, they're not so good if you're going cross-country through dense vegetation since spiky plants can easily stab your feet. I'd never do a long hike with just sandals, but I always carry spare footwear of a different type, anyway.

I've worn socks with sandals occasionally, but this isn't something to do often because socks get very dirty very quickly. Your feet do, too, of course, and the dirt can get so engrained that it's hard to wash off. Very dry feet can develop painful cracks, though this is not something I've suffered. As with any problem, changing footwear would be the answer, along with applying a moisturizer.

SOCKS

Few hikers pay much attention to socks, yet socks can make a great deal of difference to foot comfort. Ones that fit badly or that are made from harsh materials can cause blisters and sore spots, whereas ones that are cold when wet can lead to chilly feet. Conversely, socks that are too thick can lead to hot, sweaty feet. Some socks sag badly or even slip down and roll into folds under your feet. Socks that are fine on day hikes or weekend backpacking trips may not be suitable for longer walks, for the long-distance hiker needs socks that can be worn for days on end, with just the occasional rinse in cold water, without matting down.

Sandals are ideal to wear when crossing creeks.

Materials

Feet sweat more than any other part of the body except for the head and hands, giving off as much as a pint of water in 12 hours when you're active. Some of this moisture can escape quickly through your footwear, especially at the ankles. Much, however, is held in your socks until it can slowly pass through your footwear to the outside. Socks need to be able to handle this moisture so that your feet don't feel cold and wet. Your socks also need to keep their shape when damp, as wrinkles are uncomfortable and can lead to blisters.

Wool is still the most popular and most common fiber for hiking socks, although synthetics are making inroads, especially for warm weather wear. The main claim for synthetics is that they wick moisture far faster than wool and dry out much more quickly when damp. Although this is true, it needs to be tested carefully to see how much use it is for hiking socks. I've found that while CoolMax, polypropylene, and other wicking synthetics do remove moisture quickly and dry fast when worn with sandals, approach shoes, and light fabric boots, they can become wetter than wool in leather boots, especially medium and heavyweight boots. These socks then feel quite slippery and unpleasant and slide around in your footwear, which is likely to cause blisters. When damp, they're not as warm as wool either, I think because the moisture from your feet can't escape quickly from leather boots and remains in your socks. Because synthetics are nonabsorbent, a little trapped moisture can make them feel very wet and clammy. Wool retains much of its warmth when damp and doesn't become slippery because it absorbs moisture, which make it better for wearing in leather boots. Wool also recovers its shape well after stretching, resists wrinkling, and allows body moisture to pass through.

Wool socks usually have synthetics added for greater durability at the toe and heel and to add elasticity. My preference is for socks with a high percentage of wool (at least 50 percent) in all but the warmest weather. When it is hot, I prefer thinner synthetic or synthetic-rich socks because they keep my feet cooler and drier by moving moisture away more quickly than wool. Of the various synthetic fibers available, I've found CoolMax excellent.

The quality of the materials matters, too. Merino and other top-grade wool has long fine strands and is softer and more durable than shorter, coarser wool. Its appearance in socks in the 1990s led to a big improvement in comfort and durability. I find this wool stays softer and more comfortable than other grades of wool or synthetics. It mats down much less when socks are worn for days on end without washing, making it particularly good for long-distance hiking, and it fluffs up better when washed. I've also found it stays soft and fluffy and holds its shape much longer than other wool, making it well worth the high price. Worsted wool also has long fibers and performs better than lower-grade wool, though it's not as soft as merino.

Some socks, usually warm weather ones, have cotton in them. I'd avoid these. Cotton absorbs a lot of water, is cold when wet, and takes ages to dry. And when it's wet it doesn't hold its shape very well, which means that socks can sag and wrinkle. Silk, however, absorbs moisture and is warm when wet. It's sometimes found as a component of socks for cold weather and also makes good liner socks.

Construction

The fit and the materials they're made from are the most important factors to consider when choosing socks, but the construction does matter, too. Although they appear outwardly simple, socks are quite complex items. How they are knitted makes a big difference to comfort. Densely knitted socks—that is, ones with a high number of stitches per square inch—cushion well and feel very comfortable against the skin. Coarsely knitted socks, with a low number of stitches per square inch, are less comfortable, and the rough fibers can rub, leading to blisters.

For warmth and softness, terry loops inside the sock are worth having, though these can mat down very quickly underfoot unless the socks are made from top-quality materials. Having experienced this several times, I went back to old-fashioned, flat, knitted, ragg wool socks for long-distance hiking despite the very coarse knit because they could be worn for days on end and remain comfortable. Terry-loop socks were more comfortable than the ragg wool ones the first day out, but after a week the terry-loop socks would be hard and matted while the ragg ones hadn't changed. (And yes, I did wear a terry-loop sock on one foot and a ragg sock on the other to check this.) These early terry-loop socks were fairly coarsely knitted themselves, which was part of the problem. Now there are many excellent terry-loop socks, especially those made from merino wool, that don't mat when worn for many days and that I now choose over ragg ones.

For cold-weather hiking, socks with thick, densely knitted terry loops over as well as under the foot are warmest. In warm weather, however, a thinner, flat, knitted section over the arch allows for quicker moisture removal, while terry loops underfoot and on the sides provide cushioning. Many socks also have different densities of material under the heels or balls of the feet that are claimed to give more cushioning or warmth in these areas, but I can't say that I've noticed any difference between socks with and without these. Elasticized sections over the instep, achieved by adding Spandex or similar elastic fibers to the knit, give a close, snug fit and help keep the sock in place.

Elastic fibers help keep the legs of socks from falling down, too. The leg of a sock may have terry loops, which is very warm in cold weather, or may be ribbed, which also helps it to stay up. Most hiking socks are calf length, though you can get shorter ones to wear with sandals or low-cut shoes. Longer ones for wearing with knickers are now hard to find—but few people hike in knickers anymore.

Hiking socks should have a heel pocket, which gives a good fit. Stitching in the form of a Y at the heel is best. This holds the sock in place better than a straight line of stitching because it is closer to the shape of your heel. Tube socks are best avoided for hiking, as they tend to slip and wrinkle under the foot.

Socks with bulky raised toe seams can rub and cause blisters. The best socks have a toe pocket with the seam set back from the end of the toes. This is both more comfortable and more durable. The seam should be flat and smooth. If you do have problems with toe seams, one trick is to wear the socks inside out.

Liner Socks

Liner socks are designed to wick moisture quickly away from your feet and into your outer socks so that you have a dry layer next to your skin. The damp outer sock then rubs against the liner rather than your foot, at least in theory. Liners are normally very thin, though thicker cold weather ones are available. The best ones are made from wicking synthetics; these dry fast and are easily rinsed out. Silk liners are okay, too, but cotton or cotton-rich liner socks are a disaster in my experience, as they rapidly become damp and wrinkled. Liner socks are a good idea for wearing with coarse knit socks because they keep the rough fibers away from the feet, but they're not as useful with dense terry-loop socks, in my opinion. I've tried wearing a liner sock on one foot but not on the other and haven't noticed any difference in foot comfort or dampness. If your feet sweat heavily, however, liner socks could help keep them dry. Liner socks generally need washing very often, usually every day, as they quickly go stiff with the salts from your perspiration. I sometimes wear liner socks on their own in low-cut shoes in hot weather, and I often carry a pair for wearing on layover days while my thicker socks are being washed.

Choosing and Fitting

A good fit is important, and care should be taken to get this right. The sizing of socks is different from that for shoes (it's done by the length in inches) so a size 9 sock is not the same size as a size 9 shoe. A good store should have a sock conversion chart and be able to tell you which size you need. As with boots, sock sizes don't take foot width or volume into account. If you have wide or high-volume feet, you might need to go up a size for your socks, whereas a size smaller might fit narrow or low-volume feet better. Most socks stretch and will fit two to three foot sizes, however. Ideally, you should try socks on to get the right fit. Socks should be close fitting if they are to be warm, wick moisture efficiently, and not rub against your feet, which can lead to hot spots and blisters. If there is loose fabric at the toe or heel or over the instep, the socks aren't the right shape for your feet.

Just finding the right sock size in a store isn't enough for long-distance hiking. Socks that will be worn regularly day after day and week after week need to retain their shape and not mat down underfoot. The way to find out which socks will do this and which won't is to test them in advance of a long hike. When trying new socks, I measure the length before I wear them, when I return from a day hike, and after washing. Socks that stretch during a walk can wrinkle and sag, leading to discomfort and possibly blisters. If those socks don't return to their original shape after washing, they really aren't very good. (Less common are socks that stretch after washing.) After wearing socks, turn them inside out and check the terry loops. If they look at all matted after a day out, they probably won't be much use for long-distance hiking. Check the terry loops again after washing, as some socks fluff up nicely while others stay partially matted. When I test socks, I wear a different one on each foot so I can compare the stretch, how much they mat down, and the degree of recovery after washing.

Short backpacking trips are an even better place to test socks to see how they stand up to prolonged hiking. Again, I measure them every day and check the terry loops for matting. I take pairs on a long-distance hike only once I am convinced they will stand up to hard usage.

There are several good brands of socks—I've been pleased with models from Fox River, Thorlo, Wigwam, Bridgedale, and SmartWool—but just because one model from a range of styles works well doesn't mean all the socks in that range will. Also, designs and materials change, so you can't assume that socks currently produced by a company will be identical to the same brand of socks that you bought several years before. No one remembers details of the construction or materials of their socks, of course. In fact, most people can't even remember which brands they have. If you find a sock that really performs well, I suggest you keep the label or write down the name so you can look for the same brand and style again in the future.

Socks come in different weights as well as materials. The thickest ones are great for cold weather but can be too hot most of the time. Medium-weight socks are fine in all but the hottest weather, when lightweight or even liner socks are best. Hikers whose feet are usually cold and clammy would do best with thicker socks most of the time and also ones with a high wool content. Those whose feet overheat easily, like mine do, should look at medium- and light-weight socks with a wicking synthetic content for fast removal of moisture for warm weather wear. Your socks must fit your footwear, however. If you have low-volume feet, a thick sock can take up some of the room in your footwear. Similarly, thin socks make for more room. This is why wearing your own socks is important when fitting boots. Socks can also be used when hiking to increase or decrease the volume of boots. I often start a day in thick socks because my feet are cold and need warming up. Later on, when my feet have heated up and expanded, I change to thinner socks that are both cooler and give me a bit more room in my footwear.

The weight of socks isn't a major factor unless you're going to carry many pairs or you're doing an ultralight hike. Heavy socks weigh around 5 ounces a pair, medium-weight ones 4 ounces, lightweight ones 3 ounces, and liner socks just 1 to 2 ounces. In temperate and cold weather I usually take two medium-weight pairs and one lightweight pair, giving a total weight of around 11 ounces, at least 3 ounces of which is being worn. When it's hot, I take just one pair of medium-weight socks, mostly for wearing in camp, one lightweight pair, and one pair of liners. Of course, temperatures will vary enormously on many long-distance hikes. Shuttling different types of socks around in supply boxes is the way to deal with this. If the weather does turn out colder than expected and you haven't a single pair of socks that are warm enough, then wear two lighter pairs.

Sock Care

Clean socks are best. However, keeping socks clean can be difficult on a long-distance hike, particularly as you don't want to carry many pairs because of the weight. Of the three pairs I carry, one is reserved for camp wear so I can always have warm dry feet in the evening. The others I wear for two or three days each, rinse them out in cold water, and hang them on the pack to dry. That's in sunny weather. When it's wet, rinsing socks out isn't a good idea because getting them dry is impossible. At those times I wear the same pair day after day. Sometimes the best thing to do is to change your socks every day. When I sloshed through wet spring snow on the High Sierra section of the PCT, my socks were soaked by the end of every day because I could never dry out my leather boots. The weather was dry and sunny, so I hung the wet pair on the pack to dry each morning and wore the ones that had dried the day before. That way I only had wet feet and socks for part of each day.

Whenever possible, socks should be rinsed out thoroughly to get rid of at least some of the sweat, dirt, and other muck and to restore some of the softness. However, I don't use soap for washing socks, as even biodegradable versions are pollutants best kept out of the wilds. It can also be difficult to rinse socks fully, and soap residues can impede the wicking away of perspiration and irritate your skin. If there's a fast-flowing sizeable stream nearby, I rinse my socks out there. If the only water is still or the creeks are tiny, I carry water several hundred feet away (two hundred is the recommended minimum) in a cooking pot and rinse my socks there, spreading the waste water on the ground far from anywhere anyone might camp.

Anywhere there's a laundry I wash my socks properly with pure soap flakes or nondetergent washing powder. I also use a small amount of fabric softener, which really makes a difference in how soft they get, especially with socks that have been worn for many days. Turning them inside out helps to fluff up the terry loops and remove any dead skin. If socks are really matted and dirty, they may require washing twice. Drying should be done at cool to moderate temperatures because high temperatures can damage and shrink fabrics. Some synthetics may even melt.

Replacement

High-quality socks are fairly durable, but none will last for months of walking. A good fit helps with longevity; socks that are too small will be stretched, putting strain on the fibers, while socks that are too big will have loose folds of fabric that can rub against your footwear until holes form. Proper-fitting footwear makes a difference, too. If your feet move inside your boots or shoes, there will be friction with your socks, leading eventually to holes in the socks. Before I started using stabilizing footbeds, I always wore large holes in the heels of my socks, caused by my heels going up and down as my feet elongated and then returned to neutral, which rubbed the socks against the boot linings. My socks last longer now.

Once socks develop holes or cease to fluff when washed, they should be replaced. Compacted fibers offer little cushioning and can rub painfully, as can the edges of holes. Holes are cold, too.

On my first long hikes I bought new socks when I needed them. However, I quickly learned that there often wasn't much choice in small towns. On a few occasions I had to buy coarsely knitted socks that didn't fit very well and weren't very comfortable. They were soon replaced. Lesson learned, I started putting new socks into supply boxes so that I had the option of new ones at every supply point.

Oversocks

Waterproof-breathable socks can be worn over ordinary socks to keep your feet dry. They are made from fabrics like Gore-Tex or proprietary materials like those found in SealSkinz. These socks are fairly thin and don't offer much in the way of insulation or cushioning, so they are most comfortable with other socks underneath. However, because they take up room in your boots, you'll need thinner socks under them than the ones you usually wear. The best oversocks have taped seams and close-fitting cuffs and are foot-shaped for comfort. The models I've tried out do keep your feet dry but don't last that long, a couple of weeks or so at most. They can be worn in shoes as well as boots and even in sandals. I wouldn't carry a pair on a long-distance hike, but they could be useful for those who suffer from cold feet and who really want to keep their feet dry. These oversocks only need to be worn when it's wet and can be replaced when worn out, so they're certainly a far better way to try and keep your feet dry than waterproof-breathable linings in your footwear.

Plastic bags can make emergency oversocks. During the last few weeks of my end-to-end of the Canadian Rockies hike it became very cold, and the creeks started to freeze over. My lightweight boots were almost worn out, with cracked uppers that had long since ceased to be waterproof. To keep my feet dry and warm I wore plastic bags, secured at the ankle by rubber bands, over thin liner socks and then put thick socks over them. This protected the thin plastic from tearing and also meant that the bags acted as vapor barriers, helping to keep my feet warm by preventing evaporative cooling since any moisture produced stayed on my skin. The bags didn't last long, of course, but a set got me through several creek fords before needing replacement.

SPARE FOOTWEAR AND CAMPWEAR

As I've already indicated, I always carry spare footwear. This, of course, can be used in camp as a change from the footwear in which I've been hiking. Often this means changing from lightweight boots or trails shoes into sandals that let my feet breathe and cool down. Sometimes, though, it's the opposite, and after a day of hiking in sandals I'll change into socks and shoes in the evening as the sun drops and with it the temperature.

I rarely carry camp footwear that I can't use for hiking, since it means an additional item to carry. On the PCT I did carry some insulated booties through the High Sierra that were very nice to slip on at the end of the day. I could have done without them, though. And on a long-distance hike in the Scottish Highlands I carried thin, lightweight, flexible, waterproof rubber oversocks when it was wet so I could pad around camp without having to put my wet boots and socks back on. Overall, though, I regard such footwear as luxuries whose weight I'd rather not carry.

GAITERS

Gaiters aren't needed for most long-distance hiking, but some hikers like them for keeping stones, twigs, dust, and other debris out of their footwear. However, if large snowfields have to be crossed, then gaiters are very useful for keeping snow out of your boots. I was very glad to have gaiters when hiking in the snows of the High Sierra on the Pacific Crest Trail and the northern Rockies on the Continental Divide Trail. When snow started building up in the Colorado Rockies on the latter hike, I had to hike for three weeks and 350 miles without gaiters because I'd long ago sent mine home, and none of the stores in the places I passed through had any in stock. What I should have done, of course, was to send my gaiters on ahead, rather than back home. The snow wasn't deep everywhere, but on many

occasions I had to suffer cold, melting snow soaking into my socks and boots. If this had happened very often, I'd have rigged up some sort of makeshift gaiters from sock tops or even plastic bags.

Most gaiters are too heavy, too complex, and too awkward to use for long-distance hiking unless you're doing a winter trip. I've spent too much time struggling with cold, wet fingers trying to do up a jammed zipper or scrabbling in the snow replacing a broken instep cord to like gaiters. I also find gaiters quite sweaty, whatever fabric they're made from. In deep snow, however, gaiters can make the difference between cold, damp feet and warm, dry feet.

In my opinion the best gaiters for hiking are short, ankle-high ones that simply seal the gap at the top of the boots to keep snow out. Knee-length gaiters are for mountaineering or ski touring. Breathability is more important than water resistance for the fabric. Wearing nonbreathable waterproof gaiters results in copious condensation that will wick down into your boots. Some form of instep strap is needed to prevent the gaiters from riding up. This should be easily replaceable in case it snaps, as it is likely to do if you cross talus and boulders while wearing the gaiters. Such short gaiters should weigh no more than 3 to 6 ounces. The best closures are Velcro flaps at the front or side; these are very quick to use and can be operated while wearing gloves or mitts. I'd avoid simple tubes of fabric, as you have to take your boots off to remove or don them. Zippers are unnecessary, too. They add weight and are prone to jamming and breaking. Hooks to attach the front of the gaiters to your laces are useful. Gaiters should fit closely around the boot and around your ankle, as gaps will let in snow.

The same desirable features apply to full-length gaiters, along with the need for an easy-to-use closure below the knee. A properly fitting gaiter should be snug around the leg without feeling tight. Weights range from around 5 ounces for basic thin nylon gaiters to 20 ounces or more for supergaiters that cover all of your boots. The lightest models aren't very durable but could be an alternative to short gaiters for those who prefer full-length ones.

TREKKING POLES

Trekking poles are one of those items of gear that generate very strong feelings. Some people love them; others hate them so much they object to anyone using them. I am a convert, but I don't think trekking poles are essential, just an aid that I find useful. On my first three hikes of more than 1,000 miles, on six hikes of 200 to 550 miles, and on many shorter trips I didn't use a pole, never mind two. I occasionally picked up sticks to aid river fords, but that was it.

A two-week hike in appalling weather in Iceland, during which my route was partly determined by whether I could safely ford the many streams and rivers, persuaded me that carrying an adjustable pole was worthwhile. Deep rivers and shifting, slippery pebble and gravel beds mixed with large areas of soft, thawing snow made for a difficult walk. If I'd had a staff, it would have been much easier and safer. Two poles would have been even better. But Iceland is treeless, so there were no handy sticks to use. Without one I was constantly off balance, slipping, and stumbling along. After that experience I started carrying a pole on every trip, including my next three 1,000-mile hikes.

It was ski touring that taught me that two poles were useful for hiking, though it took a long time. When I had to carry the skis on my pack, which makes for a high, unstable load, I always used my ski poles, and they improved my balance enormously. It seemed obvious to make use of the poles, and eventually it dawned on me that two poles might be useful even without skis on my pack. I've since done one 1,700-mile hike with two trekking poles and many much shorter ones, and as I say, I'm converted.

There are many benefits to using trekking poles. The reasons I started using them are good ones: balance on rough terrain and a third leg during river fords. With trekking poles

Trekking poles are a great help when climbing steep hills.

steep scree and talus slopes, boulder fields, boggy ground, and other rough terrain can be crossed more quickly, more safely, and without fear of falling or being tipped over by your pack. On steep slopes, especially descents, you can always have three points of contact with the ground, which gives much greater stability. Poles are also useful on ascents, for you can push down on them for greater power and stability. I can go uphill faster with poles than without. For river fords two poles can give even greater security than one, as again you can always have three points of contact.

Perhaps the most useful benefit of using poles is that they can save wear and tear on your legs and lower back by taking some of the weight off

Crossing a small creek on a log, with a trekking pole for balance.

your feet and legs. Many people doubt this, but usually only those who haven't used poles. There are studies that back up the claims, but my belief in poles comes from my own experience. With the trekking poles I can walk further and faster without my legs feeling tired than I can without the poles. Also, my knees don't feel as hammered on long, steep descents as they did before I started using poles. In fact, it is now many years since I last had to slow down on a descent because my knees were hurting so much. Of course, some of the weight taken off your legs is transferred to your arms and upper body, and when people first use poles they do sometimes find their shoulders aching. I used to find this on the first few ski tours of the winter, but this doesn't happen now that I use poles year round. Hiking usually only works the leg muscles. Using poles also improves the muscular strength and fitness of the upper body, which I regard as beneficial.

I also think that poles are a safety item, especially for solo hikers. Having them could make the difference in being able to hike out with an injured leg or having to wait for help. I've lent poles to people with minor injuries on a number of occasions, and the difference they made has been enormous. Further, injury is less likely when using poles because of the greater stability you have.

Poles have other virtues. On level ground and good trails they help maintain a hiking rhythm. When crossing marshy ground or snowfields, you can use them to probe for hidden rocks and deep spots as well as to provide support. They can hold back bushes, barbed wire, stinging plants, and other obstructions as well as fend off aggressive dogs.

At rest stops and in camp, trekking poles can turn a pack into a backrest, two poles being much better here than one since in conjunction with your pack they form a stable tripod. In camp the poles can be used to turn a tent fly-sheet door into an awning. In fact, they can become the tent poles. Why carry tent poles in your pack that are less strong than your trekking poles? Using them with a tarp means you don't need to seek out sticks or trees from which to suspend it when you want to camp. There are now a few tarp-tents available designed to be used with trekking poles, and I expect the number to grow (for more on tarp-tents, see page 152).

As with any gear, trekking poles have to be used properly to be any use. Holding the grips tightly doesn't allow you to use the poles correctly and is also a good way to make your arms ache. Instead, the straps should be used for support by putting your hands through them from below so that the strap runs between thumb and fingers and then over the back of the wrist. This is how cross-country skiers hold their poles. The

Crossing a steep, loose slope above a creek, with a trekking pole for support.

best way to use poles when hiking on fairly gentle terrain is to swing one in front of you, plant the tip, press down on it, and walk past it before taking the pressure off. As you walk past this pole, the other one can be swung forward. A really good rhythm can be achieved like this, and if you hold the poles properly, you can flick them back and forth as you walk without having to jerk your arms around. On ascents I keep both poles in front of me, letting each pole take weight in turn as I step up with the opposite leg. This is a very powerful way of climbing, and long ascents can be made surprisingly quickly like this. On descents I do the opposite and keep the poles below me so they support my weight.

I can think of only two disadvantages of trekking poles. First, they get in the way when you're scrambling. The solution is to strap them to your pack until your hands are free again. That's why I like three-part adjustable poles that compress to a small size. Hand freedom is the

other disadvantage. If you want to take a photograph, check your map or compass, or unwrap a snack bar, you need to let go of your poles. The easiest thing to do is to dangle them from your wrists. If I think I'll be needing my hands free for more than a few seconds, I usually slip them out of the straps and prop the poles up against a tree or boulder or even, if there's nothing nearby, against my chest.

Choosing Poles

There are many poles available, some of them offering all sorts of wonderful-sounding features, usually at a high cost in both money and weight. In my opinion many of these features are gimmicks that aren't really needed. The best poles are simple, lightweight ones. There are good poles available that weigh only 16 to 18 ounces a pair but that are just as strong and durable as heavier models. I certainly wouldn't consider poles for long-distance hiking that weighed more than 20 to 21 ounces for the pair.

Length and Adjustability

There's no correct length for trekking poles, but the most comfortable length is when your arms are bent at right angles at the elbow when the poles are held vertically with the tips on the ground. If the poles are shorter than this, you don't get as much support, and if they're longer, your arms will get tired. The exception is on steep ascents, where shorter poles are useful so that you don't have to lift your arms high, which is tiring and which pushes you away from the slope. Conversely, on descents, longer poles mean you can reach down the slope without having to lean too far forward and risk losing your balance. And when you are traversing steep slopes, a short pole on the uphill side and a long one on the downhill side are useful, again so you don't end up leaning away from the slope. Altering the length of your poles is the obvious thing to do in these cases, but messing about with adjustments is not something I like to be bothered with every time the terrain changes. Instead, when descending steep terrain

I lengthen my poles by placing my hands on top of the grip, whereas on ascents I slip my hands out of the straps and grasp the poles lower down the shafts. On steep traverses I've sometimes ended up holding the uphill pole only a foot or so above the tip.

The usual way of locking and unlocking pole sections is by twisting them. This releases or tightens an internal expansion plug into which a screw fits. This system can jam, especially in the cold, and slip, which is one reason I rarely adjust my poles. An alternative system, used by Gipron and Black Diamond, that is easier to use and less prone to problems is the external FlickLock. This mechanism can be flicked open and shut with gloved hands and can be adjusted with the sort of small screwdriver found on most small pocket tools and Swiss Army knives.

The maximum length of most poles is in the range of 55 to 65 inches, which is more than adequate for most people. If you're over six feet tall, you might need to search out longer poles. I have mine set at 45 inches. Packed size is also important. Most three-section poles collapse to 20 or so inches, short enough to fit inside a large pack or to be attached to the outside of any pack without getting in the way.

Shock Absorbers

Many poles come with shock absorbers in the form of springs built into the upper section, which are claimed to take the stress of the arms and shoulders. In my experience these don't work. They add weight, complexity, length, and cost to the poles, so I'd avoid them. To check this, I went out on several day hikes with a shock-absorbing pole in one hand and a regular pole with no shock absorber in the other. I was never able to tell the difference, and on no occasion did I feel any aches or tiredness on the side without the shock absorbency. However, I did find there were places where I really didn't like shock-absorbing poles. When descending steep, rocky places, I found that if I placed a shock-absorbing pole downhill for support, it gave way a little when I put my weight on it, which I found disconcerting and which made me feel less stable.

Baskets

Trekking poles are generally fitted with small solid baskets that help keep them from sinking into soft ground but that don't catch as much on vegetation or rocks as larger baskets. These baskets aren't essential, so if they break or fall off it doesn't really matter. In deep snow bigger baskets are needed. These are usually available as optional extras for most poles.

Handles and Straps

Although the differences between pole handles aren't huge, some materials are more comfortable to hold than others. On short trips this isn't an important factor, but on a long-distance hike

Black Diamond's FlickLock pole-length adjustment mechanism.

it can matter. Hard plastic is inexpensive and durable, but it can be sweaty in hot weather, which can lead to blisters, and feel cold in cooler temperatures. Softer plastics are slightly better, and PVC, rubber, and rubber compounds better still, but none are as good as cork, cork compounds, and foam grips, which I find cool in summer and warm in winter.

I find handles that are angled forward more comfortable than straight ones, as you don't need to cock your wrist when holding them. Again, it's not a big difference.

Straps need to be adjustable. Some use buckles; others slide in and out of the handle. Being able to get your hands in and out of the straps quickly is useful, especially if you often want to use a camera or binoculars. The best straps I've found in this respect come from Leki. The system is called the Trigger and consists of a wide strap that clips in and out of the pole handle. When you're not using the pole, the strap stays around your hand.

In theory, wider straps are more comfortable than narrow ones, but I can't say I've noticed any difference. The softness of the material from which the straps are made is more significant.

Tips

Hard metal tips on poles give good grip on hard snow and ice. Carbide is the hardest and strongest material, but carbide tips can make an irritating clicking noise on rocks and hard surfaces and can even damage the terrain by breaking down the edges of the trail and scratching rocks. Rubber or hard plastic tip covers can be used to minimize this. Some poles come with these.

The tip of a pole can become trapped between rocks. Plastic tips that aren't as strong as the alloy pole shaft will snap before the pole does, so these are best. Most tips are easily replaced, and the pole can still be used until you can do so. Not that tips break often—in my thousands of miles of hiking with poles, I've broken a tip only once.

A range of trekking pole handles.

Poles on Snow

For walking on gentle snow slopes, trekking poles are more useful than an ice ax. However, they are no substitute for an ice ax on steep, icy terrain. Just try stopping a slide down a gentle slope of hard, packed snow with a pole, and you'll soon find their limitations. You also can't ram a pole deeply into the snow for security when climbing a steep slope. For steep, snowy slopes, an ice ax is needed.

Hadlaskard mountain lodge in Hardangervidda National Park in Norway.

7

Controlling the Load: Selecting Equipment

The glad, rejoicing storm in glorious voice was singing through the woods, noble compensation for mere body discomfort.

— John Muir, *Travels in Alaska*

You don't need special equipment for long-distance hiking. Whatever backpacking equipment you already own can be used. And if you need to buy new equipment, it needn't cost a fortune. Many long-distance hikes have been completed with very basic gear. Indeed, much expensive equipment isn't designed for long-distance hiking and is too heavy, bulky, and complex. Simplicity is best.

The chances are that some of the equipment you own isn't ideal for long-distance hiking, however, either because it's too heavy and bulky or because it has features that might cause problems during long-term use. If you are looking to replace any or all of your gear, this chapter contains my thoughts on what works best and which features to look for and which to avoid. I haven't discussed the details of materials and designs, though. That is covered in *The Backpacker's Handbook*.

Gear needs to be comfortable and easy to use as well as functional, durable, and lightweight. It doesn't matter how well-made something is if it has features or quirks that get on your nerves. Irritating aspects of gear that you can put up with during short trips can become unbearably annoying during a long-distance hike. Zippers that jam, buckles that slip or are hard to fasten or undo, pockets that aren't quite big enough for your hands or are hard to access, and other inefficient features can drive you crazy on a long-distance hike. It's one thing to mutter about these over a weekend, but quite another to put up with them day after day, week after week.

WEIGHT

I'd guess that many weekend backpackers have no real idea how heavy their packs are. Many aren't really interested either. It's just not that important. However, once you start hiking for weeks and months at a time, weight takes on a new meaning. Yet it's surprising how many long-distance hikers don't know how much individual items of gear weigh and only have a hazy idea of their overall pack weight. Do you know how heavy your rain jacket is or your water bottle or your sleeping bag? It all adds up, and the total makes a big difference to whether a long-distance hike is a pleasure or a pain. All too many people attempt a long-distance hike with a too-heavy load and give up. Long-distance hiking doesn't have to involve backbreaking loads. And having a light pack doesn't have to mean risking safety or suffering discomfort by leaving vital items behind. What it does mean is the difference between feeling burdened and feeling free.

How light a load should you aim for? The answer is as light as possible as long as you have adequate gear for comfort and safety. Quite simply, the lighter the load, the less tiring the hiking. The great relief felt when you take off a heavy pack is a joy I'm happy to do without as often as possible. There is also a direct relationship between the weight of your pack and how far you can walk each day. The heavier the load, the

more often you'll need to stop for a rest and the sooner you'll want to make camp. On the flat you probably won't actually walk any slower with a heavy load, but you will uphill—much, much slower. If you're not aiming for a high daily mileage, you may say this doesn't matter. But even for low mileage hikers those miles will be more enjoyable the lighter your load.

Over the years I've found that loads above 30 pounds start to slow me down noticeably. With 50 pounds I can manage 12 to 15 miles a day without feeling exhausted, as long as I'm on a good trail and there aren't thousands of feet of ascent. When I was planning my walk over all the summits of more than 3,000 feet in the Scottish Highlands, I knew there would be a huge amount of ascent and that the terrain would be very rough. (I ended up averaging 5,300 feet of ascent a day for a total of 575,000 feet; the most in a day was 11,000 feet.) Because of this I worked hard at bringing down the weight of my load. The Highlands have a wet and windy climate and there is little shelter available, so I couldn't skimp on tent and rain gear too much. Even so, I ended up with a basic pack weight of 20 pounds of hiking equipment plus 5 pounds of camera gear to give a total of 25 pounds. I usually carried food for only a few days, so the average weight of the pack was 30 pounds or less. Just once I had to carry food for six days, and that time I set off with a pack weighing more than 40 pounds. Although it was near the end of the walk and I was very fit, the extra weight slowed me down noticeably and made climbs much harder.

My personal experience that 30 pounds seems a significant weight concurs with the findings of Roland Mueser, who interviewed through-hikers on the Appalachian Trail, as described in his book *Long-Distance Hiking*. Mueser reports that 82 of the hikers interviewed carried loads of more than 30 pounds. They averaged 14.5 miles a day. How much more than 30 pounds they carried didn't seem to make much difference (though it obviously would at some point). But 19 hikers whose packs weighed less than 30 pounds averaged 17 miles a day. Did the lower pack weights allow them to hike 2.5 miles a day more on average? I imagine it certainly helped a great deal.

I say this having carried some very heavy loads at times, loads that I wouldn't consider carrying now. I did this because I knew no better, because I thought that I needed all that heavy gear if I was to survive in the wilds. With those heavy loads I had to rest often, and it was always great to get the weight off my back at the end of the day.

As a rough guide, I now plan on a maximum basic pack weight of 25 pounds (the basic pack weight means without food supplies and not including clothing and footwear worn) for a solo long-distance hike in summer. Two people hiking together could get the basic pack weight below this by sharing tent and cooking gear. These are suggested maximums; it's quite possible to get weights much lower. With a 25-pound basic load I can add food and fuel for a week at 2.5 pounds a day and have a starting weight of 42.5 pounds. When I hiked the Pacific Crest Trail, eighteen years before writing this, my basic pack weight was 45 pounds before I added any food. I regularly carried two weeks' worth of food on that trip, which meant I started out from supply points carrying 80-pound loads. Today, with a 25-pound basic load, that would be 60 pounds, which although still heavy is a lot easier to carry. I would now also plan on shorter times between supply points, too, which could be accomplished carrying a lighter pack.

Few long-distance hikers manage to carry such light loads, however. Mueser found in his interviews that the average weight carried by men on the AT was 35 pounds before re-supplying and by women 34 pounds. After resupplying, the average weights went up to 47 pounds for men and 45 for women. The heaviest packs carried were 75 pounds (men) and 65 pounds (women), and the lightest were 20 pounds (men) and 30 pounds (women).

Now if hikers are happy with the weight of their loads, that's fine. However, my experience is that many are not. Long-distance hikers I meet often complain about the weight of their packs, and how to reduce pack weight is a major topic at any gathering of long-distance hikers, whether at an organized event or informally on the trail.

All efforts to reduce pack weight are worthwhile. Just how do you do this though? First, it's best to know the weight of every bit of gear you have, however small. Then you need to decide just which items are essential and which optional. Be ruthless when doing this. It's surprising how many bits of gear are carried out of habit. Do you really need a candle lantern in midsummer, a nesting set of cookpots, enough moleskin to cover a thousand blisters?

You can't significantly change the weight of items you already have. However, some can be adapted or not carried. That candle lantern can be left at home, as can that second pot. Instead of a sleeping bag liner, consider sleeping in your spare clothing. What about all those long straps hanging off your pack? How many do you ever use? Those that are superfluous can be cut off or at least trimmed. Real fanatics cut the handles off toothbrushes, remove labels from garments, and trim the edges from maps—not that these save very much weight.

Ultimately, though, it's the weight of the big items—pack, tent, sleeping bag, stove, waterproof jacket—that really counts, so you can't beat gear that is lightweight to begin with. How can you ensure that the gear you buy really is lightweight? The best way is to weigh comparable items yourself, so I suggest taking a scale with you to check weights when you shop for gear. I wouldn't rely on manufacturer's claims. Much gear that's described as "lightweight" or even "ultralight" isn't; the description is just a marketing ploy. Or it may be that in the context of that company's range of products the item is lightweight, even though it's not when compared with alternatives from other makers. Some companies don't even know what items weigh yet still label them lightweight. You rarely, if ever, see gear described as heavyweight, even though much of it is. Catalog weights, when given, are unreliable and may not always include all components. For instance, tent weights often omit pegs, guylines, and stuff sacks, while stove weights sometimes omit fuel bottles.

To avoid even considering gear that is too heavy, I have a list of maximum target weights for every item (see sidebar, page 188); I compiled this list by reviewing the weights of many items I have tested over the years. If a product weighs more than this, I don't consider it, however tempting it is. And generally I choose items that weigh much less than these maximums.

It's also important to avoid being seduced by complexity. The lightest backpacking gear is usually simple in design. Extra features always mean extra weight. How many pockets does a fleece sweater really need? (None!) Does your rain jacket need zippers for attaching a fleece jacket, inside water bottle pockets, six outer pockets, and shoulder and arm reinforcements? Not for long-distance hiking.

One reason so much gear is heavy is that it's designed for and by mountaineers and intended for hard usage on expeditions in harsh climates and harsh terrain. Are you going to hike in such places and conditions and subject gear to such rough treatment? Probably not, but because there aren't enough mountaineers to provide a big market for such gear, it's also sold as being suitable for backpackers. It's mostly overkill, though, due to the weight, bulk, and complexity, and it's especially unsuited to long-distance hiking. Gear advertised with pictures of climbers scaling vast snowy mountains in the Himalaya or battling through blizzards in the Arctic is almost certainly completely over the top for hiking the AT or the PCT.

Ultralight

I believe that long-distance hiking is more enjoyable with a light pack and that hikers are more likely to complete their walks if they carry as light a load as possible. However, that doesn't mean I carry the lightest pack possible. I would describe my own style as lightweight but not ultralight. Ultralight hiking really does mean cutting gear to the minimum and carrying astonishingly light packs. Ray and Jenny Jardine, leading advocates of this approach, hiked the Pacific Crest Trail with packs whose basic weights were 8.5 and 7.75 pounds, respectively. I've tried hiking with almost that little weight for short periods (my lightest overnight load ever was about 11 pounds), and although I appreciated the light load, I wouldn't want to do a longer hike with so little gear. I found the absence of certain items and the minimalist nature of others detracted from my pleasure in the walking and, particularly, in the camping. I'd rather carry a bit of extra weight. If you are interested in the ultralight approach, it's explained in detail in Ray's *Beyond Backpacking*.

The ultralight approach is fine if you are fit and experienced. You need to know how to handle storms with minimum gear and be able to move fast if necessary, since you'll have little backup gear. Those new to ultralight hiking would be advised to first try out the techniques and gear on short trips in familiar country before they set out on a long-distance hike.

Good-quality ultralight gear was hard to find until the late 1990s. However, an upsurge in interest, stimulated by Ray Jardine's books, has led to an increase in the amount of gear available. Jardine himself has designed some gear that is marketed under the GoLite name. His book also describes how to make ultralight gear.

I use many ultralight items of gear, but I mix them with more standard items to build a set of equipment that suits my style of hiking. I also like to carry items that many ultralight hikers would consider unnecessary weight, such as minibinoculars and a paperback book.

THE RIGHT GEAR FOR THE HIKE

The same set of gear won't be the best choice for every long-distance hike. On the Appalachian Trail you need good rain gear. On the Arizona Trail sunscreen, a sun hat, and plenty of water containers are more important, though carrying lightweight rain gear would still be advisable. Some trails, like the Pacific Crest and Continental Divide, go through a variety of climactic zones. Their length also means you'll be out in different seasons. The same gear won't be appropriate the whole way, so it's best to send items home when you're finished with them or send them ahead to a resupply point if you think you'll need them again (see pages 87–92 for information on resupplying). I can tell you from personal experience that it is not necessary to carry an ice ax, crampons, and snowshoes across the Mojave Desert! Tents that will withstand mountain storms aren't needed on trails where you can camp in the shelter of the forest every night. However, in some areas the wind resistance of your tent can be very important. On my long-distance walks in the Scottish Highlands and the mountains of Norway and Sweden, I often camped on exposed sites where a good wind- and waterproof tent was essential. On the PCT my tent was never tested by the wind.

When you're planning a hike, before you buy any new items of gear find out what the weather and terrain are like and see what types of gear are recommended in trail guides. That way you can avoid carrying a sleeping bag rated to 0°F for a hike where the overnight temperatures are unlikely to drop much below freezing or a stove that burns fuel that isn't available along the trail you're hiking.

CHECKLISTS

I keep a detailed list of all my gear along with the weight of each item. That way I can quickly make a list for a specific hike and see what the weight is. I start off listing all the items I think I might want. This inevitably produces a total weight that is more than I want to carry, so I then go through the list again and again, slowly whittling it down.

Once I have a final list (usually a few days before I depart!), I tick off every item as I pack it to ensure I don't leave anything behind.

GREEN GEAR

Most long-distance hikers are very concerned about the environment. There's nothing like spending months walking through the glory of the natural world to make you want to help preserve it. Yet the equipment hikers use is not, overall, very environmentally friendly. It's mostly made from petrochemicals and is often shipped large distances and wrapped in too much disposable packaging. To minimize its impact, you can do a number of things. If you buy quality items, they will last longer than cheap ones. When you're finished with gear, it can be passed on to someone else, sold, or donated to a charity store so it continues to be used. Keeping equipment well maintained and repairing it when necessary will make it last longer. Find out how to keep your gear in shape in Annie and Dave Getchell's *The Essential Outdoor Gear Manual*. As well as information on how to repair and maintain gear, their book lists repair centers where you can send items that you're unable to repair yourself.

Some gear, especially fleece clothing, is made from recycled materials. Even more gear comes in recycled packaging. Many outdoor equipment companies also support environmental causes, donating money to them and promoting them in their literature. Supporting companies that use recycled materials and help conservation bodies enables these organizations to continue doing this and encourages other companies to do the same.

COLOR

Bright colors are highly visible in the backcountry, making you stand out, which is something some people like, probably because it makes them feel safer. I find bright colors overwhelming, however. I don't like being conspicuous, as it makes me feel separate from the natural world, more of an intruder, more an outsider. I prefer to blend in, to merge with the woods and landscape, so I can feel part of it. So I mostly choose soft earth tones like browns and greens or dull reds and blues or blacks and fawns for my gear. In my work as an equipment tester, I am often sent brightly colored gear to try, some of it so lurid that I am reluctant to be seen using it and only do so where I think I will meet no one else, so I know the difference bright colors make in how I feel.

My particular dislike is for bright-colored tents or tarps. A single orange or yellow tent pitched in the corner of a mountain bowl draws the eye and dominates the landscape. A green or brown tent in the same place will be almost invisible. With clothing, I used to carry a bright item or two for safety in case I needed to be seen and for photography, when a bright item can lift a picture, but I never felt happy doing so and now mostly stick to duller colors.

QUALITY AND COST

Good-quality gear and expensive gear are not necessarily the same thing. Some quality items can be quite inexpensive. The most costly gear

A heavily laden porter ascending the Tehari Khola Valley in Dolpo, Nepal.

is often overdesigned and too heavy for long-distance hiking anyway. Hikers need simple but durable and well-made equipment, not fancy designs. Glossy advertisements may imply that you should venture into the wilds only if you have top-of-the-range equipment, but in fact this isn't so. Rudimentary, inexpensive items will do in many cases.

Long-distance hiking gear undergoes far tougher treatment than most backpacking gear, so it needs to be well made from durable materials. Failure on the trail can be a major problem. With some items it could even be dangerous. A rain jacket that leaks badly in a cold rainstorm could lead to hypothermia. A tent that collapses in a gale in the middle of the night, leaving you without shelter, could do the same.

All gear should be checked carefully for flaws before you buy. And when you get home, check it again. Trying it out on a short hike is advisable, too. It's best to pick up any faults and have them repaired or the item changed before you start a long-distance hike.

PACK

The pack is the most important item of gear after your footwear for enjoyable hiking. An uncomfortable pack that hurts your hips or shoulders or gives you a backache can ruin a long walk. I've twice changed packs during a long-distance hike because the problems caused by the packs were dominating the walk. To avoid having this happen, I'd suggest taking time in choosing a pack and making sure that it fits properly and will carry enough weight comfortably.

Size

How big a pack is needed depends on the bulk of the gear you'll be carrying, including food supplies. I don't like packs in which I can only just squeeze all my gear, since these are hard to pack and gear is more likely to be damaged. Conversely, carrying a pack that's never full means carrying more weight than you need as bigger packs, of course, weigh more than smaller ones.

The figures that pack makers give for the volumes of their packs should be regarded only as a rough approximation when comparing packs since there is no standard way of measuring volume. Packs with the same stated volume may not actually hold the same amount of gear. Also, many packs are listed as having a volume range rather than a single volume, such as 5,500 to 6,500 cubic inches. The first figure is the key one, for this is the volume of the main pack. The second figure includes the volume of an extension sleeve or collar, a tube of fabric sewn into the top of the pack that can be used for packing extra items when the pack is full. When it's full, this extension sleeve raises the height of the pack. As it's unsupported by the frame or any padding, a packed extension sleeve makes the pack top heavy and unstable. For short periods of time, such as when leaving a resupply point with some bulky goodies you'll eat within a day, such extra storage is useful, but I wouldn't want to hike very far with a full extension sleeve, and I certainly wouldn't do so anywhere that balance was important for safety. For carrying comfort your load needs to fit into the main pack.

The position and size of compartments and pockets make a difference, too. If your sleeping bag won't fit in the lower compartment or your water and fuel bottles won't fit in the side pockets, it doesn't matter what the overall size of the pack is. One way to check this is to take your gear into the store when choosing a pack and see if everything will go in and if items will fit where you want them to go. I can remember doing this in a store called the Fifth Season in the town of Shasta in northern California during my Pacific Crest Trail hike. The internal frame in the pack I'd carried so far had broken, and since it was riveted into place and was of a nonstandard shape, I couldn't easily replace it (a bad design point). I needed a new pack. I tried several before I found one in which all my gear would fit where I wanted it. On the Continental Divide Trail my pack also failed when a shoulder strap snapped (it had been rubbing against the plastic reinforcement in the hipbelt, another bad design

point). I lugged my gear to the only outdoor store in the little town of Creede and tried to fit it into the packs they sold. This time, though, none were big enough and I had to order one from a store in Durango and wait a few days for it to arrive, wondering if it would really be big enough and if it would fit and be comfortable. (I was lucky. It was all these and more—I used the same pack on the Yukon walk.)

If you don't check in the store that all your gear will fit, I'd certainly do so once you get the pack home. Of course, if you already have a pack and are buying other items of gear, you can do the reverse and take the pack into the store to ensure that bottles will fit in the pockets or a sleeping bag in the lower compartment before you buy them. On a long hike you don't want to have to struggle to pack or access gear every day.

Ultralight hikers may get by with a pack that's 2,000 to 3,000 cubic inches in volume, though if many days' food or large quantities of water have to be carried, a bigger pack might be better. The ultralight GoLite Breeze pack holds 2,850 cubic inches without using the extension sleeve, which increases the volume to 4,070 cubic inches. Most hikers will need at least 4,000 cubic inches. I've mostly used packs with 6,000 to 7,000 cubic inches, as I'd rather have more space than too little. However, on the Scottish Highlands walk I used a lighter-weight 4,200-cubic-inch pack since I had less gear and never needed to carry more than six days' food. I'm planning on using the same size pack on the Arizona Trail, where I hope my gear will be even lower in bulk and weight, though I'll have to carry more food plus lots of water at times. In fact, however, I used a 5,350-cubic-inch pack, as I needed the extra space for the two to three gallons of water I had to carry.

Weight

The fact that bigger packs weigh more than smaller ones would seem obvious, but it's not just size that enters in. Most packs, whatever their size, are made from heavy fabrics and have complex carrying systems, myriad straps and clips, and large, often unnecessary, amounts of foam padding. For their size, most packs are heavy. Some are very heavy.

What constitutes a heavy pack? It depends, I think, on the weight of the load you'll be carrying. Many years ago when I began backpacking I remember reading that a pack shouldn't weigh more than 10 percent of the total load, and that still seems a good yardstick to go by. So if you expect to carry no more than 40 pounds maximum, your pack should weigh no more than 4 pounds. However, for 60 pounds a 6-pound pack is acceptable. Of course, a lighter pack is always better.

The weight of an empty pack has to be balanced against the comfort, though. The lightest packs are simple bags with no frames, padding, or hipbelts. These are fine with ultralight loads, below 20 pounds, but they're uncomfortable with anything much above that, at least for me. As the weight carried goes up, I need a thicker hipbelt and better frame if a pack is to be comfortable. And if it comes to a choice, I'd rather carry a moderate load in a heavy pack that supports it well than in a light pack that may cut the total weight by a few pounds but that is uncomfortable to carry.

The ratio of weight to volume can be used to assess the relative weights of packs. A 3,000-cubic-inch pack that weighs 5 pounds (and there are several of these) is very heavy, for example. If you divide the capacity by the weight in ounces you get just 37.5 cubic inches of capacity for every ounce of weight. The average is 60–65 cubic inches per ounce. There are packs that give 70 to 90 cubic inches per ounce, and these are the ones I would consider first. There aren't many packs this light, though. Quite often packs that are marketed as lightweight are, in fact, just lower in volume than other packs and not lighter in weight for the capacity. One genuinely lightweight pack that has been reviewed positively, though I haven't used it myself and I received no response when I contacted the makers for more information, is the Mountainsmith Mountain-Light 5000, which has a capacity of 5,000 cubic

inches and weighs 64 ounces. This works out at a creditable 80 cubic inches per ounce. The GoLite Breeze referred to above holds 2,850 cubic inches and weighs 12.5 ounces in the large size, which gives 228 cubic inches per ounce. This is astonishingly light, but the weight is achieved by dispensing with the frame, back padding, and hipbelt. GoLite representatives say the pack is designed for loads of under 20 pounds, for which it would be fine, but will carry up to 50 pounds if necessary. Maybe so, but my shoulders and back won't carry 50 pounds in a pack with no frame or hipbelt. I wish I could carry a big load in a pack as light as this, but after a few hours with much more than 20 pounds in such a pack my back and shoulders start aching badly.

Kelty has made lightweight packs from Spectra cloth for a number of years now. These are extremely light, just 17 ounces for the 2,750-cubic-inch Vapor 45 and 18 ounces for the 3,400-cubic-inch Cloud 60, which give 161 and 188 cubic inches per ounce, respectively, when stripped of all accessories including frame and hipbelt. When fitted with the frame and padded belt, they weigh 30 and 31 ounces, which yield 92 and 110 inches per cubic ounce. This is still very light. Unfortunately these packs are quite expensive and available in white only.

The North Face make what they call a "technical mountaineering" pack called the Thin Air with a capacity of 4,300 cubic inches and a weight of 54 ounces, which is 80 cubic inches per ounce. The design is more suitable for climbing than hiking, though. It would be good to see The North Face put the same design effort into making a lightweight backpacking model.

A simple and quick way to roughly assess whether a pack is heavier or lighter than average is to allow a pound or so for every 1,000 cubic inches. Looked at this way, the MountainLight 5000 at 4 pounds is clearly light in weight, whereas a 3,000-cubic-inch pack at 5 pounds is heavy.

I mention these companies by name because so few seem interested in developing lightweight packs for hikers. Most pack companies seem to view the weight of a pack as unimportant, so I feel that the few makers of high-quality light-weight packs deserve encouragement. All the figures mentioned here are from the makers' specifications. I haven't used any of these packs, so these references are not an endorsement. These packs do show what can be achieved in cutting the weight of packs if designers concentrate on this element. Oddly, the lightest packs in many makers' ranges are the budget models, for these are made from lighter, less-expensive materials and have fewer accessories and simpler frames than top-of-the-range models. I've tried a few of these lightweight packs, and although they are adequate at carrying moderate loads (up to around 40 pounds), none have been well made enough for me to take on a long-distance hike. For other products—sleeping bags, tents, stoves—the lightest models are usually the top-of-the-line ones and often expensive. It does seem strange that while one designer is cutting ounces off the weight of sleeping bags, another is unconcerned about adding pounds to packs.

To repeat, although the weight of a pack is important, if I'm faced with a choice, I would always put fit and comfort before weight. A pack that doesn't carry a load well is not worth considering for a long-distance hike, no matter what it weighs. The problem with having only a few lightweight packs available is that they won't fit everybody. And if they don't fit, the weight becomes irrelevant.

Carrying System

The heart of a pack is the suspension system. This is what supports the weight and spreads it over your shoulders, lower back, and hips.

The basic choice is between frameless, external frame, and internal frame packs. The simplest of the frameless models have no padding in the back and no hipbelts, though there may be a webbing waist strap. Sizes run from 2,000 to 3,000 cubic inches. Except for ultralight loads, these packs are too small and not supportive or

comfortable enough for long-distance hiking. Next up are packs with padded backs and padded hipbelts but no frame. These will carry loads of up to 35 pounds in reasonable comfort and 40 or so if carefully packed.

Most long-distance hikers use packs with frames, since these transfer the weight to the hipbelt, which is the most comfortable way to carry a load unless you have very strong shoulders. External frames on which the packbag is hung are the traditional load carriers and are still popular with many hikers. External frames are very good at shifting the weight to the hips so you can walk upright rather than having to lean forward. Extra items can be strapped to the frame when necessary, and the gap between your back and the packbag means that sweat is less likely to form, and when it does, it can dissipate more quickly. The main disadvantage of external frames is that they are less stable than internal frames because their rigidity keeps them from moving with the body.

Internal frame packs have the frame hidden inside the back of the pack. There are various types of internal frame; the best transfer the weight to the hipbelt and don't buckle under the weight of the load. Internal frames are flexible, which allows the pack to fit closely to your back. This makes them more stable than externals when hiking over rough terrain or scrambling. Internal frame packs also carry the weight lower than do external frames. This, too, improves stability but can mean you have to lean forward when you walk, which can be tiring and uncomfortable. Packing heavy items high up in the pack can help counteract leaning, as can choosing your pack carefully. The best internals don't cause discomfort.

Whether you go for an external or an internal frame is a personal choice. I started out using external frames, carrying one on my first hike of more than a few days, the 270-mile Pennine Way in England, but soon decided that I preferred the closer fit of an internal frame because I was usually hiking in rough terrain, often off-trail. I did, however, use an external frame on the northern

An external frame pack at Cutthroat Pass on the Pacific Crest Trail in the North Cascades.

1,000 miles of the Pacific Crest Trail after the internal frame in my pack snapped. I also used a pack with a plastic external frame for all but three weeks of my end-to-end of the Canadian Rockies walk. (The pack I set out with had a hipbelt that wouldn't support the load. I'd used the same model before, but the makers had changed the hipbelt design. The lesson I learned from this was to test all new gear.) This external frame was the most comfortable pack I've ever used with really heavy loads (60+ pounds). Unfortunately it was only on the market for less than a year due to the production costs (or so the company told me). I really regret not buying up a few before it disappeared. Although I've mostly used internal frame packs since my Pennine Way hike, I wouldn't say there was a great difference between the two types for long-distance hiking. The quality of the design and the fit are more important.

In my view the key feature of the suspension system isn't the frame anyway; it's the hipbelt, since I carry almost all the weight on my hips. A good belt should spread the load over your hips so there are no pressure points. The belt shouldn't slip down or twist when loaded and should be easy to adjust over different layers of clothing. Side tension straps that pull the sides of the pack into the belt to stop the load swaying are just about essential on internal frame packs when good stability is needed. I keep mine tightened all the time as this gives a better weight transfer to the hips.

With most of the weight transferred to the hips, the shoulder straps are really only needed to prevent the pack from falling off backward. They don't take much weight, so I'm not that concerned about how padded they are. If you carry much weight on your shoulders, you'll want to check that they fit comfortably and are well padded. I do look for top tension or load-lifter straps, which run from the top of the shoulder straps to the pack, as these lift the shoulder straps off the shoulders when tensioned and also pull in the top of the pack toward the body to stop it swaying. This takes pressure off the shoulders and helps transfer weight to the hipbelt. It also helps you to walk upright rather than with a stoop.

Virtually all packs come with sternum or chest straps. These are designed to pull the shoulder straps into the chest and lock the pack to your body so it doesn't sway. I find sternum straps restrictive and remove them for pure hiking trips. They are useful for skiing when maximum stability is required. If the shoulder straps of your pack are too wide and tend to fall of your shoulders a sternum strap can keep them in place. A pack that fits properly would be better, though.

Many packs come with thickly padded backs. Often this just adds weight and bulk. Padding that doesn't touch your back does nothing for comfort. The key areas for padding are the lumbar region and the shoulder blades. As long as these are protected, other padding isn't needed.

Fit

A simple bag with two shoulder straps, no hipbelt, and no frame will fit most people, as the length of the back isn't important. Once you add a hipbelt, the back length does matter, for the belt must fit correctly around your hips. Too high and it'll cut into your stomach and won't support much weight; too low and it'll impede leg movements, cut into your thighs, and again won't support much weight. A correctly fitted hipbelt cups the hips with the upper edge of the belt about an inch above the top of the hipbone. Women may prefer the belt a bit higher than this for a comfortable fit.

To find a pack with the right back length, you need to know the length of your torso. This is the distance from your seventh vertebrae, which lies at the base of your neck, to your upper hipbone. Your height is not relevant, though store staff may try and persuade you it is. If you have a short back, you'll want a shorter-length frame than someone of the same height with a longer back. A pack with the right back length will ride

comfortably on the hips. The top tension or load-lifter straps should rise from just in front of the top of the shoulders at an angle of 25 to 45 degrees. Too steep an angle and the top of the pack will wobble; too shallow an angle and the straps won't lift the shoulder straps off the top of your shoulders, and it'll be harder to get most of the weight on your hips. The shoulder straps themselves should wrap over your shoulders and attach to the pack a few inches below the top of your shoulders. In the front the padded part of the strap should curve well below your armpit so it doesn't cut in or pinch, with enough webbing below it to allow for adjustment over different layers of clothing.

Because hips and shoulders vary in size, the same belts and straps won't fit the same people

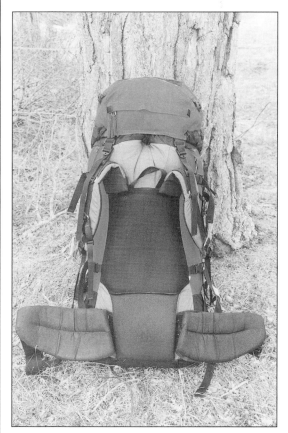

Back of a nonadjustable pack showing padded hipbelt and lumbar pad.

An adjustable back.

even if their back lengths are the same. Many pack makers offer a choice of sizes in hipbelts and shoulder straps. The width of the shoulder straps and the angle at which they wrap over the shoulders are important. You don't want straps that slip off your shoulders all the time or that pinch your neck. Some packs have adjustable shoulder straps.

Many packs have adjustable-back systems whereby the shoulder straps can be moved up and down the frame. An adjustable back is okay for fine-tuning the fit, but if a pack with a frame isn't the right length, this adjustment won't make it fit.

It's important to get the fit right, so I suggest taking time when choosing a pack. Any pack that you try should be fully loaded. Stores will usually provide something heavy like a climbing

rope to dump in the pack, but this results in all the weight being at the bottom, which doesn't replicate an actual backpacking load very well. Many perfectly good packs will feel uncomfortable loaded like this. If you load the pack with your own backpacking gear and some food, you'll get a much better idea of how well it handles a load and whether it fits properly. Walk around the store, including going up and down any stairs, to see how the pack feels. Try on several if necessary and don't buy one until you're sure it's right. Remember you'll be carrying it every day for weeks or months at a time.

Packbags

A packbag is very much a personal choice. As long as it's big enough for all your gear, how many pockets or compartments it has depends on how you like to pack. I find single compartment sacks with minimal pockets hard to use, as I can't get at most of my gear unless my load is very small. I prefer packs with two compartments, a large lid pocket and side or rear pockets. In the lower one I keep my sleeping bag and clothes I'm not wearing. When I'm carrying my self-inflating sleeping mat, it goes in here, too, folded into a square. My food and cooking gear plus items not needed during the day, like candles and a repair kit, go at the bottom of the upper compartment. On top go my spare footwear, a bag containing a paperback book and spare maps, and then my tent or tarp so it's accessible without unpacking the rest of the gear in case it's raining when I make camp. The tent poles are slid down inside the compartment. The items I need or might need during the day go into the top pocket along with other small items that might get mislaid otherwise. The result is a motley collection of hat, gloves, notebook and pens, tent stakes, snacks, insect repellent, sunscreen, and more. Water bottles and fuel bottles go in the side pockets along with a flashlight or headlamp and a first-aid kit. Many packs these days have mesh pockets on the outside. These are useful for fuel and water bottles and for wet rain gear and tarps or tent fly sheets.

Rain

Few packs are waterproof. The material may be, at least when new, but the seams and zippers won't be. There are some packs with welded seams that are fully waterproof, but the choice isn't great. They could be worth looking at if you're going somewhere really wet, but I've always managed with a standard pack without ever getting my gear wet by using pack covers or waterproof liners and stuff sacks. I used covers for many years, but now I prefer the second option. Pack covers tend to catch the wind unless cinched down tight and can collect rain in the base. Once they're on, you have no access to your gear. Further, covers can't be used if you have items such as ice axes, crampons, or trekking poles attached to the outside of your pack.

Instead of using a cover, I now use waterproof stuff sacks, available from several companies, that have sealed seams and closures that fit tightly. They are available in a wide range of sizes. Note that most stuff sacks are water-resistant only, as the seams will leak. I keep my sleeping bag and spare clothes inside waterproof stuff sacks inside a heavy-duty plastic bag. In wet weather I line the main compartment of my pack with a heavy-duty liner, too. A big advantage of having several liners and stuff sacks is that if you have to pack a wet fly sheet or tarp or wet rain gear, it won't dampen other gear.

Durability

When you're setting out on a summer-long hike, you want your pack to carry the load comfortably the whole way without any problems. Unless you travel ultralight with a very simple pack, this may not happen. On the seven 1,000-mile hikes I've made, I've had to replace packs on five of them; on the 800-mile Arizona Trail I had to reinforce the hipbelt with foam cut from my sleeping mat when the padding collapsed near the end of my hike. The causes in four cases were a broken frame, a broken shoulder strap, an inadequate hipbelt, and slipping buckles (on the hipbelt and

on the shoulder, load-lifter, and side tension straps). In the fifth case I was testing a prototype pack on a walk where I could change it fairly easily, so I can't really complain about problems. All these packs were top-quality models, yet the fault lay in poor design or poor manufacturing quality.

Am I particularly unlucky with packs? I don't think so. Packs take quite a beating during a long-distance hike. The three Pacific Crest Trail hikers with whom I went through the High Sierra all had to replace their packs during the hike. When he interviewed Appalachian Trail hikers, Roland Mueser found that about 40 percent of them had to have their packs repaired or replaced.

You can minimize the hassles caused by pack problems. First, buying a top-quality pack makes it less likely that anything will go wrong. You can check each pack carefully to see if there are any obvious weak points. If I'd done this with the pack I took on the Continental Divide Trail, I'd probably have noticed that the shoulder straps ran over a hard plastic edge in the hipbelt. Examining the pack for signs of wear during the hike is advisable, too. Again with that CDT pack, if I'd noticed the wear on the shoulder strap, I could have padded or trimmed down the plastic edge to prevent any more rubbing.

Packs that are easy to repair or with components that can easily be replaced are a good idea. If the broken shoulder strap on that CDT pack had been removable and not sewn firmly into the back of the pack, I could have easily replaced it. There wasn't anything I could have done to prevent the frame breaking on the pack I used on the Pacific Crest Trail, but if it hadn't been riveted and stitched into place I could have easily removed it without damaging the rest of the pack and replaced it. After these hard-learned lessons, I now look for packs with frames, shoulder straps, and hipbelts that can be removed and replaced if necessary. I also have a spare pack ready and waiting to be sent out if needed. (I've needed it twice.)

Most pack makers have a good reputation for repairing or replacing packs that fail during a long-distance hike. It would be worth having the telephone number with you in case you need to call them. If the problem occurs days from the nearest trailhead, as is likely, you may still have to make a repair that will get you out of the back-country. The contents of a repair kit are discussed on pages 182–83, but the most important item I've found for pack repair is duct tape. I've used this to hold a frame in place when the top of the retaining sleeve ripped out and to keep a hipbelt attached to the frame after the plastic attachment snapped. Thick thread and a heavy-duty needle are also useful in case any stitching breaks or comes undone.

Accessory Pouches and Waist Packs

Various pockets and pouches are available that attach to the front of your pack. They are designed to give you access to items needed while hiking and also sometimes to balance the load on your back. Studies suggest that they indeed accomplish the latter. I find such pouches restrictive and awkward to use, however. They block my view of my feet and make me feel clumsy. I also find them hot because they restrict ventilation.

However, I do like having quick access to some small items, particularly a map, so I often wear a small, very basic, lightweight waist pack. This isn't attached to the pack and doesn't interfere with movement, either physically or psychologically.

SHELTER

My favorite way to spend nights out is under the stars. With no walls between me and the outside world I feel in contact with nature, rather than cut off from it. I love waking in the night and looking up to a sky full of stars and the dark silhouettes of trees and peaks. And in the morning the sight of the sun's rays touching distant mountains or a deer stepping out into a dew-soaked meadow is far more involving than opening my eyes to see a sheet of nylon. I have spent many nights like this when I've been glad to be under the stars, but there have been many other nights when I was very glad for nylon walls, nights when the wind howled and the rain lashed down or biting insects buzzed incessantly. On such occasions a shelter is essential.

There are various shelters that are suitable for long-distance hiking. Which is best depends on personal preference and on when and where you are going.

TARPS

A tarp is the lightest, roomiest shelter available for long-distance hiking. It's also extremely versatile; you can pitch it in different ways depending on the weather conditions.

I first used a tarp on the Continental Divide Trail. I initially bought it because I had problems with the poles of my tent, which were cracking and falling apart. (From this experience I learned that dome and hoop tents are fairly useless if the poles fail.) I soon discovered that I preferred the tarp to the tent, as it didn't cut me off so much from the outside. It was also quicker to pitch and had better ventilation. However, when the mosquitoes were biting, the tent was much more preferable, and I ended up getting new poles for the tent and sending the tarp home.

My next two long walks were in grizzly bear country, where the advice was always to sleep in a tent. I did so, but I also carried a tarp for use as a kitchen shelter so I could cook and eat under cover when it was wet or windy. The tarp was retired completely for the walks through Norway and Sweden and the Scottish Highlands, as I felt that a tent was needed to cope with the exposed terrain, stormy weather, and biting insects found on those hikes. However, during these walks I did find it ironic that I was using trekking poles yet carrying the weight of tent poles, and I determined to try a tarp again, using the trekking poles for support.

Since then I have been experimenting with tarps in all sorts of conditions, and used one on my two-month Arizona Trail hike. I have come to the conclusion that they're the best type of shelter for most long-distance hikes. I wish I'd realized this years ago—it would have saved me carrying so much weight and made many camps more comfortable.

The tarp I have used most is made from 1.1-ounce silicone-coated ripstop nylon, the best material for tarps and lightweight tents, as it is very light and very durable. The only disadvantage is that it is so slick that tape won't stick to the seams. You can seal seams with silicone sealant, but I've never done so in tarps or tents, and I've never had any serious leakage. This tarp weighs a pound and measures 9 by 8 feet, which gives masses of room for one and would sleep two. Combined with a lightweight nylon groundsheet weighing 8 ounces and stakes and guylines weighing 6 ounces, it gives me a shelter whose total weight is 1 pound, 14 ounces, and yet it is roomier than a tent weighing three times as much. This tarp was used as a cooking shelter

In dry, calm weather no tent or tarp is necessary, as shown at this Grand Canyon campsite.

on both the Canadian Rockies and Yukon walks and frequently since and is still in excellent condition.

The tarp I used on the Arizona Trail is larger but made from the same material, and has rubber loops for attaching stakes and guylines and a reinforced hole for a trekking pole spike in the center. It measures 9.85 feet square and weighs 27 ounces. This is very roomy for one, ample for two, and could sleep three or even four. With a groundsheet, stakes, and guylines, the total weight is 2 pounds, 10 ounces.

Unless the weather is really wild, I generally have at least one side of the tarp completely open. With a tarp I don't have the feeling of either being inside or outside with a sharp difference between them that I have with a tent. The absence of a door feels like a barrier has been removed, a barrier between me and the wilds.

On a more practical level, tarps are great for cooking under in stormy weather, as there is so much space and ventilation. You can easily store all your equipment under cover, too.

Another aspect of tarp camping that I like is being able to change the shape to suit the weather. On sheltered sites I often pitch the tarp as a lean-to or an open-ended ridge. In more exposed places I usually pitch it as a pyramid, with a pole in the center and another holding up one side as a large entrance.

Pitching a Tarp

I use trekking poles with my tarp. This frees me from needing to find natural supports every night and makes the tarp far more versatile. I've pitched mine well above timberline many times. In forests a tarp can be strung between trees, the traditional method, or sticks can be used if you don't have trekking poles. You could carry a couple of light tent poles, but this would add to the weight. A few stakes and lengths of cord for guylines are needed as well. My current tarps have attachment points for stakes and guys. When these aren't present, you can wrap the tarp fabric

A tarp pitched using trekking poles.

round a smooth pebble and then loop a length of cord round this and tie it tight.

Pitching a tarp isn't difficult, but it does require a bit of practice, which is best not done on a stormy night in the middle of nowhere. When erecting the tarp as a ridge, I first stake out the ends of one side. I then slip the tip of a trekking pole through the grommet or loop in the center of one of the sides at right angles to the staked side. The pole is then stood up, and a guyline is slipped over the spike and staked out. The corner on the other side of the pole can now be staked out, keeping the material under tension as you do so to prevent the pole falling over. The other pole is then erected and as many stakes as needed for stability are fixed in position.

To pitch the tarp as a pyramid, I again stake down the ends of one side. Then I fit a pole into the center of the tarp, pushing the handle into the fabric if there's no hole here or the tip of the pole if there is. In the former case, to keep the pole from moving, a length of cord can be wrapped tightly around the fabric and the

A tarp pitched as a low-profile pyramid using a single trekking pole.

handle and then tied off. Once the pole is in place, the other two corners can be staked out, leaving the side of the tarp between them quite slack so the other trekking pole can be used to hold up the middle of that side to make a door. If it gets really stormy, I can shorten the front pole (an advantage of using trekking poles) to lower the profile. If this doesn't give enough protection, I remove the pole altogether and peg that side down to the ground, too, leaving just a low entrance through which I can crawl in and out. This can be done from inside the tarp. In really strong winds I also lower the center pole to give a very low wind-shedding profile. The lower the tarp, the more wind-resistant it is.

In any configuration the sides of the tarp can be raised well above the ground for greater ventilation or staked at ground level for better weather protection. I attach short guylines to each of the attachment points, which may be grommets in the tarp or short loops attached to the tarp.

Staking these out allows the tarp to be raised above the ground. If I want it down to the ground, I put the stakes through the attachment points.

Condensation

Tarps are not perfect, of course. Although they are much better ventilated than a tent, they are not free of condensation. I've had moisture drip on me from the inside of a tarp on a still, humid night, even though it was pitched as a lean-to with three sides open. And if you have to peg the tarp down to ground level in heavy rain, condensation is likely. However, the air is still fresher than in a tent, and condensation that runs down the walls will sink away into the ground. And there's plenty of room to sit up and move around without brushing the wet walls.

Insects

The other problem with tarps—the one that stopped me from using them on some long hikes unless I had a tent along as well—is that they don't keep out biting insects. When the mosquitoes or no-see-ums or black flies are swarming, I want a shelter into which I can seal myself. I considered various netting screens and minitents, but these all seemed very restrictive, which defeated the main point of using a tarp. Now, however, there are larger net tents that give much more room. The most interesting I've come across is GoLite's NetTent, which weighs 18 ounces and measures 7 by 4 feet. Since this has a floor, the tent can be used just as a groundsheet when you don't need the netting, saving the weight of a separate groundsheet.

Models

The NetTent hooks to the underside of the GoLite Cave, a silicone ripstop nylon tarp that weighs 18 ounces and measures 8.75 feet square. The twelve stakes needed for pitching it together weigh another 5 ounces to give a total package of 2 pounds, 9 ounces.

There are few other really lightweight tarps available. The only other one I've seen that I like is the Sil Shelter from Integral Designs, which comes in two sizes. I've tried the smaller one, which is 8 by 5 feet and weighs just 8 ounces, and which requires careful pitching to give adequate protection for one person. I like a slightly larger tarp, so I'd prefer the larger 9-by-10-foot Sil Shelter. This weighs 14 ounces and is easily big enough for one and would sleep two. Both are made from silicone nylon.

Very light small tarps like the 8-by-5-foot Sil Shelter could be carried for use as cooking shelters, tent awnings, or protection for the head of a bivouac bag (for which the Sil was designed).

Groundsheets

When you are using a tarp, a groundsheet is needed unless the ground is very dry and you make do with just a sleeping mat. Polyethylene sheeting can be used but doesn't last long and can't be staked out when it's windy. I prefer a nylon groundsheet, and there are now many available, often sold in the same shapes as popular tents. The lightest ones weigh 6 to 8 ounces and measure 4 by 7 feet, just big enough for two. A slightly heavier alternative that I've also used successfully is the All Weather Blanket (also sold as the Sportsman's Blanket), which measures 4 by 6.5 feet and weighs 12 ounces. These groundsheets are made from a laminate of different materials and have a reflective silver coating on one side, the other being red, blue, or camouflage. These blankets are particularly useful for desert hiking, since they can be erected as a sunshade with the silver side outward. Used like this, they are much cooler than a nonreflective tarp. They could also be used to attract attention in case of emergency.

I don't use a separate groundsheet with a tent. Tents are heavy enough anyway. I've never had a tent groundsheet leak badly, so it doesn't seem necessary. Small holes can be easily patched with duct tape or sticky-backed ripstop nylon.

TARP-TENTS

Shelters with more shape and features than a tarp but without the full specifications of a tent have been around for many years. One of the first was Black Diamond's Megamid, a pyramid-shaped ripstop polyester tarp-tent that weighs 3.5 pounds. The floor area is 81 square feet. Like a tent, this has a zippered door and can be pitched in only one way. It comes with a pole, but a trekking pole could be substituted to save some weight.

The latest tarp-tent is the Nomad Lite, designed specifically for long-distance hiking by a hiker named Kurt Russell when he couldn't find a tent he thought would be suitable for an Appalachian Trail hike. It's designed to be pitched with two trekking poles and is made from silicone ripstop nylon. The total weight is 2 pounds, 1 ounce, give or take an ounce. The size is 10.5 by 5.5 feet, with an internal height of 3 feet, 4 inches. Halfway between a tent and tarp, the Nomad Lite has a bug-proof interior with a Velcro-fastened mesh door, a mesh window, and a vestibule. It pitches with just three stakes. If you want something more like a tent than a tarp, it sounds like a good choice for roominess combined with protection from insects.

BIVOUAC BAGS AND TENTS

Bivouac, or bivy, bags and tiny tents with one or two hoops might seem ideal for long-distance hiking due to their light weight. However, there is minimal space inside these shelters, a big disadvantage. Bivy bags are simply waterproof-breathable envelopes into which you can slip your sleeping bag to keep it dry. They weigh between 8 and 32 ounces, depending on materials and design. I've kept dry in nights of steady rain using a bivy bag, and I've also used them in snowholes, damp mountain huts, and even tents at times. I carried one on the Pacific Crest Trail so I could sleep outside without worrying about my sleeping bag getting wet. On the Scottish Highlands walk I also had one for use in damp huts and for extra warmth on very cold nights (a bivy bag adds a few degrees of extra warmth to a sleeping bag). However, I haven't taken one on other long-distance hikes, and I wouldn't use one

A bivouac tent—very light as long as you don't mind the lack of space.

again. I'd rather have a tarp. And I've never hiked with just a bivy bag due to the fact that there's nowhere to cook, store gear, or do any of the other things you can do under a tarp or in a tent. A bivy bag is a sleeping bag cover and that's it.

Add one or two tiny poles to a bivy bag and you have a bivy tent. The poles hold the fabric off your head, but there isn't room to sit up inside, never mind cook or store much gear. Weights run from a pound and a half upward, more than a tarp for a fraction of the space. I wouldn't choose a bivy tent for a weekend away and certainly not for a long hike. I did meet a long-distance hiker on the Pacific Crest Trail who had started out using a bivy tent. He found the lack of room so frustrating that he'd sent it home and was carrying an 8-pound mountain tent instead.

TENTS

Most long-distance hikers use tents. Many tents, however, are not that suitable for long-distance hiking in my experience (and I've tested a large

A two-pole tunnel tent.

number over the years). The main reason is that they're too heavy, but an additional problem is that the designs are often inadequate for prolonged use.

Tents come in various designs. For long-distance hiking only a few designs are light enough, namely single hoop, tunnel, and semi-geodesic designs. A solo tent need weigh no more than 4 pounds, a tent for two no more than 6 pounds. Only if you're going to be camping high in the mountains in winter is a heavier tent than this required. The weight should include all necessary components such as stakes. Note that many catalog weights are only for tent, fly, and poles.

The very smallest tents weigh less than the figures given above, but you can't sit up in them or store much gear or cook, all things I think important in a tent I'll be using for months at a time.

Features I look for in a tent, in addition to headroom, are a fly sheet that comes down to the ground all the way around for protection against wind-driven rain, a large vestibule for cooking and for storing wet and muddy gear, insect netting as inner doors, and large outer doors that give a spacious view when open. Two-way zippers and vents to allow airflow through the tent are also important, since all tents suffer from condensation at times.

Condensation

Indeed, condensation is the biggest problem with lightweight tents. There's no way to avoid it, but a good design can minimize the detrimental effects. The position and angle of doors and door zippers are important here. On far too many tents the door slopes at an angle to the ground. When condensation forms on the part of the fly sheet that lies above the door, as it will, it then drips inside when the door is open, landing on you, your sleeping bag, or the ground-sheet. Unless biting insects are around, I prefer to sleep with the tent door open for better ventilation. A number of times in tents with sloping doors I've been awakened in the night by drops of condensation falling on my face and had to close the door. On tents with sloping doors the fly-sheet zipper often runs above the tent door, so that if you open it when it's wet outside, the rain comes in. A good design has a vertical inner door and a vestibule with a door positioned so that it can be opened without rain coming into the tent. This way you can unzip the top of the door for ventilation. Tents like this do exist, but they're in the minority. Most tents seem to be designed mainly for fair weather, but on a long-distance hike you're almost certainly going to have storms and heavy rain at some point.

Trekking poles or trailside sticks can be used to hold up the door of a tent to create an awning

Geodesic-dome tent with fly sheet plus extra pole to support vestibule.

and give good ventilation as well as better views. If the fly-sheet door has two zippers, the whole panel between them can be held up, which usually gives such good protection against rain that the door only needs to be closed when the rain is being driven sideways by a strong wind.

Inner or Outer Pitching

With most designs the main tent is pitched first and then the fly sheet thrown over it. This can be a problem in wet weather, as the tent can get wet while you're pitching or striking it. I prefer designs where the fly sheet is pitched first and the inner tent is then hung inside and remains dry. With this style you can pack all your gear, including the inner tent, in dry conditions, leaving just the fly sheet to be taken down and packed in the rain. You can also erect the fly sheet as a lunchtime shelter or cook inside it before you

Hilleberg Akto single-hoop tent—the author's favorite tent.

pitch the inner tent. Very few tents available in North America are designed for the fly sheet to be pitched first. VauDe make some of the few models. In Europe such designs are more common, and my favorite tents come from Swedish tent maker Hilleberg. Their single-pole Akto weighs 3.75 pounds and performed superbly on the wet Scottish Highlands walk. I was able to cook under cover in the rain with a door zipper open to let steam out but not let rain in and to store all my gear inside. The Akto has protected vents at each end, but I still had lots of condensation at times. Due to the design, none ever dripped into the inner tent, though. The Akto is also very easy to pitch and take down and is made from silicone ripstop nylon. If this sounds interesting, check out the Hilleberg Web site, <*www.hilleberg.se*>.

The only circumstance when it seems suitable to pitch the tent before the fly sheet is when rain isn't common but biting insects are. The inner tents of some fly-sheet-first models can be pitched on their own, however, which gives you the best of both worlds.

I would now take a tent on hikes only if I thought a tarp would be harder to use, which is to say hikes where I expected to have to camp in exposed places and where big storms were likely. On trails where you can camp in the forest most every night, such as the AT, PCT, and CDT, I would use a tarp, with a mesh tent to keep out bugs when needed.

SLEEPING BAG

A good sleeping bag for long-distance hiking is one that keeps you warm almost all the time without you needing to wear warm clothes in it.

I say almost, because a bag that will be warm enough for the coldest nights will probably be too hot much of the rest of the time. On any long-distance hike there will be a huge range of overnight temperatures. On my Continental Divide Trail hike the coldest night was 23°F, and the warmest, 65°F. Most were between 35° and 45°F. On the coldest nights I closed the hood and wore long johns, a thermal top, and socks in the bag. As well as the most comfortable system, this is also the most weight-efficient, since you're not carrying the weight of a sleeping bag warm enough for the coldest nights.

Warmth and Ratings

How warm a sleeping bag you need depends on whether you sleep warm or cold. I'm lucky. I'm a hot sleeper and can sleep warm in many bags at below their rated minimum temperatures. My partner Denise sleeps cold and needs a bag rated 20°F lower than mine.

Bag ratings are comparative only. There is no standard, although makers are working toward this. In many years of testing sleeping bags I've found that synthetic-filled bags are frequently overrated whereas the ratings of down-filled bags are more often fairly accurate.

Fill

The big choice to be made in sleeping bags is between down and synthetic fills. The latter have improved greatly over the years, but I still prefer down for long-distance hikes because it's much lighter, lower in bulk, more comfortable over a wider temperature range, more breathable, and more durable. In my opinion the best synthetic fill at the time of writing is Polarguard 3D. In particular, it's softer than other synthetics and drapes around the body better, though still not as well as down.

Down recovers quickly from repeated compression. A down bag can be stuffed into a small sack and carried in the bottom of a pack crushed by the weight above it every day for months on end and still loft fully every night. I have a down bag I first used on my Canadian

A mummy sleeping bag showing zipper baffle and insulated draft collar, good features to have in cold weather.

Rockies walk. Eleven years later, it's still as warm as it ever was. A synthetic bag will slowly lose its loft, however, and so it won't keep you as warm as your hike progresses. I used a synthetic bag on my first-ever long-distance hike. This was only 10 weeks long, but that bag was almost flat by the end. Today's synthetic bags should last longer than that, but I'd still treat one very carefully on a long-distance hike if I wanted it to last the whole way. Because compression reduces the loft (thickness) and therefore the warmth of a synthetic bag, I wouldn't carry it in the bottom of the pack crammed into a small stuff sack. Instead I'd pack it in an oversize stuff sack and carry it near the top of the pack, with little weight on top of it. The very worst thing to do with a synthetic bag is to use a compression stuff sack, yet because of their bulk, synthetic bags often come with such stuff sacks.

Drying out sleeping bags and bivouac bags after sleeping in the open at 12°F in Lapland.

Wetness

The often-quoted argument against down is that it's useless when wet. When I hear this remark, I always wonder if the speaker has tried sleeping in a sodden synthetic bag. I have. It feels cold and clammy, and though it is true that synthetics will dry much quicker than down, this will still take a long time and isn't something to try and do with your body heat on a cold night. Sleeping bags, whatever the fill, need to be kept dry. This can be done by carrying them in a waterproof stuff sack inside a heavy-duty plastic bag or pack liner and by sleeping inside a tent or under a tarp in wet weather. I've used down bags on all my long walks except for the first one, and I've never had one become damp enough not to keep me warm, even after days of rain.

Airing the bag on dry mornings and evenings by spreading it over dry rocks or hanging it over a branch or the tent will get rid of any residual moisture. If a bag gets really wet, it can be dried in the sun or, with great care, in front of a campfire. Keep the bag far from any sparks, which will

melt the shell fabric, and don't let the bag get too hot, since excessive heat can damage the nylon shell. Dark bags will dry more quickly than light-colored ones because they absorb heat better. If the bag's just a little damp, then body heat should dry it out adequately.

Weight

The best down gives the most warmth for the least weight, so this is the stuff to go for if you want the lightest sleeping bag. Look for down with a fill power of 700 or more (fill power is the number of cubic inches an ounce of down will fill).

The weight of your sleeping bag will depend on how warm a sleeper you are and how much protection from the cold you need. I can use a 23-ounce down bag in temperatures down to 32°F without added clothes, down to 25°F with clothes. Colder sleepers would probably need a 32-to-40-ounce bag in the same temperatures. I carry a 32-to-40-ounce bag on hikes where I expect temperatures to dip to 20°F or below. The lowest temperature I recorded on the Pacific Crest Trail was 14°F. I kept warm enough in a down bag weighing 36 ounces by wearing thermal underwear and thick socks.

Shells

Quick-drying wind- and water-resistant nylon is usually used for sleeping bag shells and linings. Some down bags come with waterproof-breathable shells. Since the seams aren't sealed, these don't make the bag waterproof, but they do greatly increase the water resistance. They're not quite as breathable as ordinary shells, however, and they're slightly heavier. I've never used a bag with such a shell on a long hike, and I don't think they're necessary. But if you're really worried about getting a down bag wet, they could give you peace of mind.

SLEEPING PADS

Whatever type of sleeping bag you use, a sleeping pad will be needed underneath to keep out the cold from the ground and to provide a

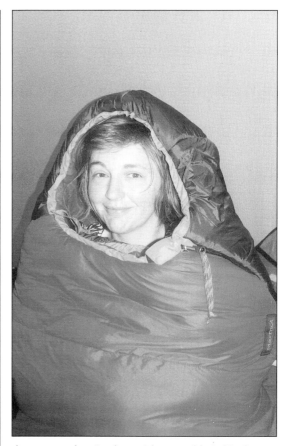

A mummy sleeping bag with a good hood is the most efficient design for keeping you warm.

degree of comfort. This pad needn't be bulky or heavy. I've always used a three-quarter-length pad that runs from shoulder to hip, using clothing for a pillow and more clothing under my lower legs and feet if necessary. Simple closed-cell foam pads are the lightest type, weighing 6 to 9 ounces for the three-quarter length. They're pretty tough and can be chucked down on any sort of ground. However, they're not that comfortable and don't compress for packing. Self-inflating mats are very comfortable, but you need to take care they're not punctured. Unfortunately most of them are too heavy, in my view, for long-distance hiking. The lightest is the three-quarter length Cascade Designs Therm-A-Rest Ultralite at 14 ounces. I've used one of these on several long-distance walks and found it comfortable and warm. It can be folded into a square for packing inside the pack.

KITCHEN EQUIPMENT

Stoves

Nearly all long-distance hikers now carry a stove for cooking. Of 126 Appalachian Trail hikers interviewed by Roland Mueser (see *Long-Distance Hiking*) only 4 didn't carry a stove. This is good news, for the traditional campfire leaves scars and uses scarce resources. This is not to say that campfires should never be lit, but that along popular trails there are too many fire rings, blackened rocks, and patches of charcoal in mea-

MSR Whisperlite gas stove—a well-established backpacking stove popular with long-distance hikers.

dows. It is now time to let the wounds heal. In many areas campfires are banned because of this. It is possible to have a fire without leaving a trace in areas where they are permitted. For information on campfires, see pages 219–21.

Liquid Fuel

Most long-distance hikers on North American trails use stoves that burn white gas for the simple reason that the fuel is inexpensive and easy to find in trailside towns. (This is not true for much of the rest of the world. In Europe white gas can be hard to find, and it's expensive when you do come across it. If you're thinking you might want to hike abroad, a multifuel stove is worth having. Kerosene is available almost everywhere, and you can run the stove on automotive fuel if necessary.) Of the various gas stoves available, I used the venerable Optimus Svea 123 (18 ounces) on the Pacific Crest and Continental Divide Trails and the MSR Whisperlite (14

Primus Himalaya Multi-Fuel System stove—the most versatile of the gas stoves.

ounces without fuel bottle/tank) on my two Canadian long-distance hikes. On the Norway and Sweden end-to-end walk I used a multifuel MSR X-GK (15.5 ounces without fuel bottle/tank) and ran it on kerosene, as this was easily obtainable. All these stoves worked well, with one caveat: it was hard to simmer on them. The Svea and the X-GK are both very noisy, too. Newer models have overcome these problems. The MSR Dragonfly (17 ounces without fuel bottle/tank) has very good flame control but is noisy. The Primus Himalaya Multi-Fuel System (MFS) stove (18 ounces without fuel bottle) also simmers well and is reasonably quiet. Uniquely, it will run off butane/propane cartridges (see below), which makes it far more versatile than other gas stoves.

The other interesting new stove is the Optimus Nova (15 ounces without fuel bottle), which is possibly the safest and easiest-to-use multifuel stove. This has a new design of a burner with ribs that transfer heat to the vaporizing chamber so that it lights in seconds, unlike standard burners that need preheating. You just pump it a little, release some fuel, light this, and wait a few seconds—it's lit. The Nova will also run off just about any petroleum product without needing the jet changed. It simmers well and isn't that noisy. To turn it off, you turn over the fuel bottle. This self-purges the stove and depressurizes the fuel bottle, so there are no drips when you disconnect the fuel line from the pump and you don't have to unscrew the pump to release the pressure, which always lets out a spray of fuel. I used a Nova with success on the Arizona Trail.

Both the Primus MFS and Optimus Nova are claimed to work with most types of petroleum. How well they do so I don't yet know. However, the MSR X-GK is well established as an efficient stove for use in areas such as the Himalaya, where clean gasoline is unlikely to be found and dirty kerosene is the most common fuel. If

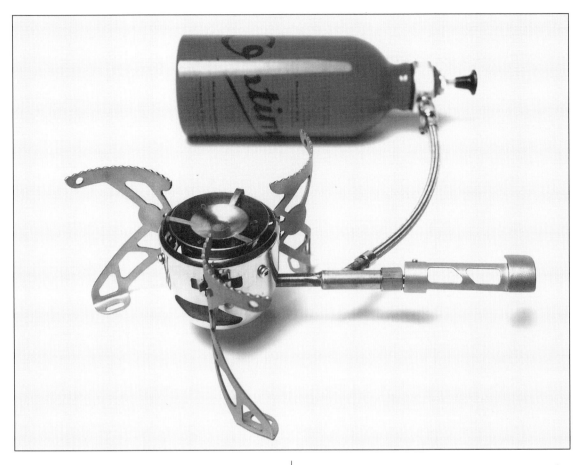

Optimus Nova stove—one of the quickest and easiest-to-use gas stoves.

you're planning ventures in remote areas where fuel quality and type are uncertain, the X-GK is a good choice. For European trips, however, I would choose the Primus MFS. Butane/propane cartridges are quite easy to find, and you could run it off kerosene if you couldn't find cartridges. Whatever stove you use, filtering liquid fuel is always a good idea.

Most gas stoves need occasional maintenance if they are to work efficiently over the long haul. The one I've used that needs the least attention is the Svea 123, probably because it's a very simple design. On other stoves leather pump cups need greasing every so often, or the pump won't pressurize the fuel

tank. I've used margarine and sunscreen for this when I've had no oil, though tiny tubes of oil are provided in the repair kits of some stoves. Jets can get blocked, too. Many stoves have a built-in jet-cleaning needle that is operated by either shaking the stove or turning the control valve a certain way. For stoves without a built-in needle, a separate needle should be carried. In an emergency a toothbrush bristle will do. To avoid pushing the blockage back into the fuel line, it is advisable to remove the jet before unblocking it. Built-in needles push the dirt out, of course. The tube between the fuel bottle and burner may also become blocked, especially if you use dirty fuels. Stoves suitable for long-distance hiking should have fuel lines you can easily clean. All the stoves mentioned above are field maintainable. I wouldn't consider a stove that wasn't. And I always carry a tiny repair and maintenance kit with spares in it.

A quart (32 fluid ounces) of fuel will last me for 10 days of cooking, so I rarely need to carry more than this. With most stoves the fuel bottle acts as the fuel tank. These shouldn't be filled fully because the fuel needs room to expand when pressurized. MSR, Sigg, Optimus, and Primus all make fuel bottles. Weights are around 3, 5, and 7.5 ounces (11, 22, and 33 fluid ounces).

Cartridges

The lightest-weight, easiest-to-use, and quietest stoves are those that run on butane/propane cartridges. The tiny Snow Peak GigaPower Titanium weighs just 2.5 ounces and the Primus Alpine Titanium a mere 3 ounces, yet both are powerful enough to boil a quart of water in less than four minutes. Titanium stoves are costly, however. Much more reasonably priced and still ultralight

Svea 123 stove—a traditional gas stove.

are the Snow Peak GigaPower Stove at 3.1 ounces, the Primus Alpine Micro at 4 ounces, and the Peak 1 Micro at 5.5 ounces. All of these stoves screw into the same type of self-sealing cartridge. None of these stoves will fit Camping Gaz CV self-sealing cartridges, which are common in alpine countries such as France. For these you need a Camping Gaz stove such as the 7-ounce Bleuet 270 Micro.

The big problem with these stoves is that cartridges aren't often available at resupply points along long trails. If you include cartridges in supply boxes, they can't be sent by airmail though they can go by ground if you request this. Overall, this means cartridges are not a good choice unless you know you can buy them along the way or you are regularly being resupplied in person by friends or family. The only long walk I've used a cartridge stove (the Peak 1 Micro) on was in the Scottish Highlands, where my partner resupplied me regularly. A standard 9-fluid-ounce cartridge lasted me four days.

Cartridge stoves aren't a good choice for very

cold weather because the fuel doesn't vaporize quickly, making for slow boiling times. Below 20°F, stoves may not work at all unless the cartridge is warmed with the hands or inside clothing. I wouldn't choose a cartridge stove for a hike where I expected regular subfreezing temperatures. The only exception to this are the Peak 1 X series stoves, which run off special cartridges that are said to work down to 0°F. I've used the Xpert stove in 20°F temperatures, and it worked fine. However, cartridges for X series stoves are much harder to find than standard cartridges.

If you like the convenience of cartridge stoves (and they are much easier to use than gas stoves), the answer could be the Primus MFS. You can run this on cartridges when they are available and on white gas or other liquid fuel when they aren't. Another advantage of the MFS is that it's field maintainable, unlike most cartridge stoves.

If you do use cartridges, please pack empty ones out. They can be recycled if completely empty.

Solid Fuel

Solid fuel is very light but has an uncontrollable flame that isn't very hot. For minimalist cooking it may be adequate. It was for a hiker I met on the Pacific Crest Trail who lived on three instant eat-from-the-bag freeze-dried meals a day. He heated water for these in a metal cup balanced on two stones or earth walls above a large solid fuel tablet. There are tiny stoves, really just pot supports and a burning plate, for solid fuel tablets. Esbit is one brand.

Denatured Alcohol

Denatured alcohol is more efficient than solid fuel, especially if used in stoves like the Trangia. However, it has only a little more than half the heat output of gas or butane/propane, so twice as much fuel has to be carried. Trangia models vary from the Mini-Trangia, consisting of burner, minimal windscreen–pot support, 1.5-pint pot with lid, and pot grab and weighing 12 ounces, to the 25K, which has nonstick pots, kettle, fry-

ing pot, full wraparound windscreen, and a weight of 45 ounces. I used a Trangia 27, which comes with two pots, lid, and pot grab and weighs 35 ounces, on my first long-distance hike. It worked fine but did use up fuel fast, with a quart barely lasting a week. That walk was in Britain, where stove alcohol is fairly easy to find, as it is in some other parts of Europe. Fuel isn't so easy to find along trails in the United States and Canada, however. Hardware stores are the places to look rather than outdoor recreation stores. It's also sold under the names "rubbing alcohol" and "marine stove fuel."

The advantage of Trangia and similar stoves is that they're virtually indestructible. There are no moving parts, no pumps, and no fuel lines. All except the Mini-Trangia work very well in strong winds due to the efficient windscreen. And because they burn unpressurized fuel, they don't flare, which means they're safer than other stoves when cooking under a vestibule.

Despite this, I've never used my Trangia on another long-distance hike, mainly due to the unavailability of fuel but also because of the weight, both of the stove and the fuel, and the slow boiling time.

Natural Fuels

The final option is for a stove that runs on small twigs, pine cones, and other flammable natural materials. These stoves, sold as Sierra stoves by ZZ Manufacturing, also have a small battery-operated fan to ensure a draft. Some people really like them; others describe them as requiring too much attention. I've never used one. Weights start at 18 ounces, but you don't need to carry any fuel, though having a tiny bit of dry kindling might be advisable in wet weather. A problem with these stoves is that they are illegal in some areas where campfires are banned because the hot embers, if dumped without being thoroughly doused with water, could cause a forest fire.

Carrying Fuel

Fuel bottles are strong and durable. I've only had one bottle leak once. The spilled fuel didn't

Trangia alcohol stove with pan set.

damage anything because it was packed, as always, away from food in the bottom of a side pocket. Although leaks are very unlikely, it is wise to keep fuel bottles away from food and other items that could be damaged. White gas and alcohol will evaporate if spilled. Kerosene, however, leaves a smelly, greasy stain, so I'm especially careful when carrying this fuel, wrapping the bottle in a plastic bag or storing it in an exterior mesh pocket.

Transporting Stoves and Fuel by Air

Transporting fuel by air is allowed only in accordance with strict regulations. You probably won't want the hassle of sorting out these rules, so if you're flying, plan on buying fuel when you reach your destination. Flying with your stove may not be possible either. Different airlines have different policies regarding the transportation of stoves and fuel bottles. Federal Aviation Administration regulations say that stoves and bottles that have been properly purged—that is, aired until there is no trace of a fuel smell—can be carried. Many airlines have tougher rules, however. Some won't carry any stoves at all; some will only carry unused stoves; some will carry butane/cartridge stoves but not gas stoves; and some will carry stoves but not used fuel bottles. It's always best to call airlines and ask before you book your tickets. I've only once been unable to fly with a white gas stove and fuel bottle. On that occasion I checked and found I could buy cartridges at my destination, so I took a cartridge stove, which the airline accepted. I've also twice had to wash out fuel bottles and stove with soap before I was allowed to take them on a return flight with an airline that had been happy to transport them on the way out.

Windscreens

In a strong wind an unprotected stove will take ages to bring water to the boil, if it does so at all, and will use much fuel in the process. A foil windscreen will save fuel and speed up cooking times and is well worth the few grams it weighs. Many stoves now come with windscreens; if your stove doesn't have one, they are inexpensive to purchase. Stoves that sit on top of the fuel tank or cartridge shouldn't be fully encircled with a windshield in case the tank or cartridge over-heats. Leave a large gap on one side and check every so often that the tank isn't too hot to touch.

Safety

Stoves are potentially dangerous items and need to be handled with care. Knowing your stove

A stove windscreen will save fuel in windy weather and, more importantly, speed up boiling times dramatically.

well means you should be able to operate it properly even when you're exhausted at the end of a long day or half asleep first thing in the morning.

Ideally, stoves should always be used outside, well away from tarps and tents. However, on any long-distance hike there are bound to be times when it is stormy or the bugs are biting and you don't want to cook outside. Cooking inside the tent is very risky and not to be recommended. However, vestibules are a different matter, as long as they are big enough. On my Scottish Highlands and Scandinavian walks I cooked in the vestibule of my tent most nights due to the wet, windy weather or the midges and mosquitoes. The tents I used had large vestibules where the stove could be placed on the ground well away from the fly-sheet walls and the inner tent. I was also able to leave the fly-sheet door zipper open above the stove so fumes could escape. Only in the very worst weather or insect attack did I use the stove with the fly-sheet doors fully closed.

With great care you can cook in the vestibule of a tent in stormy weather.

When you're cooking in a vestibule, good ventilation is essential because stoves give off carbon monoxide, which is a colorless, odorless gas that can kill you. If you'll be cooking regularly under cover, denatured alcohol, kerosene, and butane/propane are safer fuels than white gas.

Stoves are extremely unlikely to catch fire or explode, but it does happen. Keeping a stove well maintained is the best way to avoid this. Rubber seals should be checked regularly and replaced if they show signs of damage. Always check too that cartridges and fuel bottles are attached firmly and there is no fuel leakage anywhere. Never change a cartridge or open a fuel bottle or fuel tank if there are naked flames any-

where nearby. Fuel can ignite very quickly. It's best to always refill stoves and change cartridges outside your tent, just in case of a leak or spill.

Cookware

The problem with cookware usually isn't the weight of individual items but the number of items carried. A solo walker needs no more than a single quart-size pot plus a mug and spoon. If the mug is a metal one, it can be used as a second pot. Meals can be eaten straight from the main pot. Twosomes need a larger pot and maybe some plastic bowls to eat from. A second pot could be useful, too. But that's all. Kettles, backpacker's ovens, frying pans, gourmet coffee-makers, and more are great for base camps and short trips but too heavy for long-distance hiking. Lids for pots are worth carrying because they speed up boiling times, which saves fuel. Heavy metal lids aren't necessary, though. Sheets of foil are fine.

Aluminum pots are the lightest and also transfer heat efficiently, but they dent and scratch easily and can be hard to clean. A simple one-quart pot need weigh no more than 4 ounces. Aluminum pots give a metallic taste to some foods, and there is some evidence that cooking in aluminum pots isn't good for your health, though this is unproven. Titanium pots are slightly heavier, at about 5 ounces for a quart size, but more durable and easier to clean. Unfortunately, the cost is very high. Stainless steel is much less expensive than aluminum and even tougher, but it is also heavier, with quart pans weighing at least 7 to 8 ounces. Steel doesn't transfer heat as well as aluminum or titanium and is more likely to scorch and burn food. Composite pots with stainless steel on the inside and aluminum on the outside weigh marginally less than stainless steel and have the best properties of both materials. Nonstick pots are also available, but I wouldn't use them on a long-distance hike. Food may be less likely to stick to them, though it happens at times, but keeping them in good condition requires too much care. I want pots I can scour and scrape when necessary. I doubt that the nonstick coating is very good for you when it comes off into your food, as happens if it's scratched.

I now use a titanium pot. It has survived a four-and-a-half-month hike, a two-month hike, and many shorter ones unscathed. When I used aluminum pots, they were so battered after a long-distance hike that I retired them. Stainless steel and composite pots survived better, and I still use them for short trips, but when weight is crucial I prefer titanium.

Whatever pots you use, it's worth blackening the outsides as then they'll transfer heat to the contents much quicker, speeding up boiling times and saving fuel. You can do this with stove paint or simply by holding the pot over a campfire. Alcohol stoves blacken pots anyway. I am always baffled when people complain how difficult it is to clean the soot off Trangia pots. To me this is an advantage.

Some pots have very smooth bases that easily slide off stoves, dumping your dinner in the dirt. It's happened to me. Sandpaper or even gravel can be used to roughen the base of the pot to help prevent this from happening.

As well as a pot, I carry a pint-size stainless steel mug called a Cascade Cup. It weighs 4 ounces and with its wide base can double as a second pot. For cutlery I carry two Lexan plastic spoons weighing a quarter of an ounce each. Titanium spoons weighing half an ounce are available, but they're pricey. Lexan is strong enough for me.

My pot, mug, and spoons together weigh only 9.5 ounces, less than some pots alone.

Water Containers

Many hikers give little thought to their water containers, yet these are important, especially on hikes that go through desert terrain or other areas where water is scarce and where a leaking bottle could be serious. Carrying containers with enough capacity to hold all the water you need for an overnight camp is also important. It means you won't keep going back and forth to water, starting a trail and perhaps trampling the bank or scaring away wildlife. You can also camp between water sources at times, which can make hiking much easier where there is little water.

Water containers come in three different forms: rigid bottles, compressible bags and the latest gimmick, hydration systems with long tubes on which we can suck while we walk, ensuring an effortless drink whenever we want. I find the last unnecessary when hiking. I would also worry about keeping the hose clean on a long hike. I've found it hard enough to clean and dry them at home after a day out.

On a long-distance hike I find a mix of rigid containers and soft bags best. The first I use for carrying water to drink during the day; the second is for use in camp.

Empty soft-drink or mineral-water bottles can be used for the rigid containers. The first ones I used didn't last more than a few weeks, which put me off using them, since I don't like having a water bottle leak while on the trail. I also don't like using plastic bottles that don't last long because they're a big environmental problem, clogging up too many landfills. However, some drink bottles do last. A quart-size bottle bought for a two-week hike in the Grand Canyon I then used as my main water bottle during my Scottish Highlands walk. It's still in use and has proved tougher than many bottles sold in outdoor recreation stores, yet it's lighter than most at just 3 ounces.

Unlike my cheap soft-drink bottle, many of the bottles found in outdoor recreation stores aren't actually very good. In particular, the lids often leak. Before buying an unfamiliar brand, I'd fill it with water and shake it to see if the lid leaks. Bottles with push-pull drinking spouts seem particularly prone to leakage. Even a slight leak can result in a lot of liquid escaping into your rucksack over a period of several hours, so a bottle with a properly sealed lid is well worth having. This is particularly important when hiking in deserts or other places where it's very hot and water sources are many hours or even days apart. Here you can't afford to lose any water.

Nalgene makes probably the toughest plastic water bottles around. They come in two food-grade materials, a polycarbonate called Lexan and HDPE, a high-density polyethylene. Both are guaranteed leakproof. Lexan is also shatter-proof, withstands subzero and boiling temperatures, resists staining, and doesn't retain odors. HDPE is pretty tough but doesn't have these properties. It is much cheaper, though. Of the two types, I prefer the slightly heavier Lexan ones because you can fill them with different drinks without any lingering taste or odor remaining. A quart-size wide-mouthed Lexan bottle weighs 5 ounces. The caps are permanently attached to the bottles, a feature you come to appreciate after you spend an hour or more searching in a stream for a dropped lid, as I have done twice. I've used Nalgene Lexan bottles for years, and they've proved very durable.

The advent of Cascade Designs collapsible Platypus bottles has drawn me away from Nalgene bottles because of their very light weight — the quart size weighs just under an ounce—and the tiny space they take up when empty. These bottles are made from a three-layer plastic laminate with welded seams. The inner layer is made from food-grade polyethylene that doesn't make water taste of plastic. However, it may absorb flavors from other liquids so it's best to put only water in them. Unlike most other collapsible containers, the Platypus bottles will stand up when a quarter or more full and can be used just like a rigid bottle. There are several different versions with options such as squirt caps, push-pull caps, and drinking tubes. For long-distance hiking I think the basic model with screw cap is best. Although the mouth of the Platypus bottle is narrow, the flat shape when empty means it's easier to fill from small streams than rigid bottles with small mouths.

For many years before I discovered Nalgene bottles, I used aluminum Sigg Drinks Bottles. I carried these on the PCT and CDT. They are very durable—I have one a few decades old that is badly scratched and dented but still functional. The insides of the bottles are coated to stop acids from fruit juices or alcoholic or isotonic drinks from eating into the aluminum. This coating also helps prevent the bottles smelling and ensures the aluminum can't contaminate the contents. An advantage of aluminum is that it keeps drinks much cooler in summer than plastic. The only minor disadvantage of these bottles is that the narrow openings make them hard to fill from seeps and trickles. Sigg Drinks Bottles are colored red, blue or green. Plain silver ones are designed for stove fuel and aren't coated inside. They're about the same weight as Nalgene Lexan bottles.

For camp use I now use two 2.5-quart Platypus bottles that together weigh just 2.7 ounces. These are easier to use because they stand up and weigh less than the gallon-size water bags I used to use. The last are still worth considering, though. My Ortlieb one (3.5 oz.)

has proved extremely tough. Nalgene, MSR, and Platypus make similar models.

On hikes where water sources aren't too far apart, I carry a quart-size bottle and the two 2.5-quart Platypus bottles. On the Arizona Trail, where water is scarce, I carried four quart bottles, two 2.5-quart ones and a gallon water bag so I could carry up to three gallons if necessary. Having seven containers means that if one leaks it's not too serious.

If a bottle springs a leak, it can be temporarily repaired with duct tape. This works particularly well on cracked lids.

CLOTHING

Many long-distance hikers carry more clothes than is necessary. This is somewhat of a generalization, but it certainly seems true based on the comments of those to whom I talk and also on the astonishment often expressed at how few clothes I carry. It may be nice to have a complete change of clothes in the evening, but with modern quick-drying synthetics it's not necessary.

This doesn't mean that I don't have other clothes to wear but rather that my clothes can all be worn together if necessary. There are no duplications.

Layering

The most efficient way to dress is in many thin layers that can be peeled off or added according to how warm or cold you feel. When hiking, you should feel comfortable but not so warm that you start sweating, as that will dampen your garments, making them likely to cool you when you stop. When you do start to overheat, you can strip a layer or two off and open up garments for ventilation. When you feel cool or stop for a rest, you can add layers so you don't get too cold.

I always carry a minimum of four layers for my upper body: wicking inner shirt, lightweight fleece top, windshirt, and rain jacket. This is all I carry if I don't expect temperatures to drop below about 35°F. If I do expect subfreezing temperatures, whether during the day or at night, I carry a second, warmer insulating garment. The basic clothing system for my legs is shorts, trail pants, and rain pants. When cold weather is expected, I add long underwear.

These layers give great versatility. I usually hike in shorts and wicking shirt, donning windshirt and trail pants if the wind picks up and I start to feel chilly. When I stop, I put the fleece top on over the other layers if necessary, removing it just before I start hiking again. If my shirt is damp with sweat when I stop to make camp and I begin to feel cold, I remove it and put the fleece on next to the skin. If this doesn't prove warm enough, the windproof shirt goes on over the fleece and then the second insulating layer if I have it. The rain garments are normally worn only when I'm hiking in rain, since overheating in them is almost inevitable, no matter what they are made of. If I feel chilly in camp with all my other clothes on, I wear my rainwear as well.

The last item in the layer system is the sleeping bag. Slipping into this, or even unzipping it and wrapping it around your shoulders, should warm you up if all your clothing doesn't.

All my hiking garments are made from synthetic materials—polyester, nylon, and polypropylene—which absorb little moisture and dry quickly when damp. They're not warm when wet. Nothing is. It's the speed of drying that makes synthetics superior to other materials. Cotton is too cold when wet and too slow drying. In cold and wet weather it can be dangerous to wear cotton next to the skin because it takes a great deal of body heat to dry it, heat that is needed to keep you warm. I don't wear cotton even in the heat, since it sticks to my skin and feels clammy. Wool does provide some warmth even when it's damp, but it's also slow drying and heavy when wet. It's fine for socks, but synthetics are lighter and more efficient for other clothing.

Next to the Skin

Base-layer garments (sometimes called *thermal underwear*) should quickly transport or wick perspiration away from the skin so it stays dry and warm. There are many wicking synthetic garments available—usually made from various polyesters or polypropylene. None of the many I've tried are quite as good as claimed by the makers, as all can be overloaded with sweat so they end up soaked. They then take longer to dry than stated, too. They're still pretty good though, keeping me fairly dry most of the time. There's little difference between the top brands in terms of performance. Fit, design, and thickness are the real differences. To work at their best, wicking synthetics need to be close fitting. Thin fabrics remove moisture and dry faster than thick ones and so are the best choice for hiking. A high collar with a zipper means you can close it up for warmth and open it for ventilation, which is useful in really cold weather. For summer hikes crew necks are fine, as are short sleeves.

Appropriate clothing in hot weather: wicking shirt, shorts, and sandals.

Long underwear is useful in cold weather. I carry a pair in all but the warmest weather. If I think I won't need a pair for a few weeks or longer, I put it in my running supply box (see pages 90–91).

Conventional-style shirts made from smooth, quick-drying polyester or nylon are good in warm weather. Ones made for hiking usually have a wicking treatment, though they aren't as efficient at removing moisture as base-layer garments. Many designs have vents under the arms that, combined with a fully opening front and sleeves that roll up, make them easy to ventilate. They're also sun-resistant and have a fair degree of wind resistance. I wouldn't carry one of these shirts instead of a wicking base layer since they're not as efficient worn under other garments in cold weather. However, I often carry one in hot places—I took one on the Arizona Trail—wearing it on its own in the heat and over the base layer when it's cool. One reason I like these shirts is their breast pockets, in which I carry maps, binoculars, and other items.

Shorts

Shorts are the ideal garments for long-distance hiking, and I wear them as often as possible. They keep your legs cool and allow complete freedom of movement. Any type will do, but I prefer ones with built-in briefs as then no underpants are needed. I also like thin, lightweight shorts so I can pull long pants over them without them feeling bulky or restrictive.

Trail Pants

On days when the wind or the temperature makes wearing shorts seem a little masochistic, I wear light polyester or nylon pants of the type often sold in stores as trail pants or wind pants. These are windproof, quick drying, breathable, durable, and bug proof. Some trail pants are made from thick materials and can be quite heavy, especially if they have lots of pockets, reinforced areas, articulated knees, and more. The lightest materials and simplest designs are best. There's no need for long pants to weigh more than 10 ounces. Pockets for your hands are nice, and that's all that's really needed in the way of features.

Because of the warmth generated by my legs, I rarely need to wear more than trail pants when hiking in the cold. If it's really wet and my legs start to feel cold I put on my rain pants (see at right). While in camp or when starting out on a really cold morning I wear wicking synthetic long pants under the trail pants if I'm carrying them.

Windshirt

My favorite upper garment and the one I wear more than any other is a thin, single-layer nylon or polyester windshirt. This can be worn over a wicking base layer or a shirt, over or under a fleece top, under a waterproof jacket, and even next to the skin. It protects against wind, showers, sunshine, and biting insects and adds a surprising amount of warmth for the weight. Many windshirts and windproof jackets are quite heavy because they have double layers of fabric, lots of pockets, drawcords, and other features. I don't use ones weighing more than 8 ounces. I like very simple designs with a full or half zipper in the front, sleeves with wide, adjustable cuffs for ventilation, and a chest pocket big enough for a map. I don't need to have a hood, as a hat will keep my head warm.

I always carry a rain jacket, so I don't require my windshirt to be water-resistant. Breathability is far more important. Shirts made from fabrics that are almost waterproof are the worst of both worlds for hiking. If it rains really hard they leak, but in dry, breezy weather they don't breathe well enough, so you get damp through condensation. They may be fine for mountain biking, trail running, or spring ski touring, but they're not suitable for long-distance hiking.

Windshirts with thin, wicking linings are also available. These are very warm for the weight, which may be no more than 8 or 9 ounces. They're not quite as versatile as a single-layer windshirt, however, and are best suited to cool- and cold-weather hikes. They can be worn as wicking underwear with other layers on top or over a wicking base layer as a shell.

Rainwear

Waterproof clothing is the most controversial and probably the most cursed item of hiker's clothing. Despite all the claims made, it is still impossible to hike in prolonged heavy rain in any rain jacket without getting damp inside. Most hikers simply produce too much moisture for it to escape through a waterproof barrier, especially one with an outside running with water.

Rain clothing is still essential because getting wet and cold can lead to hypothermia, that chilling of the body that will result in collapse and death if not checked. Being hot and sweaty inside rainwear is preferable to being sodden and shivering without it.

Waterproof-breathable garments that let some moisture out are more comfortable than ones that are just waterproof. In windy, showery weather the best fabrics stay quite dry inside. It's when it rains continuously for hours that the breathability fails. This applies no matter the fabric, in my experience. There is a difference between various waterproof-breathable materials, though. In some I get wetter sooner than in others. Gore-Tex is the market leader and the best known (it was, after all, the first), which is reflected in the price. It's still near the top in terms of performance, but there are less-expensive materials that perform at least as well. I used Sympatex garments on three long-distance hikes, including the very wet Scandinavian hike, and they performed well and proved very durable, in that all the garments were still waterproof at the end of the hikes. Both Gore-Tex and Sympatex now come in lightweight versions under the names PacLite and Sympatex Ultra-light. I've tried both and found them very breathable. Other fabrics that have worked well for me, though I haven't used them on a long hike, are Lowe Alpine's Triple Point Ceramic and Marmot's MemBrain.

Long-distance hikers need rain garments that are light in weight, low in bulk, and simple in design. That excludes most of those you'll find in the stores. Top-of-the-range garments are usually designed for mountaineering and have huge hoods designed to fit over climbing helmets, armpit zippers for ventilation, heavy reinforcement patches, internal water bottle pockets, and other weight-accumulating technical features that are unnecessary for hikers. Most of the other rain jackets are aimed at day hikers or designed for mainly street use and again have lots of weight-adding features such as myriad pockets, detachable and rollaway hoods, and lots of drawcords. The fabrics for both these types of garment are usually quite thick and heavy. They may be called lightweight or even ultralightweight, but they aren't.

There are truly lightweight rain garments available though, by which I mean jackets at 20 ounces or less and pants at around 8 ounces. They are made from light fabrics without reinforcements and have a minimum of features. All I look for in a jacket are a hood with drawcords, a front zipper with a protective flap, wide adjustable cuffs for ventilation, and a chest pocket big enough for a map. It's hard to find a garment without at least two pockets however. In that case I like two chest pockets made from mesh so that when they're open they help to vent the jacket. I also like jackets long enough to cover my backside and upper thighs. Many lightweight garments are very short, which means your upper legs get wet. Rain pants need no features at all except for a waist drawcord. Zippers at the ankle, so you can pull them on over your footwear, are nice but not essential. As I wear rain pants far less often than a rain jacket, low weight is the most important criterion.

Depending on how much you have to wear it and what it's made from rainwear may or may not still be waterproof at the end of a long-distance hike. It is very likely that the outer water-repellent treatment, which makes rain bead up on the surface and then run off, won't last. When the water no longer beads, this doesn't mean the garment isn't waterproof but that the outer layer will absorb rain and become very wet. This, in

Rain pants are easy to put on over boots if they have full-length zippers.

turn, reduces breathability so more condensation forms inside, and you feel damper. Restoring the water repellency can be done by putting the garment in a warm, not hot, tumble dryer (with all fastenings done up to prevent them damaging the fabric) or ironing it. The first may be possible in self-service laundries in trailside towns; the second seems unlikely unless an iron is available where you are staying. Both the dryer and the iron will revive the repellency to some extent, but eventually you'll have to restore the repellency with one of the various sprays and wash-in treatments. I've used Nikwax TX-Direct with success. I've never bothered during a long hike though; I leave this task until I'm back home.

Wearing rainwear only when necessary will keep it waterproof and water-repellent longer. This is where the windshirt is useful, since it can be worn in windy or showery weather. If you have only a rain jacket, it has to be worn on these occasions.

Insulating Garments

Insulating garments are needed to keep you warm at rest stops in cool weather and in camp. I always carry at least one warm top. I generally find that I get too warm hiking in an insulating garment, though in strong winds and very cold weather I might need to do so. Usually the combination of inner shirt, windshirt, and rain jacket is enough to keep me warm.

The start and finish of a long-distance hike often see the coldest weather. When this is so, I carry two insulating garments, sending one on ahead when no longer needed. Very occasionally I've carried three warm garments to cope with subfreezing temperatures. In keeping with the layering principle, I find this much more efficient than having a single, very warm garment. Shuttling garments around means not carrying more weight than necessary. For example, on the south-to-north walk through the Yukon, which started on the still partly snow-covered Chilkoot Trail, I began with three warm layers—a light fleece top, a medium-weight fleece jacket, and a down sweater. After the first few weeks I sent the light fleece and the down sweater to a resupply point a few weeks from the end of the walk, as I no longer needed them. Toward the finish, when temperatures began to drop again as summer came to an end, I was glad I had them again.

As with rainwear, most of the insulating garments available are unnecessarily heavy for long-distance hiking because they are mainly designed for either high-altitude mountaineering or current street fashion. When selecting insulating clothing, always look for lightweight fabrics and a minimum of features.

Fleece is the standard material for warm wear; my basic insulating top is made from fleece. Fleece is quite warm for the weight, comfortable over a wide temperature range, breathable, durable, and quick drying. Many fleece garments are heavy and bulky, though. As this first warm garment is one I may wear when hiking if it's really cold, I want one that fits into the layering system. The lightest, thinnest fleeces are best for this, by which I mean ones lighter than 200-weight fleece. Fleeces like this need weigh no more than 12 ounces. Some are less. The Polartec 150 fleece sweater that was my only warm clothing for most of my Scottish Highlands walk weighs just 9.5 ounces. It's a simple design, merely an over-the-head top with a neck zipper and high collar and no pockets, drawcords, hoods, or reinforcement patches to add weight. An alternative to a thin fleece is an expedition or winter-weight base-layer top. Indeed, some of these are just about indistinguishable from fleece. Only the labels are different.

When temperatures in camp or at rest stops are likely to regularly drop below 40°F, I carry a second, warmer insulating garment. If subfreezing temperatures are likely, I have sometimes carried a third warm top. The choices here are between a heavier fleece and a synthetic or down-filled top. Having carried different combinations on different walks, I have decided the filled tops are a better choice than the fleece if I'm carrying only one piece of extra-warm wear because they are lighter and more compact for the warmth.

When I have taken along a fleece top, it's been a medium-weight one made from 200-weight fabric. Thicker fleeces take up too much room in the pack and weigh too much. Fleece jackets weighing 18 to 20 ounces were my main warm garments on the Pacific Crest Trail and on the Yukon and Scandinavia walks. These worked fine and proved very durable.

Ordinary fleece isn't windproof, which is one of the reasons it's very breathable. Windproof fleece (whether with a membrane laminated to it or a separate shell or lining) might seem ideal for the long-distance hiker, but it lacks the versatility of a fleece-windshirt combination while performing no better and weighing no less. It's usually too hot to wear when hiking unless temperatures are well below freezing and winds are high.

Of the insulating fills, down is the lightest for the warmth given and wonderfully warm and luxurious to wear. I carried a 14-ounce down vest in the High Sierra on the Pacific Crest Trail, and throughout the Arizona Trail, and an 18-ounce down sweater in the Yukon. The cold dry conditions found in those places were ideal for down

A full-length waterproof jacket suitable for the worst winter weather.

garments. For hiking, very basic down garments are best. Lots of features and complex constructions aren't needed. Down garments designed for mountaineering can be quite heavy. I regard any down top weighing more than 20 ounces as too heavy for long-distance hiking.

In really wet climates, synthetic fills are probably better. I prefer down for sleeping bags, but I don't want to sit outside at rest stops or in camp in a down garment when it's wet. Synthetic fills aren't as warm, weight for weight, as down, but since cold wet weather is usually milder than cold, dry weather, this isn't a problem. On the Continental Divide I had a rather heavy 23-ounce synthetic-filled jacket, while on the Canadian Rockies walk I had an even heavier 26-ounce one. That was back in the 1980s. Since then lighter, more compact synthetic fills and shell fabrics have appeared. Of the few lightweight garments available, I've found the Moonstone Cirrus Pullover excellent, though I've not used it on a long-distance hike. It's filled with Microloft and weighs 12 ounces for the medium size. Its packed bulk is quite a bit less than a 200-weight fleece. Alternatives include GoLite's Cool Parka, filled with Polarguard 3D and weighing 13.5 to 19.5 ounces, depending on size, and Patagonia's Puffball Pullover, filled with Microloft and weighing 13 ounces. Synthetic-filled vests weigh even less, around 8 to 10 ounces.

Whatever type of insulating garment you choose, it's a good idea to get one that is oversized so you can pull it on over all your other layers. Having to take off your windshirt or rain jacket in order to put your warm top on means losing some warmth, especially when it's windy.

Having tried various combinations of garments, I would now carry a thin fleece and an insulated garment. I think this is the lightest and most efficient combination. The total weight need be no more than 24 ounces, less than the weight of many fleece garments that wouldn't provide the same warmth or versatility. I'd choose down for hikes where the weather should be fairly dry, synthetic fills for hikes where it's likely to be damp much of the time. On the hot, dry Arizona Trail, I carried a 10-ounce fleece top and a 14-ounce down vest as my warm clothing. This combination proved to be ideal because I could wear the fleece for hiking on chilly mornings without overheating and back it up with the vest in camp.

Hats

A warm hat is one of the most important items of clothing to carry. Because the supply of blood to your head is constant, you can lose masses of heat in cold weather if you don't put a hat on. I always carry a simple watch cap (or stocking cap) made from a thermal wicking fabric or a thin fleece. Such hats weigh only around 2 ounces yet provide an amazing amount of warmth. Because hats are so important, I usually also carry a thin thermal balaclava or neck gaiter as spare headwear. (I did once lose a hat on a

Putting on windproof clothing, hat, and gloves on a windswept summit in the Scottish Highlands.

long-distance hike and don't want to repeat that experience.) This can be worn under the watch cap in really cold weather. Again the weight is only a couple of ounces. If there's likely to be much rain or snow, I prefer a fleece-lined waterproof-breathable peaked cap. These are great in stormy weather because you can wear one instead of a jacket hood in most conditions, which means much better ventilation around your neck and more freedom of movement, or under a hood when the weather is really extreme. The peak keeps rain and snow off your face, and the fleece lining keeps your head warm. The most efficient designs have stiffened peaks that don't flap in the wind and neck cords or attachments for cords to keep the hat on your head in strong winds. Weights are around 3 to 4 ounces.

Hats are needed to keep off the sun as well as the cold. It took me a while to realize this. I hiked through the deserts of southern California on the Pacific Crest Trail without a hat, though I did wear a bandanna around my head to keep

the sweat out of my eyes. In New Mexico on the Continental Divide Trail I discovered that a light, brimmed hat helped keep me cool as well as protecting my face and neck from the sun. Sun hats come in two styles: ones with wide brims all the way around and others with a peak and a flap to shade the ears and neck. I have both designs and overall prefer the brimmed hat because I've found the neck flap on peaked caps can be a bit hot. Indeed, as mine is detachable, I've often taken it off, which rather defeats the purpose. In theory, lighter-colored hats are cooler because they reflect rather than absorb heat, but I can't say that I've actually noticed any difference. Pale hats do show dirt and sweat stains more, however. A sun hat is the one garment I'm happy to purchase in cotton because absorbing lots of water and drying slowly are positive attributes in this case. Soak a cotton hat and put it back on, and your head will feel cool for ages. A wet synthetic hat will give you the same initial refreshing feeling but will dry very quickly. My favorite sun hat is the Canadian-made cotton Tilley Hat. Mine has gone on three long-distance hikes and masses of shorter ones. It looks very battered—which I think gives it character—but still keeps the sun off. For some reason, it's one of the few bits of gear to which I've developed a sentimental attachment, as I discovered on the Scottish Highlands walk when I left it behind at a rest stop. My reason said to leave it behind, it's only a hat, you can get another. Emotionally I felt upset at this. Tattered and faded it might be, but it was full of memories. Sentiment won, and I went back to search for it, feeling unreasonably happy when I found it.

Gloves

A pair of light gloves or mitts can make a huge difference to your comfort on a cold day. Cold hands can be painful and can make routine tasks difficult. I nearly always carry at least a pair of thin thermal gloves weighing 1 or 2 ounces. If cold weather is expected, I also carry a thicker pair of fleece mitts or gloves with a waterproof-breathable shell. Or at least I almost always do. I have twice been caught out without adequate hand coverings. The first time was near the end of the Canadian Rockies walk. My thermal gloves and thin wool mittens were completely inadequate in the subfreezing temperatures and snow showers I experienced for the last week. I solved the problem by wearing a spare pair of thick wool socks on my hands. Eight years later, the lesson not fully learned, I set off on the Scottish Highlands walk with no gloves at all, even though cold and stormy weather was predicted. Three days out I found myself floundering around on a steep, rocky, mountain ridge in a whiteout. Wet snow blown by a strong wind soon froze my bare hands, which I couldn't put in my pockets because I needed them for balance and to grab the occasional rock. Again a spare pair of socks came to the rescue.

Rather than separate mitts and shells, I carry shelled fleece mitts because these are lighter in weight (around 4 ounces) and lower in bulk. I get them big enough to wear over the thermal gloves, if necessary. Most of the time the thermal gloves are adequate because my hands heat up really quickly, but it's nice to have the mitts as a backup. At the height of summer I mail them forward to be picked up when the temperatures start to drop again.

Color

As with hats, light-colored clothing is meant to be cooler in the sun. Again, I can't say I've actually noticed any difference. Light clothing is also supposed to be less attractive to biting insects. I haven't noticed this either. Ticks are more visible on light clothing though, which could be a reason to choose light colors. The main reason I prefer at least some light-colored clothing is because it stands out better in photographs. Bright colors, especially reds, are even better, but as I've already said, I prefer not to stand out in the wilds. Pale clothing is a good compromise.

Carrying Clothes

If you arrive at a campsite wearing sweaty or rain-soaked clothes, you'll want to be able to change into dry clothing so you don't get chilled. To ensure I can do this, I carry items like trail pants and insulated garments in a waterproof stuff sack. Note that the stuff sacks that come with many items of clothing are not usually waterproof. They might be fine for organizing other items, but they're not good for storing clothes unless carried inside a waterproof stuff sack or pack liner. I don't bother with stuff sacks for rainwear—they just add weight. Rain gear gets squeezed into a corner of the pack. If it's wet I lash it to the outside or stuff it into a mesh pocket if my pack has any.

Caring for Clothes

Sweat-soaked, dirt-encrusted clothes do not work efficiently at transmitting body moisture or keeping you warm. Rinsing garments out every so often keeps them fairly fresh and maintains a reasonable performance level. I don't use soap for this, just water carried well away from the source (at least 200 feet) in a water bag. I dunk the clothes in a cook pot to wash them. Wet garments can be hung on the pack to dry or, in camp, on a line strung between trees. If I don't think I can get clothes dry quickly and easily, I don't wash them. Clothing that has been washed in the rain does feel very soft, so if there are heavy showers I do sometimes hang clothes out in the rain. If it's mild enough you can just wear clothes in the rain and have them wash on you. I did this inadvertently on the Scottish Highlands walk when I left my pack on a pass while I climbed the summit above. I was wearing a windshirt and pants, but not rain gear. Just as I approached the summit, the sky turned black and a cloudburst ensued with huge drops of rain and soft hail. I was quickly soaked to the skin, though not cold, since there was no wind. By the time the storm finished 45 minutes later, the hillsides were white with foaming streams. After hiking for an hour, I was dry again, and my clothes (and hair) were fresh and soft.

Many trail towns have self-service laundries. When I find one, I wash everything that needs it, sometimes sitting there in just my rainwear.

When using a self-service laundry, check the heat settings on the machines and the labels in your clothing. Some synthetics melt and shrink very easily. I reduced some long underwear to doll's size in a hot dryer on the Pacific Crest Trail by failing to check the heat setting. Luckily I'd just finished the coldest section of the hike.

ACCESSORIES

Umbrella

Until I hiked the Arizona Trail I'd only ever carried an umbrella for a couple of days, just enough to show me the value of carrying one. Using an umbrella means you don't need to wear a rain jacket and so don't have problems with overheating and condensation. However umbrellas are hard to use when it's windy and can break in strong, gusty winds, so I always carry rainwear. Once the wind builds and the rain starts coming sideways, my experience suggests umbrellas are too much hassle. I prefer to don my rain jacket. On calm days or in the shelter of a forest an umbrella is useful. One is also useful as a sunshade in hot, open country, as I found on the Arizona Trail. If my umbrella had had a reflective outer (which can be made by taping a layer of Mylar over it) it would have kept me even cooler, as I realized when I briefly tried another hiker's umbrella. The umbrella I used in Arizona was a GoLite Dome, which weighs 9.5 ounces and is only umbrella I know of specifically made for hikers. The Dome was designed by Ray Jardine, who has used umbrellas on many long-distance hikes, and is both stronger and lighter than standard models.

Using an umbrella and two trekking poles isn't really feasible. On the Arizona Trail I tried tying the umbrella to the top of the pack and simply balancing it there, but that didn't work well as the umbrella kept slipping to the side. I ended up using it with just one pole.

I found the umbrella easiest to use on good trails and when crossing open terrain. On rough trails or where there was dense vegetation above waist height, carrying the umbrella proved awkward and interfered with balance, so I strapped it to my pack.

Bandanna

The uses for a bandanna are limited only by your imagination. I always carry one and often thread it through the webbing on the shoulder straps of my rucksack so it's handy for wiping sweat off my face. Other possible uses include headband, potholder, dishcloth, washcloth, towel, sling, and handkerchief. Because absorbency is an important property, I prefer 100 percent cotton bandannas. Ones made from a cotton and synthetic mix don't soak up as much moisture.

Lighting

Some form of lighting is just about essential at night in camp and also on the trail if you find yourself hiking after dark, which can happen if the place you hoped would be suitable for a campsite turns out not to be and you have to keep going. Inexpensive flashlights are fine for short hikes but usually aren't very reliable. For a long-distance hike, a top-quality light is best.

A headlamp is great when setting up a tent or tarp or when cooking in the dark because it leaves both hands free. I've used Petzl headlamps for decades and have always found them reliable. When nights are long, the Petzl Zoom is excellent, as it has a powerful 100-foot beam, and the flat MN1203 4.5-volt battery lasts for up to 17 hours. However the Zoom is quite heavy at 11.5 ounces, and a spare battery weighs another 5.5 ounces. Flat batteries are also hard to find in many small towns. Instead of the flat battery you can get an adapter that weighs 2.5 ounces complete with three AA batteries, which last up to 8 hours each. That makes the weight for the Zoom 8.5 ounces, 11 ounces with spare batteries. Even lighter, though, is the Petzl Micro, which weighs just 5 ounces complete with 2 AA batteries. This has a 30-foot beam and a battery life of around 5 hours. I find it's all I need in summer, and it's the light I've carried on most long-distance walks.

While headlamps are a boon in camp, a handheld flashlight is better for walking since you can hold it low down to the ground. This makes it easier to see the definition of the ground ahead than with a beam mounted on your forehead. A flashlight gives strong shadows, whereas a headlamp gives very flat light with little detail. A handheld light can also be easily directed anywhere. Of course, you can hold a headlamp in your hands, and you can mount a flashlight on your head by attaching it to a headband. For example, I can convert my Mini-Maglite flashlight, which weighs 5 ounces complete with 2 AA batteries, into a headlamp with a Nite Ize headband that weighs 1 ounce. It's not quite as comfortable as a real headlamp and the light can't be swiveled up or down, but it's still functional.

It's advisable to carry spare batteries and bulbs, or you might find yourself without a light when you really need one. Alkaline batteries fade rapidly in cold weather (the times quoted above are for 70°F). Lithium batteries last much longer and weigh less, too. Petzl and Maglite headlamps and flashlights come with spare bulbs lodged in the housing.

Candles

I prefer to use batteries only when absolutely necessary due to the weight, the cost, and the pollution caused during manufacture and disposal, so I carry candles for light in camp. Candlelight is softer and more pleasing than electric light anyway. It feels friendlier and natural since it has a warm glow rather than the cold light of a bulb. It also gives a little heat on cold nights. I like it for reading and for writing in my journal. A headlamp is best for cooking, as you need to be able to see into the pot. Candle lanterns are convenient, but I don't bother with them on long-distance hikes due to the weight. Instead I stand a candle on the ground or on top of a pot or pot lid with my stove windscreen behind to reflect the light and keep breezes off. The short stubby candles designed to fit candle lanterns are ideal for this because they're fairly stable. These could be put in supply boxes to ensure you always had some. They last for 10 to 30 hours depending on the size and weigh 4 to 7 ounces. Stores along the trail are likely to sell only household candles. These can be cut in two to make them more stable. Whichever sort of candle I use, I always make sure it's placed so that if it falls over it won't set anything on fire. I never bring a lit candle into the inner tent.

Wash Kit

Very little is needed in the way of a wash kit. In a small plastic or nylon bag I carry a tooth-brush and either moist wipes in a sealed bag or phosphate-free biodegradable soap. I don't bring along toothpaste, so I can clean my teeth when I want and not have to bother with where I spit. Toothpaste should be kept out of backcountry water. It's best if you spit it into sand or mineral soil, rather than vegetation. The wipes and soap are so I can wash my hands after going to the toi-let. Washing my hands with soap seems a wise precaution against catching giardiasis or any other bug carried in feces (see pages 94–95). The advan-tage of wipes is that they leave no trace behind because they can easily be carried out of the wilderness as garbage. They are also useful when water is in short supply since they are premoist-ened. When using soap you should use the mini-mum amount and wash at least 200 yards from any water source. Water for this can be carried in a bottle or cook pot.

For washing other parts of the body I don't use soap, just water. A bandanna will do as a wash-cloth, and a fleece jacket can double as a towel. A water bag hung from the branch of a tree makes a good shower, but I don't bother carrying the var-ious shower attachments that are available to fit water bags. If the bag is left in the sun for a few hours, the water will be quite warm, especially if the bag is black or dark in color.

A traditional way of wilderness washing is simply to jump in a lake or stream, with clothes on if you want to wash them as well. However, in addition to trail dirt, a hiker's body is likely to be sticky with sunscreen or bug repellent, chemicals that should be kept out of backcountry water. Also, someone may be camping or hiking down-stream and taking drinking water from the same

source. It's probably okay to bathe in a large lake or river where the grime from your body will soon be diluted and washed away, but it's best to stay out of small creeks and pools. Never use soap if you go swimming.

A hot shower is one of the joys of a resupply point. Small plastic bottles or sachets of sham-poo plus small bars of soap can be put in your running supply box so you don't have to buy more than you want and then dump it every time. You can use what you need and then send the rest to the next resupply point.

Comb

Hikers who've been on the trail for a week or more are never going to look clean and shiny when they arrive in a town. However, not look-ing too grubby or scruffy only seems fair on local people and may also mean you receive a friend-lier reception. Combing your hair makes a huge difference to your appearance, so I carry a small plastic comb in the wash kit.

FIRST AID

Training is more important than equipment when it comes to first aid. Having some knowl-edge as to what to do in an emergency and also how to treat minor injuries is important for long-distance walkers. Taking a wilderness first-aid course is a very good idea, especially for solo hikers. A first-aid manual is a good reference work to have at home, too. The standard here is *Medicine for Mountaineering*, edited by James Wilkerson, but this comprehensive volume is far too heavy to carry in the pack. There are first-aid leaflets that could be carried, though.

First-aid kits for long-distance hiking are always a compromise. You cannot carry every-thing you might need. I used to carry a fairly hefty kit weighing a pound. Now I carry a few items in a nylon bag with a total weight of 4 ounces. I usually include the following:

- first-aid leaflet
- 2- by 3-inch sheet of Second Skin for blisters

- roll of 1-inch adhesive micropore tape for holding Second Skin and other dressings in place and for taping up a sprained ankle
- 2 4- by 4-inch nonadhesive absorbent gauze dressings for burns and other wounds
- 3 or 4 antiseptic wipes for cleaning wounds or blisters
- 12 assorted plasters for cuts
- 2 safety pins for fastening slings and bandages
- 10 foil-wrapped painkillers—ibuprofen or aspirin
- scissors (if not part of knife)
- tweezers (if not part of knife)

If scissors and tweezers are part of your knife (see page 182), you don't need to carry separate ones in the kit. Items carried for other purposes can be called into play if necessary for first-aid purposes. A bandanna makes a bandage for a large wound and can be used to tie up a sprained ankle. Clothing can also be utilized for these purposes. Extra first-aid items can be placed in the running supply box so the kit can be refilled whenever necessary.

On a long-distance hike in a really remote area it may be advisable to carry prescription painkillers and wide-spectrum antibiotics. Talk to your doctor about this. I carried both in the northern Canadian Rockies and the Yukon.

SUN PROTECTION

Long days of hiking in the sun can be wonderful—but not if you get sunburned. Red, raw skin is very painful, and if sunburn is repeated over time, it can lead to skin cancer. The sun is at its strongest in the middle four hours of the day, so this is when protection is most needed. It's also stronger at higher altitudes due to the thinner air. To avoid sunburn when you are hiking in the open, you can wear a sun hat, hike under an umbrella, and wear long clothing. Not all clothing keeps out the ultraviolet rays that cause burning, by the way, though most tightly woven synthetics do. Some clothing now comes with a SPF rating—see below.

However, most hikers prefer to hike in the heat wearing shorts and short-sleeved shirts. Also, sun can reflect off snow (or water or sand) and burn you from below. A hat or umbrella is no use then. Sunscreen should always be carried and applied to any exposed skin when it's sunny, even if the sun is hazy.

Sunscreen

All sunscreens have a sun protection factor (SPF). The higher the number, the greater the protection. For example, a sunscreen with a SPF of 10 means that you can stay in the sun for 10 times longer than without sunscreen before your skin starts to burn. Once the SPF gets above 15, however, the extra protection gained is apparently minimal. Whatever the SPF, sunscreen needs reapplying every couple of hours or so, as it's likely to get wiped off or washed off in sweat, even if it's labeled "waterproof." Be aware that the ingredients of some sunscreens can cause allergic reactions in some people, so it's best to try sunscreens in advance of a hike. Para-aminobenzoic acid (known as PABA) seems to be the component most implicated in this.

Sunscreen can be applied to the lips but some types taste unpleasant. Lip balm is a better bet—a small tube weighs only a fraction of an ounce.

Sunglasses

Sunglasses are needed when you are hiking on snow. Otherwise the surface of the eyes can burn, leading to a very painful condition called snow blindness and a temporary loss of vision. It's best to buy sunglasses from a specialist outdoor equipment retailer, as some cheap glasses won't keep out ultraviolet light. Unless you'll be spending much time on glaciers or big snowfields, glasses with side shields aren't necessary. Glasses should have large curved lenses, though. In addition, sunglasses are useful to cut down the glare from very bright sand or rock.

KEEPING INSECTS AWAY

Insect Repellent

On most long hikes there will be times and areas where biting insects can make life almost unbearable. Although there are several ways to minimize the aggravation (see page 216), insect repellent is just about essential. The standard for years has been repellent containing N,N-diethyl-meta-toluamide (known as DEET), a powerful chemical that can melt plastic and damage some synthetic fabrics. DEET is absorbed into the bloodstream and can provoke a bad reaction in some people. Even for those people who don't react to DEET, it's probably not wise to use it frequently or in high-strength concentrations. Studies have shown a concentration of 35 percent DEET to be just as effective as higher concentrations. Repellents containing 35 percent DEET or less are widely available.

Alternatives to DEET include citronella and eucalyptus oil. I've found the latter quite effective, and it's what I now use. I put repellent on any exposed skin as well as on my hat, which helps keep insects from buzzing around my head.

Mosquito Coils

Green coils of pyrethrum or other insecticides will keep some insects away, especially if used in a tent vestibule or under a tarp. I find them effective against mosquitoes and, to a lesser extent, no-see-ums. A pack of 12 coils, each lasting 8 to 10 hours, weighs 7 ounces.

Head Net

Repellent doesn't stop all insects from biting— black flies in the Yukon ignored it completely— and even when it does, it may not stop them from buzzing in clouds around your face and crawling over your hair. In those circumstances the answer is a head net made of fine mesh and worn over a wide brimmed hat so that none of it touches your skin, to prevent insects biting through it. The neck end should have a drawcord and be long enough so as not to leave a gap between it and your clothing. Nets weigh an ounce or so. I've found dark colors best because I can see more clearly through them than pale ones.

SANITATION

How to deal with human waste is dealt with on page 219. Apart from toilet paper, the only equipment involved is a small plastic trowel, weighing around 1.5 ounces. Heavier metal ones (6 ounces or so) are less likely to break and are worth carrying by groups. Of course, if you have an ice ax, it can be used for digging "catholes," so there's no need for a trowel.

KNIFE

A small, folding knife is essential on a long-distance hike. A large heavy knife isn't required, however. I've always used one of the lighter Swiss Army Knives (SAKs). The features other than a blade that I find particularly useful are scissors and tweezers. On my last long hike I carried the tiny Victorinox Classic SAK, which has a file-screwdriver in addition to the above blades, and which weighs just 0.7 of an ounce. I use the blade for slicing food, shaving feather sticks for fire lighting, and more. The scissors are used for opening food packets and for cutting all manner of things, from cord for guylines or shoelaces to Second Skin and tape for blisters and toenails and fingernails. Tweezers are useful for tick removal (see page 216).

If the Classic SAK seems too small, the Spartan, which weighs 2.5 ounces, is a good alternative. As well as bigger blades and scissors, it has can and bottle openers plus a corkscrew, which may well appeal to some people.

REPAIR KIT

During a long hike it is almost inevitable that some items of gear will need repairing. Usually these repairs are quite simple to carry out as long as you have the right tools. I carry a very basic

The tiny Victorinox Classic Swiss Army Knife.

lightweight repair kit in a small stuff sack. The total weight is about 4 ounces. The usual contents are

- sticky-backed ripstop nylon for patching any nylon items from clothing to sleeping bag
- duct tape for holding together broken items such as pack frames and tent poles
- 12-by-18-inch piece of nylon for patching large holes or tears
- tiny tube of epoxy or seam seal for coating stitch holes in rain wear, fly sheet or tarp to prevent leaking
- 2 sewing needles in different sizes
- 2 sewing machine needles for heavy-duty sewing
- sewing awl for heavy-duty sewing
- several long lengths of sewing thread in different weights
- cotter pin for rethreading drawcords

I also carry the stove maintenance kit with the repair items along with a self-inflating mattress repair kit if appropriate.

Nylon Cord

The repair bag also contains 50 feet of nylon parachute cord, which weighs 4 ounces. I've used lengths of this cord to lash together a companion's broken pack frame and to replace broken shoelaces and snapped underfoot gaiter straps. However, it has many other uses: bearbagging food, guylines for tarp and tent, clothesline, tying items such as wet clothing to the pack, lowering a pack down or pulling it up steep ground, and as a chin strap for a hat. When cut, the ends of cord need sealing with a flame to prevent their unraveling.

WRISTWATCH

Escaping from the constraints of a clock-dominated society is one of the pleasures of the wilderness. Time is measured in days, not hours and minutes. The sun going down and the sun coming up are the only crucial times of day. Until, that is, you're approaching a resupply point and need to get there before the post office shuts, or you're wondering whether you can cross the next pass before dark. It's also surprisingly easy to forget which day of the week it is, as it doesn't matter until you realize you'll be arriving at the next post office on a Sunday. For these reasons I always carry a watch that tells the date and day of the week as well as the time. An alarm can be useful if you have to get up early in order to reach a supply point before it closes. Generally, though, I don't like being woken up by an alarm when on a long hike (or at home either). I prefer to wake naturally when my body has rested enough. After a week or so on the trail I find I settle down into a routine that means I wake at roughly the same time each day anyway. A watch is also useful for navigation as you can use it to time sections. My Suunto Altimax is also a wrist altimeter (see pages 185 and 187) and barometer (see page 205), which makes it even more useful for navigation and weather forecasting. It weighs 2 ounces.

BINOCULARS

A small pair of binoculars has many uses. I started carrying them for watching wildlife but soon found they were good for checking the terrain ahead, especially when hiking cross-country, and surveying valleys from high points for possible river fords. I also use them to examine rock features and patterns high on cliffs and flowers and other plants that I can't get close to. My 8 x 21 pair weighs 5.5 ounces and is small enough to carry in a pocket so it's always accessible.

SAFETY ITEMS

A few items are occasionally carried purely in case of difficulty or danger.

Cellular Phones

Cellular phones have become quite controversial for backcountry use. This is partly because many people go hiking in part to escape from such things and partly because they have been misused by people calling for help when they didn't really need it. However, there have been some cases where a rescue was effected, and lives saved, because a cell phone was used to call for help.

If you're considering carrying a cell phone on your hike, you first need to check whether it will work where you are going. On trails near towns it may do so; in remote wildernesses it probably won't. Even if the area is covered, reception may not be possible in deep valleys or thick forest, as it's dependent on line of sight. Batteries can fail, too. A cell phone should be regarded as a backup that might be useful and not as a substitute for good wilderness skills.

Signaling Devices

I don't think signaling devices are needed on popular trails, though solo hikers may want to carry one for peace of mind (for both the hiker and those family or friends back at home). A pack of miniflares weighs 8 ounces, and each flare reaches 250 feet and lasts 6 seconds. The only item I carry that is purely for signaling is a small plastic whistle that produces an amazingly loud and piercing sound. Mine weighs 0.8 ounce. A headlamp or flashlight can also be used for signaling. With a whistle or flashlight, the international distress signal is six blasts or flashes, followed by a pause and then repeated.

In wooded country the quickest way to attract attention would be to build a large smoky fire. To attract attention from searching aircraft you could also spread light or bright colored articles of gear on the ground. A shiny object such as a mirror, stove windscreen, watch face, or camera lens could be used to reflect sunlight in the hope that this would be seen.

Rope

On most long hikes ropes aren't needed. Hikers used to carry them, as I did, for roped river crossings. This is now regarded as highly dangerous and should not be done (see chapter 8, pages 194–98). Ropes can be used to safeguard hikers as they cross sections of steep snow early in the season. I used a rope for this once in the High Sierra on the Pacific Crest Trail. That section of the PCT and the start of the Continental Divide Trail, where again there was still much snow, are the only times I've carried a rope on a long-distance hike. Full-weight climbing rope isn't needed—7 mm line is fine. About 50 or 60 feet should be adequate. If you do carry a rope, you need to know how to use it, of course, which means the right knots to use and being able to belay.

Bear Repellent Spray

Capsicum-based pepper sprays are said to be effective at repelling bears, if used correctly. They could be worth carrying in grizzly bear habitat. To be of any use, the spray would have to be carried in a quick-draw holster. You'd have to react very quickly, too. I've never carried one, though I may do so on my next hike in grizzly country. A pepper spray isn't a substitute for taking proper precautions in bear country. (For safe food storage, see page 83; for hiking in bear country, see page 215.)

NAVIGATION

Navigation and route finding are covered in chapter 8. Here I just look briefly at the equipment needed.

Trail Guide

On well-documented trails like the Pacific Crest Trail and the Appalachian Trail, a trail guide is likely to be your main navigational tool. Where trail guides are bulky and heavy, like the two volumes that cover the PCT, you can split them into sections so you don't carry more than is necessary between supply sections. Sections can be mailed in your supply boxes.

Maps

Some trail guides come complete with maps. Where the trail is well marked and clear on the ground, these may be all you need. Elsewhere large-scale topographic maps will be needed. Maps weigh from 1 to 4 ounces, depending on the size.

Compass

A small orienteering compass such as one of the basic Silva models is all that a hiker needs. On some trails it may hardly, if ever, be needed—I used mine only once or twice on the Pacific Crest Trail. In other areas it might be used every day or even many times a day. I always keep my compass handy in a pocket where I can find it quickly. A good way to become lost is to have your compass in your pack and decide you can't be bothered getting it out when you need it.

Altimeter

An altimeter can be a useful navigational tool when hiking cross-country, especially in poor visibility. I wear a wrist model that is also a watch.

Global Positioning System

Global positioning system (GPS) receivers are the latest navigational aid. I've tried several of these, and used one on sections of the Arizona Trail in order to follow the proposed line of the trail in areas where it has not been built. They can be useful for confirming or ascertaining your position in featureless terrain and for directing you to a point whose coordinates you have entered into the GPS. I can see that one might have been valuable on my Yukon and Canadian Rockies hikes, but I wouldn't carry the weight of one on a trail hike such as the Pacific Crest or Appalachian. If you do use a GPS, you still need to carry and be able to use a map and compass. A GPS may not be able to receive signals in dense forest or when surrounded by high mountains or with a cliff above you. Batteries can run out, and the GPS may not work if dropped. A GPS works best in conjunction with a map and compass.

SNOW GEAR

These specialist items are covered in chapter 9.

RECORDING

Journal

Virtually all long-distance hikers like to have some record of their adventure. A journal can be a detailed account of every day of the hike or just brief notes listing distance traveled, place camped, weather, and other data. I actually do both, keeping a data record at the back of my journal and a day-by-day account at the front. The data record acts as an index so I can quickly refer to the day I camped at a certain spot long after I've forgotten which month it was, never mind which day. The amount of detail you keep determines how large a journal you need. I

Writing in a journal at a rest stop in the mountains of Norway.

mostly use small (7 by 4 inches) black notebooks with waterproof covers that weigh 4 to 6 ounces and have 130 to 180 pages. One of these lasts me a month at most, so I need several per hike. New ones I send in supply boxes. Logically, full ones should be sent home but I must admit that my journals are so valuable to me that I prefer to carry them to ensure they are safe. In addition to your writing, you may want to include drawings, cuttings, and any other embellishments in your journals.

Weather Data

For years I've carried a small thermometer and kept records of the overnight temperatures at every camp. That's how I know that the coldest night on my Pacific Crest Trail hike was 14°F on 27 May near Bullfrog Lake in the High Sierra.

Now, rather than just a thermometer, I carry a Brunton/Silva Alba WindWatch that records the wind speed and barometric pressure as well. With battery this weighs 1.75 ounces.

Altimeter

My wrist altimeter can calculate the amount of footage climbed each day, which I then record in my journal. When I've checked this against the contour lines on a map, it's been pretty accurate—though it is affected by rapid changes in air pressure, since that's what the instrument measures.

Photography

A photographic record of a long-distance hike can bring back great memories and also be a way to show others what the country you walked through was like. The problem with photography is the weight of the equipment and the time it takes. Because I make part of my living from selling photographs and giving slide shows, I carry more equipment than most long-distance hikers, though far less than most professional photographers regard as the bare minimum.

For most hikers, a quality compact camera or lightweight single lens reflex (SLR) should be adequate. The weight need be no more than about 8 ounces for the compact and 12 ounces for the SLR (without a lens). Zoom lenses are useful for composition, though not essential. A 28 to 80 or 28 to 105 zoom lens is the most versatile single lens. If you want good-quality photographs, remember that the lens is more important than the camera. Rather than being impressed by the modes and features a camera has, most of which you'll never use, the sharpness of the lens is the factor on which to concentrate. The film you use matters, too. For slide shows and paper publication, transparency film is needed. Slow speeds, 100 ISO or less, provide the best quality. Prints are the easiest photographs to show to others and can be pasted into your journal of the hike. With print film, higher speeds can still provide good-quality pictures.

Film can be sent in supply boxes along with prepaid processing mailers so that film can be sent straight to the processing lab and then home. You might have someone back home check your developed film and let you know if you need to correct such problems as consistent under- or overexposure. I average a 36-shot film a day. Most people would use less film, but it's better to have too much film than too little. Film weighs around an ounce a roll.

Films can be scanned into a computer for viewing, manipulation, or downloading to a Web page. If this is your main intention, a digital camera could be a better choice. With a digital camera you can see each picture on a screen straight after taking it and delete it if you don't like it. You don't need film, though storage cards would be needed. These are very thin and weigh a fraction of an ounce. They can be reused, too, so they could be returned to you after the images had been downloaded to a computer at your base. Prints can be made from digital images, of course.

Cameras are vulnerable to dust, rain, grit, snow, and being dropped or knocked on hard surfaces. It makes sense to carry your camera in a padded pouch. This can be attached to your pack hipbelt or slung bandolier style on a sling across your body so you can use your camera whenever you want. Cameras stored in packs don't take many pictures.

ENTERTAINMENT

Is entertainment needed on a long-distance hike? Isn't the natural world enough? Much of the time it is, but when you're stuck inside the tent during a long stormy evening, listening to the drumming of the rain on the fly sheet palls after a while. You can write in your journal, of course, and study the maps or guidebook, but there are times when some sort of distraction is welcome. This is especially so for solo hikers.

Books

As a fanatical reader, I always have a book with me, often more than one. Because I am interested in the natural history of the areas through which I hike, I often carry nature guides. The tiny regional "Finder" booklets to the flowers, trees, birds, and

Target Weights

Footwear	Target Weights (in ounces)
sports sandals	25
running shoes	25
trail shoes	32
lightweight boots	40
medium-weight boots (for crampons)	48

Note: *these weights are for a men's size 10; scale up or down for other sizes*

Packs	
3,000 cubic inches	40
4,000 cubic inches	64
5,000 cubic inches	90
6,000 cubic inches	104

Shelter	
groundsheet	10
bivy bag	16

tarp, solo	18
tarp, duo	26
tent, solo (three-season)	64
tent, duo (three-season)	96
tent, duo (winter mountain)	128
sleeping bag (summer)	25
sleeping bag (three-season)	40
sleeping bag (winter)	64
closed-cell foam mat	9
self-inflating mat	17

Kitchen	
stove (cartridge)	8
stove (multifuel/white gas)	16
stove (alcohol with solo cookset)	35
stove (alcohol with duo cookset)	44
quart pot with lid	8
cookset with 1- and 2-quart pots and lid	26
mug	4

Clothing	
lightweight synthetic T-shirt	4
midweight synthetic shirt	8
long base-layer pants	8
shorts	6
trail pants	10
lightweight fleece top	12
midweight fleece top	20
synthetic fill top	20
down top	20
windshirt	8
waterproof jacket	20
waterproof trousers	8
warm hat	2
microfleece cap with peak	4
sun hat	4
liner gloves	2
fleece/wool gloves/mitts	4
shell gloves/mitts	5

Note: *Please remember these are intended as maximum weights. There are items available that weigh less than this. Also, not all these items would be carried at the same time, of course.*

---

other subjects are excellent. They weigh just 2 ounces. I have carried heavier books at times. On the Canadian Rockies walk I carried Ben Gadd's comprehensive and excellent *Handbook of the Canadian Rockies* the whole way, despite its 25.5-ounce weight. Unfortunately, the latest all-color edition weighs 34.5 ounces. On the PCT I carried a series of regional nature guides, including the 18-ounce *A Sierra Club Naturalist's Guide to the Sierra Nevada* by Stephen Whitney. The weight of these books was worth it to me because they enhanced my appreciation of the places where I was hiking.

As well as nature guides, I usually carry an inexpensive lightweight paperback of some sort, either a novel or an outdoor story. The weight of these can be reduced by using pages that have been read as toilet tissue or as tinder for campfires. Books that don't get destroyed in this way I leave in shelters or huts for others to read, sometimes swapping them for books that other hikers have left.

Books can be bought in towns along the way (a method that sometimes produces local gems you'd miss otherwise, though you might end up with little choice), or put in supply boxes.

Radios, Cassette Players, and CD Players

I like books because they don't cut me off from the sounds of the natural world. Some hikers who like to listen to music in camp or even while hiking carry tiny radios or cassette players. I've never done so, though I can see that a radio could be useful for listening to weather forecasts. Spare batteries and new cassettes could go in the supply boxes.

Ascending the Tarap Gorge in Dolpo, Nepal.

8

On the Trail and in Camp

For the first time I saw quite clearly what mattered in The Walk were the simple things—snow and vivid light and sharp-grained bobcat tracks.

— Colin Fletcher, *The Thousand-Mile Summer*

After all the route planning, the gathering of gear, the sorting of supplies and supply points, and the last-minute rush to complete a mass of little details, it is a relief to leave the trailhead and actually start hiking. In some respects the hardest part of the journey is now behind you. All you have to do is put one foot in front of the other and enjoy the hiking. It's not that simple, of course. If it were, it would be a less fulfilling experience.

FOLLOWING A TRAIL

Established trails are usually clear on the ground and often well marked. The white blazes of the Appalachian Trail are famous among long-distance hikers. Most other trails are not quite so well signed, however. In wooded areas there may be blazes—ax cuts in the shape of a *T* or dotted *i*—on the trees, while in open areas cairns (or ducks) may show the way. Cairns, which are piled-up stones, occur worldwide, but there are other forms of marking used in some countries. In Europe (but not the United Kingdom) red paint is often used to mark trails. This may take the form of a simple red blotch, or it may be two parallel red lines, as in the French Alps, or a red *T*, as on many trails in Norway, where it is the symbol of Den Norske Turistforening (the Norwegian Mountain Touring Association, see Resources), the organization that runs the backcountry hut system.

In many places, in my opinion, there are too many cairns or other trail markers, especially above timberline. A line of cairns leading across a hillside beside a clear trail is an unnecessary visual intrusion. If the trail can be easily followed, markers aren't needed. It's only when the trail is indistinct or there are side trails that the main route needs marking.

If you're on a well-marked trail and don't see a blaze or cairn for a while, it could mean you've strayed onto an animal trail or a side path. It would be worth returning along it to see if there was a junction you missed. Sometimes you'll find a marked trail that doesn't fit with the map or the trail guide. This could be a trail relocation. If there are no alternatives, it's best to follow it. On the PCT in northern California I spent several days following a relocated trail I couldn't place on the map. If you do follow such a trail, keep an eye on the compass to check that the trail is heading the right way.

On many trails there are signposts at junctions, which makes staying on the trail easy. In some places, however, such as many designated wilderness areas, signs have been removed as part of projects to minimize human impact, while in others the signs were never there in the first place. At unsigned junctions it's wise to check your map or trail guide. What seems the obvious direction

Boulder field in the Jotunheim Mountains in Norway, with hiking route marked with painted *T*s on rocks.

for the trail to take may not be the right one. Sometimes a trail divides, and either branch could be the right way. If only one trail has blazes or cairns, it's almost certainly the correct one. If both are marked, you need to consult the map.

Occasionally an unsigned junction may not be marked on the map or indicated in the trail guide. In that case you need to take a compass bearing on each trail and check the map or guide to see which direction you should be going. In open country you may be able to see ahead to places the trail should reach and then take whichever trail heads that way. In poor visibility or forests this won't be possible. Then you can look on the map or in the trail guide for an obvious feature such as a river, lake, cliff, or campsite that you should reach soon. Calculate how long it should take you to reach this feature, check your watch, and then set off along the most likely trail. Glance at the compass every now and then to make sure the trail is still going the right way. Abrupt changes in direction are easily noticed but a gradual curve can end up with you heading at right angles to where you want to go without you realizing it. If any features appear, check the map or guide for them. If the feature you are seeking appears, you're on the right trail and can relax. If you don't spot the feature and you're past the time it should have taken to reach it, you're probably on the wrong trail. You need to retrace your steps and try another trail. Sometimes you eventually find that your first choice was actually the right one. The trail may not have matched that on your map because the trail has been relocated. All you can do then is accept it as part of the journey and be glad you're on the correct trail.

Though not knowing which trail to take can be frustrating, it's much worse when there is no trail at all. If the trail you're on simply peters out, it's likely that you took a wrong turning at the last junction and are on a side trail. Then it's better to go back to the turn and take another trail than to continue on or try to go cross-country. The only exception to this is in open country where you know in which direction the correct trail must be and know it will be quicker to cut across to the

Swedish signpost along trail.

trail. However, if you're in doubt, turn back.

Sometimes the trail may be blocked by blow-downs or avalanche debris or patches of old snow, and you won't be able to see where it continues. Finding where the trail lies on the far side of an obstacle can take a long time, particularly in a forest. First you need to safely circumvent the obstruction. Once you're on the far side, as well as looking for the trail itself, which you'll see only when it's almost under your feet, look for signs of it, such as a straight line through the trees, snipped branches and twigs, cut logs, or other signs of ax or saw use. Logs may not lie on the trail itself—maintenance crews may push them some way off—but they indicate that the trail is nearby. In my experience it's always worth spending time searching for a trail until you find it. It may be tempting to regard this as wasted time and simply head off cross-country in the right direction. Having succumbed to this on occasion myself, I have learned that it usually leads to much longer delays, again particularly in forests where fallen trees and undergrowth can make cross-country travel very difficult. When you're above the timberline and in open areas such as deserts, if you really can't find the trail, you should be able to take a compass bearing on a feature that lies on or near the trail and walk to that feature, hoping to pick up the trail on the way or when you arrive.

Early and late in the season trails may be obscured by snow. I followed hundreds of miles of snowbound trail in the Sierra Nevada on the Pacific Crest Trail and in the Montana and Colorado Rockies on the Continental Divide Trail. In open country you can navigate by features. You may not follow the actual line of the trail, but you should be able to follow the approximate direction as long as you check the map regularly. In places, particularly south-facing slopes, the trail may be exposed for anything from a few feet to a few hundred yards. By scanning ahead—binoculars are useful here—you can pick up these bits of trails and can then aim for them, confident you're heading in the right general direction. In forest you have to rely on lines through the trees, cut branches, blazes, and the edges of the trail, which sometimes appear above the edge of the snow. In the dense forests of the northern Sierra I became quite adept at finding the snow-covered trail by way of old blazes and ax cuts. If you're completely confused, turn around and look back at the last sign of the trail. Try to work out where it would logically go from there.

CROSS-COUNTRY HIKING

Planning a cross-country walk is covered in chapter 4 beginning on page 59. Here I look at some of the problems that can arise during the actual hiking.

Choosing a Route

Whatever rough route was planned in the comfort of home, the specific course you hike has to be worked out on the ground. You may have planned on hiking up a certain valley, but until you get there you won't know which is the best route. If the valley bottom is brush-choked, it may be best to climb above the bushes and traverse across the hillsides above. In areas of rolling hills the bare or sparsely vegetated ridges and summits may make for excellent hiking. I found this in the Richardson Mountains north of the Arctic Circle in the Yukon. The valleys were narrow and thick with brush and small trees, and the mountainsides were steep. But once on top I could stride out for miles along the arctic tundra of the undulating ridges and gentle summits. Alternatively, large meadows and open forest may make hiking along a valley floor much easier than on the boulder-covered slopes and steep rocky summits to either side. Animal trails are often the easiest routes through dense brush or forests. Keep a check on their direction, though. The creatures that made them won't be going where you are. On a cross-country hike you are always considering where the best route lies and constantly revising your plans. It is much more immediate and intense than hiking on a good trail. Surveying the land ahead from a good vantage point such as a pass or mountaintop is always worthwhile. A pair of binoculars helps here.

As you hike through an area day after day, you can learn about the topography and the vegetation types and can work out where the best hiking will be. I did this in both the northern Canadian Rockies and the Yukon, and although I still encountered difficulties, once I understood how the landscape was put together, route finding became much easier.

A compass can be useful on any long-distance hike, though it may not get much use on a well-marked trail. On the Pacific Crest Trail mine was only used when the trail was snow-covered and even then only a few times. On a cross-country hike a compass is essential and should always be

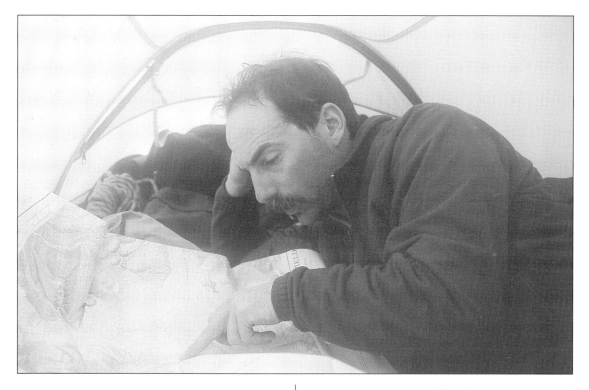

Planning the route while sheltering from a storm.

close at hand. As well as using it to check the direction, you can use it for taking bearings off the map to get you to a lake or river or other feature you want to reach and for working out your position by taking bearings on visible features. I would say good compass skills are a basic necessity for cross-country hiking.

Unlike a compass, an altimeter isn't essential, but it can be very useful. On trail hikes it really tells you only how much ascent is left before you reach the next pass. When you're going cross-country, knowing your altitude can be very helpful, however, especially in poor visibility, whether in dense forest or mist, and it can be very difficult or impossible to work this altitude out from the map. I wouldn't undertake a long cross-country hike without an altimeter. I can remember one journey along a forested hillside where we needed to locate a shallow, narrow gully that from the map looked as though it would provide a safe

descent through the cliffs below us to the head of a drainage where we wanted to camp. By using the altimeter I was able to stay at the right height so that we arrived at the head of the gully, which we could indeed descend. With just a compass it would've been much harder and would've taken more time to do this. In fact, I would've aimed off so that I knew when I reached the edge of the drainage that the gully was to my left or right. With the altimeter I just traversed at the right height. I've used the altimeter when I need to drop off a ridge at a certain height or leave a stream and start to climb the slopes above. If I can't see the features, the altimeter tells me where I am. On my Scottish Highlands walk the altimeter was very useful when climbing featureless slopes in mist (which are common in the Highlands—both the mist and the featureless slopes) because knowing my height made route choices much easier. I could also estimate how much time it would take to reach the next summit or pass or descend to a glen.

Bushwhacking

Sometimes, though, despite all your efforts (and it's worth every effort you can make), bushwhacking becomes necessary. Fighting through dense bushes that grab and catch at your clothes and pack is the most exhausting and slowest form of hiking I know. Staying calm can be very difficult. Whenever possible, link any open areas—meadows, riverbanks, lakeshores—you can to minimize the amount of time spent in the bushes. In a densely forested trail-less area just south of Banff National Park in the Canadian Rockies, I hiked up the Palliser River for many miles, either on shingle banks or in the cold ankle-to-knee-deep water. This gave the easiest walking and also excellent views of the surrounding mountains that I wouldn't have had if I'd stayed in the forest. The hardest bushwhacking I've ever done was in the Tombstone Mountains, north of Dawson City in the Yukon. In the narrow, steep-sided Little Twelve-Mile River valley I was forced into the tangled jungle of willow and alder that covered the valley floor. The springy branches caught at my pack and clothes as, hot and bothered, I crashed onward in a haze of mosquitoes. While my energy expenditure soared, my rate of progress declined to a mile an hour, and very hard-won miles at that.

MINIMIZING THE IMPACT

A good trail is a narrow thread of dirt winding through the forest or across the mountainside. A poor trail is a spider's web of wide ruts and eroded ground or a series of deep parallel channels cut into the earth. To keep a trail in good condition, it's best to stay on it and not take shortcuts or walk off the edges. When descending switchbacks, resist the temptation to cut across them for a quicker descent, since the routes made by doing so can quickly become eroded scars. When the trail is wet or muddy, stay with it and put up with damp feet or dirty legs. Trails get widened by hikers walking along the edges to stay out of the wet or muddy segments. If the trail is really narrow, go in single file if you're in a group. Trails that are already damaged need proper repair or even relocation. In the meantime, though, hikers can try not to do more damage by staying on the trail and trying to follow the original line.

Your goal when cross-country hiking should be to avoid leaving the beginnings of a trail. This is easiest to do by sticking to durable ground such as dry vegetation, decaying forest matter, sand and gravel, rock, and snow as far as possible. Wet ground is more easily marked. Groups should walk apart because several pairs of feet soon start a trail. Cairns should never be built to mark cross-country routes. Others may follow these cairns, and a trail will start to appear.

Lightweight footwear with a fairly shallow tread (see page 119) almost certainly does less damage to the ground than a heavily lugged hefty boot. This is not just because of the weight of the boots but also because you can walk more gently in light, flexible footwear.

RIVER CROSSINGS

One of the most dangerous things hikers do is ford rivers and creeks. Flowing water is amazingly powerful, and it is very easy to misjudge the strength of a creek. Never try to cross a creek if you're not sure you can do so safely. No long-distance hike is worth the risk. In summer, high water levels in streams crossed by long-distance trails are very unusual. On most unbridged streams keeping your footwear dry is then the biggest concern. However, long-distance hikers are likely to pass through areas early in the season where the spring snowmelt has turned normally placid creeks into raging torrents. I found this in the northern Rockies on the Continental Divide Trail and even more so in the Yosemite region of the High Sierra on the Pacific Crest Trail. When you plan your own route, there may be river fords at any time of year. I had many in late summer in the northern Canadian Rockies on my walk the length of the range. In some areas the whereabouts of a safe crossing place determined my route.

What do you do when a creek you can't easily cross bars your path? First, check the map or trail guide to see if there is a bridge nearby. I learned this after following a river many miles upstream in search of a safe crossing place, only to discover from the map that there had been a bridge not far downstream. Sometimes, however, a bridge marked on the map may have been washed away. The sight of the last remnants of a bridge on which you hoped to cross a river, sticking out of a foaming mass of glacier-gray water, can be very disheartening, as I found at the Blaeberry River in the Canadian Rockies. I'd had a difficult bushwhack down to the river anyway. In one direction cliffs barred the way; in the other lay an unfordable side creek. My only choice was to follow the side creek upstream. Very soon, though, I came upon a trail heading upward. The map showed it led to the logging road I'd left for the bushwhack down to the river. And that road led

Crossing a snowmelt-filled creek on logs on the Pacific Crest Trail in Yosemite National Park.

to a bridge on the other side of the cliffs. Back up 1,000 feet I went and then down to the bridge. My shortcut had led to an unnecessary six miles of hiking. The lesson is that if the trail or track you're on leads to a bridge, stick with it even if it doesn't seem the most direct route and even if, as in this case, another bridge is marked on the map. The lack of a road or trail on the map leading to or from the washed-out bridge should have warned me it was no longer in use.

In really wild areas there won't be a man-made bridge. And in some areas bridges may be present only in summer. On my walk through Scandinavia I hiked through the southern Norwegian mountains early in the season and had to ford several streams because the bridges hadn't yet been installed. They are taken out to prevent them from being damaged by heavy snow or washed away in the spring melt. If there are no man-made bridges, the next thing to look for is a natural bridge such as a fallen tree. On the Pacific Crest Trail I used tree trunks to cross several creeks swollen with snowmelt in the

Bridges are the best way to cross rivers. This one is in the Hardangervidda National Park in Norway.

Yosemite backcountry. If the log is big enough and free enough from branches and a fall into the water would not be serious, confident hikers with good balance could walk across, using a stick or trekking pole for balance. Usually, though, it is much safer to straddle the log and edge yourself slowly across. If there are several logs you could walk across one and hold onto another. Before crossing on any log, check that it's secure and isn't going to roll when you put your weight on it.

When there are no bridges, natural or man-made, you have to seek out a safe crossing point. First, look at the map to see if there are any areas nearby where the river is braided or very wide because it will be shallower in these areas. If there are none, it is better to explore upstream for a ford rather than downstream, since streams get smaller toward their source. Sometimes, though, a steep ravine, a waterfall, or cliffs may

prevent you from doing this. Occasionally you can't go downstream either. I was faced with this situation once in the Canadian Rockies. Upstream I could see the creek I wanted to ford rising in a series of cascades to the foot of the glacier that fed it, while just a few yards downstream it joined a much bigger river. The far bank was 25 feet away. The water was murky with glacier silt, and I couldn't see how deep it was. Taking off my pack, I gingerly stepped into the edge of the water, holding onto a bush for security. Just a couple of feet from the bank the water was over knee deep and was so strong I could barely keep on my feet. I scrambled back out and made camp. I would have to wait until the next morning. The volume of water in glacier-fed creeks falls during the night as the temperature drops and the thaw stops. Such creeks are at their lowest early in the morning. I stuck a notched stick in the water. At 5:00 A.M. the level had dropped six inches, the water was clearer, with boulders visible in places, and I forded the creek safely. As well as waiting for the water level in glacier-fed creeks to decline overnight, you can also wait for rain-fed creeks to subside. In heavy rain, streams in steep mountain areas can turn from trickles you can boulder-hop across to deep foaming rapids in a matter of hours. Luckily they can go down just as quickly. On the Scottish Highlands walk I had one very wet day high on a mountain ridge. When I finally descended out of the cloud, it was to see white streaks of water roaring down the hills all around. The stream in the valley below, which I needed to cross, was a tumbling mass of whitewater. Attempting a ford would clearly have been madness, so I managed to find a slightly less than totally sodden campsite on the top of a knoll. By morning the stream was more normal looking, and the white hillside cascades had vanished.

When selecting a crossing point, look for straight sections of water. The banks of creeks are often undercut on the outside of bends, and the water is usually deeper there. Choose a quiet section, too; whitewater is to be avoided. Shingle banks, small islets, and boulders can all be used as safety points where you can rest. Be careful around boulders, though, as there can be big holes in the creek bed beside them. Boulders and tangles of fallen trees under the water can be very dangerous and should be avoided. Check the map for rapids or waterfalls downstream of your proposed ford. If there are any, don't cross there, since if you fall in you could be swept over them. Take into account the width of the river—if it's very wide, it may be difficult to assess what it's like near the far side. You may get tired or very cold, too.

Before crossing a creek or river, you should undo your pack hipbelt and sternum straps so you can discard it if you have to. The chances are it will float, as there's a lot of air inside. If it does, it could be used as a life raft, though I haven't tried this myself. If you haven't a staff or trekking poles, find a long, stout stick to use for support. Cross facing upstream so the water can't buckle your legs from behind. Keep your feet about hip width apart and move one foot at a time, shuffling sideways. Don't commit your weight to a

foot until it feels secure. Don't hurry. Not slipping is the main objective. If the creek bed is very slippery or the stones or gravel are moving with the force of the current, turn back. Turn back, too, if the water rises up above your knees, unless the current is very weak. If at any point you feel unsafe, retreat as well. It's always better to hike many miles upstream in search of a log bridge or to a point where the creek is much smaller and you can ford safely—don't risk a dangerous crossing.

It's best to wear footwear for grip and to protect your feet when fording creeks. Sandals are ideal for this. I cross barefoot only if I can see the

When fording a shallow creek, keep your boots on, take short steps, and use a trekking pole for support.

bottom and if it's sandy or fairly smooth and the current isn't very strong. If the water is very cold, boots or shoes are warmer than sandals, or you could wear socks with the sandals. Long trousers are not a good idea, as they will drag in the water. Bare legs are better.

A group can cross together by holding onto each other's waists and shuffling across with the first person facing upstream and holding a pole. Three people can put their arms around each other's shoulders and shuffle across, with two people facing each other across the stream and the third facing upstream. Three of us used this method for creek crossings in the High Sierra on the PCT and found it very effective.

Ropes can be used to protect river crossings, and I have made roped crossings in the past.

When making a deep, difficult ford—such as crossing Strawberry Creek in the Bob Marshal Wilderness on the Continental Divide Trail—move slowly, face upstream, and use a trekking pole for support.

Current thinking, however, is that the chances of being swept away and trapped in the water by the rope are too great, and roped crossings are no longer recommended.

If you can't find a safe ford, and if the water doesn't go down after an overnight wait, turn back and seek another route. I've completely replanned routes at times because of rivers that were too dangerous to cross.

TYPES OF TERRAIN

Much long-distance hiking takes place on good trails in forests or mountain terrain. However, there are a few places that are different enough to these places to warrant adaptations of techniques and gear.

Deserts

Both the Pacific Crest Trail and the Continental Divide Trail go through desert and semidesert areas at their southern ends, whereas the Arizona

Temperate Deserts: Cold and High

Deserts are not all hot, sandy wastes. Some are stony mountain lands, rough, steep, harsh, and cold. Such temperate deserts, as they are known, are usually fairly high in elevation and further north than hotter areas.

The Great Basin, which covers much of Nevada and Utah and parts of Oregon, Idaho, Wyoming, and Colorado, is this type of desert, the coldest and highest as well as the largest desert in the United States. Most of it is over 4,000 feet in altitude, and the typical plant is gray-green sagebrush rather than the cacti found in hotter deserts to the south.

Much higher and colder, however, is the desert mountain plateau lying to the north of the Himalaya that makes up much of Tibet and parts of northern Nepal. This arid land lies between 14,000 and 16,000 feet. Despite the dry, cold snow that falls in winter, it is a desert, as can be seen from the lack of vegetation and the dry stony valleys and rocky hillsides. It's part of the huge desert lands of Central Asia, the largest temperate desert in the world.

Trail is in such terrain for much of its length. Until I hiked the PCT I'd never seen a desert, never mind walked across one. The first few days north of the Mexican border were a real shock. The heat and scarcity of water and shade were overwhelming. But so were the scenery and the light. I was enchanted with this land, so totally different from anywhere I'd been before. Deserts have a cleanliness, a clarity, a simplicity not found elsewhere. Arctic tundra has the same sense of openness and space and the same huge skies, but the tundra is cool, a land of blue and green with cold gray air. The desert is red and yellow and warm.

The two big linked concerns in the desert are heat and water. When you first start hiking in the heat, your body won't produce enough sweat quickly enough to keep you cool. It takes about a week to acclimatize to hiking in hot weather. After that time you will sweat more but lose less salt. While you acclimatize it would be best to plan for a lower daily mileage and more time spent resting than later in the hike.

Water and how much to carry and drink are covered in detail beginning on page 92. Drinking plenty of water, of course, is essential to coping with the heat. On desert hikes it's very important to know the location of water sources and how reliable those sources are. If there's any doubt, enough water should be carried to get you to the next certain source. Know, too, where sources off your route are located, as even the

most reliable water can fail in some years. Natural water sources include creeks, pools, seeps, and springs. Most desert areas have manmade ones, too, such as cattle troughs, containment dams, wells, and windmills. I used many of these in New Mexico on the Continental Divide Trail and throughout the Arizona Trail. I remember how wonderful the sight of a distant windmill was on a long, hot day in flat, almost featureless desert, even though I knew it would take hours to reach it.

Maps mark many (but not all) water sources but give no indication as to their reliability. Trail guides should have this information, but it won't be up-to-date. For this you need to ask rangers and local land management agencies. They should always be consulted anyway in case a spring has dried up permanently or a well or windmill has failed or been abandoned. Be prepared, though, for imprecise and sometimes inaccurate information. Along the Arizona Trail I was often told potential water sources "should" or "might" have water. Sometimes they did. Sometimes they didn't.

Shade is important but is lacking in most deserts. Indeed, one definition of a desert is a waterless and treeless area. Carrying your own shade, in the form of a sun hat and maybe an umbrella (see page 178), can make hiking in the heat of midday surprisingly comfortable. I didn't use either on the Pacific Crest Trail, and in the Mojave Desert I found the few hours

Near the head of the Hermit Trail in the Grand Canyon.

around noon just too hot for hiking on the warmest days so I sat them out with my companions in the shade of groundsheets erected as sun shelters. With the right gear I could have kept walking, as I did on the Arizona Trail. To escape the heat we tried night hiking on the PCT, which was very pleasant. However, even with flashlights we couldn't tell the difference between bits of dead plants and rattlesnakes so after a couple of scares we abandoned night hiking. Instead we began hiking at dawn, had a siesta in the middle of the day, then hiked until dusk.

As well as providing shade, umbrellas and sun hats protect against the sun. Hot desert sun can burn you quickly, so plenty of sunscreen is needed on any exposed skin. Long-sleeved shirts and long pants keep the sun off, but I find them too hot and clammy.

Deserts look hard and tough, stony landscapes that are resistant to damage. This isn't so, however. Because of the lack of water, dry desert soils are often fragile and crumble easily. To avoid causing harm, it's best to stay on trails where they exist. When hiking cross-country, the most durable surfaces are rock and sand. Dry washes, where these surfaces are common, are often good routes, too. The banks of flowing streams are usually suitable for walking on, as the well-watered soil and vegetation will be tougher and more quickly renewed than that away from water. Desert plants are usually widely dispersed and thus are easily walked around. Plants grow very slowly and can be quickly damaged or destroyed. Recovery takes a very long time. In particular, the strange, black, raised clumps of cryptobiotic soil should be avoided. This isn't in fact soil, but a community of mosses, lichens, algae, and fungi that is incredibly delicate and can crumble to dust if walked over. Cryptobiotic soil is very important, as it is part of the process of building real soil in which other plants will grow.

Rocks

Trails in the mountains are often rough and stony, wending their way through boulders and across scree and talus slopes. They're still trails, though; they give you a line to follow, and they're usually flat and secure underfoot, even when crossing a steep, unstable mountainside. Once you venture cross-country, rocky terrain requires much more thought and care.

When you need to cross rocky ground, it's best to work out a route before you start out, if possible going all the way to the far side. When you can't do this, pick out distinctive boulders or flat areas, walk to these, and then work out the next stage of the route. While hiking you need to concentrate on your balance and footing, rather than on which way to go.

Rocky terrain varies from the small stones called scree that move under your feet to larger rocks and small boulders, which are known as talus. In some places you may have to negotiate huge boulders the size of cars or even small houses. Good balance is needed, no matter the type of rock, and can be aided by the use of a staff or trekking poles. Keep your weight over your feet and test each foothold before you put weight onto it, in case the rock is loose. This means taking short steps rather than big strides so if a rock does move, you're not committed to standing on it. When descending, resist the temptation to lean back. It may feel more secure, but it isn't. If your feet are ahead of your body, you're much more likely to slip and sit down suddenly, especially when carrying a heavy pack. When traversing or ascending, you need to stand away from the slope rather than leaning in, again so that the weight is over your feet.

The balance of your load makes a difference, too; close-fitting internal frame packs are better than externals for this. The balance of both types of pack can be improved by packing heavy items low down or in the middle of the pack and close to your back. Heavy gear carried above shoulder height will cause the pack to sway; if heavy items are far from your back, the pack is more likely to swing from side to side. Tightening up shoulder

Hot Deserts

Hot, sandy deserts, often scattered with red-rock cliffs and canyons, are the most common type of desert and include the Sahara and the Kalahari in Africa as well as the deserts of Australia, South America, and the Middle East.

In the United States these deserts are typified by the Mojave Desert in southeast California, which includes Death Valley, the Sonoran Desert of southern Arizona, with its instantly identifiable saguaro cacti, and the Chihuahuan Desert in Texas and New Mexico. Monument Valley and the Grand Canyon are some of the most spectacular hot desert landscapes. Hiking can be superb in hot deserts, but water and heat are always major concerns.

straps and using the sternum strap also help with balance. You want the pack to cling to your back and move with you, not against you.

Scree can be very frustrating stuff, especially if you try to climb it, as your feet keep slipping. I'd suggest staying off scree except in descent, unless there's really no alternative—and there may not be if a scree-filled gully is the only route between cliffs. If you have to climb scree, kick steps in it as you would in snow. You'll still slip a little, but not as much as when you tread more gently. On a really steep slope you can try zigzagging back and forth, though sometimes this is harder than going straight up because you slip even more. Ascending scree is always very hard, slow work. When you're descending scree, you have to let the stones roll under your feet; trying to stop them is very exhausting and ultimately futile. Don't move too fast, though; running down scree can damage the slope and can also result in more serious injuries if you fall. When there are other hikers on the same slope above you, there may also be a danger that they will dislodge stones, which then crash down and hit you. A group can stick close together to avoid this happening, moving in an angled line or arrowhead formation so no one is directly above anyone else. If a rock is knocked down and there are people below, yell "rock" at the top of your voice to warn them. And if you hear a cry of "rock!", protect your head with your arms (and pack, if possible) and *don't look up.*

Talus is easier to hike over than scree because it is more stable. Testing individual rocks for security is important, though, because the occasional rock may tip over when weighted, especially on a slope that is rarely if ever walked on. Hikers with good balance can boulder hop from one rock to the next. However, you need to be confident to do this and prepared to react very quickly if a rock throws you off balance, since a slip can be serious. If the rocks are wet or covered with moss or lichen, they'll probably be slippery, in which case you'll need to move more carefully.

Steep Slopes

Trails sometimes switchback up very steep slopes that would be difficult and possibly dangerous

Rough ground in the Cairngorm Mountains in Scotland.

to ascend otherwise. Where there are no trails, great care has to be taken to find a safe way up and down steep slopes. It is best to scan the slope, with binoculars if you have them, and select a route before you set out. Where you can't see all the way up or down the slope, you'll have to plan the route in stages. Particular care is needed when you can't see what is below you. In ascent, if you reach a cliff or section that is too steep to climb, you just have to go around it. You won't see these drops from above, however. In descent, approach "blind" edges very cautiously in case the ground is slippery or falls away very suddenly. Long grass and shrubs can overhang drops, too, so don't go the edge of these. If in doubt, turn back and traverse across the mountainside in search of a safer way down.

Zigzagging across a slope is often easier on the legs and feet than going straight up or down and sometimes easier on the nerves as well. Sometimes you'll reach a section you think you could get down quite easily if you weren't carrying a pack. If there is flat ground below, you

could lower your pack down on a long length of cord and then climb down after it. But don't do this unless you're certain you can descend safely. Hauling your pack back up will not be easy, and it may jam. On occasion I have climbed down a steep section without my pack to check if I could do so and then climbed back up, lowered my pack down, and climbed down again. When ascending, remember that it's generally easier to climb up than down. Don't climb up anywhere if you're uncertain that you could climb back down again. You may need to retreat due to unseen obstacles higher up.

High Altitude

Many trails climb high into the mountains. Both the Pacific Crest and Continental Divide Trails go over 13,000 feet and are above 10,000 feet for significant distances. The John Muir Trail reaches 14,494 feet on Mount Whitney. Once you go this high, the altitude has an effect on your hiking performance and can affect your health. If you hike overseas, much higher elevations may be reached. Many trekkers' destinations in the Himalaya such as Everest Base Camp are over 17,000 feet high.

Alpine Mountains: A World of Snow and Ice

Soaring pyramids of rock and snow with glaciers tumbling down the flanks are magnificent to look at, but climbing them is the province of the mountaineer, not the hiker. In alpine regions, whether it is the Alps themselves, the Himalaya, the Andes, the Alaska range, or other steep mountains with permanent snow, routes for hikers wind through the mountains from valley to valley, crossing high passes and perhaps ascending an occasional lower, gentler peak.

Alpine mountain ranges are superb places for long hikes, for they contain some of the wildest, most spectacular scenery on earth. Whether it is walking hut to hut in the Alps, following trails from village to village in the Himalaya, or backpacking through the Canadian Rockies, a hike in big mountains is always an inspiring adventure.

Climbing steep scree to the Breche de Roland on the Spanish–French border in the Pyrenees.

Some hikers notice the effects of altitude when they go above 5,000 feet, but it's above 8,000 feet where altitude sickness may occur. Acclimatizing to high altitudes is necessary both for health and for enjoyment of your hike. The best way to do this is to ascend gradually and, when possible, sleep as low down as possible.

When you're hiking above 14,000 feet, the advice is to ascend no more than 500 to 1,000 feet a day and rest every third day. This is what I did on a high-level trek in Nepal, where we were above 13,000 feet for ten days and crossed three passes over 17,000 feet. Because the initial ascent was up a steep gorge that gained altitude rapidly,

Good balance is required on narrow rocky ridges.

problems with the altitude because I'd gradually ascended over a period of many days. However, when I visited the Colorado Rockies for a shorter trip and arrived at 10,000 feet in a matter of hours, I found going upstairs in a hotel hard work, and it was two days before I was fit to hike.

Altitude sickness comes in several forms. The symptoms of acute mountain sickness (AMS), which is caused by ascending too high too fast, are headaches, tiredness, dizziness, loss of appetite, nausea, and vomiting. Figures reproduced in James Wilkerson's *Medicine for Mountaineering* (which has an excellent chapter on altitude problems) show that 47 percent of trekkers who flew to 9,275 feet and then started hiking to Everest Base Camp at 17,500 feet suffered from AMS. With climbers ascending Mount Rainier in Washington State, who went to high altitude in just one to two days, 67 percent suffered from AMS. It's not a rare problem. The symptoms usually pass in a few days and can be alleviated by descending. You certainly shouldn't climb any higher until you've recovered. Aspirin can relieve headaches, and it's important to drink plenty of water. Even mild dehydration can make the condition worse. If the sufferer deteriorates, however, dropping down 2,000 to 3,000 feet is essential, as it could mean that a more

Forest Mountains

Most mountain ranges outside of the polar regions have forests on their lower flanks. In some places, though, the forests cover the summits or rise very close to them. This is so in ranges such as the Zuni Mountains and Mogollon Mountains in New Mexico, the mountains of southern and central Arizona, and throughout much of the Appalachian Mountains. This means that trails such as the Appalachian Trail and the Long Trail can climb steeply up and over many mountain summits yet only occasionally leave the confines of the forest. Forested mountains make great walking country as long as there are trails. Going cross-country can be very difficult, however, due to thick underbrush and fallen trees.

we hiked only 3 or 4 miles a day for three days so as not to gain too much height too soon. Even so, I really noticed the effects of altitude on my performance on the first pass we crossed, at 17,380 feet. Four days later, however, all spent above 15,000 feet, I found the going much easier on a 17,875-foot pass.

If you hike without stopping to over 10,000 feet from a low elevation, the altitude is likely to affect you greatly, and the chances of altitude sickness are quite high. Far better to spend three or four days hiking at 6,000 to 8,000 feet and then go up to 10,000 feet. Luckily this is what happens on long trails such as the PCT and CDT anyway. When I hiked the CDT through the Colorado Rockies and the PCT through the High Sierra, the highest parts of those trails, I had no

Stone Mountains

Many mountain ranges have little or no permanent snow or glaciers, which can make the summits more accessible to the hiker, at least by the easiest routes in summer.

These mountains may be found in otherwise snowy ranges, such as the Queyras Mountains in the Alps, but are usually distinct ranges, such as the Sierra Nevada in California, the Pyrenees, and the Norwegian mountains. The last area has many summits that are easily attained by hikers, as do lower, even more snow-free mountains, such as those of the Scottish Highlands. In these areas there are often trails leading to the summits.

Snow and ice may be absent due to the low altitude of the mountains, as with the Scottish Highlands, the location in a rain shadow, such as the Queyras Alps, and location in a hot southern area, such as the desert mountain ranges of Arizona.

---

serious illness is developing. This may be either high altitude cerebral or pulmonary edema, a fluid buildup in the brain or the lungs. Either can be fatal, which is why AMS sufferers who get worse rather than better should descend quickly.

Different people acclimatize at different rates, and the same person may acclimatize more slowly or quickly on different occasions. It can't be predicted. Just because you've never suffered from AMS in the past doesn't mean you won't in the future. It has nothing to do with fitness either.

WEATHER

The weather plays a critical part in a long-distance hike. People have abandoned hikes when they couldn't cope with the weather, either psychologically or physically. This shouldn't happen if you've done your planning properly, since you'll have an idea of what to expect and will have packed the gear to cope with it, but even so the chances of atypical weather occurring somewhere along the way are quite high. I've been rained on in the Mojave Desert and at the bottom of the Grand Canyon, hiked in heat waves in the Yukon and the Montana Rockies, and had unseasonal snow in the Colorado Rockies.

Forecasting

Having an idea of what the weather might do can help with planning, especially if there's a choice of routes. I always get a weather forecast whenever I can, usually in towns or at resupply points. Occasionally I have had a day off when a big storm was forecast; at other times I have left sooner than planned when I heard that the weather would be good for a few more days and then a storm was due.

On the trail you could carry a small radio for listening to forecasts. I rely on observing the clouds and the wind direction and, particularly, on my altimeter-barometer, which records changes in air pressure. Each evening I set the barometer to measure overnight change in pressure. If the pressure starts dropping rapidly, a big storm is almost certainly on the way within the next 24 hours. In the morning I may change my route for the day if the pressure has fallen greatly and if I was planning on hiking on exposed ridges or over summits. Conversely, if the pressure is rising, I may decide a high-level route is the best choice. Such knowledge is particularly useful on self-planned hikes where you're going cross-country and selecting your own routes most days. There are sections of long-distance trails, such as the Continental Divide Trail in the Wind River Range in Wyoming, where there are high- and low-level alternatives. Here having an idea of what the weather might do could be useful in determining which route you'll take.

Most wrist altimeters will show pressure changes and also give the temperature (which will be accurate only when the altimeter is not on your wrist). However, the Brunton/Silva Alba WindWatch also has an anemometer that records the wind speed and gives the windchill factor as well as the ambient temperature. The main display is a very clear bar chart showing the air pressure for the last 16 hours. I use the WindWatch for weather forecasting and recording wind, temperature, and windchill data. I also carry a Suunto Altimax altimeter for navigation purposes, so I have two altimeters with me. However, each records different data, and the combined weight is only 3.75 ounces.

Rain

Prolonged rain is the hardest weather to deal with. A big storm can be exhilarating or terrifying, but it doesn't usually last that long. Steady rain can go on for day after day, though, falling out of a dull gray sky. Coping with rain is a matter of keeping yourself and your gear as dry as possible and looking for the positive side of wet weather.

First you need to make sure everything sensitive to water is packed in waterproof bags, whether nylon stuff sacks or plastic zipper-lock bags. Even more so than when it's dry, items you'll need during the day should be in outside pockets or at the top of the pack so you don't have to take out other gear. Your shelter should be at the top, too, so you can make camp without getting other gear wet.

While hiking, wear the minimum needed to feel comfortable. It is very easy to overheat in the rain. Waterproof-breathable clothing will not let body moisture through as fast as when it's dry, so condensation is more likely. If you're too warm inside, condensation will occur even more quickly. And lots of condensation means damp inner clothing that will be chilly when you stop hiking. However, if you start to feel cold, pause, preferably in the shelter of a rock or tree, and put on extra clothing under your rain jacket. A warm hat under your hood can make a huge difference, while condensation can be reduced by wearing a waterproof hat instead of your rain jacket hood, as this allows for warm damp air to escape at the neck. In strong winds the hood has to go up, but in much rain it doesn't need to. I like wearing my Tilley Hat in the rain. The broad brim keeps

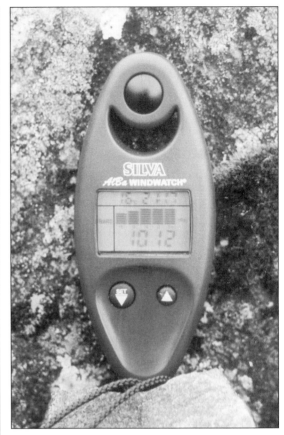

The Brunton/Silva Alba WindWatch records air pressure, wind speed, and temperature.

rain from dripping down my neck, and because it's cotton, it stiffens when wet, which gives more protection because the brim doesn't flop down. In torrential rain it does eventually leak, but in most rain it's much more comfortable than a hood.

Often rain starts gradually with a few light drops that slowly turns to gentle drizzle and then to heavier rain. It is tempting when this happens not to bother with rain gear at first, in the hope that it'll stop before you get very wet. Sometimes it does, of course. But when it doesn't, donning rainwear over already damp clothing increases the likelihood of condensation and of feeling chilly and uncomfortable. I speak from experience, having often neglected to stop and put on rainwear until I'm already quite wet. It's much better to put rainwear on as soon as the first drops fall. You can always take it off if the drizzle peters out. In country where rain is likely, having rainwear easily accessible rather than buried deep in the pack makes it more likely that you'll put it on sooner rather than later.

If the rain is coming straight down and it's not very cold, I usually don my rain jacket but not my rain pants, as I find these restrictive and hot. I only wear them when it's cold and windy as well as wet. In warm, wet weather bare legs stay comfortable while you're hiking. When it's cool, synthetic windproof long pants are fairly warm when wet, and they dry very quickly.

When there's no wind or the wind isn't very strong or gusty, an umbrella can be very useful. When using one you don't need to do up your rain jacket or even wear it at all, which means you won't get damp through condensation. When you stop, the umbrella forms a minishelter, too. It can be held over the pack while you get items out so nothing gets wet and over you while you have a snack.

Stopping for long in the rain is a good way to get chilled, so stops should be kept short. You do need to eat, though, as calories will help keep you warm as well as provide the energy to keep you going. Frequent snacks of trail mix, granola bars, and the like are the easiest way to eat in the rain, since you don't need to stop for long. When you do stop, look for a bit of shelter such as a large, spreading tree or an overhanging boulder. Don't forget to drink either. Just because it's raining doesn't mean you can't get dehydrated.

If you want a long stop in the rain—to check the route perhaps, or because you're tired—you can erect a tarp or even pitch your tent. Once under cover, you can don warm clothing, even get in your sleeping bag if you're really cold, and you can eat, drink, and relax. The stove can be fired up so you can have a hot drink or meal.

A shelter for a rest stop can be pitched almost anywhere, as it'll be used for only a short while. When you make camp in the rain for the night, much more care is needed with site selection. In particular, you need to find a site that drains well so you don't get flooded out. A slight slope helps, as does a site that is higher than the surrounding ground. This was made starkly clear to me at a camp in the Pyrenees. Three of us had pitched our two tents on some bare ground in a deep valley just before a torrential rain storm began that lasted all night and half the next day. The smaller solo tent had been pitched on ground that was no more than a few inches higher than the larger area occupied by the two-person tent. It made all the difference. The two of us in the larger tent had water running under the groundsheet and through the tent porch. Our companion was perfectly dry.

It's when you're pitching and striking camp that gear is most likely to get wet. Once I've selected a site, I take my tent or tarp out of the pack and then close the pack and try and find somewhere sheltered to put it, such as under a tree. If I can't find a place, I prop it up with a trekking pole or stick or lean it against a boulder. If it is lying down, it is far more likely to leak, since much more of it is exposed to the weather and more of it is on the wet ground. I then pitch my shelter as quickly as possible (if I'm using a tent, this is where it's a boon to have one where you pitch the fly sheet first). I put my pack under cover, take out my water bottles, go and fill them, and then get inside myself. If it's a tent, I'm careful to remove my wet rainwear in the porch so the inner tent stays dry. It's actually easier to get in and out of a tarp in the rain, as there's no inner tent that needs to be kept dry. Once inside, I change into dry clothing and stay there. Any cooking is done in the porch, after priming the stove outside the door if that's necessary, unless I'm in country where bears may be a problem. If that's the case, I'll set up my cook tarp some distance away, running between the two with my rain jacket on when necessary.

However good your gear is, if you hike in rain for several days or longer, you'll slowly get wet— from condensation inside your rainwear, from rain getting in at the neck, wrists, and hem, and from the general dampness of the air. All your garments will feel damp, and your feet will be sodden. There's no way around this, so it has to be accepted. Instead of feeling miserable because you're damp, look around to see what the rain is bringing to the world. Waterfalls and rivers are spectacular during rain, the earth smells fresh and clean, leaves and flowers sparkle with raindrops.

Even so, there comes a point when drying out seems an attractive option. A night under a roof gives you the opportunity to dry all your gear and feel warm and dry for a while. After many days in the rain, I usually stay in a hotel or other accommodation for a day when the opportunity arises, even if I'd planned to camp. I also use backcountry shelters or mountain lodges more often in prolonged wet weather if any are available. If you know the location of any of these near your route, you can alter your route a bit if you want a night in the dry.

Clouds sweeping over the mountains—conditions that call for hikers to use good navigational skills.

When the rain finally clears away and the sun reappears—and oh how welcome that is!—take the time to dry out all your gear, if you haven't already done so inside somewhere. It might be raining again the next day.

Mist

Mist can shroud forests, making them mysterious and otherworldly, but it's most common high in the mountains above the timberline. Mist can come from above or below. Sometimes you can see a white wall sweeping up a valley toward you and rearing up as it engulfs you and blots out the sun and the sky. At other times the sky turns gray, and distant peaks become fuzzy and then fade from view as clouds sink down and enshroud you.

Inside mist you are in a strange insubstantial world. Visibility may be only 10 yards or so. Scale and size become hard to judge. Rocks rear up in front of you, looking like huge cliffs, and then in a few steps dwindle into small boulders.

A cloud inversion over the Scottish Highlands with Ben Nevis in the distance.

The problem in mist is that if you lose your way, there are few clues to guide you back again. What little you can see looks featureless. On a good trail this shouldn't be a problem, as the trail will still be clear. When hiking cross-country, careful map and compass work is needed in mist to avoid getting lost. Be very careful when descending in mist if you're not on a trail, for the ground could steepen abruptly.

It can feel quite claustrophobic to be in a thick mist, making you feel hemmed in and restricted. After hours of walking in a thick, gray, damp blanket that deadens sounds and gives no views, it can be quite a relief to drop below it and see the world suddenly spread out all around you. Even better is when the mist starts to disperse and the landscape begins to materialize, slowly solidifying and gaining color as the mist evaporates. This has happened to me on many occasions and is always magical. One outstand-

ing occurrence was in the Pyrenees. A companion and I had climbed into the Encantados (Enchanted) range on a dull, rainy day with the mountains covered in cloud. As we approached a high pass, we were enveloped in mist. But at the pass the mist started to dissipate and patches of blue sky appeared above. Tall, pinnacled summits and rocky peaks floated, vague and hazy in the swirling cloud. Below a blue lake appeared and then the bright green, grassy floor of the bowl, dotted with rocks. Brilliant sunlight pierced the shrinking clouds, and the spectacular scene became sharp and clear. The mountains truly were Enchanted.

The other glorious spectacle mist can bring is a cloud inversion, which is when the valleys are filled with mist but the peaks are bathed in sunshine. As you climb, you can walk through the mist into a bright, high-level world that feels cut off from the grayness below. All around you islands of cloud-free peaks push through the cotton-wool mist into the blue sky. Camping on the edge of a cloud inversion, you can watch white tendrils creep up the valley to break up as they reach the high ground. Sometimes you wake to find the mist gone, but often the mist rises during the night, and by morning your camp is clammy with gray cloud, and the world has shrunk to a few dull yards.

Mist is usually quite wet, so camping below it is advisable. However, if you are unsure of your whereabouts, it is better to camp and wait for the mist to clear than to push on and possibly become even more lost.

Wind

Strong winds can be frightening and dangerous. Lying in the tent waiting for the next gust to come roaring down from the mountains above and shake the tent violently is an unnerving experience. Trying to walk into a powerful wind that buffets and knocks you about is exhausting and, if the wind strengthens enough, ultimately futile. The roaring of the wind can be disorienting in itself and can make thinking difficult. Wind whips away heat, too, an effect known as windchill. You cool even more quickly if your clothes are wet—hence the need for windproof and waterproof clothing.

On many long hikes the wind isn't a major concern, at least most of the time. I never encountered winds that caused problems on the Pacific Crest Trail, which is not to say that they couldn't occur. The Continental Divide Trail isn't particularly subject to strong winds either, but I encountered one that snapped branches off lodgepole pines and made me glad I was not high in the mountains at the time. I later learned that gusts of 70 miles per hour had been recorded. The third of the Big Three trails, the Appalachian Trail, is mostly in forest and so not too troubled by high winds, but the trail does cross the White Mountains in New Hampshire, where winds of more than 100 miles per hour are not unusual.

In 100-mile-per-hour winds you can't stand up. At 60 miles per hour, walking into the wind is just about impossible, and even if you try walking with the wind at your back, you'll be blown all over the place. The strongest gust I've recorded on my anemometer is 62 miles per hour, and I couldn't stand still while I held the instrument up in the air. I know that winds over 30 miles per hour are difficult enough to walk in, so if these are forecast, I plan on staying at lower altitudes. Of course, high winds can't always be predicted, and on a long hike you won't often have a forecast (though if you carry an altimeter, watch for very rapid changes in pressure, which often mean strong winds). When the wind picks up and walking becomes hard, don't try to fight the wind and continue into it. You can quickly become totally exhausted and in danger of hypothermia. Instead, look for an escape route that puts the wind at your back and that will eventually take you down to shelter. It's better to stay up high with the wind at your back than to try to walk into it to a nearer descent route. People have died struggling into strong winds because that was the way to the nearest safety. When the wind is very strong, I wouldn't hike over exposed passes or summits. It's always safer to descend with the wind behind you and take a lower route or wait until the wind drops.

One of the strongest winds with which I've had to cope on a long walk was in the Richardson Mountains north of the Arctic Circle on the Yukon end-to-end walk. The Richardsons are notorious for strong winds, but for the first three days I spent hiking high on their bare rounded ridges the weather was fine. Then a big storm blew in with strong winds and lashing rain. I spent one day camped in the shelter of a forested valley head. The next day, as the storm seemed to be easing, I attempted to walk along a level, 10-mile-long, 3,500-foot-high ridge. Initially the ridge was quite broad and covered with soft vegetation. The wind, though, was very strong and gusty, blowing me sideways at times. Soon the ridge became narrower with small rocky pinnacles and large boulders covered with slippery moss. Skidding and stumbling along, clinging to boulders at times, I was having a harder and harder time trying to keep going as the wind rose. Eventually a gust blew me off my feet, after which I could only progress by almost crawling, my hands on the rocks all the time. Realizing this was a very dangerous location, I decided I had to descend. The only road in the northern Yukon, the gravel Dempster Highway, lay to the west, but the wind was coming from that direction, and I knew I couldn't walk into it, so I descended the steep, loose moss and boulder slope to the east. For the first 1,200 feet I had to take great care, clinging to my staff to avoid slips and to prevent gusts of wind knocking me over. Once the angle of the ground eased, I was able to walk more normally, though the strongest gusts still knocked me about.

Only on one long-distance hike have strong winds played a major part and that was my walk in the Scottish mountains. This was partly because any walk over summits is going to expose you to the worst weather but also because the Scottish Highlands are a very windy range. The weather station on Cairn Gorm, one of the eight peaks in the Highlands over 4,000 feet high, regularly records winds more than 100 miles per hour in winter. In summer the speeds are a bit lower, but there were still many days on the walk when the wind forced me to retreat and descend to the glen below.

Camping in wind can also be difficult if a sheltered site can't be found. Even if your shelter can be pitched and stays standing, the noise of the wind and the shaking of the fabric can prevent sleep and leave you feeling quite stressful, so it's better to keep going in search of a protected site. If you have to pitch your tent or tarp in the wind, do it very carefully. Don't let go of anything that can blow away, or you'll probably lose it. That includes the tent and the fly sheet. Firmly stake down one end before you connect the tent to any poles. Once the tent is up, stake out all guylines tightly. Facing the narrowest end of the tent into the wind is usually best for stability and also gives you a more sheltered door. If you're pitching a tarp, stake down one side and erect it as a low-profile pyramid, since this is the best configuration for shedding wind.

When pitching in a forest in strong winds, look around for dead branches or trees that may be blown down and camp well away from them. Deep in the forest at a low point is usually the safest place to be. Trees on the edges of meadows or out in the open are more likely to come down or shed branches in a storm. In Waterton Lakes National Park near the start of the Canadian Rockies walk, I arrived at a backcountry campsite in oppressive weather that suggested a storm was on the way, so I camped deep in the woods. The only other tent there was pitched right in the middle of a flower meadow next to a creek, an intrusive site where it would be hard not to damage the ground. Not long after dark the storm broke with a rumble of thunder followed by a strong wind and heavy rain. A loud crack echoed through the forest. At dawn I found a tall, dead tree had blown down very close to where the other tent had been pitched. The tent itself had gone, the owner probably having packed up in the night.

Snow

Snow can fall at any time of the year in the mountains. In summer it mostly melts off very quickly, though sometimes it can stay for a day or so, especially on the summits. Spring snow can last longer, and the remnants of the previous winter snowpack may still be present. The first snows of autumn usually melt away fairly quickly, but eventually a heavier snowfall arrives and marks the start of the winter snowpack. Predicting to the week or even the month when the first snow that sticks will fall is impossible. When I hiked the Continental Divide Trail snow began to build up in the Colorado Rockies as early as mid-September. In other years it has been two months later.

Here I'm going to deal with hiking in the occasional summer and early autumn snowfall. Winter and spring travel, when the snow can be heavy, is dealt with in chapter 9.

In terms of clothing, rainwear is the best protection against wet snow, which will quickly melt and soak into any nonwaterproof clothing. Dry

Cornices on the rim of steep slopes can last long into the summer.

snow can easily be brushed off windproof garments, however, and as these breathe much better than rainwear, you won't get damp from condensation when wearing them. In rain, you often don't need to wear mitts or a hat. In snow, you almost always need them. You'll probably want more in the way of insulation on your body, too. Don't wear too much, though. If you avoid overheating and the resultant damp garments, you'll stay drier and warmer in the long run.

Visibility in snowstorms can be very difficult. In strong winds you may encounter whiteout conditions, where the sky and ground merge and it's hard to tell whether the ground in front slopes up or down. In these conditions it's best to descend, as long as you can do so carefully, and make camp. Pushing on is foolhardy unless you are on a clear trail and there is shelter not too far ahead.

I was caught out by late summer snow in the northern Colorado Rockies on the Continental Divide Trail. It was early September, and I was climbing up into the Never Summer Range (aptly named, as it turned out) when snow began to fall. I went on up the trail for two miles to 11,900-foot-high Farview Pass (an inapt name this time), by which time I was in driving snow, strong winds, and thick mist—a blizzard, in fact. Although I had adequate clothing to deal with the storm, I was hiking in running shoes. My feet were soaked and very cold, so I descended some 600 feet to the first flat ground I could find and pitched the tent in the shelter of some stunted timberline spruce trees.

Making camp in the snow is similar to doing so in the rain, in that the main aim is to keep the moisture out of the tent. Where possible, it is always best to camp on bare ground rather than snow. Earth is warmer, and it's easier to pitch your shelter. On that occasion in the Never Summer Range I had to camp on snow, but it was only a few inches deep, so the stakes went through it into the earth below. Once the tent was up, I stood the pack in the vestibule and emptied the contents into the tent. The frozen, snow-covered pack itself was left outside. I then filled my water bottles, crawled into the tent, put dry socks on my now very cold feet, and slid into my sleeping bag. The temperature inside the tent was 38°F. Along with the sleeping bag and warm clothes, several hot drinks and a hot meal warmed me up.

Like many summer snowstorms, that one didn't last, and I emerged later that evening to see the snow-covered mountains turn gold in the last rays of the sun. The snow made the next day magical as I walked through crisp snow below peaks shining and sparkling in the sun.

Most summer and early autumn storms deposit soft snow that presents no real problems, though you can end up with wet feet. If the snow gets deeper, trails start to be hard to follow and walking becomes difficult. Then dropping down to a lower altitude and sitting out the storm is probably the best option. At some point in the autumn the snow usually starts to build up rather than melt away. Then you have to accept that your hike has changed and that you need snow gear and skills. On the CDT in the Colorado Rockies when the snow began to accumulate, I replaced my running shoes with light-weight leather boots. Later I bought some gaiters and rented an ice ax so I could continue a high-altitude route.

Lightning

The sight of bolts of lightning flashing through the sky is impressive. If the storm is approaching and you are in an exposed place, it can also be terrifying. The first thing to do if a thunderstorm is building is to descend by the most direct safe route to a low point. If this is in a dense forest, that's even better. You don't want to be the highest point around, so out in the middle of a meadow or other flat area is not a good place to be. Because there is a danger from ground currents, you also don't want to be near the highest point either, so move away from summits, ridge tops, the edges of cliffs, and single trees. Small groves of trees and the highest tree in a forest can

be dangerous places to be, too. Sheltering in a deep cave is fine, but not in a shallow one. When a storm breaks out, you can estimate how far away it is by counting the seconds between a flash and the following crack of thunder. Five seconds means the storm is a mile away.

Thunderstorms can usually be identified by towering dark cumulonimbus clouds, which look like enormous cauliflowers. If you see these developing, stay away from dangerous places even if it means cutting short the day's hike. Sometimes due to trees or mountains you don't see a storm until it's upon you, however. On the Pacific Crest Trail in the High Sierra two of us were crossing a snow-covered meadow when a huge and unexpected storm suddenly broke nearby with many big lightning flashes. The meadow suddenly seemed enormous as we ran for the shelter of the trees, which luckily we reached before the storm was overhead. Another occasion, when I was on the Continental Divide Trail in the Teton Wilderness, I discovered how fast I could run with a heavy pack when fear produces enough adrenaline. I was on a 10,000-foot-high plateau admiring the superb view west to the Grand Teton when the sky turned black, thunder rumbled all around, and lightning flashed not far away. I covered the distance to the nearest forest in a surprisingly short time.

If safe places are far away and you cannot escape the storm—and when it is above you, it is safer to sit tight than to run—the advice is to crouch on all fours on your insulating mat, minimizing contact with the ground. Keep away from cliffs and peaks and shelter among boulders, if you can. Gear made from metal or containing metal, such as your pack, should be placed some distance away. You can suffer burns from metal after a nearby strike.

In some areas such as the Rockies and the High Sierra thunderstorms occur at much the same time on most days, usually late afternoon or early evening, so you can plan to be over high passes and off any high ground by early afternoon. In other areas thunderstorms are not so predictable, and you just have to keep an eye on any clouds in exposed areas.

Because lightning affects the brain, which controls breathing, if someone is struck by lightning and knocked unconscious (which doesn't happen when most people are struck), breathing is likely to stop, so mouth-to-mouth resuscitation will probably be necessary.

NIGHT HIKING

Hiking in the dark can be exciting and stimulating. The world is different at night. Your senses are enhanced, especially your hearing. It's surprising what you can see, too, once your eyes adjust to the dimness. Except on the darkest nights with dense clouds covering the sky or when beneath trees, I can hike in the dark without need of a flashlight, though I keep one handy. After a while you learn to differentiate between different shades of darkness, knowing that total blackness means a hole in the ground, that pale gray lumps are rocks, and that silvery lines and patches are water. However, more concentration is needed than when hiking in daylight, and you won't hike as fast. Care also needs to be taken to stay on the correct route. Trails can become invisible when in shade. Moonlit nights are actually worse for this than nights with no moon because the contrast between the bright and dark areas is greater, and the dark areas become black holes in which nothing can be seen.

The only places where long-distance backpackers are likely to choose to hike in the dark is the desert, where night hiking can provide relief from the heat of the day. As I point out on page 200, however, the problem with this is telling the difference between sticks and rattlesnakes. A flashlight can help, but using one will spoil your night vision.

Because bears are active at night, I would avoid night hiking in bear country unless it's absolutely essential. And if you do find yourself still on the trail as it gets dark, make a lot of noise to warn bears of your presence.

There are times, though, when night hiking becomes necessary, something that is more likely to occur on cross-country hikes than trail hikes. If there are no water sources or campsites you may have to keep going until dusk and beyond. This may be because a source has dried up or cannot be found or because a campsite that looked good on the map turns out to be a boggy morass in reality.

On rough or steep ground, in a forest or when the sky is cloudy, a flashlight is needed. Once you switch on your flashlight, your night vision will be reduced greatly and you'll basically see what the beam lights up and not much else. With a typical hiker's flashlight that illuminates only a small area, I find it best to light up the trail for some way in front for a general outline of the way ahead and then to shine the light down to pick out the detail at my feet. I then walk a few steps and repeat this. Holding the flashlight low down gives better definition to shadows and lets you see the terrain more clearly.

PROBLEMS WITH WILDLIFE

Encounters with animals are one of the joys and highlights of long-distance hiking. I find that after a few weeks in the wilderness I become more attuned to wildlife, more sensitive to its presence, and so I see more animals more closely. Wildlife often seems less afraid of me, probably because, without being conscious of it, I am moving more quietly and gently. Wolves moving silently through a meadow at dusk in the Yukon, a bright-eyed stoat watching me from a rock crevice just a few feet away in Norway, an otter sliding down a bank at my feet and swimming away upstream in the Scottish Highlands; these and many more are my memories of wildlife.

Generally meetings with wildlife are to be relished, not feared. Most animals simply want to be left alone and will not disturb you if you don't disturb them. Even the few potentially dangerous animals rarely cause any problems.

If you're hiking in a foreign country, you

should always inquire as to dangerous animals you may encounter and what precautions you should take. Here I discuss creatures found in North America. If leopards, crocodiles, tigers, malaria-bearing mosquitoes, or other potentially deadly creatures are found where you're going to hike, up-to-date local advice is required.

Bears

The chances of meeting a bear while hiking are not very high, even in areas where they are common. In over 8,000 miles of hiking in black bear country, I've encountered only 10 bears, while in over 3,000 miles of walking in grizzly bear country, I've seen only 3 grizzlies, and 2 of those were far away. Most bears simply want to keep out of your way. The danger is in coming upon one suddenly so that it feels threatened—then it may attack in self-defense. To avoid this, you need to make sure that any bears will know you are there. Most of the time your smell and the noise you make will be enough. If the wind is in your face, or a creek or strong wind drowns out the noise you are making, or you're hiking through dense undergrowth, a bear may not be aware of you until you are very close. In these situations making a noise is a good idea. It needs to be a loud noise. The tiny bear bells that some hikers wear are inaudible at any distance if there's much other noise. Shouting, singing, and clapping hands are much better choices. Keep an eye open, too, looking for bear signs, such as scat, dug-over ground, and scratches on trees, as well as actual bears. In open country a pair of binoculars is useful for spotting bears at a distance. In the northern Yukon I saw a grizzly a quarter mile away through my binoculars and changed my route in order to avoid it.

The only time I've met a grizzly bear fairly close up—about 50 yards—it moved away once it realized I was there. It was my fault we came so close. I was above timberline in the Canadian Rockies on a rainy day, hiking into the wind and with a noisy creek not far away. Because of the weather I had my head down and was not looking round. The bear didn't smell or hear me, and

I spotted it long after I should have seen it. I made a noise so it knew I was there, and it moved on.

For hikes in grizzly country, a bear-repellent spray could be worth carrying (see page 185), but this is a weapon of last resort and not a reason to neglect sensible precautions.

Protecting food from bears is covered in chapter 5 (see pages 83–87). If you want to learn more about bears, Stephen Herrero's *Bear Attacks: Their Causes and Avoidance* is recommended reading.

Poisonous Snakes

Snakes are beautiful and interesting creatures. They will only attack if they feel threatened, so, as with other wild animals, leaving them alone is the way to avoid bites. Not all snakes are poisonous, and those that are may not inject much if any venom when they bite someone. Rattlesnakes are quite common along the lower sections of some long-distance trails. I saw and heard many along the Pacific Crest Trail in southern California. The bite isn't likely to be serious for healthy adults, but it's sensible to seek treatment. The chances of being bitten are very low anyway, and you can reduce the odds even more by taking a few simple precautions. In snake habitat, be wary of bushes and rock piles in case they harbor a snake. Don't put your hands behind logs or under rocks or anywhere you can't see. Snakes are active at night, so be careful around campsites then, especially if barefoot. Hiking in boots and loose-fitting long pants also gives protection—few snakebites are higher than the ankle.

For treatment in case you are bitten, you could carry a venom extractor—this can also be used for tick, spider, and insect bites. Old-style cut and suction devices are no longer recommended as they are likely to cause as much or even more harm than the bite itself, as are tourniquets. Although you won't know immediately whether venom has been injected or not—indeed, it could be many hours before this becomes clear—the extractor should be used straight away if it is to have any effect. If there's someone else who can go for help, the victim should rest with the site of the bite cleaned thoroughly and then bandaged snugly and kept at the same level as or lower than the heart. Any activity will speed the spread of the venom through the blood stream, and so it should be avoided. Solo hikers will have to walk out themselves however.

Wilkerson's *Medicine for Mountaineering* contains an excellent section on snakebite for those who want to go into this in more detail.

Biting Insects

The creatures that are most likely to cause serious problems on a long hike aren't bears or snakes or other large animals but biting insects. While day hikers and backpackers on short trips can plan their hikes to avoid peak insect times, the long-distance hiker can't. On most long trails—including the AT, PCT, and CDT—you are likely to go through areas where mosquitoes, black flies, or no-see-ums (midges) are swarming. Having clouds of insects buzzing around your head and being covered in itchy bites is very maddening. The gear to cope with biting insects—repellent, netting hoods, mesh tent doors, tightly woven clothing—is discussed in chapter 5. Other precautions you can take are to hike briskly—insects are more of a problem when stationary or moving slowly—and to take rest stops and camp in windy spots, the opposite of usual practice. Strong breezes prevent insects flying and so are a bonus.

Ticks are a more serious threat than some other insects because they can spread dangerous diseases. Ticks transfer themselves from vegetation when you brush against it, so it's where you can't avoid long grass or trailside shrubs that you're most likely to pick them up. When hiking through brush and vegetation, regular body searches are advisable. Ticks don't attach themselves immediately, so you have a good chance of catching them before they do. Ticks are dark so show up better on light-colored clothing. Putting insect repellent on your socks and tuck-

ing your shirt into your pants can help, as can wearing long-sleeved shirts.

Sharp tweezers are good for pulling out embedded ticks. You can also get special tick removers that make getting them out a bit easier. Don't twist the tick when you do this; instead, pull it straight out, holding it as close to the head as possible. Try not to crush it as the fluids inside may bear disease, and you don't want them on your skin or inside the wound made by the bite. Once the tick is out, a venom extractor can be used if you have one. The bite should then be washed with soap or antiseptic. If you become ill after being bitten by a tick, even if it's a few weeks later, seek medical advice. There are many symptoms. Look out in particular for rashes.

POISONOUS PLANTS

Plants that scratch or sting are annoying but not really a problem. Most long-distance hikers will come into contact with them at times, especially on cross-country routes. The only plants that can cause more than irritation are the members of the *Rhus* genus: poison oak, poison ivy, and poison sumac. The last is found in marshy areas in the eastern United States and Canada and is not often a problem for hikers. However, the first two grow at low elevations throughout the United States and southern Canada and can be found alongside the AT, PCT and CDT. Poison oak and poison ivy are vinelike bushes with long, thin branches. They can be identified by the leaves, which grow in clusters of three. Just brushing the plant can transfer sap containing urushiol to your skin or clothes. This chemical causes contact dermatitis, which means a very itchy rash plus a burning sensation and small blisters. These symptoms can take up to a week to clear. If you know you've been in contact with poison oak or ivy, rinse the affected area thoroughly in cold water as soon as possible to try to remove some of the sap. Hot water, soap, and other cleansers apparently do not help and are not needed. The sap also sticks to clothing and equipment, so these should be washed if they've been in contact with the plants. Otherwise you could transfer the sap from them to your skin.

Wearing long pants and a long-sleeved shirt when hiking along brushy trails is a good defense against poison oak and ivy, as is keeping a close eye on any shrubs next to or hanging over the trail. I saw much poison oak on the Pacific Crest Trail in northern California but never had any problems, as I was careful not to touch it. In particular, I remember a 6-mile descent down 36 very steep switchbacks overgrown with poison oak to the little town of Belden. Wanting to reach the post office before it closed, my companion and I raced down the trail, weaving round the shrubs reaching out on either side. There was no time for identification. We just tried to avoid touching any of them.

Calamine lotion and cool saltwater compresses are said to relieve the itchiness caused by urushiol. Some people suffer badly from poison oak and ivy dermatitis and require medical care. If this includes you, you'll have to leave the trail if you are affected.

CAMPING

Camping techniques are the same however long the hike. When you are out for many weeks or months, the techniques become automatic, and you find you can set up camp with barely a thought. As you hike, good campsites are noted almost subconsciously. During the first few days or possibly weeks of a long hike there are often concerns as to whether you'll find anywhere to camp each evening. Soon you know that you'll find a place and also that if you don't find a good location, you'll make do with a less-than-ideal spot.

In some areas, particularly U.S. and Canadian national parks, you're restricted to camping at certain sites, which will be specified on your wilderness permit. Long-distance hikers can sometimes have difficulties convincing rangers that they hike further each day than weekend backpackers do. Yellowstone National Park is notorious for permit problems with Continental Divide Trail hikers. At the Old Faithful Ranger Station I had difficulty convincing the ranger that I was hiking 20 miles a day. She wanted me to camp at sites about 8 miles apart, as that was how far backpackers walked each day. I got my permit in the end, but it took quite an argument. Where you have to use these sites, be prepared to alter your plans slightly to take their whereabouts into account. I found more understanding in the Canadian Rockies National Parks, where the rangers accepted that long-distance hikers couldn't guarantee where they would be weeks in advance and issued me with a permit that listed sites and dates but with a note that said these were approximate only.

Finding campsites is not usually difficult. Not creating new ones or causing more damage to existing sites isn't so simple, however, but it is something long-distance hikers should do for the sake of other hikers who follow in their footsteps.

Campsite Selection

Along popular trails you will find many campsites, some of them large and bare, with all ground vegetation gone, the lower branches missing from the trees, and little trails shooting off to water, viewpoints, and toilet sites. Fire rings probably dot the ground, too. Unappealing though the most overused sites may be, camping on them prevents new sites from developing. Don't enlarge these sites—stick to the already worn areas.

Sites that are still relatively unspoiled should be passed by and left to recover. If you've time, break up any fire rings, pick up litter, and scatter firewood so the site looks better than when you came upon it. Above the timberline campsites are often marked by circles of stones that have been used to hold down stakes. I've broken up far too many of these over the years, removing the stones to a creek shore or patch of bare ground so the crushed vegetation beneath can start to recover. If you do put rocks on stakes, which is rarely necessary, return the rocks to their original location when you leave.

Camping on bare ground, as at this campsite in the Grand Canyon, has the least impact on the environment.

If you don't camp on a well-used site, it's best to camp where no one has camped before. On such pristine sites it's important to leave no trace that you have camped there. The first way to do this is to camp some distance—at least 200 feet—away from the trail and preferably out of sight of it. Keep at least the same distance from water, if possible (it sometimes isn't in narrow valleys or marshy areas, where the only dry ground is on riverbanks or lakeshores), as camping close to water makes polluting it more likely and can disturb animals and birds. Look for durable ground that won't show any sign that you have been there. Rock, bare ground in

forests, sand and gravel, and dry grass and similar vegetation are all pretty tough. Damp ground is more easily damaged, as are forest floors with broad-leaved and woody plants rather than grass, as these are easily crushed. Basically, if you think you can walk on a surface without leaving any sign that you've done so, then you can probably camp on it without impact, too. If your feet will do damage, then a tent certainly will.

A site should never be altered in any way. If there isn't room for your tent without moving rocks or pruning vegetation, then go elsewhere. Try to avoid creating trails by repeatedly walking to and from the nearest water or between tents. This is where having enough water containers to collect all you need for a camp in one go is environmentally friendly as well as convenient. Cooking next to the tent or tarp means you don't have to walk to and from your kitchen. Where bears mean this isn't advisable, choose a durable site for your kitchen, such as a rock outcrop or gravel bank and try not to walk between tent and kitchen too often. Bare feet, sandals, and shoes have less effect on the ground than boots around camp.

Sites where no one has camped before should be used for one night only, which isn't a problem for long-distance hikers. When you depart, make sure you take everything with you. Use your fingers to fluff up flattened grass and other vegetation. You want it to look as though no one has ever camped there so it will not attract other campers.

Finding such sites can take time, so it's best to start looking for one well before dark. If I can't quickly find a suitable site, I take off my pack and search without it. That way I am less likely to choose a site that is uncomfortable or that could cause damage. When I do end up looking for a site in the dark, I still seek out a durable area where I'll leave no impact. Once I'm looking for a site, I also note the time I pass water sources. Then when I find a site I know how long it will take me to fetch water. More than half an hour for the round trip, and the site has to be very good for me to stay there. If I suspect that a water source may be the last one for many miles (though water can often be found where none is shown on the map—see pages 95–98 for information about water sources), I fill my containers so I can camp far from water.

Although using pristine sites is the norm in little-visited areas and when hiking cross-country, they have some advantages along popular trails, especially in areas where bears raid campsites regularly. Camp where no one has camped before and well away from popular sites, and bears are unlikely to be a problem. If you cook and eat late in the afternoon and then hike a few more miles before camping, you are even less likely to be visited by bears. (See pages 83–87 for information on food storage in bear country.)

When searching for a site, go uphill rather than down unless you can see there is no flat ground above you. Cold air sinks at night, so a terrace on the side of the valley is likely to be warmer than the valley bottom. It's often damper low down as well, and biting insects are more likely to be found there. You don't have to climb very far; just a few hundred feet can make an enormous difference. Whether you're low down or high up, look for ground that isn't in a dip or hollow that could flood if it rains heavily.

I also like to camp where I will catch the early morning sun as soon as possible. Knowing where the sun will rise means I can select a site partly on this basis or even decide on which side of a tree or rock I'll camp. This doesn't apply around midsummer in northern places, where the sun rises early. When the sun will be up at 4:00 A.M. and doesn't set until after midnight, I don't want to be woken up when it rises, so I look for a site that provides early morning shade. Of course, go far enough north, and the sun doesn't set, so this becomes irrelevant. I can get used to sleeping in daylight quite easily in those locations. If you can't, eye shades can help.

Sanitation

The incorrect deposition of feces is a problem along many trails. Too often people defecate too close to water or to a campsite and don't cover up the result. To avoid other people coming into contact with feces, they should be buried in what is known as a cathole. This is a shallow hole just deep enough for a couple of inches of soil to cover the feces. Around six inches deep should be adequate. It can be dug with your heel, a trekking pole, an ice ax, or a special toilet trowel. Catholes should be sited at least 200 feet from water, actual and potential campsites, and trails. Heading uphill is usually best. The idea is to leave your feces where other people won't find them and where they can't pollute water supplies. Once you have finished, mix the feces in with the soil with a stick, as this is said to aid decomposition.

Many backcountry campsites in popular areas have outhouses. Where these are found, they should always be used. They may detract from the wilderness feel, but they do reduce the health risks.

Campsites along popular trails are often surrounded by bits of pink and white toilet paper sticking out from under stones or even just lying on the ground or decorating bushes and plants. This is very unsightly and also a potential health hazard.

There are three solutions to the toilet paper problem: pack it out, burn it, or don't use it. The first means carrying a supply of plastic bags and double-bagging the used paper. It's now the recommended method of dealing with toilet paper (and any substitutes such as book pages). Burning is no longer recommended because of the fire risk. However, if you're having a campfire anyway, you might as well burn any used toilet paper you're carrying. The third method is to use natural materials such as pebbles, snow, sand, or soft fallen leaves. After use these can be deposited in the cathole before it's filled in. For further information and advice, consult Kathleen Meyer's *How to Shit in the Woods*.

Campfires

The campfire has a visceral appeal. It feels right when camping to sit around a fire. However, too many campfires have left too many scars that are very slow to heal. In many areas campfires are now banned, and in others their use is inappropriate because of the damage they can do.

One problem is that traditional campfires have a high impact. Every hiker has come across rings of stones with blackened ground in the middle of them. Usually there will be no down wood for some distance around the campsite, and the lower limbs of trees and shrubs may have been broken off.

At times, though, campfires are welcome, especially on cold or wet nights in really remote areas. One I remember with real affection. After a long day making slow progress hiking cross-country up a brush-, marsh-, and pool-choked valley in the Yukon, I pitched my tarp in the rain between two large spruce trees. Although the temperature was 54°F, I felt cold once I'd stopped hiking due to the dampness, so I cleared away the spruce needles from in front of the tarp and lit a fire. The bright cheerful flames and the

warmth had an immediate impact, and I suddenly felt much more cheerful and quite relaxed. Outside lay a vast wilderness. I knew I was far from any other human beings, but sitting in front of the fire I felt secure and content. I watched the fire for hours, hypnotized by the flickering flames and the glowing coals.

I lit many other fires in the Yukon and also in the northern Canadian Rockies, but only in places where I could leave no trace. The best place is on sand and gravel bars beside rivers that are regularly swept by floods. In these places there is often plenty of wood that has been washed downstream, too. Ocean beaches below the high tide level can be used as well. Away from water look for rocky and mineral soil. Never light a fire on vegetation or forest duff. Rocks can be covered with sand or soil so they don't blacken. On bare ground dig a shallow pit that can be covered up when you depart. Any dead organic matter—pine needles, forest duff—should be removed and put to one side so it can be replaced later. Fire rings aren't needed and

Campfire on a riverside sandbank that is regularly cleaned by floods in Yukon Territory.

shouldn't be constructed. Instead, ensure there is a foot or more of bare ground all around the fire. For safety and to avoid forest fires, there should be nothing flammable—trees, shrubs, dry grass, your tent—anywhere near a campfire.

Building a new fire, even a minimum-impact fire, cannot be justified in places where there are existing fire rings. I use these rings if I have a fire, which is rarely. I lit no more than a dozen fires on the Pacific Crest and Continental Divide Trails. In some areas such as the national parks in the Canadian Rockies, land managers have decided campers can't be stopped from lighting high-impact campfires. Metal fire pits are provided along with ready-cut fuel so that nearby trees won't be damaged. Again, where these are provided they should be used rather than new fire sites created.

I usually cook over any fire I light, so I keep it small. This uses up less wood and means there is less heat to cause damage to the ground than with a big fire. I never break off twigs or branches, even dead ones, from trees, and if I can't easily find enough wood nearby, I don't have a fire. I also collect only small pieces of wood to make sure they are burned to a fine ash so no charcoal or charred logs are left. Dry moss, tiny twigs, pinecones, and any scraps of paper I have about me are used as tinder.

Before leaving the site of a campfire, ensure that it is completely extinguished and cool to the touch. If you created the fire site, scatter the ashes widely, preferably on bare or rocky ground. Then fill in and smooth over the pit so there is no visible trace left.

The Cloudy Range in Yukon Territory.

9

Snow Travel

The winter! The brightness that blinds you,

    The white land locked tight as a drum,

The cold fear that follows and finds you,

    The silence that bludgeons you dumb.

The snows that are older than history,

    The woods where the weird shadows slant;

The stillness, the moonlight, the mystery,

    I've bade 'em good-by—but I can't.

    — Robert Service, *The Spell of the Yukon*

Under snow a landscape becomes wilder and more challenging. Trails disappear and familiar landmarks look different. The scars of summer vanish, hidden beneath the snow and ice, and overused, worn places look pristine. Far fewer people venture deep into the backcountry, so it becomes less crowded. All this makes snow country very appealing to hikers who love wild, empty places.

Winter, of course, is the season for snow, but spring, in fact, is a better time for long hikes in the snow because there is more daylight, it's warmer, and the weather is usually more settled. The further north or the higher the altitude, the sooner the snow usually arrives in the autumn and the later it lasts into the spring. The amount of snow and how long it remains on the ground varies enormously from year to year. The year I hiked the Pacific Crest Trail there was continuous cover above 9,000 feet in the High Sierra in May. The year before the snow was virtually all gone by the same time of year.

Backpacking in winter and early spring is a very different activity than summer hiking. It requires more skills and extra equipment. Occasional snow patches or light falls of snow can be easily dealt with (see pages 211–13). Continuous snow cover is a different matter, however. The snow hiker needs to be able to cope with the cold, to know how to camp on snow, and to be aware of the best ways to travel through deep snow. There are new dangers, too, from avalanches, cornices, blizzards, and extreme cold. More clothing and warmer sleeping bags are needed, probably along with ice axes, crampons, skis, or snowshoes. That means heavier packs and lower daily mileage, especially in midwinter when the days are short. There is so much involved that there are whole books about travel in the winter wilderness. I've written one myself—

A spring camp in Onion Valley in the High Sierra.

Wilderness Skiing and Winter Camping. Another useful book with a different perspective is *The Winter Wilderness Companion* by Garrett and Alexandra Conover. If you're venturing into the realm of alpine mountaineering, you'll want to be familiar with the classic *Mountaineering: The Freedom of the Hills,* edited by Don Graydon. Below I outline the major topics, but if you're serious about undertaking journeys deep into the snowy wilderness, I recommend that you take a look at the books mentioned above.

WINTER WITHOUT THE SNOW

Of course, not everywhere is snow-covered in winter, and not all hikers like the cold or want to learn the skills for dealing with snow. In the deserts of the Southwest, winter is a good time to undertake a long-distance hike, as they are much cooler than in summer. If you want to venture abroad, you can have a second summer by heading south of the equator to Australia, New Zealand, South America, or southern Africa.

EQUIPMENT FOR THE SNOW

In light, soft snow cover no special equipment is needed. Once the snow deepens or there is much ice around, various items make travel both safer and easier. Which items you need depends on where and when you are going.

Ice Ax

Ice axes are needed for safety on steep slopes of hard snow and ice. For hikes in flat areas or in dense forests they may be of little use. In the depths of winter, when the snow is deep and soft, an ax isn't needed either, unless you go above the timberline onto harder, wind-blasted snow. Spring is the time when ice axes are most used, when the snow has compacted and hardened. This means that early-season hikers on long-distance trails may well need an ax. I used one frequently in the High Sierra on the Pacific Crest Trail and the northern Rockies on the Continental Divide Trail.

An ice ax is needed to prevent slips that could send you hurtling down a snow slope and to stop a slip if it does occur. This means you need to know how to use it. I outline basic techniques below, but I don't believe you can really learn them from a written description. The best way to learn is from an instructor or an experienced friend. Teaching yourself is difficult and can be dangerous.

The time to learn to use an ice ax is not during a long-distance hike. I found this out on the Pacific Crest Trail when I teamed up with three other hikers to go through the snowbound High Sierra. All of us had ice axes, but only three of us knew how to use them properly. The fourth hiker, Larry, had only had his ax for a few weeks. At first there was no real need for any skill with the ax, for the snow was soft and the slopes gentle. However, we wanted to climb Mount Whitney, for which ice axes were essential and which was not an ascent for someone with no ice-ax skills, so the day before our planned climb we spent a few hours teaching ax techniques to Larry. This wasn't adequate, of course, but it was all we could do.

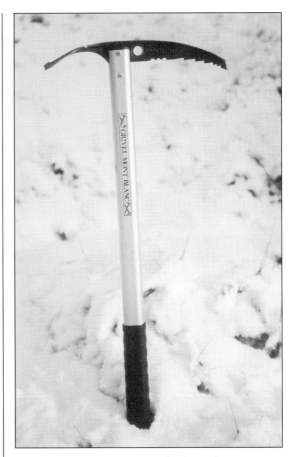

A lightweight ice ax suitable for long-distance hiking.

During the ascent all went well, though the snow was hard and crampons were needed throughout the climb. On the descent, to avoid a rather unnerving traverse below some pinnacles and to shorten the time needed to get back to camp, we went straight down from the summit to the top of some gullies we'd passed below on the climb and which we reckoned could be descended with care. From the top the narrow, twisting, and steep gullies, 1,000 to 1,500 feet in length, didn't look so appealing, but we found one that looked safe. Dave went first and then Scott, both of them sitting on the snow and glissading downward, their axes held ready to stop their slides if necessary. At one point each of them disappeared around a narrow twist in the gully but quickly appeared again to eventually reach the wide, safe runout at the base of the gully. Larry went next, picking up speed at a great rate, and soon going much faster than the others. At the bend he sped out of view in a flurry of snow and rocks. A loud yell echoed upward; then came silence, a deep, profound silence. I waited, stunned. Larry didn't appear below. Was he injured, dead even? Then came a distant shout: "I've lost my ice ax." Not daring to glissade in case I slid into Larry, I carefully scrambled down the rocks next to the gully. Near where he'd disappeared I found his ax to the side of the gully, wedged between some rocks. Larry lay not far below, spread-eagled on his back on the snow. He couldn't move without slipping, so, facing inward and using both axes, I kicked steps down to him. When I reached him, I found out what had stopped him. We'd shared a pack for the day, and our crampons were on the back of it, removed because we didn't want to glissade with them. Larry was carrying the pack, and the crampons had stuck in the snow and stopped his slide. Once I returned his ax to him he was able to finish the descent. (I don't, by the way, recommend glissading. It is potentially very dangerous, as this story shows.)

Designs and Materials

A basic ice ax of the sort labeled "walking" or "general mountaineering" is the best for long-distance hiking. Fancier models with weirdly curved heads and handles are designed for ice climbers and mountaineers and aren't suitable for hiking.

The pick of the ice ax should be gently curved with a few teeth underneath, while the adze should be broad for stopping a fall in soft snow and making step cutting easier. The head of an ax can be made from a single piece of metal or from two pieces welded together. Although not strong enough for serious climbing, two-piece heads are cheaper than single piece ones and are fine for hikers.

Most ax heads are made from forged steel, but the lightest models have alloy heads. These become blunt quickly, but this shouldn't be a problem for occasional hiking use. I have a Camp HL250 ax that weighs only 10.5 ounces and that is fine for my needs. The light weight is welcome, as the ax spends far more time strapped to my pack than in my hand. Steel-headed axes can weigh up to 30 ounces, though there are lightweight ones like the Grivel Air Tech Racing ax, at 12.5 ounces, and the Charlet Moser Helium Racing ax, at 11.5 ounces. I certainly wouldn't choose any ax for hiking that weighed more than 14 ounces.

Shafts are usually made from aluminum alloy because it's strong and light. However, it's also cold to hold and slippery when wet. A rubber handgrip or synthetic coating overcomes this.

Length

For hiking, you want your ax long enough that the spike is an inch or so above the ground when the ax is held by the side at arm's length. For most people, this means an ax should be between 25 and 30 inches in length. Some people, including some experienced mountaineering instructors, reckon that axes this long are difficult to use on steep slopes and for self-arrest. They recommend much shorter axes. For climbers who are confident on steep snow and ice, this may be fine. I've used both 22- and 28-inch axes frequently, and I feel much more secure with the longer ax, as I have no need to stoop over it when using it on relatively gentle slopes. It's also better for descending steep slopes as you can reach further down the slope, either to cut steps or to simply plunge the ax in the snow for security.

Wrist Loops

Many axes come fitted with wrist loops, and a sling can easily be attached through the hole in the head if one isn't provided. Do you need one though? It depends. If you use a wrist loop, you're unlikely to lose the ax if you drop it. However, there is a danger of the ax injuring you if you drop it in a fall and it's lashing about still attached to you. Wrist loops are also awkward to switch from hand to hand as you change direction when zigzagging up a slope. I like to have a wrist loop fitted, though I don't always use it. A wrist loop is a very good idea while you're learning to use an ice ax, as you're more likely to drop your ax then than when you're experienced.

Using an Ice Ax

The most important use of the ice ax is to stop yourself from sliding down a slope if you slip. This is called *self-arrest* and should be practiced until you can do it without thinking. And once you've learned the technique, you should still practice it regularly. In an emergency your reactions must be automatic. If you have to think what to do, it'll be too late. The first time I had to stop a fall with an ice ax—on the Pacific Crest Trail in the San Bernardino Mountains—it happened so fast I couldn't remember falling or stopping. One minute I was traversing across a steep slope; the next I was lying on some snow about 20 feet lower down with the ice ax tucked under me.

A slope of hard snow with a long, safe runout is needed for practicing self-arrest. The self-arrest position is with the ax held across the body with the upper hand on the adze, which is tucked into the shoulder, and with the pick pressed into the snow. It's important to have the ax head close to your shoulder, for holding the ax at arm's length may lead to it being ripped out of your hands. The other hand holds the shaft near the spike. If you pull the shaft upward with the lower hand, it helps push the pick into the snow and also keeps the spike from catching on the snow. Arching your back exerts even more pressure on the pick. Feet and knees can act as brakes, but note that you should keep your feet off the snow if you're wearing crampons (which you shouldn't do when practicing), or they may catch and flip you over.

Initially it's best to practice by lying on your stomach with the ax held off the snow. Slide down the snow until you pick up a little speed and then push the pick into the snow until you come to a halt. Once you're happy doing this, you should try it lying on your back with your head up the slope and then with your head down the slope on both back and stomach. You need to practice in these different positions because you could end up sliding down a slope in any position. In the first case you have to roll sideways toward the head of the ax and onto the pick. When sliding head down the slope on your back, you need to ram the pick into the snow out to the side so you can pivot around it while rolling onto your stomach until your feet are downhill and you can stop.

Stopping a head-down slide on your stomach is difficult. Thrusting the pick into the snow at your side and pivoting around it to get your legs downhill is relatively easy. The problem is that you end up with the ax out at arm's length above your head, where it can easily be ripped out of your hands. To avoid this, the pick has to be lifted out of the snow and the ax pulled in close to your shoulder.

Most of the time an ice ax is used like a walking stick with the spike pushed into the snow as a third point of contact to help with balance. This is also good for safety since if you do slip, you can push the shaft farther into the snow and stop your slide before it has really started. When angling up a slope, it's best to have the ax in your uphill hand, which means changing it over each time you change direction. That way you can lean on it if you slip. On really steep ground or if you're above a small cliff or steep ravine, you should move your feet only when the ax is firmly thrust into the snow.

When you're descending, you can thrust the ax shaft into the snow below you for security and then "heel down" by leaning forward and stamping your heels into the snow.

The most comfortable position for holding the ax is with the pick pointing forward so the hand can rest on the wide flat top of the adze. With it in this position you are also less likely to impale your leg on the pick if you stumble. However, for quick self-arrest, the pick should be pointing backward, so I carry my ax like this if I think a slide is possible.

If you have to cross ice or snow so hard that you can't kick adequate steps into it, and if you

Kicking steps up a snow slope with an ice ax for security.

don't have crampons, the adze can be used for cutting steps. This isn't as easy as it sounds, and you'll need to practice doing it. It's also quite difficult and tiring with an ultralight ax, since you have to use a lot of force due to the lack of weight. Crampons may seem to have made step cutting redundant, but it's still quicker to cut steps across a short section of hard ice or snow rather than to don crampons.

Carrying an Ice Ax
When not needed, the ax can be strapped to your pack. This is fine when approaching the snow or when on low angled snow but not when the ax needs to be handy, as you have to take your pack off to get at it. If there's any chance you'll need it, the ax should be in your hand, not attached to your pack. If you don't want to hold it, you can slide it between your back and the pack so the head rests on the top of the shoulder straps and it's easily accessible. Ice-ax picks and spikes are sharp and can tear fabrics and puncture skin, so you need to cover them when not in use. Rubber protectors are available, but wine bottle corks work just as well. I've even seen the end of a toothpaste tube used.

Crampons
Rubber-soled footwear won't grip on ice and really hard snow. Instead, they'll go skidding across it as if on a skating rink. Crampons make the difference between safe walking and sliding about dangerously. Indeed, in conditions where

ice-ax braking is difficult or impossible due to the hardness of the ice or snow, crampons may be essential for safe hiking. Crampons can also be useful in places where you don't need an ice ax, such as flat or gently sloping terrain that is very icy.

Hikers on long-distance trails don't often need crampons, however. If a snow slope is too hard to cross or climb safely with an ice ax, it will probably be softer later in the day. Early-season hikers may need crampons, though. In the High Sierra on the Pacific Crest Trail I used them frequently, particularly when climbing to a high pass early in the day. Those slopes were softer later on, but unfortunately the snow in lower areas was also softer, much softer. So soft and deep, in fact, that we found traveling, even with snowshoes and skis, so slow and difficult by late

Cornices, overhanging masses of snow or ice on mountain ridges, can be extremely dangerous. This is the peak of Braeriach in the Cairngorm Mountains in the Scottish Highlands.

afternoon that we stopped early. In order to make much progress we needed those early starts, which meant we also needed crampons.

Crampons are mountaineering tools, not hiking tools, and skill is needed in their use. As with ice axes, I'd recommend taking instruction in their use (the two usually go together in a general mountaineering course).

Types

The various types of crampons can be differentiated by how much they bend along their length. The three basic types are generally known as rigid, articulated, and flexible. The first are designed for ice climbing and aren't suitable for hiking as they are likely to break or fall off if used with semistiff hiking boots. They're also heavy. Articulated crampons (hinged would be a better description) will fit some hiking boots but are still unnecessarily heavy for hiking. Flexible crampons are designed to fit flexible boots and are the lightest full-length crampons, making

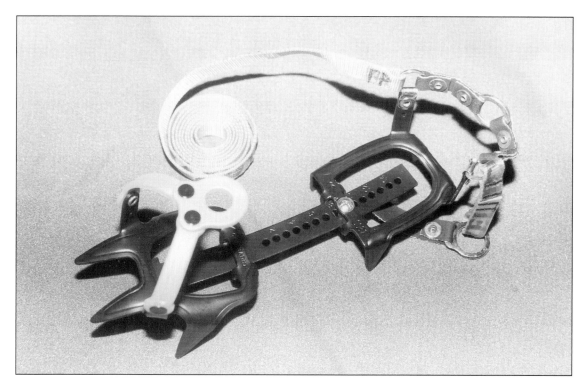

Lightweight flexible crampons designed to fit hiking boots.

them the best choice for the hiker. Crampons may have 8, 9, 10, or 12 points; the number doesn't matter for walking. Neither does it matter if there are front points—that is, points that stick out at the front since these are for climbing, not hiking.

Materials

Most crampons are made from hardened steel, which is very durable, stays sharp a long time, and can easily be sharpened when it does get blunt. However it's also relatively heavy. The lightest crampons are made from alloy, which doesn't stay sharp very long and is harder to sharpen. In fact, it's impossible to get the same edge on alloy as on steel. Durability isn't as good either. For occasional hiking use on hard snow alloy crampons are satisfactory, but they won't penetrate hard ice very well and thus don't give the security of steel ones.

Straps

Some crampons come with quick-fit bindings with heel levers and toe bales. These are much easier to use than straps but, unfortunately, they can only be used with boots with pronounced welts, which most hiking boots lack, so walkers still have to put up with fiddling with frozen straps with numb fingers. The easiest system I've found comes from Grivel and has hinged flexible plastic toe and heel harnesses, which close around the boot and are then secured with a single strap.

Whatever system your crampons have, attaching them to your boots should be practiced at home so that, if necessary, you can put them on in a blizzard relatively quickly.

Fit

Crampons must fit your boots properly or they may fall off, which is always inconvenient and may be dangerous. All crampons are adjustable, but it's still best to take your boots to the store so you can be shown how to fit the crampons to your boots and how to do up the straps. To check the fit, attach the crampon to the boot but don't fasten the straps; then pick up the boot and shake it. A properly fitted crampon won't fall off.

Even flexible crampons won't fit all hiking boots. Firm uppers and semistiff soles are needed. If straps are tightened up on boots with soft uppers, they can press on the feet, which is painful and could lead to frostbite due to constricted blood flow. And if the boots aren't torsionally stiff, then crampons may twist off, especially when traversing steep slopes.

Walking

Walking in crampons isn't difficult, but it does require a little practice. You need to keep your legs well apart so you don't trip over the crampons and fall flat on your face, or catch a side point in your gaiters or pants and rip them or even gash your leg. For maximum security on slopes you need to put your foot down flat so that all the points are in contact with the snow or ice. If your crampons have front points, you can kick them into the snow and balance on them. This, however, is getting into the realm of climbing rather than walking and is very hard to do for more than a few steps with flexible boots.

Carrying

Crampons are not the easiest items to pack. Rubber spike protectors are available, but they are prone to tangling and can be hard to sort out with cold fingers. I use tough Cordura or polyvinyl chloride (PVC) bags that can be carried inside the pack without danger to other items of gear. Many packs come with straps or patches for carrying crampons on the outside, the best place when they are likely to be needed often.

Snowshoes

Ice axes and crampons work well when you can walk on the snow. However, they are no help at all when you sink deeply into it. Floundering— or *postholing*, as it is known—through deep snow is an incredibly tiring and slow method of travel,

as I found in the southern ranges of California on the Pacific Crest Trail. After slogging through relatively short stretches of deep snow in the San Gabriel and San Bernardino Mountains, I knew that postholing for hundreds of miles through the Sierra Nevada just wasn't feasible, so I bought some snowshoes. With these I could stay on the snow, rather than sink into it.

Snowshoes are great if you just want to get out into the snow-covered backcountry and not spend time learning new skills. There's not much technique needed to walk on snowshoes, and you can, as I did in the High Sierra, set out on a long journey the first time you use a pair. You can wear them with ordinary hiking boots, too. Ski poles are a great help but not essential. I went through the Sierra with just an ice ax for support.

In recent years snowshoeing has boomed, and there is now a large choice of snowshoes available. Some, though, are designed for racing or climbing rather than hiking. For backpacking, fairly large snowshoes are needed to support the weight of you and your load. Lightweight shoes designed for fast movement on packed tracks are unsuitable for hiking with a load on soft snow. I'd suggest snowshoes at least two and a half to three feet in length. The bindings are the only complex bit of a snowshoe. Check that they fit your boots in the store, then practice fastening them at home so you can do so easily in a blizzard with numb fingers. Try and find snowshoes with simple bindings and ones that you can easily fix with a length of cord if they break. Pivoting bindings are useful in the mountains, for you can kick your toes into a slope with the shoe lying on the surface.

If you're not bothered about speed, especially downhill, snowshoes are a good alternative to skis. In some circumstances they're better than skis, such as soft, deep snow into which even the widest skis can sink and in dense forests where skis can be unmanageable. Because of their greater flotation, snowshoes could be carried on some ski tours as a backup in case the skis won't support you. This especially applies in very cold places where deep unconsolidated snow lasts for

Snowshoes are useful in deep, soft snow.

months. I've done ski tours in the Canadian Rockies and the Yukon where a pair of snow-shoes would have been a great boon as the skis sank in deeply and made progress very difficult. You can also keep snowshoes on when crossing snow-free sections of ground and even, as I did in the High Sierra, for fording creeks without worrying about damaging them. Finally, when strapped to the pack, snowshoes don't protrude and catch on branches the way skis do.

Skis

On that snowshoe trek through the snowbound High Sierra, I traveled with two companions who used skis. Or at least I traveled with them some of the time. Whenever there was a long flat section or a downhill slope they were quickly dots in the distance. The next winter I learned to cross-country ski. As well as returning to the

High Sierra, since then I have backpacked on skis in Greenland, Spitsbergen, Lapland, Norway, the Canadian Rockies, the Scottish Highlands, the Alps, the Groulx Mountains in Quebec, and the Tombstone Range in the Yukon Territory. When the backcountry is snow-covered, skis are my favorite means of travel.

Unlike snowshoeing, however, skiing takes time to learn. Very few people can head out into the wilderness after only a short time on skis and get very far, especially when carrying a heavy pack. The quickest way to learn is at a skiing class.

Types of Skis

There are many types of skiing and many types of skis. Lightweight, narrow, cross-country skis designed for zooming around cut tracks aren't suitable for ski backpacking as they won't support the weight of you and your pack in soft snow and are very difficult to control on de-scents. At the other extreme is the current trend for very wide skis and high, heavy, plastic boots. These boots may lock down at the heel for Alpine-style descents or flex at the toe for telemark turns. Such skis and boots are great for ski mountaineering, where the aim is to climb high into the mountains and then descend very steep slopes, but for ski backpacking they're heavy, quite slow, and hard work on flat and undulating terrain.

Rather than the widest skis and plastic boots, I prefer more traditional Nordic touring or mountain touring skis and leather boots. These skis and boots are a good compromise and will do everything adequately. The skis should have metal edges so the edges will hold on ice and hard snow. These types of skis are 50 to 70 millimeters wide in the middle and 10 to 20 millimeters wider than that at the tip. This *sidecut*, as it's called, helps the skis to turn when going downhill. More sidecut makes skis easier to turn but

A backcountry lodge almost buried in the Norwegian mountains.

harder to ski in a straight line on the flat. Touring skis should have a bit of a bow in the middle so that pressure is needed to flatten them onto the snow. This is called *camber* and helps a ski to glide on the tips and tails with the middle section off the snow. When you're carrying a heavy pack, a fast glide is very hard to sustain for more than a few strides, but you can get some glide on firm snow. Touring on skis with virtually no camber is hard work on the flat. The length of skis is a matter of great debate. For touring skis, your height plus 8 to 10 inches should be fine. For ski mountaineering, a shorter ski may be best, especially if you go for a wider model.

Waxable or Waxless

Skis are either waxable or waxless, which means that either you apply a grip wax to the smooth base to keep it from slipping on flat and undulating terrain or the ski has a pattern cut into the base that grips the snow and thus doesn't need wax. The advantage of a waxable ski is that there are different waxes for different temperatures and types of snow, so you can fine-tune the ski to the

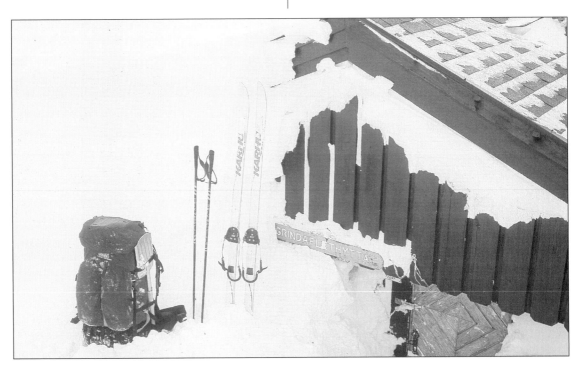

Crossing Tombstone Pass between the Tombstone and Cloudy Ranges in Yukon Territory.

conditions. The disadvantages are that you have to learn how to wax properly, and carry a wax kit with you. With waxless skis, you can just put them on and go. However, you can't alter the waxless pattern for different types of snow, and in some situations the pattern won't work very well. Waxless bases work best in snow that's around the freezing point, which is just the snow where waxing is hardest because snow at this temperature changes texture very quickly. If you ski only very occasionally, or if all your skiing is in fairly warm conditions, waxless skis could be the ones to choose. However, waxless skis are like riding a bicycle with one gear and can't compare with the ease of skiing on a well-waxed ski. Actually, waxless skis are more accurately called "less wax" skis for they still work best if some wax is used. Like all skis, they glide and turn better if the tips and tails are waxed with glide wax,

usually applied at home with a hot iron. You can also get a grip wax for waxless skis that helps if they start slipping.

Waxing for touring doesn't have to be complicated. There's no need to carry lots of waxes. I usually just take three or four broad-spectrum waxes that cover all the conditions I'm likely to meet plus a cork for rubbing them in and a scraper for removing excess wax.

With waxless skis, you won't be able to climb directly up anything more than a fairly gentle slope; with waxable skis, you'll be able to do so only if you apply so much wax that the you have to walk down the other side. To make ascents easier, climbing skins are needed. These are ski-length strips of synthetic fabric with a brushed raised surface that won't slip backward on the snow on one side and glue on the other to stick them to the bottom of the skis.

Boots and Bindings
Nordic touring boots attach to the ski binding at the toe only so that you can raise your heel when

skiing on the flat and uphill. There are a number of different boot and binding combinations. These aren't compatible with each other, so you need to ensure your boots and bindings match. The oldest system is called the Nordic Norm and is probably the best for ski backpacking. Boots for this system have a square front to the sole that is 75 millimeters wide and juts out beyond the toe of the boot. This sole has three holes in the bottom of it that fit onto three pins on the binding. A bail arm then clamps the boot into place. Three-pin bindings, as these are called, are simple and lightweight. An alternative that gives slightly better downhill control is a cable binding that wraps around the heel of the boot. You can also get combination three-pin/cable bindings. For touring, my preference is for a cable binding. I find these easier to get in and out of and less likely to damage boots than three-pin bindings.

There are two other systems suitable for ski backpacking that are similar to each other but not compatible. These are the Rottefella New Nordic Norm Backcountry (NNN-BC) and the Salomon Nordic System Backcountry (SNS-BC). With both systems, a metal bar under the toe of the boot clips into the binding. These systems are excellent when gliding on the flat (lighter weight versions of them are standard for cross-country racing) and give good downhill control with the right boots. However, there is a limited choice of boots for each system, unlike with the Nordic Norm.

Ski touring boots look much like medium- to heavyweight hiking boots. They need to flex at the toe for easy gliding but be rigid from side to side for turning. With any ski boot, hold it at the toe and heel and see if you can twist the sole. If you can, the boot will twist off the ski when you try to make a turn. Some boots come with one or two buckles and stiffened ankles. These make turning the skis easier, but skiing on the flat is a little more tiring. I use a boot with a single buckle for skiing in steep mountain terrain and a lighter boot without buckles for more undulating tours.

Most touring boots are leather, but the lightest plastic models can be used for mountain skiing. They have the advantage of keeping your feet dry and do give more control on descents. However, I don't find them as comfortable on the flat.

Poles

Trekking poles work fine as ski poles—indeed, quite often the only difference between adjustable trekking poles and adjustable ski poles is the graphics—though a wider basket will be needed for soft snow. For skiing, poles should be armpit length, a bit longer than is normal for hiking. Aluminum is the best material for ski backpacking poles. Fiberglass is too easily broken.

Repairs

Extra items are needed for repairing ski gear. I carry binding screws in case of loss, a screwdriver for tightening loose binding screws, quick-drying epoxy for bindings and for gluing together delaminating skis, and vise grips or hose clamps for holding delaminating skis together while glue dries, a spare cable if using cable bindings, and a spare pole basket. On long tours I also carry a spare ski pole and a spare binding.

Shovel

A snow shovel is a vital safety item. Being able to build a snow shelter has saved lives, and if an avalanche occurs, victims can be dug out much more quickly if you have a shovel. It can also be used to build a snow wall round your camp and dig a kitchen site. There are many shovels available in weights ranging from 8 to 32 ounces. Shovel blades are made from either poly carbonate or aluminum. Polycarbonate is almost unbreakable but doesn't cut into hard snow very well. Aluminum is better for hard snow but not as durable; nevertheless, it is still pretty tough. The simplest and lightest shovels are just blades that can be fitted onto a ski pole shaft, whereas the heaviest have full-length telescoping shafts with snow saws inside them. Small blades are

Sleds can be used for hauling gear on ski tours. This skier is approaching Kearsage Pinnacles in the High Sierra.

good in the confines of a snow hole; large blades are better for shifting large quantities of snow.

Avalanche Beacon

A beacon transmits a signal that can be picked up by searchers who also have beacons and can be used to locate someone buried in an avalanche. If beacons are used, everyone in the party should have one (and should practice using it regularly). A beacon won't protect you from an avalanche nor necessarily save your life if you're caught in one, so wearing the beacon doesn't mean you can ignore other precautions (see pages 242–43 for more on avalanches).

Packs

For stability on skis, internal-frame packs are best. Large ones (5,000 cubic inches or larger) are needed to accommodate bulkier sleeping bags, more clothing, and other items.

Sleds

To reduce the weight on your back, you can pull some or all of your load on a sled. These work well on flat and undulating terrain but can be awkward on steep ground. Sleds are available that are built for this purpose, or you can adapt a child's plastic toboggan.

Clothing

The same principles apply to hiking clothing year round. Layers are best. (See page 170 for a detailed discussion of clothing.) In winter it's even more important not to overheat, as damp clothing will chill you even more than in summer, and drying clothing can be impossible. For above timberline trips, heavier shell garments are warmer and give more protection than thin summer ones. In below-freezing temperatures, garments that are windproof but not waterproof are better than waterproof-breathables as they will let out far more body moisture. Warmer hats and gloves are needed, and spares are essential, both in case of loss and in case they get wet. Gaiters are necessary for keeping snow out of your boots. Super-gaiters also add a bit of warmth. When you stop in really cold weather, you cool down very quickly, so a thick insulating garment big enough to go over all your other layers is a great item to have. If rain is unlikely, down is best for this as it's more compact for carrying and gives more warmth for the weight. In damper climates a synthetic-filled top or even a heavyweight fleece might be better.

Vapor barriers are an alternative way to stay warm when it's very cold. Vapor barrier (VB) clothing is made from thin synthetic fabrics with nonbreathable waterproof coatings that prevent evaporative heat loss by preventing body moisture from escaping. To do this, VB

Down clothing is ideal for camp wear in cold weather.

clothing needs to be worn either next to the skin or over a very thin wicking synthetic garment. VB clothing works best when it's cold and dry because that's when evaporative heat loss is greatest. I find VB clothing so efficient that I can't ski or hike in it without breaking into a sweat within minutes, so I don't wear it when I'm moving. In camp, however, it provides much extra warmth at very little extra weight or bulk, and I often carry a VB jacket and trousers in case of extreme cold. It's especially good for sleeping in if your sleeping bag isn't warm enough. VB gloves and socks are also useful. Plastic bags can be used as socks if your feet are really cold, but they won't last long.

Camping Gear

A sleeping bag that is comfortable in summer won't keep you warm in winter. You either need a much warmer bag or a second lightweight bag that will fit over or inside the one you already have. Cold ground is much more of a problem in winter, and a thin foam pad won't keep it out when the temperature is much below 25°F. Two pads are better or a thick, self-inflating model.

The same tent will do year-round, though larger models are nice to have in winter, as you'll spend more time inside due to the cold and the longer nights. Tents that can be pitched with mitts on are also useful. Vestibules big enough to cook in safely are worth having, particularly when you're stuck in a storm for several days.

The best stoves for winter cooking use liquid fuel, since these stoves aren't affected much by the cold. With cartridge stoves, apart from the Coleman X models, the cartridges have to be kept warm if they are to work properly in temperatures below 25°F. This can be done by keeping the cartridge in your sleeping bag or inside your clothing when not in use and by warming it with your hands when in use. A cartridge can also be stood in a pan of warm water to keep it warm. All stoves will work more efficiently if the fuel supply is insulated from the snow. With stoves where the fuel tank or cartridge is under the burner, don't use closed-cell foam or anything plastic, since this will melt if it gets too hot. A metal snow shovel or piece of wood is better. (In the High Sierra I used a paperback book under my Svea 123.) Foam pads or even stuff sacks can be used under hose-attached fuel bottles and cartridges. When refilling fuel bottles, be very careful not to spill any fuel on your skin because it could cause frostbite. When handling stoves with gloves on, wear ones made of cotton, silk, or wool. Unlike those made of synthetics, they won't melt if you touch a hot part of the stove or get too near the flame.

Large pans are useful when snow has to be melted. You can produce more water more quickly than with a small pan. Vacuum flasks and insulated water bottle jackets will ensure water doesn't freeze.

Melting blocks of snow, with a shovel placed under the stove for insulation.

SNOW CAMPING

How to pitch a tent or tarp on snow depends on what sort of snow it is. On very hard snow or ice you may have to hack holes in it to get the stakes in. Usually, though, the softness of the snow is the problem. Then you need to stamp out a platform for your tent, first with skis or snowshoes and then just with boots. Once this is done, leave it to harden before pitching the tent. Skis, ice axes, and ski poles can be used to anchor guylines and staking points. Stakes can be buried horizontally with the guylines wrapped round them and then the snow stamped down on top. You can also fill stuff sacks or plastic bags with snow, tie guylines around the mouth, and then bury them. In the morning, however, care will be needed to dig up the now-frozen sacks without damaging them. Getting the snow out may be a problem, too. I prefer to use stakes, which can be hacked out with an ice ax.

If the campsite is exposed to the wind, a wall of snow can be built to shelter it. This needs to

be far enough from the tents so that any snow that falls on the lee side of it doesn't bury the tents. When snow does start to cover the tent, it must be knocked off; otherwise the poles may bend or break and the tent collapse. Snow on the fly sheet can usually be knocked off by banging it from inside. Snow around the perimeter of the tent will have to be dug away with a shovel.

Cooking in winter can be done in the tent vestibule in stormy weather, as long as there's ample ventilation. In fine weather a kitchen area can be dug out with benches to sit on (line these with your foam pads for warmth) and a table to cook on.

In camp, don't leave anything lying on the snow, including garbage, as it's very easy for items to get buried. When leaving a winter camp,

In spring it is often possible to find snow-free patches of ground to camp on. This is Crabtree Meadows in the High Sierra on the Pacific Crest Trail.

dismantle all structures and hide the signs that you have been there so the area will look wild for future visitors.

Toilets are a problem in deep snow. Just burying feces means they'll reappear come spring. If you do use catholes, make sure they are well away from water (check the map for this—it may not be apparent on the ground) and away from any place where people might come across the feces when the snow melts. It could be better to leave feces on the surface as they decompose much more quickly in sunlight, as long as you do so in places where no one is likely to come across them. Toilet paper should be burned or packed out, if used. Snow makes a good alternative. In popular areas consider packing out feces, too. This is not as unpleasant in winter as in summer, since the feces will freeze. Pick them up with an inside out plastic bag over your hand, turn the bag right side out, and then put it in another bag. Unsightly yellow pee stains should be covered with snow.

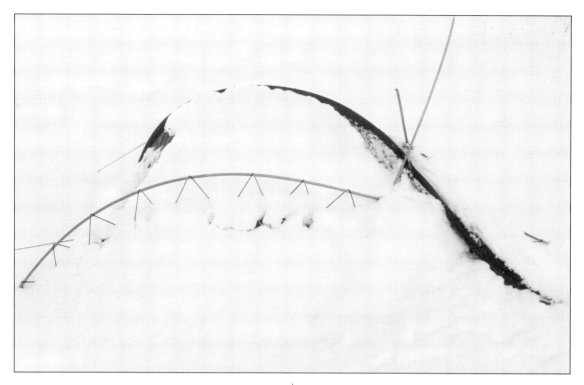

Tents need to be cleared of snow buildup frequently to prevent them from collapsing.

SNOW SHELTERS

In very windy weather a snow shelter is a much more pleasant place to be than a tent. Inside you won't even know what the wind is doing. A snow shelter can be drier, warmer, and roomier than a tent, too. Building one can be done surprisingly quickly with a snow shovel. You can dig into a steep bank to make a snow hole or snow cave, or you can heap up a large mound of snow and then hollow it out to make a snow dome. The quickest shelter is a snow trench, dug straight down into deep snow and roofed with a tarp, groundsheet, or tent fly held in place with skis, ski poles, or fallen branches. With all types of shelter, make sure you have plenty of ventilation and don't leave any gear lying round where it can get buried. Entrances should be small and low down so warm air doesn't escape through them.

To make a snow cave, dig a trench straight into a bank of snow at least 6 feet deep and then dig out either side to make sleeping platforms. Keep these higher than the trench so that cold air will sink into the latter (don't leave your boots in it!). The roof should be at least a foot thick. Smoothing the roof down makes it less likely that melt water will drip onto you. Poke a ventilation hole in the roof with a ski pole, which can be left in place so you can keep the hole open. Stop up most of the entrance with snow blocks to stop snow blowing in and warm air escaping. A pack can be used to close off the door at night.

A snow dome big enough for three or four people can be built very quickly. Just heap up a pile of snow some 12 feet across and 6 to 8 feet high; then dig out the middle. The walls should be at least a foot thick. To achieve this, ski poles and ice axes can be pushed a foot into the dome at various points from the outside so it looks like a rather strange giant pincushion. When the end of one of these items appears, those digging out the inside of the dome know to stop at that point.

When camping in deep snow, you can dig your own seats and build a table.

In case you need to build one in an emergency, it's worth practicing building snow shelters. It's a good occupation for a stormy day when you're not going to continue your journey.

Snow domes should be flattened and snow trenches filled in when you leave so there is little sign you've been there.

ROUTE PLANNING AND ROUTE FINDING

Trips into snow-covered terrain are often much more exploratory than summer hikes, especially when there are no tracks to follow. Heading into an untouched wilderness can feel like entering an unknown land, as in a sense it is. The weather and the state of the snow play a major part in the success of a venture, especially in remote, little-visited places. On one two-week trip to southwest Greenland we progressed just 10 miles from our starting point before having to retreat. The slow progress was due at first to an early melt of the low-level snow, which left us carrying sleds packed with two weeks worth of supplies through boulder fields, up steep loose scree slopes, and across arctic tundra. Then, when we finally reached the permanent snow, we had just one day of skiing before a series of storms blew in that kept us trapped in the same camp for four days. When the weather cleared, we retreated back down while we could. Despite the tiny distance covered and the long hours spent in the tents, during which paperback books became incredibly valuable, the trip was enjoyable because of the location. We were in a remote and spectacular wilderness where we saw no other people or signs of them—not even a plane high overhead—for 10 days.

Most trips aren't like that, of course, but it's sensible to accept that you may not always be able to complete a route. The joy is in being in the wilderness, rather than in covering many miles. Sometimes a trip can be improved by retracing your steps, odd though that may sound. This is because in difficult snow conditions, once you've made a track, whether with skis or snowshoes, it is much easier to return along it. On one trip in the Tombstone Mountains in the Yukon the snow in the valleys was very soft and deep, and trail breaking was very hard—so hard, in fact, that we took turns breaking trail and during our own stint would leave our pack behind and then ski back for it when the stint was over. In two eight-hour days we progressed just 10 miles. If we'd continued on our planned through-hike, we'd have been breaking trail through this snow almost the whole time. Rather than do this, once we were high in the mountains where the snow was much firmer, we stayed there, moving camp occasionally and exploring the area on day trips

Snow shelters like this snow dome are warmer and more stable than tents.

before returning on the track we'd made, which took less than half the time and a fraction of the effort needed on the way out. The lesson from this is to be adaptable on trips in the snow and change your plans if doing so will give a more enjoyable or safer journey.

When planning a route, don't aim for high mileage, especially in unknown terrain. In soft snow progress can be very slow, whereas every stop takes much longer than in warmer weather. Allow more time for pitching and striking camp and for camp chores, too. Hours can be spent melting snow in really cold conditions.

Deteriorating weather conditions can force changes in plans, especially above the timberline. Pushing upward into a blizzard is foolhardy. Sorting out a new route on the map can be very difficult in a storm, so it's best to have alternative routes already planned.

Navigation in snow-covered terrain is more difficult than in summer. Much of the time you will be traveling cross-country. Good map and compass skills are needed, as is the ability to

select a safe route. Altimeters and GPS receivers can be useful, especially in featureless terrain above the timberline or in whiteouts. Snow can change features so much that the terrain and the map may not appear to match. Hollows and dips can fill up with snow and disappear while snow-covered lakes can be almost impossible to locate in large flat valleys.

In forests you may be able to locate trails by the long, straight, open lines they leave between the trees. You can't rely on this, however, and above the timberline you can forget about trying to follow trails in deep snow. There will be so little sign of them that it's not worth the effort. Also, the lines taken by summer trails may not be good winter routes. They may even be potentially dangerous. Trails often traverse high up along the side of valleys, which may be avalanche prone in winter, or along narrow ridges, which may be corniced. Valley bottoms that are boggy or brush choked in summer can make good, safe routes in the snow, as can broad ridges and wide plateaus. In some areas frozen lakes and rivers are the best routes. Make sure they are safe before venturing onto them, though, especially in spring. Running water can often be crossed on snow bridges, but again you need to check these are safe. View the bridge from further up or down the stream bank to see how thick it is and cross one at a time.

AVALANCHES

Avalanches are terrifying forces of nature. Watching a wall of snow thunder down a slope in a great spray of white is a tremendous and awe-inspiring sight. Avoiding avalanches is a major concern when backpacking in snow-covered mountains.

An avalanche occurs when a layer of snow slides over the layer below because the two haven't bonded well together. Most avalanches occur on slopes between 25 and 45 degrees. In gentle terrain they're not a hazard. They are more common in some areas than others and in some years than others, as their likelihood depends to

Snow covers trails—even signs can be buried.

a great extent on how the snowpack has formed. Bowls, gullies, and convex slopes are likely places for avalanches, while ridge tops are generally safe. The risk is greatest during and immediately after heavy snowfall, so potentially dangerous terrain should be avoided for 24 hours after a big dump of snow. Once it's fallen, snow starts to settle and bind together, a process known as *stabilization*. This happens most quickly when the temperature remains just below freezing. Prolonged cold weather can mean the snow doesn't stabilize for weeks or even months, and then the avalanche hazard remains high.

Avalanches can't be accurately predicted, but a

good estimate of the hazard can be made. For many areas avalanche conditions are posted regularly, on the Internet, in local newspapers, and at ski areas. Avalanche information worldwide can be accessed via the excellent Cyberspace Snow and Avalanche Center Web site, <*www.csac.org*>. In avalanche reports the risk is given on a scale from low to very high. Heeding these warnings is common sense, yet every year people die in avalanches in areas where the risk is high or very high.

As far as possible, avalanche terrain should be avoided. While you're traveling, keep an eye out for recent avalanche debris, a sign that the avalanche risk may be high. If you intend crossing a potentially dangerous slope, test it first by digging a pit in the snow (in a safe place but facing the same way as the slope). Smooth down the back of the pit and then push a finger into each layer of snow, feeling for signs of instability such as sudden changes in the hardness of different layers, layers of ice or hail, air spaces, very soft layers, and loose, unconsolidated snow. You can also cut out a column in the back of the pit, put your hand or shovel blade down the back of it and see how easy it is to pull off a block of snow. Do this for each layer of snow. If any blocks slide off easily, the avalanche risk is likely to be high.

It takes time and experience to learn to assess avalanche risk. Taking a course is a good idea, as is studying one of the many books on the subject, such as *Avalanche Safety for Skiers and Climbers* by Tony Daffern and *The Avalanche Handbook* by David McClung and Pete Shaerer.

An ancient bridge in the Rio Ara Valley in the Spanish Pyrenees.

10

Afterword

It's all still there in heart and soul. The walk, the hills, the sky, the solitary pain and pleasure—they will grow larger, sweeter, lovelier in the days and years to come.

— Edward Abbey, "A Walk in the Desert Hills," *Beyond the Wall*

Toward the end of a long summer in the wilds, hikers' minds start to turn toward life after the trail and the world beyond the wilderness. Such thoughts may be welcome. You may be looking forward to returning to your family or enjoying again those things you have been without—sleeping in a bed, eating at a table, fresh food every day, television, films, concerts, newspapers, nights out with friends. Often, though, the thought of leaving the trail, of not hiking every day, can leave you feeling sad or worried or even frightened. Life on the trail is simple in its regular routines, in the basic action of walking, but it's also complex in its variety and particularly in the connection with the wilderness, the subtle interaction with nature that can make modern civilization seem shallow and out of touch with what is really important.

Any change in your way of life can be both challenging and threatening. It's just as great a change to cease hiking after months on the trail as it was to begin. Very few people can simply return to their old life as if they've never been away. Most require some time to adjust to not being a full-time hiker, to not living in the wilderness.

There are various ways to cope with life after the trail. First, it's sensible to accept that it will seem strange and that you might feel a little anxious or even depressed for a week or so. This is less likely if you prepare yourself during the last few days or even weeks of the hike. Once I leave my last supply point I am aware that the end of the hike is near, and I start to think beyond the finish, planning what I will do. There's always a tension between my desire not to leave the wilderness and my desire to see family and friends and do some of those things I've missed. While still enjoying the last days of the hike, I try to think positively about life beyond the trail.

Once your journey is over and you're back home, it's best to spend the first week adjusting to your new life and not trying to do too much. This is a time for celebration, for telling family and friends about your hike. They may be awed by what you've done or simply be uncomprehending. Those who are hikers will have some grasp of what you've achieved and what you are feeling, but only those who've undertaken a similar journey will really understand.

The first weeks at home are also a time for reflecting on your hike, for finishing your journal, for sorting out your photographs, and for contacting those you met along the way—hikers, others you want to stay in touch with, and those you want to thank for their assistance. If you want to tell others about your hike, you could send reports to the trail association journal or your local newspaper, set up a Web page, or give slide shows.

If you do feel anxious, confused, or unhappy after a long hike, part of the reason will almost certainly be because of the lack of physical activity. It is a huge change to go from hiking all day every day to being sedentary. At the end of a long hike you will be superbly fit, your body used to hard daily work. Suddenly stopping this activity is bound to have profound effects. The answer is not to completely stop. I like to go for short walks as often as possible (short by your standards—they may seem long to friends and family), and as soon as I can, I load up my pack and take off for a night or two.

When you stop hiking, the huge appetite you've developed won't immediately decline. Also, after months of mostly living on trail rations with just brief opportunities to eat other food, being able to eat what you like when you like can be overwhelming. Unused to unlimited food supplies, your body is likely send you signals that you should eat as much as possible. The result can be that you'll put on weight very quickly. This is another reason to keep up a moderate amount of exercise. For the first week I indulge my appetite and the joy in being able to eat all sorts of food I've not had for months, but then I try, not always totally successfully, to cut down on what I eat.

Moving from a life spent outdoors to one mostly spent indoors, from a sleeping mat to a bed, from a tent to a house, can also be disruptive. Some people find they can't sleep in a bed and end up on the floor; others camp in the backyard while they gradually become used to spending time indoors. This isn't unusual, though friends and family may find it strange, and it's better to adjust slowly rather than to force yourself back into the constraints of living indoors.

The initial feelings of dislocation after a long hike usually dissipate in a few weeks. Often though, even though you may outwardly appear to have readapted to "normal" life, there is a background feeling of dissatisfaction, an awareness that you are not the same, that much of modern life now seems shallow or inappropriate or unsatisfying. The life you led on the trail can seem more real than the way you are living now, more sharply focused, more in touch with both yourself and the outside world.

To share these feelings you can talk to other long-distance hikers by letter and e-mail and via Internet Web sites. Joining a long-distance hikers' association is well worthwhile, especially if you attend meetings. In October each year the Appalachian Long Distance Hiker's Association (ALDHA) has a Trailfest and the American Long Distance Hiker's Association has a Gathering. At both you can meet other hikers, see slide shows, and discuss all aspects of long-distance hiking.

Sea stacks and cliffs on the far northwestern coast of Scotland.

The sense of being part of a long-distance hiking community found at these gatherings is wonderful and could do wonders for those feeling isolated. If you have joined the trail association for the trail you hiked, you can follow developments and read accounts by other hikers. You can also take part in work parties and contribute to the building and maintenance of the trails you've hiked.

Many long-distance hikers feel concern for the environment and the places they have been. On many long-distance trails you will see spots where damage has been done or hear about other areas that are under threat. You may feel you want to do something about this so that others will be able to enjoy the wilderness as you have done. It's easy to get involved. There are many organizations such as the Sierra Club and the Wilderness Society working to protect wild places. Of all of them I'd single out the Wildlands Project, an organization dedicated to the conservation and restoration of huge areas of North America, as especially relevant to long-distance hikers. One of the lessons I've learned from long-distance hiking is that you can't put boundaries on nature, that you can't draw a line and say this is to be protected but this isn't. Walk the length of a mountain range or other ecosystem, and you understand its integrity, its essential wholeness in a way that is impossible by any other means of travel. I began to grasp this on the Pacific Crest Trail and had my feelings confirmed when I walked the length of the Canadian Rockies.

Finally, when the pull of the trail grows too strong and you feel a growing restlessness, a desire to sleep under the stars far from any town or village, a craving to explore unknown wildlands and see what is on the other side of the next mountain and the one after that and the one after that, there's only one thing to do. Start planning your next long-distance hike.

Resources

FURTHER READING

General

Berger, Karen. *Advanced Backpacking.* New York: W. W. Norton, 1998.

Getchell, Anne, and Dave Getchell. *The Essential Outdoor Gear Manual.* 2nd ed. Camden ME: Ragged Mountain Press, 2000.

Graydon, Don, ed. *Mountaineering: The Freedom of the Hills.* Seattle: Mountaineers, 1997.

Herrero, Stephen. *Bear Attacks: Their Causes and Avoidance.* New York: Lyons & Burford, 1988.

Jardine, Ray. *Beyond Backpacking: Ray Jardine's Guide to Lightweight Hiking.* La Pine OR: AdventureLore Press, 1999.

Mueser, Roland. *Long-Distance Hiking: Lessons from the Appalachian Trail.* Camden ME: Ragged Mountain Press, 1998.

Sobey, Ed. *The Whole Backpacker's Catalog: Tools and Resources for the Foot Traveler.* Camden ME: Ragged Mountain Press, 1999.

Townsend, Chris. *The Backpacker's Handbook.* Camden ME: Ragged Mountain Press, 1997.

Waterman, Laura, and Guy Waterman. *Backwoods Ethics: Environmental Issues for Hikers and Campers.* 2nd ed. Woodstock VT: Countryman Press, 1993.

Whitney, Stephen. *A Sierra Club Naturalist's Guide to the Sierra Nevada.* New York: Random House, 1982.

Abroad

Dudley, Ellen. *The Savvy Adventure Traveler: What to Know Before You Go.* Camden ME: Ragged Mountain Press, 1999.

Strauss, Robert. *Adventure Trekking: A Handbook for Independent Travelers.* Seattle: Mountaineers, 1996.

The Far North

Molvar, Erik. *Alaska on Foot: Wilderness Techniques for the Far North.* Woodstock VT: Countryman Press, 1996.

Morton, Keith. *Planning a Wilderness Trip in Canada and Alaska.* Calgary AB: Rocky Mountain Books, 1997.

Food

Kesselheim, Alan. *Trail Food: Drying and Cooking Food for Backpackers and Paddlers,* Rev. ed. Camden ME: Ragged Mountain Press, 1998.

Miller, Dorcas S. *Backcountry Cooking: From Pack to Plate in 10 Minutes.* Seattle: Mountaineers; Emmaus PA: Backpacker Magazine, 1998.

Miller, Dorcas S. *Good Food for Camp and Trail: All Natural Recipes for Delicious Meals Outdoors.* Boulder CO: Pruett, 1993.

Guide Books

Appalachian Trail Conference Guidebooks. Menasha Ridge Press. Regularly updated trail guides.

Bezruchka, Stephen. *Trekking in Nepal: A Traveler's Guide.* 7th ed. Seattle: Mountaineers, 1997. Classic combined general guide and trail guide.

Birkett, Bill, ed. *Classic Treks: The 30 Most Spectacular Hikes in the World.* Boston: Bulfinch Press, 2000. A selection of worldwide hikes.

Bruce, Dan "Wingfoot." *The Thru-Hiker's Handbook.* Conyers GA: Center for Appalachian Trail Studies. Planning guide for the Appalachian Trail.

Cleare, John, ed. *Trekking: Great Walks of the World.* London: Unwin Hyman, 1988.

Copeland, Kathy. *Don't Waste Your Time in the Canadian Rockies: An Opinionated Hiking*

Guide to Help You Get the Most from This Magnificent Wilderness. Berkeley: Wilderness Press, 1998.

Gadd, Ben. *Handbook of the Canadian Rockies.* 2nd ed. Jasper AB: Corax Press, 1995.

Jacobs, Randy. *The Colorado Trail: The Official Guidebook.* Englewood CO: Westcliffe, 1994. Trail guide.

Jones, Tom Lorang. *Colorado's Continental Divide Trail: The Official Guide.* Englewood CO: Westcliffe, 1997. Trail guide. Further volumes covering Idaho/Montana, Wyoming, and New Mexico are promised.

Lukei, Reese F., ed. *American Discovery Trail Explorer's Guide.* Helena MT: Falcon Press, 1995.

Lynx, Dustin, and Julia Lynx. *The Great Divide Trail.* Calgary AB: Rocky Mountain Books, 2000. Trail guide.

Miller, Arthur P., Jr., and Marjorie L. Miller. *Trails across America: Traveler's Guide to Our National Scenic and Historic Trails.* Golden CO: Fulcrum, 1996. Overview.

Patton, Brian, and Bart Robinson. *The Canadian Rockies Trail Guide: A Hiker's Guide.* Banff AB: Summerthought, 1971. Many revised editions (some with different subtitles), but all currently out of print.

Reynolds, Kev. *Walking in the Alps.* Milnthorpe England: Cicerone Press, 1998. Comprehensive guidebook with details of many long-distance trails.

Roper, Steve. *Sierra High Route.* Seattle: Mountaineers, 1997. Trail guide.

Schaffer, Jeffrey P., and Andy Setters. *The Pacific Crest Trail.* 6th ed., 2 vols. Berkeley: Wilderness Press, 2000. Two-volume trail guide.

Tighe, Kelly, and Susan Moran. *On the Arizona Trail.* Boulder CO: Pruett, 1998.

Unsworth, Walt, ed. *Classic Walks of the World.* Somerset England: Oxford Illustrated Press/Interbook, 1985.

Veron, Georges. *Pyrenees High Level Route.* Goring England: West Col, 1990. Regularly updated trail guide.

Wolf, Jim. *Guide to the Continental Divide.* 6 vols. Baltimore: CDTS, 1991–99. Trail guide. Regular supplements.

Long-Distance Hiking Stories

Berger, Karen, and Daniel R. Smith. *Where the Waters Divide: A Walk Across America Along the Continental Divide.* Woodstock VT: Countryman Press, 1993. Story of a CDT through-hike.

Berger, Karen, Daniel R. Smith, and Bart Smith. *Along the Pacific Crest Trail.* Englewood CO: Westcliffe, 1999. Account of a through-hike with spectacular photographs.

Brown, Hamish. *Hamish's Mountain Walk: The First Traverse of all the Scottish Munros in One Journey.* London: Gollancz, 1978. A classic account of the first walk over the individual 3,000-foot mountains in Scotland.

coyote, o.d. "Slackpacking Revisited." *Appalachian Trailway News.* (Nov.–Dec. 1994).

Crane, Nicholas. *Clear Waters Rising: A Mountain Walk across Europe.* London: Penguin, 1996. A 6,000-mile hike from Cape Finisterre to Istanbul.

Dudley, Ellen, and Eric Seaborg. *American Discoveries: Scouting the First Coast-to-Coast Recreational Trail.* Seattle: Mountaineers, 1996.

Fayhee, M. John. *Along the Arizona Trail.* Englewood CO: Westcliffe, 1998. Account of a through-hike with beautifully illustrated photographs.

Fletcher, Colin. *The Man Who Walked through Time.* New York: Vintage Books, 1989. First trek through the whole of the Grand Canyon. A classic.

Fletcher, Colin. *The Thousand-Mile Summer.* New York: Vintage Books, 1989. Walking the length of California. A classic.

Hillaby, John. *Journey through Britain.* Boston: Houghton Mifflin, 1970. Hiking Britain from end to end.

Hillaby, John. *Journey through Europe.* Boston: Houghton Mifflin, 1972. Hiking Europe north to south.

Hillaby, John. *Journey through Love.* Boston: Houghton Mifflin, 1977. Includes account of an AT hike.

Matthiesen, Peter. *The Snow Leopard.* New York:

Penguin, 1987. A story of a long trek in Nepal interwoven with personal philosophy.

Muir, John. *A Thousand Mile Walk to the Gulf.* Many editions since original publication in 1916. Muir's journals written during his first long walk.

Ross, Cindy. *Journey on the Crest: Walking 2600 Miles from Mexico to Canada.* Seattle: Mountaineers, 1987. Story of a PCT through-hike.

Steger, Will, and Paul Schurke. *North to the Pole.* New York: Times Books, 1987.

Styles, Showell. *Backpacking in Alps and Pyrenees.* London: Gollancz, 1976.

Townsend, Chris. *The Great Backpacking Adventure.* Somerset England: Oxford Illustrated Press, 1987. Includes accounts of PCT and CDT walks.

Townsend, Chris. *High Summer: Backpacking the Canadian Rockies.* Seattle: Cloudcap, 1989. First continuous walk along the whole range.

Townsend, Chris. *The Munros and Tops.* Edinburgh Scotland: Mainstream Press, 1997. Story of a 1,700-mile walk over all the 3,000-foot-high summits in the Scottish Highlands.

Townsend, Chris. *Walking the Yukon: A Solo Trek through the Land of Beyond.* Camden ME: Ragged Mountain Press, 1993. Story of a 1,000-mile south to north walk through Canada's Yukon Territory.

Medicine and Safety

Daffern, Tony. *Avalanche Safety for Skiers and Climbers.* Seattle: Mountaineers, 1992.

McClung, David, and Pete Shaerer. *The Avalanche Handbook.* Seattle: Mountaineers, 1993.

Wilkerson, James A., ed. *Medicine for Mountaineering and Other Wilderness Activities.* 4th ed. Seattle: Mountaineers, 1992.

Minimum Impact

Hampton, Bruce, and David Cole. *Soft Paths: How to Enjoy the Wilderness without Harming It.* Harrisburg PA: Stackpole, 1995.

McGivney, Annette. *Leave No Trace: A Guide to the New Wilderness Etiquette.* Seattle: Mountaineers; Emmaus PA: *Backpacker* magazine, 1998.

Meyer, Kathleen. *How to Shit in the Woods: An Environmentally Sound Approach to a Lost Art.* 2nd rev. ed. Berkeley: Ten Speed Press, 1994.

Snow Travel

Conover, Garrett, and Alexandra Conover. *The Winter Wilderness Companion: Traditional and Native American Skills for the Undiscovered Season.* Camden ME: Ragged Mountain Press, 2001.

Gorman, Steven. *The AMC Guide to Winter Camping.* Boston: AMC, 1991.

Townsend, Chris. *Wilderness Skiing and Winter Camping.* Camden ME: Ragged Mountain Press, 1992.

Magazines

Backpacker
Rodale Press Inc.
33 E. Minor St.
Emmaus PA 18098
800-666-3434
www.bpbasecamp.com

Explore Canada
301 14th St. N.W., Suite 420
Calgary AB
CANADA T2N 2A1
800-567-1372
www.explore-mag.com
E-mail: explore-mag@explore.mag.com

Outside
Mariah Media Inc.
400 Market St.
Santa Fe NM 87501
800-678-1131
www.outside.starwave.com

TRAIL ASSOCIATIONS

American Disscovery Trail Society
P.O. Box 3672
Frederick MD 21705-3672
301-668-2202
www.discoverytrail.org
E-mail: cvoell@aol.com

Appalachian Trail Conference
799 Washington St.
P.O. Box 807
Harpers Ferry WV 25425
304-535-6331
E-mail: appalachiantrail@charitiesusa.com

Arizona Trail Association
P.O. Box 36736
Phoenix AZ 85067
602-252-4794
www.primenet.com/~aztrail
E-mail: aztrail@primenet.com

Bruce Trail Association
P.O. Box 857
Hamilton ON
CANADA L8N 3N9
800-665-HIKE (800-665-4453), 905-529-6821
Fax: 905-529-6823
E-mail: info@brucetrail.org

Colorado Trail Foundation
American Mountaineering Center
710 10th St., #210
Golden CO 80401-1022
303-384-3729
www.coloradotrail.org
E-mail: ctf@www.coloradotrail.org

Continental Divide Trail Alliance
P.O. Box 628
Pine CO 80470
303-838-3760
www.CDTrail.org
E-mail: CDNST@aol.com

Continental Divide Trail Society
3704 N. Charles St., #601
Baltimore MD 21218-2300
410-235-9610
www.gorp.com/cdts
E-mail: cdtsociety@aol.com

Florida Trail Association
5415 S.W. 13 St.
Gainesville FL 32604
800-343-1882

www.florida-trail.org
E-mail: fta@florida-trail.org

Iditarod National Historic Trail
P.O. Box 637
Kasilof AK 99610
907-260-5618
www.anchorage.ak.blm-gov/inhthome.html
E-mail: mzaidlic@al.blm.gove

Long Trail
Green Mountain Club
4711 Waterbury-Stowe Rd.
Waterbury Center VT 05677
802-244-7037
www.longtrail.org
E-mail: GMC@greenmountainclub.org

North Country Trail Association
49 Monroe Center N.W., Suite 200B
Grand Rapids MI 49503
616-454-5506
E-mail: NCTAssoc@AOL.com

Pacific Crest Trail Association
5325 Elkhorn Blvd., P.M.B. #256
Sacramento CA 95842
888-PCT-RAIL (888-728-7245)
www.pcta.org
E-mail: info@pcta.org

Pacific Northwest Trail Association
P.O. Box 1817
Mount Vernon WA 98273
www.pnt.org/
E-mail: pnt@nwlink.com

HIKERS' ORGANIZATIONS

American Hiking Society
P.O. Box 20160
Washington DC 20041
301-565-6704
Fax: 301-565-6714
www.americanhiking.com
E-mail: AMHIKER@aol.com

American Long Distance Hiking
Association–West (ALDHA–West)
P.O. Box 651
Vancouver WA 98666
www.gorp.com/nonprof/adhaw/

Appalachian Long Distance Hikers' Association
(ALDHA)
10 Benning St.
P.O. Box 224
West Lebanon NH 03784
www.connix.com/~adlha/
E-mail: aldha@connix.com

Den Norske Turistforening
(Norwegian Mountain Touring Association)
Oslo Region
Pb. 7 Sentrum
0101 Oslo
NORWAY
22-82-2805
Fax: 22-82-2855
www.turistforening.no/
E-mail: info@turistforening.no

Fédération Française de la Randonnée Pédestre
(French Hiking Federation)
14, rue Riquet
75019 Paris
FRANCE
1-44-89-9393
Fax: 1-40-35-8567
http://asp.ffrp.asso.fr/index.asp
E-mail: ffrp.paris@wanadoo.fr

WILDERNESS CONSERVATION ORGANIZATIONS

Canadian Parks and Wilderness Society
401 Richmond St. W., Suite 380
Toronto, ON
CANADA M5V 3A8
800-333-9453
Fax: 416-979-3155
www.cpaws.org
E-mail: cpaws@icomm.ca

Leave No Trace
P.O. Box 997
Boulder CO 80306
800-332-4100
Fax: 303-444-3284
www.lnt.org
E-mail: LNT@Nols.edu

Sierra Club
85 2nd St., 2nd Floor
San Francisco CA 94105
415-977-5500
Fax: 415-977-5799
www.sierraclub.org
E-mail: information@sierraclub.org
Newsgroup: alt.org.sierra-club

Wilderness Society
900 17th St. N.W.
Washington DC 20006
202-833-2300
Fax: 202-429-3957
www.wilderness.org
E-mail: tws@tws.org

Wildlands Project
1955 W. Grant Rd., Suite 148A
Tucson AZ 85745
520-884-0875
Fax: 520-884-0962
www.wild-lands.org
E-mail: wildland@waonline.com

INTERNET NEWSGROUPS

These newsgroups are open to posts from anyone and as such have a mixture of useful information, turf wars, and bizarre opinions. All have informed and helpful regular posters. Read them for a while, and you'll work out who these people are (and who to avoid).

alt.rec.hiking
rec.backcountry
rec.skiing.backcountry
uk.rec.walking

WEB SITES

Great Outdoor Recreation Pages: *<www. gorp.com>*. There are many outdoor Web sites, ranging from individual hikers' home pages to big corporate ventures. *<www.gorp.com>* is a good source for information and links, but it's always worth doing a search to see what you come up with. Key words and phrases for a search include *backpacker, hiker, long-distance hiker, trail,* and *long-distance trail* (depending on the search engine, results could vary with and without hyphens, so try both ways).

MAPS

National Resources Canada
Canada Map Office
130 Bentley Ave.
Nepean ON
CANADA K1A 0E9
800-465-6277
Fax: 899-771-6277
E-mail: info@GeoCan.NRCan.gc.ca

U.S. Geological Survey
Map Distribution
P.O. Box 25286
Federal Center
Denver CO 80225
800-872-6277
Fax: 303-202-4693
www.usgs.gov
E-mail: ASK@USGS.gov

Overseas Maps

Maplink
25 E. Mason St., Dept. G
Santa Barbara CA 93101
805-965-4402
www.maplink.com

MEDICAL INFORMATION

Centers for Disease Control
1600 Clifton Rd. N.E.
Atlanta GA 30333

888-232-3228, 800-311-3435, 404-639-3311
www.cdc.gov
Gives U.S. Public Health Service advisories on health, immunizations, specific diseases in countries around the world. You can reach the CDC International Traveler's Hotline at 404-332-4559 or *<www.cdc.gov/travel.html>*.

IAMAT (International Association for Medical Assistance to Travellers)
417 Center St.
Lewiston NY 14092
716-754-4883
www.sentex.net/~iamat
Provides World Climate Charts that include recommended seasonal clothing and information on sanitary conditions of local water, milk, and food by regions, e.g., East and Northeast Africa; world immunization charts and distribution of diseases; world malaria risk chart and guidelines for suppressive medication by country.

Medic Alert
2323 Colorado Ave.
Turlock CA 95382
800-432-5378
www.medicalert.com
Provides bracelet or necklace with phone number of 24-hour emergency response center that can dispatch your medical record to anywhere in the world.

World Health Organization
www.who.ch/welcome.html

TRIP AND MEDICAL INSURANCE

International SOS
P.O. Box 11568
Philadelphia PA 19116
800-523-8930
www.internationalsos.com

Travel Assistance International
9200 Keystone Crossing, Suite 300

Indianapolis IN 46240
800-821-2828
www.1travel.com/protect/press.htm

Travelex
P.O. Box 9408
Garden City NY 11530-9408
800-228-9792
www.travelex-insurance.com
Travel Guard International
1145 Clark St.
Stevens Point WI 54481
800-826-1300
www.travel-guard.com

Travel Insured International
52-S Oakland Ave.
East Hartford CT 06128-0568
800-243-3174
www.travelinsured.com

TravelSafe Insurance
40 Commerce Dr.
Wyomissing PA 19610
888-885-7233
www.travelsafe.com

Travmed (product of Medex Insurance Services)
9515 Deereco Rd., 4th Floor
Timonium MD 21093
800-732-5309
www.medexassist.com/programs/pro.htm

Wallach & Company, Inc.
107 W. Federal St.
Middleburg VA 20117
800-237-6615

World Access
6600 W. Broad St.
Richmond VA 23230
800-285-3300
www.worldaccess.com/company/forinsur.html

World Care Travel Assistance
1141 Clark St.

Stevens Point WI 54481
800-826-1300

For more firms, check with the State Department's Overseas Citizens Services Office: Office of Overseas Citizens Services, Bureau of Consular Affairs, Room 4811, U.S. Department of State, Washington, DC 20520-4818, 202-647-5225.

SAFETY AND SECURITY INFORMATION

Association for Safe International Road Travel
11769 Gainsborough Rd.
Potomac MD 20854
301-983-5252
www.asirt.org

Department of State Bureau of Consular
    Affairs
Room 4811
U.S. Department of State
Washington DC 20520-4818
202-647-5225
www.travel.state.gov
Government travel warnings are posted at the Web site. The home page has a link to U.S. embassies and consulates worldwide, and a link to foreign embassies in Washington, D.C., and foreign consular offices throughout the United States.

Department of State Citizen's Emergency
    Center
202-647-5225

Department of State Travel Advisories
Bureau of Consular Affairs
Room 4811
U.S. Department of State
Washington DC 20520-4818
202-647-5225
Automated fax 202-647-3000
www.travel.state.gov/travel_warnings.html
Warnings and safety advice for travel to specific countries and areas of the world.

Department of Transportation Travel
  Advisory Line
800-221-0673
Threats to domestic and foreign transportation systems.

Federal Aviation Administration
Flight Standard Service
Aviation Data Systems Branch
P.O. Box 25082
Oklahoma City OK 73125
405-954-4391
www.faa.gov
Rates foreign countries' safety oversight of their airlines.

International Airline Passengers Association
P.O. Box 700188
Dallas TX 73125
800-821-4272 (9 to 11 A.M. CST)
www.iapa.com
Provides information on foreign and domestic airlines, including types and average age of planes and accident rates.

Kroll Travel Watch
800-824-7502
http://kins.kroll-ogara.com/ktw1.cfm
Provides city-specific reports for subscribers (primarily business travelers), including what parts of town to avoid, safety and security considerations, getting from airport to center city, health considerations, and emergency phone numbers. Also provides updates on political unrest, health emergencies, terrorist activities and kidnappings, events such as elections and public holidays, and safety records for airlines. Issues safety and stability forecasts.

Superintendent of Documents
U.S. Government Printing Office
P.O. Box 371954
Pittsburgh PA 15250-7954
202-512-1800
www.access.gpo.gov/su_docs
Call for health and safety publications: *A Safe Trip Abroad* and booklets in the Tips for Travelers series on different parts of the world.

Metric Conversion Table

miles	1.61 kilometers
yards	0.914 meters
feet	0.3 meters
inch	25.4 millimeters
cubic inches	0.0164 liters
pounds	0.4536 kilograms
ounces	28.35 grams
fluid ounces	0.0296 liters
pints	473 milliliters
quarts	0.9 liters
gallons	3.785 liters
°F	°C x 0.555 − 32
°C	°F − 32 x 1.8

Index

INDEX

About the Author

Chris Townsend is an experienced wilderness hiker and an award-winning writer and photographer. His particular passion is for long-distance hikes that take many months to complete. He has hiked the length of the Canadian Rockies, a 1,600-mile journey that had never been done before. Another first was his 1,700-mile continuous hike over all the 3,000-foot-high summits in the Scottish Highlands. He has also through-hiked the Pacific Crest Trail, the Continental Divide Trail, and the Arizona Trail, walked 1,000 miles south to north through the Yukon Territory, 1,300 miles south to north through the mountains of Norway and Sweden, and 1,250 miles from Land's End to John O'Groats in Britain. He has also hiked in the Himalaya, the Alps, the Pyrenees, Iceland, Greenland, Spitsbergen, and many other places.

He is the author of eleven books on backpacking, hiking, and ski touring, including the award-winning *The Backpacker's Handbook*, as well as *Wilderness Skiing and Winter Camping* and *Walking the Yukon*, all published by Ragged Mountain Press. Other titles include *Long Walks in the Pyrenees, The Munros and Tops, Classic Hill Walks, Adventure Treks: Western North America,* and *Ramblers' Guide to Ben Nevis and Glen Coe.* He also writes for many outdoor magazines and Web sites. Townsend lives in the Scottish Highlands.